This card does not necessarily include the fall of the last wicket

2d. Lord's

CW00498046

R.A.F. v. R.

(R.A.F. AND R.A.A.F. CHARITIES)

SATURDAY, JUNE 16, 1945. (One-day Match)

ROYAL AIR FORCE		First Innings		Second Innings
F/O R. E. S. Wyatt	Warwickshire	c Workman b Cristofani	94	
Flt/Sgt. D. Brookes	Northants	c Miller b Roper	4	
Sqn/Ldr. W. J. Edrich	Middlesex	b Williams	1	
Sgt. G. Cox	Sussex	lbw Christofani	24	
L.A.C. E. A. Nutter	Lancs	lbw Cristofani	1	
P/O E. H. Perry	Worcester	c Carmody b Cristofani	12	
L.A.C. L. Warburton	Lancs	c Roper b Williams	1	
L.A.C. W. E. Philipson	Lancs		1	
Cpl. E. P. Robinson	Yorks			
L.A.C. J. S. Buller	Worcester			
F/O R. Beveridge	Middlesex			

B , l-b , w , n-b ,   B , l-b , w , n-b

Total ....   Total ....

FALL OF THE WICKETS

—	2—	3—	4—	5—	6—	7—	8—	9—	10—
—	2—	3—	4—	5—	6—	7—	8—	9—	10—

ANALYSIS OF BOWLING

Name		1st Innings					2nd Innings					
	O.	M.	R.	W	Wd.	N-b.	O.	M.	R.	W.	Wd.	N-b.

R.A.A.F.		First Innings		Second Innings
F/Sgt. J. A. Workman	P. Adelaide	b Nutter	27	
F/Sgt. H. S. Craig	P. Adelaide	b Philipson	12	
F/O K. R. Miller	Victoria	b Robinson	63	
F/Lt. D. K. Carmody	N.S.W.	c & b Perry		
F/O R. M. Stanford	S. Australia	b Beveridge	0	
F/O J. Pettiford	Gordon C.	b Beveridge	57	
F/O D. R. Cristofani	N.S.W.	b Perry	31	
W/O R. G. Williams	S. Australia			
S/Ldr. S. G. Sismey	N.S.W.			
F/Lt. A. W. Roper	N.S.W.			
F/O R. S. Ellis	S. Australia			

B , l-b , w , n-b ,   B , l-b , w , n-b ,

Inn. Declared Total 243   Total ....

FALL OF THE WICKETS

—27	2—49	3—	4—	5—	6—	7—	8—	9—	10—
—	2—	3—	4—	5—	6—	7—	8—	9—	10—

ANALYSIS OF BOWLING

Name	1st Innings						2nd Innings					
	O.	M.	R.	W.	Wd.	N-b.	O.	M.	R.	W.	Wd.	N-b.

MILLER'S LUCK

ALSO BY ROLAND PERRY

Cricket
Bradman's Best
Bradman's Best Ashes Teams
The Don
Captain Australia: A History of the Celebrated Captains of
Australian Test Cricket
Bold Warnie
Waugh's Way
Shane Warne, Master Spinner

Others
Monash: The Outsider Who Won a War
Last of the Cold War Spies
The Fifth Man
The Programming of the President
Mel Gibson, Actor, Director, Producer
The Exile: Wilfred Burchett, Reporter of Conflict
Lethal Hero
Programme for a Puppet *(fiction)*
Blood is a Stranger *(fiction)*
Faces in the Rain *(fiction)*

Documentary films
The Programming of the President
The Raising of a Galleon's Ghost
Strike Swiftly
Ted Kennedy and the Pollsters
The Force

THE LIFE AND LOVES OF KEITH MILLER,
AUSTRALIA'S GREATEST ALL-ROUNDER

MILLER'S LUCK

ROLAND PERRY

RANDOM HOUSE AUSTRALIA

Random House Australia Pty Ltd
20 Alfred Street, Milsons Point, NSW 2061
http://www.randomhouse.com.au

Sydney   New York   Toronto
London   Auckland   Johannesburg

First published by Random House Australia 2005

National Library of Australia
Cataloguing-in-Publication Entry

Perry, Roland, 1946–.
Miller's luck.

Bibliography.
Includes index.
ISBN 1 74051 397 5.

1. Miller, Keith, 1919–2004. 2. Cricket players –
Australia – Biography. 3. Fighter pilots – Australia –
Biography. 4. Journalists – England – Biography. 5.
Australian football players – Biography.
I. Title.

796.358092

Cover design by Darian Causby/Highway 51 Design Works
Back cover photograph courtesy Getty Images
Index by Catherine Page
Typeset by Midland Typesetters, Maryborough, Victoria
Printed and bound by Griffin Press, Netley, South Australia

10 9 8 7 6 5 4 3 2 1

To the memory of Peg Miller

Non rammentare che le ore felicia –
Remember only the happy hours.
Keith Miller's favourite saying, with an intended *double entendre*.

CONTENTS

PART 1

WEEDY'S WORLD

LORD OF LORD'S

Keith Miller took two steps down on to the Lord's arena. He was greeted by such applause that anyone not knowing he was an Australian would have thought he was English. The date was 27 August 1945. It was the last hour of the second day of a match between England and a 'Dominions' combination, made up of eight Australians, one New Zealander, one South African and one West Indian. Miller was conscious of the fact that W. G. Grace, Victor Trumper, Wally Hammond and Don Bradman had also made those two modest steps for cricket. It gave the tall, lithe and graceful athlete – with his characteristic erect back and loose limbs – a thrill to be walking the same walk. Miller loved the spirit at this ground, the epicentre of the cricket world. He had made it his own during the World War II years with brilliant performances. They had seen him compared with all the greats of the game.

Most of the 34,000 people packed into the ground had stayed in the hope of seeing Miller. They were full of expectation as he characteristically tugged at his sleeve, used his teeth to wriggle on his batting gloves, and strode to the wicket with the athletic lope of a man relishing the moment. Male fans were riveted to him as he rolled his broad shoulders and glanced skywards, as if searching for enemy planes and missiles, which he and they had done for several years. Female fans clapped and shrieked as he took off a glove and gave his ample dark locks a smoothing over, like the concert conductors he so admired just before a performance. Miller took block and settled into his upright, classic stance. There was no agitated tap of the bat. There was no need with this batsman. His stillness spelt murderous intent, as did his easy grip. It was in the province of the tail-ender, high up the handle, signalling that at every chance he would attempt to belt the cover off the ball and often send it skyward. Yet Miller was establishing himself as a batsman of the highest order. His readiness for mayhem reflected his character rather than his stroke-making prowess.

The score was 2 for 60 in the Dominions' second innings. It led England by 80. A Miller special was needed. Already this summer at Lord's he had scores for the RAAF, Australia and now a Dominions side of 105, 1 (run out), 7, 71 not out, 78 not out, 75, 63, 118, 35 not out and 26. In previous seasons he had scored several centuries here. He had just been a clear man-of-the-series in five Victory Tests for Australia against England, which celebrated the end of World War II in Europe. Miller was the runaway favourite player of the English summer and had come to symbolise the best of British life, sport and athleticism. He might have been an antipodean of Scottish descent, but he had served with the Royal Air Force as a pilot in a bomber squadron over enemy skies in Europe. The United Kingdom and Lord's had claimed him as their own. The matinée idol good looks, ready smile and willingness to engage with the spectators all conspired with his outstanding performances to make him the centre of attention with the bat, the ball, or even just fielding. It was said he could catch swallows in slips.

Miller had every motivation to perform. It would be his last big game at Lord's for the summer and his wartime stay in England. Hammond had provided a typically fine century in England's first innings. Miller had tussled with him for preeminence as a batsman all season, and wished to leave his adopted cricket 'home' with a statement. There was little to lose. If he failed, he would still be ranked as equal to the English great. Miller could deliver a swashbuckling show or go down trying.

He moved on to the front foot against the excellent bowling of Test leg-spinners Doug Wright and Eric Hollies. He was in touch from his first cover drive to the fence the second ball he faced. Miller was a player of moods. His footwork demonstrated his finesse on this day, as each movement brought his head and shoulders over the ball, which at first sight seemed exaggerated until the observer realised that this was the norm. Miller's backfoot movement also seemed overdone when, in rare moments, the spinners forced him to retreat. The elbow was erect as if an extension of a very vertical bat. Even this defence was a form of attack. The ball was rebounding through the field.

Miller was lunging at deliveries with full confidence and decisive punch, whether to kill Hollies' spin or cover-drive Wright with power and the straightest of bats. Another hint early that he was in form was his late-cutting. The artistry and precision of this fine shot were usually the preserve of shorter players, such as Don Bradman or Denis Compton. Yet the taller Miller was as adept at it as these two fine exponents.

Miller reached 49 in 49 minutes. At that score, he took one step down the wicket and lifted Hollies high and straight. Members in front of the pavilion scattered as the ball cleared the fence and bounced right. Three balls later he repeated the feat. Miller was 61 not out, and the Dominions 3 for 145 at stumps on day two.

He always slept on 'a few beers' before a game, but whatever he had on the night of 27 August, it put him in a plundering mood on the third and final morning of the match. New Zealand's dashing little left-hander Martin Donnelly (29) was yorked early by Wright. This brought West Indian Learie Constantine, the Dominions' captain, to the wicket. Miller went into overdrive, smashing Hollies and Wright with contempt to all parts of the ground. Hammond had no slip. Every fielder was in the deep, in the hope that this flop-haired belligerent would mistime a stroke and sky a catch. As writer Denzil Batchelor put it: 'The nearest fieldsman seemed in Mesopotamia, while the farther bodies were pretty well astral.'

Miller was in an ebullient mood for the second successive day. He asked umpire Archie Fowler if it were true that no one had cleared the pavilion roof with a hit since Australian Albert Trott had done it playing for Middlesex against Australia in 1899. 'Correct,' Fowler replied. 'He hit a ball from Monty Noble. It struck a chimney pot and fell to the back of the pavilion.'

'Well, Archie,' Miller said, 'I'm going to clear it myself this morning.'

He set about his task. One of Miller's sixes carried over the 170-metre (188-yard) boundary and hit Block Q to the right of the pavilion. Then he set himself for the biggest one ever seen at Lord's. It was a swing over mid-on, which kept climbing and climbing towards the broadcasting position, causing commentator Rex Alston to 'choke on his words and duck'. Only half a metre at the top of the pavilion and a small roof on the broadcasting box above the players' dressing room stopped the ball from leaving the arena and ending up on a doubledecker bus in the streets of St John's Wood. The press box had not been there for Trott's hit, which indicated that Miller's launch might well have been greater.

'On hitting the pavilion,' noted former England captain A. E. R. Gilligan, who was in the box, 'it fell into a hole that had been made in the roof of the commentary position by shrapnel [from a German bomber]. The ball had to be poked out with a stick.' It was the only poking that ball experienced.

Had Miller's match been played on another pitch to the left, the ball would not have been impeded by anything on its flight into folklore. Yet the innings itself was headed there. Experts in the pavilion, if not ducking for cover, were spellbound. As Miller's carnage continued, former England captain and Marylebone Cricket Club chairman Plum Warner, who had 60 years experience in first-class cricket, was prompted to say, 'I have never seen such hitting.'

Another member repeatedly called: 'Why don't you give Langridge a bowl?'

Hammond obliged, throwing the ball to the left-arm Test spinner, whom nobody at the ground could recall being 'seen to' by a rampant batsman. Miller corrected this by sending two of his first four balls soaring straight and over mid-on to the pavilion, causing members – including the vociferous Langridge supporter – to scatter. Constantine joined in with another six in the same over.

The destruction saw 117 runs scored in 45 minutes. Miller connected with 13 fours and 7 sixes, most of which collected the seats below or adjoining the Long Room windows. Dick Whitington, who had performed with Miller in the Australian services team in the Victory Tests, observed: 'Several elderly gentlemen who had experienced some of the severest Germany artillery bombardment [on the Western Front] of the Kaiser War [World War I], were forced to desert their favourite positions and seek sanctuary in the Members' Bar.'

Part of Miller's appeal was the pure 'Englishness' of his batting. Right through his frenetic stay he stood tall at the crease, in classic side-on pose. Each time after a huge hit, he reverted to that still position. His batting this innings and in all others was based on front-foot play, with the emphasis on the drive. Yet he still made room for the backfoot cut, which was one of his favourite hits. And from the beginning of his innings the day before, Miller had drawn appreciative applause from the connoisseurs in the Lord's Pavilion Long Room for his sweet dab of a fine late cut, which was in contrast to the lusty belting of those massive sixes. This delicacy seemed incongruous for such a square-shouldered big bloke. Yet it was part of the character of Miller, who had several gears and nuances beyond the one-dimensional in his play and his life. His shots had authority and style on both sides of the wicket, but if he were to be remembered for other than his sending good deliveries into orbit, it would be for the cover drive. He played it with textbook precision and power, opening the blade and giving full expression to the most glorious of strokes.

Even the experts watching on this sunny morning at Lord's might have been fooled by his occasional lofted shot to leg. The terrific twist of his upper body, and the thrust of shoulders, arms and whipping wrists, caused him to end up playing the shot with just his powerful left arm. To the unaccustomed eye this seemed like a loss of control; a wild hoick more in keeping with what would be expected from the village blacksmith. But Miller knew what he was doing. He executed it on purpose.

There wasn't much to hook in this innings, but Miller demonstrated a liking for this shot too with the few chances he had. It required confidence, courage, good footwork, reflexes, eye, punch and more than a touch of the daredevil and risk-taking.

Miller went on to 185 before cracking a faster Langridge ball straight to Wright, giving two of the tormented opposition a minor consolation. Miller had scored 124 in 115 minutes before lunch. The innings had taken in all just 165 minutes.

He left the arena to a standing ovation, his eyes searching the sky for non-existent Luftwaffe again, now a sign of embarrassment rather than light adjustment. With a characteristic pluck of his unbuttoned shirt away from his sweating torso, a jerk of his head to throw back his hair and a wave of his bat to the cheering fans he disappeared up the pavilion steps into the Long Room.

Whatever followed from Hammond in England's second innings, it would be physically impossible for him, aged 42, to match this sustained power hitting. Miller was being applauded as king of the 1945 season and, for the third successive season, a dominator at Lord's.

The *Times* correspondent, Beau Vincent, the next morning

wrote: 'We were beginning to wonder whether Lord's is big enough to take such terrific hitting.'

Former England Test player and a legend of the game, C. B. Fry, added some perspective for those in Australia who had not witnessed Miller's 1945 summer of brilliance. 'In our eyes, Miller is Australia's star turn,' he said in a BBC World broadcast. 'We know we have been watching a batsman already great, who is likely, later on [when official Tests resume post-war], to challenge the feats of Australia's champions of the past. Apart from his technical excellence, Keith Miller has something of the dash and generous abandon that were part of Victor Trumper's charms.'

One of the game's finest ever observers, R. C. Robertson-Glasgow, watched Miller's dominance of the summer and remarked:

He has over-matched the best bowlers in England. He has quelled them with a casual accuracy peculiarly his own. His abundant runs have kept England from victory in the [Victory] Tests; the manner of their making has revived the affection of the faithful and excited the interest of the doubtful. *Miller is a story-book batsman; were he not fine fact, he would be first rate fiction.*

***

Miller was 25 years old. His triumph at Lord's was the pinnacle of his career, and the innings an expression of his character, which had been modified by his experiences in World War II as a night-fighter pilot. After nearly losing his life on at least six occasions when many of his mates and colleagues were not so fortunate, Miller was living life on a day-by-day basis. It had become a habit forced upon him in his 30 months in the air force in England.

To understand the nature of this exceptional character and cricketer we must go back exactly a generation to the first year after World War I.

SUNSHINE BOY

Keith Ross Miller was born at a time of optimism in Australia. It was 28 November 1919. The biggest war in history had ended a year earlier, and 170,000 diggers, along with their esteemed commander John Monash, were either home or on their way after playing the decisive role in winning the 1914–18 war for the Allies. As part of the celebration of peace, the Australian Government offered a £10,000 prize for the first crew to fly from England to Australia. Four of the six entrants crashed en route. The winner was a Vickers Vimy biplane flown by brothers and pilots Lieutenant Keith Smith and Captain Ross Smith, who were both knighted for their efforts. They took off on 12 November and were just over half way to Australia when Miller was born. Father Leslie (Les Sr) and mother Edith – known as 'Edie' – reflected the excitement of the event by naming their fourth child Keith Ross Miller after the risk-taking former war aces.

Two Scottish Christian names represented a heritage: Les Sr's grandfather Joseph Bass Miller came from North Leith, the port of Edinburgh, in April 1849, and his grandmother Rose Jean was from Dundee. Edie was a Watson and also had a Scottish background. The names symbolised the hope and aspiration for a son born at an exhilarating time.

Young Keith arrived in the front room of 29 Benjamin Street in Sunshine, Victoria, an English-style, one-level terrace house. The pastoral, working-class borough, 11 kilometres west of Melbourne, had a population of about 900 in 380 houses, sprinkled over 9 square kilometres. There was no water supply (tanks sufficed), phone, radio or sanitation, and the night carter did the most unenvied job of all. Horses were more common than cars. Sunshine was dominated by the farm machinery maker H. V. McKay, which was the biggest employer in the area. It had relocated from Ballarat in 1906. Les Sr, who began his working life as a teacher in Warracknabeal and then worked as an engineer for McKay in Ballarat, was posted with the company to Sunshine.

Local entertainment for the Methodist Millers was limited to a sound-free cinema at the Mechanics Institute, a billiards room in the only guesthouse, and the simple yet fashionably underwhelming game of quoits, in which a ring of rope, rubber or metal was hurled 3.5 metres in an attempt to encircle a peg. A treat for the family was to take the train into the big smoke of Melbourne, with its restaurants, dance and concert halls, cinemas and the Mecca of sport, the Melbourne Cricket Ground. Despite its deprivations, Sunshine was an idyllic setting for the three siblings, the blonde Gladys (known as 'Snow'), 12, Les Jr, 9, and Ray, 7, to grow up in as it had plenty of bush areas, open fields and the Kororoit Creek. Snow was old enough to help Edie and became Keith's de facto mother, which ensured plenty of feminine attention, despite the masculine household with its emphasis on sport – Aussie Rules football in the winter and cricket in the summer. Les Sr set the pace. He had been a rugged footballer with country team Warracknabeal, which won a premiership in 1900. Les Jr and Ray played with a football made of bound rags.

There were old bats for cricket in the long, hot summers. Les Sr insisted that the boys learn the game with tennis balls. He preached the virtues of orthodoxy. No back leg was allowed to drift square. The leading elbow was prominent; he hammered home that cricket was a 'side-on' game. Les Sr always encouraged technique over aggression, especially until the basic strokes were mastered. His attitude was that a batsman would not learn as much from the pavilion if he had been dismissed playing a wild shot before he was set. The emphasis was on a sound defence and self-control, in the Ponsford mould. This separated park cricketers, who lost concentration easily, and first-class players. Not that it was all strict copybook shot-making in the backyard. Les always also encouraged the boys to stand their ground, drive, hook and cut, no matter how fast deliveries came at them. Counter-attack was often the best defence. Les Sr's overriding theory, especially in the use of the soft ball early in 'careers', was simple. When they came to play with hard leather balls their natural courage, good 'eyes' and skills would make the transition with ease. If leather was introduced too early and exclusively it could inhibit the lads.

This sporting environment was the world little Keith grew into. Yet not very fast. He was the runt of the litter. Even at the local preparatory school he was smaller than all the other boys. By the time he was seven, when the family moved across Melbourne to the south-east, lower-middle-class suburb of Elsternwick, the elder brothers, in the cruel Aussie tradition of mocking physical shortcomings, had an unsubtle nickname for their younger brother. Whereas tall kids might get called 'Shorty', or those with red hair 'Blue', those overweight or short were never called 'Slim' or 'Giraffe'. It would always be a confronting 'Tubby' or 'Stumpy'. Keith's nickname was even more obnoxious. He was given an altogether more demeaning sobriquet, with a layer beyond lack of centimetres. It also denoted poison and something unwanted. Long before K. R. Miller could be assessed on merit for other than his height, he was known as 'Weedy'.

The family's new home at 16 Denver Crescent, Elsternwick, cost £3,000 in late 1926. It was a jumbled, Federation-style abode with two levels, an attic and a sizeable shed out the back, befitting an engineer with a penchant for tools. The back garden, precious forever in suburban Australia, was big enough to accommodate family games of cricket. Keith, being the youngest and smallest, was regarded as less efficient at fielding than the family dog, Buttons, which was a compliment. Buttons was alleged to be the best fielder in the state, and could, the family claimed, 'almost talk'. The canine companions of a young Don Bradman at Bowral and a mature Clarrie Grimmett in Adelaide had a definite rival in Melbourne for the title of cleverest carnivore catch.

Weedy's twin handicaps of height and age made rather than defeated him in the backyard. He found it tough to get his talented older brothers out and so had to develop his fielding and catching skills. When he secured a turn at the crease, he built a sound defence and used a very straight bat. It was noticed at primary school more than his flute-playing or academic earnestness. If he wasn't in the backyard at Mum's, the diminutive Keith was playing at school or at the little field adjoining the Elsternwick Cricket Ground, or even at the ground itself.

He was a good listener and watcher. He loved observing his hero of all sports, Bill Ponsford, who lived just 400 metres away in Orrong Road, to which Denver Crescent was a dangling extension. Ever since he could remember, the mammoth-scoring 'Ponnie' – a gentle, self-effacing champion – had been his favourite. The midget Miller and his little mates would loiter around Ponsford's home in the hope of just getting a wave or perhaps a 'hello' from this affable sporting god. The solid opener had first come to national prominence in 1923 when he amassed 429 out of Victoria's mind-boggling, if not silly, score of 1059. His was then the highest ever first-class score, eclipsing the 424 by Lancashire's Archie MacLaren. Apart from an amazing capacity for accumulation, Ponsford was also a crowd pleaser. He didn't dawdle his way forward or doggedly amass his runs. His 429 took 477 minutes and included 42 fours. It represented long hours of entertainment for the watcher or the radio listener. Keith first became aware of him three years later at the beginning of the 1927–28 season when Les Sr, who ranked his own hero, the late

Victor Trumper, just ahead of Ponsford as a batsman, took the boys and Snow to the MCG to watch a match against Queensland. Ponsford, using his bat known as 'Big Bertha', set about a more studied assault on his previous quadruple century.

It was at this game that Les Sr told Keith to 'watch everything about' Ponsford, from his concentration to his stance and his impeccably straight bat. The boy had plenty of time – 10 hours and 21 minutes, spread over two playing days – to absorb the Ponsford lesson as he diligently rather than adventurously thumped his way to a new world record of 437. About the only aspect of the 177 cm, 82 kg batsman that Keith would not copy was Ponsford's crab-like, yet still effective shuffle down the pitch to spinners. Keith's short stride meant he would have to develop twinkle toes to counter the slower, turning ball, which he did.

Edie approved of Les Sr's instruction to the boys and leading the way in sport, but she did not condone his affairs with other women. Les Sr used to pretend he was going to a Masonic Lodge at night, but would instead meet a local lover, 'Liz'. One day Edie, just 148 cm but feisty, was walking with Les Sr in the shopping area of Glenhuntly Road, Elsternwick, when they came across Liz. Edie attacked her physically and told Liz in no uncertain terms to stop seeing her husband. The affair was terminated, but Les Sr, a chronic player, found another girlfriend in another suburb.

Tough Edie was the family matriarch, who ruled the family and set the standards, which, in extreme cases, included violence in attempting to achieve her aims.

In a seven-year period until the end of 1933 – year 8 of his schooling – the young Miller honed his skills under the tutelage of his father and brothers, who were both good enough to move on to subdistrict level. There was also Jack Gainey, a teacher at the primary school, who reckoned the 'little peanut of a boy', as Miller characterised himself, was a cricketing prodigy. Gainey factored in the lad's determination, something about which the consumptive former World War I digger knew quite a deal after fighting on the Western Front at Messines Ridge and Passchen-daele, where he had been gassed.

When Keith was alone in the backyard he would place a tennis ball in one of Snow's discarded stockings, attach it to a clothes line and swing a bat at it until he became bored, the stocking tore or neighbours complained of the incessant 'thunk' sound. These endless hours of singular application improved hand–eye coordi-nation to a point where he believed he could control anything coming at him, no matter what the speed, angle or direction.

Ian Johnson, himself a Test player in the making, noticed Miller in the nets at South Melbourne. The sawn-off bat looked too big for him when he first faced up, yet the disproportion was soon forgotten when the boy danced to spinners, cut with grace or hooked off his nose. Miller Junior was not daunted by the jibes or such remarks as: 'His full-blooded drives roll back to the bowler.' He was proving detractors wrong.

'The first time I struck him was when I was practising for an interstate schoolboys' side,' Johnson recalled. 'This was an under-15 team. I was 13 but he was only 12. This little kid was only knee-high to a grasshopper, but we older blokes were absolutely entranced by him. He was a glorious player.'

Test batsman Keith Rigg, Miller's third Victorian XI captain, remembered the first time he saw him play for South's under-age team. 'He was so small that when he came in to bat his pads flapped around near his waist,' Rigg said. 'Hans Ebeling [later a fast-medium state and Test bowler] was bowling. Keith hit him through the covers without power, but with style. I thought, "Crikey, who is this kid?"'

His sporting skills applied to football. He had reached just 4 feet 11 inches (150 cm). Speed and agility were essential to avoid intended damage by opponents in a contact sport, where 'ironing out' a player was acceptable, and usually praised, in under-age teams of the 1920s and 1930s. Young Miller was always playing outside his weight for age, and it took courage just to enter a football ground. Yet even at 12, when light enough to be blown over by a gust of wind, and playing against fully grown youths, he was never known to take a backward step.

The boy's lack of growth caused his head to turn to another sport for which he thought he was destined: horseracing. The Caulfield track was a manageable bike ride away from home and school. He spent many an early morning watching through the mist as the strappers and the jockeys put their sleek and graceful charges through their paces. Keith liked the rhythmic sound of galloping steeds in hard work-outs that saw their nostrils belch steam. Even the mixed stable odours of hay, sweat, leather and manure were heady to him. These intrepid riders, with their colourful race-day gear and even more colourful language, made their size an advantage in one of the few sports where it was better to be tiny. Keith related to them. He admired them. They were his local heroes. He even badgered his father into letting him have riding lessons. There was the odd practice race, when he more fully appreciated the guts of the jockeys, who all wore scars and told stories of horrific falls and crashes.

There was another attraction that caught the boy's eye. Race day was a most glamorous, vivid event. Women and men turned out in their finery and fashions, which attracted him.

Young Keith became enchanted with racing after his father took him, a few weeks before his seventh birthday, to the 1926 Melbourne Cup, won by Spearfelt. The race annually drew double the crowds of Test cricket matches or Aussie Rules grand finals. It was also the only sporting event in the world for which a state proclaimed a *holi*day, which was apt in a nation where many gambled religiously. The sport of kings was also the pastime of the masses in Australia. Over the years an added seduction for Keith became the swirl of money at the track. He had none to play with himself but became aware that the allure for those who had it, or wished they did, was the same: the mirage of sudden riches. Early on, he learned the language of the jockeys and trainers. They met eager and greedy men in smart suits and hats behind the racetrack grandstand or near stables, giving them tips out of the corners of their mouths. Mates, masters and mug punters alike would be told how a horse was performing, or not; what was a 'sure thing' and what was not. It added to an intrigue peculiar to the Australian ethos of the battler and the better, of the mystical '100 to 1 long shot', and the romantic champions such as the mighty Carbine or the legendary Phar Lap, equine excellence that you could 'bet your house on'.

This atmosphere and environment, along with the less tangible goal of 'fame', beckoned Keith to racing more than any other sport. He dreamed of riding a winner at the Melbourne Cup. His fever for being a jockey reached a peak during the 1930 Flemington spring carnival when Phar Lap won a race on each of the four days, including the Cup, for which he was odds-on favourite. Jim Pike, who rode the huge gelding, was put even higher on a Miller pedestal, for the moment, than Ponsford and Don Bradman, who had a few months earlier become Australia's hero of heroes in the 1930 Ashes contest in England. At 10 going on 11, Keith accepted that he was always probably going to be under-sized. Being a superstar jockey was a more practical reverie than playing in a grand final or a big Ashes Test.

About a year later, his brother Ray introduced him to classical music, starting with Mozart's Symphony in C, No. 41, 'Jupiter'. At this time, too, Les Sr opened him up to poetry, including his two favourite poems, Gray's 'Elegy Written in a Country Churchyard' and Wordsworth's 'Upon Westminster Bridge'. These lessons compounded over the years and influenced Miller's love for the great composers and poets.

Just before his fourteenth birthday in late 1933, Miller learned that his primary school examination marks were sufficient for entry to Melbourne High School opposite the Yarra River. There was a certain amount of prestige in going to this institution. It was non-fee-paying and controlled by the State Government. Yet its look, its position in an up-market suburb, its emphasis on scholastic and sporting achievement and general feel were more like those of the traditional private schools that aped the British system in everything except the use of corporal punishment and employment of 'fags', younger boys who had to do the older boys' bidding.

Miller fell in love with the school's architecture at first glance. Perched on a hill, its imposing four-tiered, 13-metre towers, with their mock medieval castle turrets, stood like sentinels guarding the school's sloping terrace lawn, which drifted down to a sports oval. The dominant smells wafting over the river from industrial Richmond were those of the Rosella tomato sauce factory, a meat works and a yeast factory. The unsavoury mix made for an uncertain yet permanent olfactory sense and memory for Miller. He, like many a Melbourne High old boy, was reluctant to count the meat pie and sauce as his dish of choice.

The teaching staff was to have little influence on Miller in year 9, except perhaps the music teacher, Charles Breen. He was to maintain Miller's interest in classical music, which was enhanced by Sunday visits to the house of a cousin, Albert Leviston, who lived at Ballarat. Albert was obsessive about music and cricket. He would play gramophone records, and Miller caught some of his infectious enthusiasm.

Miller's school marks were low, which was no surprise. He did very little study. He concentrated on sport: cricket, football and baseball, which had been inspired by Ponsford, who was a star at this, too. There were the occasional jockey work-outs, horse-riding and even a little swimming for his house. It exasperated the masters, especially the maths teacher, the disciplined, teetotalling, Methodist minister's son William Maldon 'Billy' Woodfull, who happened to be the Australian Test cricket captain. He was torn between a high regard for the not-quite-cheeky Miller's abilities and his disappointment at the boy's lack of application to learning. Woodfull seemed to embody the bland school motto, 'Honour the Work'. He would remind Miller and others who were study-averse that the nation was just recovering from an awful depression. They couldn't get by on their good looks or sporting prowess. They had to extract the best from their schooling and qualify for a job.

The juvenile Miller by contrast kept up a dream of being a great sportsman, which he and others believed would somehow lead to fame and then *perhaps, maybe, somehow* riches. Most of all, he wanted to be *somebody*. He couldn't see how this could happen by mastering long division or basic algebra or concern for Pythagoras' theorem. So he didn't apply himself to them. This didn't make him Woodfull's favourite pupil. Yet this pre-eminent sports icon, who had become more famous for his protest against bodyline bowling a year earlier in the 1932–33 Ashes series than for his batting, couldn't help seeing what had attracted Jack Gainey and young Ian Johnson and countless others to young Miller. He had a careless charisma.

Woodfull refused to coach cricket at the school. He would have intruded on the jobs of the sports masters. Nevertheless the Australian Test skipper was caught watching from afar as the boys performed in the practice nets after school. He couldn't help noticing the batting brilliance of his pint-sized, near-worst mathematician. Nor could the captain of the First XI, the red-headed, rugged Keith 'Bluey' Truscott, who was in his final year. Truscott wanted Miller in his team despite his size and age. Miller was selected to bat at number six in his first-ever big game, versus Swinburne Technical College.

It was a Saturday in mid-February 1934. About 50 spectators were scattered around the picturesque school oval. Marching out to bat in short pants and pads that flapped against his stomach, Miller carried a small blade that had been sawn down to make his stance at the wicket more comfortable. It had black tape to cover the hints of cracks. Coming in at 4 for 100, Miller looked the part from the start. He had all the shots but they were powerless. The 14-year-old had to be content with quiet accumulation around a strong defence, with pushes, nudges and deflections for ones and twos.

An opposition speedster tried him out with a head-high bouncer. Miller's footwork was lightning. He swivelled inside the ball and rolled his wrists as he made contact. The ball went to ground and straight to a fielder at square leg. But the shot was executed with so much assurance that the small crowd reacted, with some clapping before realising that the ball had been cut off.

As his innings progressed, those on the sidelines half-jokingly appropriated the nickname for Woodfull – 'the Unbowlable' – for Miller. He blocked a lot with an immaculate defence – a veteran of around a decade in the game in the backyard, the park and for his state school.

Miller remained 44 not out from a total of 217, which led to a win in the game. It was a promising start on such a big occasion for the youngest and tiniest competitor. His ability and grit endeared him most of all to Truscott. Less gifted, he was all determination and a leader, and he encouraged the new little battler in the team. Truscott, a prefect, took Miller under his wing and even introduced him to some clandestine drinking and smoking with older mates. Despite such distractions, Miller's first season's form was steady.

Truscott gave a pep talk before an important game. 'Don't be scared to have a go,' he implored his charges. 'Pin your ears back and get stuck into it. If you can't bowl a man out, bluff him out.' Nearly running out of clichés, he turned to his miniature mate. 'Now this business of Keith Miller is a case in point,' he said. 'Miller's only a little squirt, but he stands up to the lot of you and beats the hell out of you. The unbowlable Keith Miller! Yes, he's got a stout defence and the heart of a lion.' It was a welcome show of support. Miller, not lacking in confidence at any time, felt emboldened.

Truscott was so impressed that he took Miller down to the St Kilda club for a try-out in September at the beginning of the 1934–35 season. He had a limited batting session and made no impression. The technique was obvious to all, but the lack of power, especially in the nets, could not convey how effective he would be in the middle. His bowling fared worse. While rolling his arm over with Truscott to Hector Oakley, an established first-class player, he lost his line and length attempting to bowl fast. Perhaps it was nerves in trying to impress. But his spin and slow-medium trundlers were not penetrating.

'Son,' a frustrated Oakley said, 'take the ball and hand it to someone who can bowl.'

Miller was hurt. He gesticulated at the other nets. 'We're the only two here!' he snapped. It was a fair point, but didn't help his cause. When the five St Kilda teams were posted at the end of the week, he was not in any of them.

His next step was closer to home at subdistrict club Elsternwick. Wet weather in Melbourne's usual notorious start to a season conspired to prevent him having a bat. He didn't get a bowl, but did a lot of leather-chasing. To his further disappointment, he was dropped to the seconds. The reason given was that he was 'too slow in the field'. It was a humiliation for a young teenager trying hard. After the tease of his possibly becoming a district cricketer in the competition from which the state team was chosen, Miller had to be content with an inferior level, at a time when his self-esteem was given another blow. He did not pass one of the eight subjects he studied in year 9: English, algebra, geometry (scoring '0' in the final term exam, which displeased Woodfull), physics, chemistry, drawing, history and French. His average mark was 25 per cent. He finished bottom of his class of 40.

Miller's marks had deteriorated through the year. The reason was obvious. He had taken on a huge sports load at school with cricket, swimming, football and baseball along with the jockeying at Caulfield and the demands of cricket for Elsternwick, in a competition composed mainly of men. On top of this, Truscott's influence, although encouraging and supportive, had led to social distractions, all conspiring to keep him outdoors and away from his studies.

Just three other boys were forced to repeat year 9. One of the others – an over-sized, non-sporting character – completed Miller's humiliation by telling him: 'It's okay for you, no one will even notice.'

Yet Miller demonstrated a persistent, determined streak. He promised his father he would organise his time in 1935 and do better. But he would keep his sport as a priority over his studies. Of his own volition, in an effort to improve his already proficient batting and lift his ordinary bowling, he began attending Sunday morning practice sessions in a net rigged in the backyard of player Bill Nichols. The South Melbourne club's coach, E. V. 'Hughie' Carroll, was there, instructing. He liked the look of the Miller package, but was blocked from inviting him down to his club by the Elsternwick management, who wanted him to mature as a player with them.

Miller worried that he might never develop physically. After a nasty experience with a cigar, he gave up smoking, partly in the hope that the myth about it stunting growth was true and that he might now sprout. Yet he remained vertically challenged and relatively weak, which prevented him from taking apart an opposition attack. Instead, his scores throughout 1934–35 for Elsternwick seconds and his school's firsts in early 1935 were again steady yet unspectacular. He lifted himself for the big encounter against main rival University High, scoring 30 out of 127 in a game his school won. In the return game, Melbourne High had to at least draw the game to be the top team in their competition, and it did, thanks to a Miller score of 25 in much quicker time than his other innings.

***

A change in the ruling about poaching between Elsternwick and South Melbourne allowed Carroll to invite Miller to his club at the start of the 1935–36 season. The club's skipper, fast bowler

Frank Morton, organised a trial with two good club bowlers. They sent down about a hundred deliveries. None got through his immaculate defence, and plenty were dispatched in a wagon wheel that impressed South's selectors. They debated whether Miller should be put straight into the South firsts or eased in through the seconds. The worry was that St Kilda might reassess him when it played South in the next game of the season. They had first call on him, but since the Saints had rejected him once, South had its chance. The decision was made to play him in the firsts.

'The first thing they [Carroll and co.] did was to measure me,' Keith recalled, 'and they gave me a cut-down bat.' He was advised to bowl slow in the nets to gain accuracy, when his natural inclination was to bound in and hurl them down as fast as he could. His bowling was forced into a secondary role.

South Melbourne provided a friendly atmosphere, in which Miller reacquainted himself with off-spinning all-rounder Ian Johnson and two other lads who were almost as short as him: the impish, stylish bat Lindsay Hassett and the bouncing flea of a wicket-keeper, Cyril Parry. 'We [Johnson and Miller] got around together,' Miller told Melbourne *Herald Sun* journalist Geoff Poulter in 1998. 'We went to the boxing and all those sorts of things. We were very close pre-war.' Two other Swans who impressed were the dashing left-handed opener Ian Lee and the already legendary Laurie Nash, the champion footballer and erratic speed merchant, who had played Test cricket against South Africa in the 1931–32 Test series.

They all made Miller welcome for that first game. St Kilda scored 9 for 250, and Miller, still in short pants and with his miniature bat, came in at number seven when the damage had been done and half the Swans were out for very little. He hung on for a grim 12 not out from a disappointing 127. But astute judges at the game were already predicting a sparkling future, while always expressing the qualification, '*If he can just grow a few inches and fill out a bit.*'

His efforts for South provided a far better end to 1935 than the previous year. Even his school marks improved in his repeat year, although he fell away in the third term when at South, slipping to thirty-sixth in the class of 40, after managing to reach twelfth in second term. His results showed a sprinkling of good scores: 82 per cent in algebra in second term, 78 per cent in chemistry in first term, 71 for history in second term and 68 per cent in French in third term. These marks demonstrated that he could do well if the whim, or the muse, took him. But inspiration on the sporting field was always going to be more likely, as he showed early in 1936, aged 16, with continued progress at South and blistering form at school.

A highlight was his first international match against a visiting schoolboy side from Ceylon (now Sri Lanka). Miller saved his team by scoring a stubborn 28 not out from 5 for 74 in reply to the visitors' 4 for 105. He enjoyed meeting some talented youths from continental Asia, an experience that he later claimed helped him appreciate the people he met from backgrounds other than Australia's monochrome, isolated environment of the 1930s.

He also bowled well in this match and took a wicket. Miller experimented more in the nets during 1935–36 at South. His medium pace trundling became more accurate. He also could now deliver an effective leg break and wrong 'un, and he proved his worth by taking 3 for 5 against University High and 7 for 29 against St Kevin's.

Two mini seasons of baseball had lifted his out-fielding, catching and throwing skills. Now slip was his preferred position. He was quick and missed nothing. Prowess with the bat contin-ued, with scores in those games of 71 and 59 not out, allowing him to claim all-rounder status, at least at school level. Miller was declared Melbourne High's 1936 cricket sports champion with a batting average of 86. His 13 wickets for 120 gave him a good return of 9.2 runs a wicket.

His performances prompted Woodfull to comment in the

school magazine, *The Unicorn*, that 'Miller has Test possibilities'. This was a statement to be considered coming from the recently retired Australian captain who had assessed countless 'could-bes' in his career.

There was one other factor that would influence fulfilment of this acknowledged potential: Weedy Miller had begun to grow. A newspaper photograph of Miller taken in March 1936 by chance captured the sudden change that had come over him. It was at the beginning of an amazing growth phase, and he was now 160 cm. He had added 10 cm (4 inches) in just three months. The arms were first to elongate. They hung like a thin gorilla's at his side. The legs too were longer, but the small head was caught in a netherland of undeveloped jaw and chin, large ears and forehead, with a wad of dark hair, cut short back and sides. The torso seemed to be defying what was happening around it by remaining unmoved and tiny.

A photographer was there, not to secure this anatomical transformation like something out of the movie *The Hulk*, and not directly to snap the first flowering, perhaps, of a champion. He was at the South Melbourne ground at the beginning of South's innings because it had collapsed against Carlton, which was captained by Billy Woodfull.

At the beginning of the innings, young Miller, batting at eight, was sitting and talking to Les Sr not far from the dressing rooms and wondering whether he would get a hit at all on the day. South had a fair batting line-up, with the power-hitting Nash coming in at number six. One for 3 was an early fall; 2 for 3 was a surprise; 3 for 6 made everyone nervous. Miller headed for the rooms to pad up. He was not in the door when the score was 4 for 6. At this point, the reporter at the ground, Percy Millard, had phoned the Melbourne *Herald* to say that a photographer should be sent. Something sensational was happening.

Miller had one pad on and was shocked to hear a roar go up with another wicket down. The score was 5 for 6. The South dressing shed was in a rare state of despair as Nash crashed his way back into the rooms after being dismissed.

'We're not going to get bloody double figures!' someone said with a glance at Miller, as he straightened up, both pads on. He said nothing in response, either through nerves or a determination to stop the rot, given half a chance. All eyes turned towards the centre, with the expectation of seeing another set of stumps shattered. Woodfull, calm and stolid as he was, had a killer instinct. His Carlton Blues were set for some sort of record low score for a team in Australian club cricket.

Miller was ready. He sat outside the rooms, accustoming his eyes to the light, and waited. There were frenzied appeals that would have set the pulse racing, a dropped catch and an lbw that looked plumb. But the batsmen avoided the embarrassment of the team not reaching 10 runs. The score crawled up. Fourteen thousand fans began to fill the terraces, forming the biggest crowd for the competition that season. Twenty runs, then 30, restored a modicum of respectability. There was a sense of relief, and an urgent clap for every ball kept out or single scampered.

At 32, the sixth wicket fell. Miller was in. It was still a humiliatingly low total. Few clubs had been dismissed under 50 in the competition's history. It had only happened to South once, versus Hotham in the 1882–83 season when the team managed just 6 on a very wet pitch. Miller was conscious of his dissatisfied maths teacher standing at mid-off. He knew Woodfull would be doing his best to dismiss him. It made Miller determined to show that if he couldn't always gain a good score in class, then he could under real pressure on the field. He began slowly, intent on keeping his wicket intact. Three more wickets fell as South reached 9 for 76, with Miller on 18 not out. Last man in 'Snowy' Davidson joined him. To the delight of spectators, who loved the improbability of an under-sized kid and a 'bunny' fighting back, the pair managed a partnership of 65 in 95 minutes (Davidson 30 not out). This lifted South to a more respectable 141. Miller scored 61 with 4 fours (two leg glances and two late cuts) in a 2-hour 27-minute stay at the crease.

The entire crowd rose to him as he strolled off the ground with the concentration and nonchalance of youth. The photographer secured that look and the moment for posterity.

Millard's report, and comparisons, would have pleased his subject as much as Les Miller Sr: '"A Ponsford in miniature" describes Miller. He has all the strokes, courage and artistry. All he needs, apart from experience, is power in his shots, particularly his drives . . . Running between the wickets, Miller looked all legs and pads. His bat is the smallest in District cricket . . .' The paper featured a photo of the bat next to one of normal size. 'Discovered and coached by Hughie Carroll,' Millard added, 'Miller, who possesses cricket brains and temperament, has developed to the extent that already the Southerners acclaim him as a future Test batsman.' Another newspaper critic went further, calling him a 'Test player in miniature who revealed all the poise and artistry of a Kippax'.

Carlton went on to win on the first innings the following Saturday. When the game was decided, Morton threw the ball to Miller in an encouraging gesture. The skipper knew that the lad's confidence would be sky-high after such a courageous effort with the bat. The crowd cheered. They already admired him for his pluck. Miller hurled himself at the batsman, sending down two accurate overs. In his second over, an opposition batsman thrashed him to mid-on. It might have cleared any other fielder than Nash, who leapt high and snaffled it. Miller was destined to take many great wickets, but this first one in club cricket gave him the most joy. He would never forget it. Nor would Nash.

In another gesture meant to inspire Miller, the Carlton club donated a silver eggcup marked 'for sterling performance'. Woodfull took time off in algebra class to present him with it. The boy's prestige would have been lifted by this gesture from his teacher and an opposition club, especially in front of classmates.

Yet still Miller had the problem encountered in year 9. The distractions of cricket, playing for his school and a district club, and now the beginnings of fame in a sports-devoted town, meant his studies in year 10 were neglected. He passed only drawing and chemistry and failed his other six subjects in first term.

His geography teacher and the First XI's coach, Harry Zachariah (now aged 93), considered him 'not the best student' but someone he admired for his 'magnificent handwriting' and minor heroics off the field. Zachariah was in his first year as a teacher at the school in 1936. He took Miller and 30 other boys on a country excursion to plant trees as part of geography instruction. The teacher had forgotten the keys to a cabin used by the school for such activity. In it were the necessary spades. Zachariah panicked. If he couldn't get into the cabin, the day's activity would be wasted. The only way in was via a chimney. The only boy lean and small enough to attempt it was Miller, who was still the smallest lad in the group. Some of the boys hoisted him on to the roof. Miller, with some difficulty, eased and squeezed himself down the chimney and saved the day.

After the heady start to the year with on-field successes, he settled in term two, studied with more application and this time failed only two subjects, arithmetic and physics, and passed six. The football season was less hectic and demanding, although he did well despite a problem about where to play him. In previous years he could be hidden as the team rover or on a wing. By July, he had grown to 170 cm – a freakish 20 cm (nearly 8 inches) since his sixteenth birthday. He was about as tall as brothers Les and Ray, who were now not calling him 'Weedy'. Any lingering dreams about riding a Melbourne Cup winner were evaporating.

Miller was now put uncertainly on a half-forward flank. He was all gangling limbs, but was daring to contemplate going through packs instead of around them. He had a long memory of being flattened by bigger boys. It had toughened him, given him, in Aussie Rules parlance, 'a bit of mongrel'. Miller would never be a fringe player relying solely on skill. He wanted to demonstrate a physical presence. He knew all about intimidation, or at least attempts at it, having been on the other end of it all his short life. For the moment, he decided to go *over* packs and fly for high marks. Until this season, he was forced to crumb at the bottom of packs and rely on his agility at ground level. He had always looked on with envy at the taller lads who could fly for the 'speccy' – the spectacular mark. Miller had courage, and confidence in his eye. He would attempt the big grabs, especially with his growing legs for the leap and lengthening arms for the catch of the oval ball.

He had a middling season of transition between a rover and something else no one could predict as he settled for being a forward. Another pleasing aspect of his winter game was his kicking. He had always had poise and balance, but with little depth. Now he was drop-kicking the ball with penetration. By August he was the best and longest kick in the school.

A photograph in *The Unicorn* of the First XVIII, taken towards the end of the 1936 football season, shows Miller sitting cross-legged. He was then about average height and weight in the team. That formerly retarded torso had woken up just a fraction.

At the start of term three in September he was back at South Melbourne for the beginning of another cricket season. He stood at 178 cm – a growth of 28 cm (11 inches). Diminutive Lindsay Hassett, who had not seen him since March, asked the club's caretaker who the gangling kid in the dressing room was.

Miller continue to improve and impress. He was chosen for the Colts, the under-21 team that played in the district competition, while he was still at school in third term and not yet 17. Such a selection was recognition from the state that he was a young player with a strong possibility of becoming a first-class cricketer. This, and his games for South, were a further pull away from his studies. Miller was still playing for the school in third term, but he had gone well beyond the competition standard.

'Some of the other kids were complaining that they weren't getting a bat,' Zachariah recalled. In one match, Miller was approaching a century when the coach sent a boy out to tell him to retire. When Miller returned to the dressing room he complained: 'Sir, I was just settling in.'

The early retirement robbed him of a chance of a school century but demonstrated his dedication to the game, which was taking up all his after-class hours. It was reflected in his exam results. Miller passed five subjects and just failed three for year 10, which recorded a certain amount of diligence and a fair return given the time he devoted to schoolwork. He could have gone on to study at year 11 – 'Leaving', which was the university prepara-tory year for those bright enough or inclined to go on to tertiary studies. But Miller had had enough of school. He believed he had a future in sport and would look for employment that gave him every chance to fulfil that 'Test potential' so blithely used to describe him. Much of the judgement about him so far had been based on the way he looked with his early control of every stroke in the game. But more important was how he appeared under pressure and against tough opposition. Temperament, so evident in that club game against Carlton, was going to be the key.

Miller found uninspiring work as a trainee clerk in a car business and established himself in the Colts during 1936–37. He had reached 181 cm (5 feet 11 inches) early in 1937, and began to put on weight over the next year. His extra strength was reflected the next season – 1937–38 – with the Colts when he headed the team's averages, scoring 340 runs from nine innings at an average of 42.50. He was placed eighth in the overall district averages (445 runs for South and the Colts at 40.45), with his South Melbourne team-mate Ian Lee on top (412 at 103.00), Miller's hero Ponsford second (700 runs at 100 for Melbourne) and Melbourne's Percy Beames third (618 runs at 61.80).

Topping the Colts gained him an inscribed wooden mantel clock trophy, which Miller prized for the rest of his life, more than any other award except for the silver eggcup presented to him by Woodfull at school. The Colts bowling trophy – a silver mug – was won by his fast-bowling friend from Elsternwick school days, Bill Newton.

Miller rarely attempted to take attacks apart for the Colts. He still emulated the approach of his hero, Ponsford, with a solid defence first and the use of all the strokes second. This caused him to be an accumulator who didn't lose his wicket, rather than an aggressor like Charlie Macartney or a dasher like Trumper. Bradman, who in 1937–38 had been the dominant batsman in the world for nearly a decade, was somewhere between the dashers and Ponsford. Bradman had dwelt in 'the zone' of the big hundred, the big double, triple and once the quadruple, more times per innings than any cricketer before (and after) him in history. He had an exceptional power of concentration and an uncanny ability to judge each ball on its length and its merit, rather than a need to hit nearly everything. This was essentially Ponsford's strength, too. The difference was that Bradman was faster in his accumulation at every level of the game, and had taken big Test scores into a dimension of his own. These two were the trendsetters in the 1920s and 1930s. It was natural for Miller, especially with Les Sr's endorsement, to follow their methods, which worked to devastating effect at the highest level of the game.

At the end of the 1937–38 season, the *Argus* described him: 'A steady right-hander, he uses his feet well, and his off drives have power and good direction.' The *Age* noted his progress:

> 18-year-old Colt Keith Miller is steadily developing into a class batsman . . . Miller is now infusing punch into his smooth, natural stroke-making. With South, he had to go in fairly low on the list, and his scoring was hardly fast enough. Now he goes in earlier and has more scope. Once he fills out – he is rather tall for his weight – Miller should become a brilliant, aggressive batsman.

The key factor emerging was Miller's mental attitude. He had the basic equipment and capacity to concentrate, which led to consistent scores of 59, 72, 78 not out and a scintillating 102 against Northcote, his best performance for the district season. Technique was still the master of aggression in his mind. He had the discipline to curb the inner demon that was beginning to manifest itself in recent months since his shots had some force, especially off the front foot. He now had as much penetration in a drive as the average club cricketer.

Miller's steady form in the Colts caused him to be chosen to play for the Victorian Second XI in early February 1938 against Tasmania. Because he was playing against a state team it was his initial first-class match. It was also his first game at the mighty MCG. A decade ago Miller had sat with his father studying Ponsford. Those days were still fresh in his mind, and now he was the centre of attention, right where his hero had been. The spectator capacity had risen to around 90,000 with the completion of the Southern Stand in 1937, giving the arena the feel of an amphitheatre. But with just a few hundred spectators scattered around the colosseum it seemed to have less atmosphere than he had encountered in games for Melbourne High.

Still, Miller rose to the occasion. He unveiled a wide range of strokes in amassing 181 in 289 minutes. The extra dimension that distinguished this from performances at the start of the season was timing allied to more power, especially in his driving on both sides of the wicket, although his statistics of just 5 fours did not reflect it. Miller liked lofting the ball too, now that he could. Never again would he be accused of not having enough force in his shots. Defence and technique were still dominant in his play, but on a par with them now was an attacking intent. Yet he had not calibrated when to go on the offence and when to draw back, especially against spinners, who snared him often.

Advance was slow after such a fine start. Miller was frustrated and irritated by late in the next season, 1938–39, when he still had not been given another chance at the first-class level. But a strong batting performance for the Victorian seconds against New South Wales seconds at the MCG in late January 1939 clinched his belated advance. He scored 46 in the first innings and 60 in the second. The latter was a fighting knock when other batsmen failed in a tally of 158. Arthur Morris, a week after his seventeenth birthday, played in the game for New South Wales batting at eight, scoring 6 and 3. Miller's mate, Bill Newton, dismissed him in the second innings.

Five weeks later Miller was chosen in the First Victorian XI, led by Keith Rigg, in the last two non-Sheffield Shield first-class matches versus Western Australia in Perth. Miller had one failure with scores of 38, 55, 1 and 17 not out, which left him with that most deadly of all descriptions: 'Promising.'

Defence was the key to his burgeoning football career at the Brighton Club, which was in the Victorian Football Association (VFA), ranked one level below the top competition, the Victorian Football League (VFL). After being played in attack at school, he was plonked on the half-back flank, but it could have been just about anywhere. His versatility, natural athleticism, fitness, stamina and adaptable skills allowed options. He had height, but was still not judged strong enough to hold down full-back or centre-half back, unless as a fill in, until his third season in 1939. The VFA in the 1930s was as physical as the AFL today. A key position player had to be tough. The late teenage Miller didn't lack courage, but he was still too lean to start 'shirt-fronting' – using the hip and shoulder charge and bump that could debilitate, even concuss, an opponent. Miller was content to out-mark the opposition and use his long-legged dash to run off them. His magnificent drop-kicking meant that he had an incomparable finishing skill that turned defence into attack. As a defender, he was more and more backing his skills rather than relying on blanketing or negating his opponent. Just as with his cricket, Miller by 1939 was mixing defence with attack on the football field.

The hopes and aspirations of a generation of young Australian men around his age were thrown into uncertainty on 3 September 1939 when Great Britain and France declared war on Germany after it had invaded Poland two days earlier.

That night in Canberra, Prime Minister Robert Menzies made an announcement in a radio hook-up throughout the nation: 'Fellow Australians, it is my melancholy duty to inform you officially that, in consequence of the persistence of Germany in her invasion of Poland, Great Britain has declared war upon her . . . Where Britain stands, there stand the people of the entire British world.'

Major conflict had been coming after an uneasy twenty-year hiatus following World War I and the dictatorial power in Germany from 1933 of Adolf Hitler and the Nazi Party. Allied nations had looked away after he had ordered occupation of the Rhineland in contravention of the Treaty of Versailles in March 1936. They did nothing in March 1938 when Hitler's troops occupied Austria and incorporated it into Germany. They sat paralysed in March 1939 when Czechoslovakia was annexed by Germany and its fascist partner Italy took over Albania. The Allies then looked on in fear as Germany signed a non-aggression pact with Stalin's Soviet Union.

While heavy boots were goose-stepping in unison 20,000 km away in Central Europe, Miller and countless sportsmen across Australia were swapping stops for spikes at the start of another lazy spring. Fighting seemed remote and far away despite the headlines and Britain's engagement leading automatically to Australia declaring war on Germany, too. The ramifications for the average bloke would take time to sink in. Yet the experience of World War I, still heavily in the memory of survivors and families of those who hadn't come back alive or well, would begin to enter the consciousness of the Australian psyche again. The tyranny of distance for the antipodes would allow people to carry on in the wistful thought that surely there could not really be another world conflagration after the Great War of 1914–18, which was called, more in hope than realism, the war to end all wars. Newspapers would be read and radios listened to more intently as Europe was scrutinised in the wish and hope that leaders would come to their senses and not take it further.

In this atmosphere, Miller's expectations of a continued advance as a cricketer remained in the 1939–40 season. He received a boost when chosen to take the train to Adelaide to play against the South Australians in his first Shield game for Victoria. He was the new chum in a happy and talented squad that included friends from South, Lee, Johnson and Hassett, along with Doug Ring, the leg-spinner who had also been at Melbourne High. There were three other Test players apart from Hassett: spinner Chuck Fleetwood-Smith, skipper and keeper Ben Barnett and opening bowler Morris Sievers.

Miller could not have had a more pleasant place to begin his Shield first-class career. The Adelaide Oval dominated the parklands between Torrens Lake and St Peter's Cathedral. It featured trees. The stands and gates were distinctive. The old scoreboard dated back to Edwardian times. It had an atmosphere of play rather than that of combat that was engendered at the MCG. But any thoughts of a relaxed competition were soon quashed by a look at the South Australian line-up. The batting included Bradman, Ron Hamence and 'Jack' Badcock, who would be the Victorian bowlers' collective problem, but not Miller's. His challenge would come in facing a formidable spin trio of Clarrie Grimmett, Frank Ward and Mervyn Waite. Grimmett would be the test. At his peak he was regarded by most astute judges as the best purveyor of *slow* leg-spin bowling ever, as compared with the best bowler as such in the world, Bill O'Reilly of Australia and New South Wales. He also bowled leg-spin, but with less turn and much more pace.

Grimmett, 48 years old and past his prime, was variously known as 'Old Grum' and 'Scarl' (after the Scarlet Pimpernel) and he was still as wily as they come. His main aim was to spin a web of uncertainty around an opponent and to think him out. Scarl thought nothing of delivering ball after ball of almost the same delivery, edging his opponent closer and closer to an lbw or catch. Or he could send down eight different types of ball in succession, testing a batsman's skills to the limit.

Grimmett's approach depended on what sort of batsman he had in front of him. The opponent might receive the full variety to see if he could pick him out of his hand, whether he waited for the pitch of the ball, or again if the batsman fancied himself as a dancer to the pitch. Grimmett preferred the more cautious type above the cavalier. A defensive batsman, usually using backfoot play as a counter, would be easier for Grimmett to tie up and fool. The aggressor would be tempted by the bowler to judge the size of his ego. A smashing four, or even two in succession, would be followed by an offering inviting a third dip that would often see a mis-stroke and maybe a skyed catch.

Barnett won the toss and batted, and Victoria was soon in trouble, losing 3 for 18. Miller came to the wicket in a mini-crisis but was caught in slips for just 4 by (his later friend and co-writer) Richard 'Dick' Whitington off the paceman Harold Cotton, whose action was suspect enough to be called 'chucker' by the opposition. It was a disappointing start, especially as Miller regarded himself as a 'big occasion' performer. He would have liked to make a strong first impression on the Don.

Victoria scrambled together 207, thanks to a rearguard fight by Barnett (51) and Ian Johnson (35). South Australia responded with an equally poor beginning, losing 4 for 30. Bradman then got going. He was hurtling towards yet another century when he played a ball into the covers towards Miller. The fieldsman noticed out of the corner of his eye that the Don was dawdling. Miller whipped the ball in; Bradman made a desperate last-second scamper, but was run out on 76.

He was such a superb runner between the wickets that it was the first time he had been dismissed this way in a first-class match in a decade, almost to the day. It was one of only four run-outs he would endure in 338 first-class dismissals. Miller had made his impression, at least as a swooping cover field. The day when Elsternwick dumped him to its second team for being retarded in chasing leather was long gone.

South Australia led by 54 on the first innings. Second time around, Victoria did better. Miller came in facing spin, not pace. Grimmett judged him a 'careful' starter. He pegged him on to the back foot, tied him up, beat him several times and then bowled him for 7. It was a comprehensive victory for the bowler. Miller was left with an inauspicious start: 11 runs for the match, no bowling figures, one catch, one run-out, and a team defeat. Bradman (64) and Hamence (99) ensured a tight three-wicket win for the home side.

Miller was more disgruntled than disappointed by his performance on the train ride home to Melbourne. Such was his competitive nature that he mulled over the way Grimmett had defeated him. He wondered if he might find a few clues from the newspaper reports. The spinner had taken 5 for 118 in the second innings. Four of those dismissals were shown in a photo montage. Each batsman, including Miller, had been bowled or lbw playing back. He made up his mind that the next time they met he would play forward to Grimmett, and not allow him to dictate terms.

Miller at 20 was tall (182 cm), lean (70 kg) and, like his brothers Ray and Les Jr, good-looking. Like them, he had an easy charm. He was taller than his brothers, and his sporting prowess so far had taken him a notch above them in football and cricket, which gave him a higher and growing profile. His sister-in-law Molly (married to Ray) remembers teenage girls hiding in the bushes outside his Elsternwick home, hoping to get a glimpse of him. 'You got too much,' Molly used to say to him, meaning his looks, physique, character and athletic ability. Nicknames sometimes stuck. But 'Weedy' left him by the end of his school-days when he was still growing up and out.

Miller's first job after leaving school was in the spare parts section of a car company, followed by even more prosaic inaction but better pay with a customs and shipping agent, who promised him some time off for his cricket commitments. But it wasn't enough.

The Vacuum Oil Co. (the forerunner for Mobil Oil), an oil products distributor, offered him mundane work as a clerk in its finance and accounting department, yet with flexible time to accommodate his first-class cricket advancement. Bill Lynstead, a 15-year-old straight out of Box Hill High School, remembers joining the company on the same day as Miller. 'We had the uninspiring job of sorting invoices into numerical order,' Lynstead recalled. 'At morning tea, someone turned on the wireless, which was broadcasting the Shield game, Victoria versus Queensland, at the MCG. Percy Beames, also a state cricketer, was our new boss at Vacuum Oil. I thought that this was a pretty good job. You could listen to your workmates playing top cricket while you worked.'

Miller did enough in this second match, scoring 41 and 47 not out, to hold his place in the state team. 'I didn't mind getting out in the first innings,' he told Beames, 'after all [C. P.] Christ caught and bowled me!'

In a back-to-back match at the MCG, this time versus New South Wales, he ran into a barrage of wonderful leg-spin. The great 'Tiger' Bill O'Reilly, at the peak of his powers, troubled him and had him stumped for 14 in one innings. The highly skilled Cecil Pepper, only a rung below O'Reilly, bowled him in the other innings for the same score. Leg-spin had baffled and beaten Miller in every first-class game except his first against Tasmania. It made him anxious for the return encounter against South Australia, which began on 29 December 1939, again at the MCG.

Barnett won the toss again, and once more batted first. Percy Beames, who became a friend (and football rival) of Miller's, discussed how to play Grimmett. Miller told Beames that all the players Grimmett snared in the previous match were playing back. He was going forward at every chance. This had not worked for him against O'Reilly and Pepper. But they were faster spinners, who often speared the ball in at near medium pace. Grimmett lofted it more, and was slower.

Victoria in this game batted more consistently. Hassett managed 92, in a healthy partnership with Miller. The latter showed the firmness of his convictions, and demonstrated that it is better to have a counter-attack plan than no plan at all by going after Grimmett. The batsman did the *one, two, one* dance down the pitch to the spinner. The good batting wicket engendered confidence.

Miller found himself in a duel with the old master spinner, but refused to be trapped on the back foot. Once set, he also drove through the covers with elegance. The laconic Grimmett never, ever looked flustered. The only indication of hesitation, even some inner turmoil, was the length of his deliveries. They began shortening, ever so imperceptibly. Miller even had the temerity to feign a forward move, then rock back and smack the ball off the back foot. This was cheeky for a 20-year-old tyro. Yet it worked.

Hassett took the cue after Miller had shown the way. Together they saw off the economic leggie. It was a sweet victory for Miller. He went on to 108, his second first-class hundred and initial century in the fierce, high-standard Shield competition.

On that score, Miller drove at a ball from Grimmett when he was in his third spell. The ball seemed to squeeze out. It went straight to Bradman, who caught it. 'Well bowled, Clarrie,' Bradman said with a grin. The bowler looked relieved and pleased, having dismissed his youthful tormentor. But Miller stood his ground, asking the umpire if it were a 'bump ball'. The umpires conferred, without the benefit of replays, which themselves could be inconclusive. After a short delay, the umpire gave him out. Miller accepted the decision.

The next morning when he read the papers, he wondered whether he and the umpires had been deceived by the gamesmanship of the experienced Bradman and Grimmett. Miller's attitude was that he stood his ground if there were doubts, but that he would 'walk' if he were certain he was out. The incident, he thought, told him much about Bradman. He would stay within the rules, which he knew better than any other player, having sat and done very well in the umpire's exam at age 24. But Bradman was all about winning, and if some gamesmanship, psyching out of the opposition or bluff helped, he would use it. Miller was not a wily type. Very few cricketers were, at the age of 20, playing against men with, in Bradman's case, a decade of experience and, in Grimmett's case, up to two decades at the first-class level. They had a professional approach in an essentially amateur game. And young Keith Miller was still naïve. Whether he remained so scrupulously fair with maturity would be a matter of experience and character.

Regardless of this incident, Bradman said that he was most impressed by Miller's batting. Clem Hill, the great left-hander of the nineteenth and early twentieth centuries, forecast a big future for him.

Apart from Miller's obvious batting skills in scoring this century, the effort proved early in his career that he was a learner. He would not wallow in self-pity or defeat, but was self-confident enough to reflect on what went wrong and find an answer to a challenge. The cricket 'brains' that Percy Millard noticed in March 1936 were even more evident now in a tougher, more competitive environment.

His boss Beames learned something from his staff member and hit 104 in the Adelaide match, and Victoria reached 475.

Sizeable crowds of 30,000 turned up on days two and three in anticipation of a Bradman response. He gave an exhibition on New Year's Day 1940 that Miller would never forget, slaughtering the Victorian attack. He was severe on the talented Chuck Fleetwood-Smith, the left-arm spinner. Miller, prowling the covers, and looking to repeat his run-out of the Don, did a lot of leather-chasing. Yet he didn't mind. At least he was in the game and giving those long legs a work-out. Bradman sliced, diced, drove, dissected and deflected his way to a century, then 150, beating the clock along the way. When Bradman reached 196, Barnett stacked the covers, anticipating that Bradman would take up a challenge and attempt to drive through the five men patrolling from point to mid-off as another of his 37 first-class double centuries beckoned.

Miller was determined not to let anything through. It was the batting genius against a bowler and a wall of fieldsmen. The ball was pitched on middle stump. Bradman repositioned his feet and struck. The ball sped past Miller within a few metres of another fielder. They both turned to chase, but had hardly moved when the ball hit the pickets.

After reaching his double, Bradman delivered himself and the spectators a rare treat; he went six-hunting. For as long as Miller could remember, his father and other coaches had preached the gospel of keeping the ball along the ground the way Ponsford and Bradman always did. These two had been so dominant and successful over most of the past two decades that any other approach seemed like heresy. If a batsman wanted to succeed and help his team to a winning score, he did *not* loft the ball. A batsman rolled the wrists over cuts and hooks. He drove with a break on the follow-through. It was almost an unwritten law in top cricket. Only park cricketers, no-hopers and tail-enders, coaches claimed, lost concentration and went the long handle. Yet here, against all orthodoxy and principles, was the high priest of the game loosening up and belting balls into the stands.

Miller noted another factor. When Bradman reached 250 less than 30 minutes later, he was trying his hardest to loft the ball for a catch off the long-suffering Fleetwood-Smith, who, in front of his home crowd, had never been able to remove the Don. Knowing that the talented spinner would soon be retiring, Bradman was giving him his wicket, not an unusual thing for him to do, although never when a game was in the balance or his score was low.

The hard-headed, calculating crusher of opponents at all levels of the game had a sense of fun after all. Miller nearly took one of the five skyers, but it was just beyond him. Finally Ian Johnson snaffled one in the deep. Chuck had his prize with Bradman on a chanceless 267 in 340 minutes.

Miller received mixed messages. He had seen the greatness of Bradman with every shot in the book and more. Miller had chased many of his 27 fours along the carpet to all points of the compass. Then he had witnessed the batsman going over the top with ease against all bowlers once he had passed 200. It was a first-hand lesson in how to accumulate with discipline and exceptional skill while still entertaining the crowd. Miller would retain this unwritten instruction. He would go for big scores, too. It was fashionable. Yet Miller would loft the ball and attempt to be the crowd-pleaser even more. There was at this point a sense of the gambler, the risk-taker lurking. He was very keen to defy the odds. Technique and concentration were still ruling, but the aggressor in him liked what he saw in Bradman's finish to an unforgettable performance.

Miller was coming up against all the great characters in Australian cricket and enjoying the experience. The fiery O'Reilly intrigued him as much as anyone. In the final Shield game of the season in Sydney against New South Wales he witnessed a clash between O'Reilly and Hassett. The dainty Victorian was the only batsman in this game to have O'Reilly's measure. Miller was trapped lbw by O'Reilly for just 1 in the first innings and was run out – a too-common experience for him early in his career – for 24 in the second. Hassett scored 122 in both innings. The knocks were punctuated by repeated lofted straight drives off O'Reilly. Miller recalled batting with Hassett when the spinner reacted to two of these hits for successive fours. The next delivery turned sharply, beat the bat and just slid over the off bail. Hassett looked down the wicket at Miller and grinned. O'Reilly saw it. He gestured to a fielder to pass the ball quickly to him. Then he wheeled in with extra pace. Hassett danced down the wicket and lofted him high for a third four in four deliveries.

Miller heard O'Reilly mutter: 'A fellow may as well go and sit on the fence now!' The world's finest bowler was defeated. It was a rare moment and compliment to Hassett.

In the second innings, Miller was at the wicket again when Hassett repeated his feat of two successive straight hits for boundaries off O'Reilly. His infamous temper flared. 'You little bastard!' he said, glaring down the wicket, hands on hips. 'You're not even good-looking!'

***

Apart from the 108, Miller's first Sheffield Shield season was middling. He ended with 298 runs from ten completed knocks at an average of 29.8. Nevertheless, the skill level was there for all to see. He had the strokes and was not afraid to display them. But there were a few flaws, such as a weakness against top-class spin and a hesitancy running between the wickets. Yet they were matters he could work on. He was recognised as a versatile field, adept in slips or in the deep.

But Miller did not bowl one ball in his first Shield season.

WAR INTERVENES

Almost to the day that Miller was first recognised as a young player with a real future in Test cricket, events beyond his control were conspiring to end it. Germany and the Soviet Union had divided Poland between them. The Soviets had occupied Estonia, Latvia and Lithuania. They had also attacked brave Finland, which was finally defeated. In April 1940, while Miller was lining up for Brighton and looking forward to some excitement and advance in his football, Germany was waging an effective submarine campaign against merchant shipping bound for Britain. It also occupied several Norwegian ports and all of Denmark. Somehow, to mainly Anglo-Celtic Australia, the Nazi attacks were still confined to another world – northern and middle Europe. There was still a hope and prayer that Germany would not attack west again. In an atmosphere of concern rather than worry life went on unhindered down under. Sport was a sizeable part of it.

Miller, his confidence high after his advances in cricket, was ready for anything on the football field. Brighton was preparing for its hardest game of the season against Coburg, one of the toughest sides in football. Miller was told early in the week before the match that he would be playing on Bob Pratt. He, Haydn Bunton, Dick Reynolds and Laurie Nash were the greatest names in Victorian football in the 1930s. Pratt, a stocky, strong, high-leaping mark and prolific goal-kicker, had caused a sensation by transferring from South Melbourne in the Victorian Football League to Coburg in the Victorian Football Association. He had kicked 678 goals for South in ten seasons, with three successive seasons topping 100 goals. Pratt was 27, and not carrying any serious injuries that would curtail his goal-hungry ambitions. Miller was talented and with courage to burn, but he was still lean. Despite being several inches taller, Miller could not attempt to bullock or harass this champion off his game. Pratt thrived on players trying to match his strength. There was only one way to play Pratt, and that was to leap over him for marks and run off him, *if* a player had the height, skill, judgement and pace. Faced with another great opponent in another sport, Miller listened to his coach and decided to again follow a set tactic. If it didn't work, there would be plan B. But it wouldn't be his problem. An early goal spree from Pratt would see Miller moved off him and someone else given the hardest task in Aussie Rules.

There was another edge to this match. The coach and selectors of the VFL St Kilda Football Club would be at the game to assess any prospects they could poach from Brighton. This would be the chance for any player to impress and make the leap into the higher competition. Team-mates pitied Miller. It was plain bad luck being asked to perform against such an opponent when selectors were watching.

Miller took up the challenge, standing shoulder to shoulder with Pratt. Each time the ball came their way, Miller would wait to the last second to back his judgement. He out-marked the superstar several times in the first quarter and left Pratt cursing his team-mates for not delivering the ball properly. Miller was in terrific form. If he didn't think he could mark the ball, he would punch it clear.

In the second quarter Pratt slipped away twice for two kicks and a return of one goal and one point. Pratt took two marks in the third quarter, but Miller had forced him to chase kicks the other side of the centre. The forward missed another set shot, but in the main Miller had beaten him. In the last quarter Pratt was completely blanketed and did not get a kick.

Brighton had a rare victory against Coburg, and Pratt had the poorest day anyone could recall in years. Miller was the best on the ground. The St Kilda representatives came to him in the rooms. They gushed over his performance and wanted to sign him on the spot. The *Age* reported the recruitment: 'Miller, who is also an expert cricketer, is one of the most promising players ever to enter league ranks, and can be played anywhere in defence. It was he who kept Bob Pratt to one goal in last week's Association match.'

Almost every fantasy Miller had ever had in sport was coming true. He was now a first-class cricketer, and experienced observers and former players were saying he had a Test future. Soon he would be in the highest ranks of Aussie Rules football in the home of the code, Victoria. Just about the only dream not to come true for him was his obsession with being a jockey. His weight now would see even Phar Lap wince at the thought of Miller on his sturdy back. He would have to be content with just being in the company of jockeys, trainers and owners, and fellow punters.

Everything he did was aimed at paving the way for a career in sports, which had been his aim since he was a child. It was rapidly coming to fruition.

There was just one snag: war. A day after Miller thrashed Pratt and signed with St Kilda, Prime Minister Menzies felt compelled to broadcast that football should continue as a morale booster in the face of deteriorating circumstances abroad. A percentage of gate receipts would go to war charities. Suddenly, sport, which so dominated the Australian cultural landscape, was put into a different perspective. It could remain viable purely to keep people's spirits up. Footy and cricket, normally treated as religions, were reduced to mere entertainments. They were in danger of being cut further when, on 10 May 1940, the Germans began their western offensive. It was a move that every Australian dreaded, especially the veteran diggers, who had done so much to push them back and defeat them in 1918.

Then there was a blitzkrieg sweep of Panzer armoured divisions through the Netherlands and Belgium into France. By 22 June three-fifths of France, including Paris, was occupied, and the rest had become a 'neutral' state with its government in Vichy. The Germans would install a puppet administration there, which meant that Hitler and the Nazis in effect controlled France. This news sent thousands of volunteers in Australia scurrying to military recruiting offices to join up for the fight against Fascist forces. Miller wanted to join up. St Kilda warned that if he joined one of the services, he could be placed outside Victoria, which would end his football career. He decided to wait until the week of the last game of the season.

Miller made the most of his sporting opportunities, aware that for him the games could stop at any time. He began well at his new club, St Kilda, which was soon a toughening experience. In his first game – against Carlton – he lined up on the half-back flank against a hard-hitting star player, Ron 'Socks' Cooper from Western Australia. There was a near-capacity crowd, and Miller, aged 20, was keyed up for a big effort. The ball was bounced. Cooper looked at Miller, and then punched him in the head. It was the classic king hit – the most cowardly blow in football – delivered to a player who was unaware that it was coming. Miller went down, semi-concussed.

There had been the odd punch-up in the VFA, but no one had targeted him this way before. Miller's reputation in holding Pratt to a solitary goal had preceded him into the League. It was a delayed baptism. He would retain the memory of the incident. 'I learnt more in a second or two [from the untelegraphed punch],' Miller said, 'than I would have in a year.'

He thought he might consider getting in the first punch in his second game against Footscray if another thuggish player was on him. But he changed his mind. He was lined up on champion boxer Ambrose Palmer. Miller was apprehensive. If Cooper could deliver a blow like that, what would a professional boxer do? But Palmer was intelligent enough to leave his punching to the ring. He was a tough but fair footballer. He shook hands with Miller at the start of the game and sought him out at the end of it for another handshake and an encouraging 'well played'. 'Ambrose was a real gentleman,' Miller said, 'to me anyway!'

The next time St Kilda played Carlton in 1940, Miller gave no hint to Cooper of his feelings about the previous encounter. Less than a minute after the first bounce the Carlton player was about to collect the ball on the half volley when Miller hit him with a shoulder bump to the chest. Cooper went down hard. A trainer helped him to a forward pocket, and he was replaced at quarter time. Miller found the experience exhilarating. He had never really hit or hurt a player before. Now with added weight at the end of the 1940 football season, he had another dimension to his game: aggression. Opponents would be less likely to target him, and if they did, Miller felt more confident about retaliating within or without the rules of the game.

In another game, versus Richmond, Miller came up against Jack Dyer, who had a pugilist's nose and a matching mien. 'Captain Blood' was the player who Miller claimed 'really frightened' him. 'I was bending down to pick up the ball and I saw Dyer charging towards me,' he said. 'I thought, "Oh no!" But fortunately he slipped on the cricket pitch and missed me.'

During the season, St Kilda played twice against the reigning premier club, Melbourne, led by Alan La Fontaine. It included in its ranks his old school mate Bluey Truscott and fellow state cricketer Percy Beames, along with Norm Smith at his best, Jack Mueller, Ron Barassi Sr and a phalanx of other stars who took it to its second successive premiership. In the second game, Miller was reported for twice questioning a goal umpire's decision. The tribunal let him off, mainly because of his spotless record to that point.

St Kilda won just five games of 18 and finished second-bottom of the League table. This was no fault of Miller's. He was the runaway best and fairest player at his club for the 1940 season after performing brilliantly against a galaxy of the era's big names, including leading goal-kickers Jack Titus (Richmond), Smith, Sel Murray (North Melbourne) and Des Fothergill (Collingwood).

On 20 August 1940 Miller decided to join the army in its motor transport division, but first had to pass a medical examination. He was a fit specimen, standing just under 6 feet (182 cm), but still lean for his height at 70 kg. The only registered distinguishing mark on him was an appendix scar. The doctor attending told him that his 39-inch chest span, impressive for one so thin, meant that he would probably fill out more. When Miller told the doctor his recent growth history, he was informed that he might not have stopped growing. Not surprisingly, he had 20:20 vision.

***

In September, as Miller became a spectator in the finals watching Truscott star for Melbourne, the Luftwaffe launched massive bombing raids on Britain in an attempt to soften it up for a cross-Channel invasion. The war had moved figuratively close to 'home' for most Australians.

Miller was pleased to be sent on 30 September to an army camp at the Caulfield racetrack. There were no horses, jockeys or racing now, but at least he felt comfortable in familiar surroundings. It also meant he was able to play cricket for South Melbourne and Victoria. Yet he was never at ease with the strictures of army life. He abhorred it, and it was not long before he clashed with authority. On 4 November he was charged with 'using insulting language to a superior officer' and fined 10 shillings. It was this and his knockabout style that earned him a new sobriquet, 'Dusty'. This was a label associated with a hard-drinking Outback character; someone who didn't mind the odd 'dust-up' or brawl. Miller had resented being called Weedy. Yet he would happily live up to the new nickname attained in his first few months in the army.

He managed to get leave to play interstate cricket during the 1940–41 cricket season, which was reduced to 10 interstate matches rather than the usual 30 or so. Miller's limited opportunities saw him notch 140 runs at 28.00. The fact that he bowled a bit and was a good fielder did not come into calculations in assessments that could still only rank him as 'promising'. He took part in one featured game for the war effort: D. G. Bradman's XI v. S. J. McCabe's XI. Bradman at 31 was ill and a shadow of his former self. He scored just 0 and 12, bringing his tally to 18 runs from four innings for the limited season. Critics predicted that it was the end of his career, but made some positive noises about Miller's future – as a bowler. After failing with the bat, he was thrown the ball by skipper Stan McCabe, when he and Morris Sievers were unfit to deliver.

'Although he [Miller] seldom bowls,' the *Argus* newspaper reported, 'he performed splendidly.' The medium pacer began 'with two half-pitchers' and after that bowled 'fairly accurately. He was able to make his good length ball stand up a little, and [South Australian star bat Ken] Ridings touched one [caught by keeper Don Tallon] to give him his first wicket.' (It was a wicket that meant something to Miller for more reasons than one. Ridings would be one of several first-class cricketers to die during World War II.)

Miller took for 1 for 24. Coming off a short run, he looked every inch the athlete. His mop of thick black hair was flicked back, almost theatrically, as he loped in to deliver. He had a high arm action and could extract lift from near a good length. His surprising first-up effort was swamped by Bill O'Reilly taking 5 for 53 (including the prize wicket of the Don) and Grimmett

4 for 46. Yet Miller's cameo was not lost on Bradman, especially when he caused batsmen to hurry shots. It would stay in the Don's mind.

Cricket had suffered because of the cost and time taken for interstate games, but the VFL battled on in 1941 despite many clubs beginning to see players called up for military service. The game's standard was kept high while attendances fell just over 200,000 spectators to 1,157,000. Miller enjoyed another superb season and proved his versatility by playing forward when there was a strong wind. He would return to the back line, in the key positions of either centre half back or full-back, when St Kilda was kicking into the wind. Sam Loxton (later of Invincibles cricket fame) was the full forward pushed back to make way for Miller with the wind. On the rare occasions Miller played forward all game, he proved successful, with one eight-goal haul against North Melbourne.

At the age of 21 he had grown to 185 cm and weighed 76 kg. He was beginning to throw his extra weight around on the field. Lou Richards, the colourful Collingwood rover, wrote of him:

Keith was a very tough player. He would knock your head off at the drop of a hat. That was his make-up because he was also a tough, tenacious cricketer. As a footballer he was just as spectacular as he was with bat and ball. A strong mark at full-back, he used to put the ball well back into play with beautiful long drop-kicks.

Richards recalled Miller 'sinking the slipper' – a euphemism for kicking an opponent, usually in the lower leg or ankle. (Decades later when asked how he would stop leading goal-scorer Hawthorn full-forward Jason Dunstall, Miller replied jokingly with a throaty laugh: 'First, I'd kick him in the ankle.')

Miller paid little attention to reputation or rank when it came to battles on the football field. His boss Percy Beames was having a wonderful run with Melbourne, which had a strong chance of winning its third successive premiership. In the week before the match between their two clubs, they chided each other at work. Beames, also a rugged and talented rover, irritated Miller by calling him 'Snako'. Miller retaliated by calling him 'Kicker'. At the start of the game, Miller charged Beames and collected him with a raised elbow, which put him out of the match. It was not perhaps the way to treat a boss, although it did not affect his relationship with Beames. This type of incident was building him a reputation. Melbourne won its hat-trick of premierships while St Kilda languished at second bottom again. Miller was second in the Best and Fairest.

He was called back to service during the football season and was again stationed in and around Melbourne, mainly at Broadmeadows. Yet he was still having trouble with army discipline, and could not get used to taking orders, especially from superiors he considered his inferior, which was almost all of them. Miller left the army in late September after the grand final, and six weeks later, in early November, he went with a mate, Johnny Hosking, to join the navy. Hosking had dreams of being an admiral. But there were few places available at the top so both men filled out forms for starting more modestly – as stokers. Miller was accepted, but Hosking was not. Miller tore up his form, refusing to join any fleet that wouldn't take his mate. Hosking was scared of heights and didn't fancy the idea of the air force. The army had to be his choice, the only option Miller would not be taking. That left Miller with one option himself: the air force. He began with the RAAF on 8 November 1941.

Miller was acutely aware of the drift of friends and acquaintances into the armed services and action in Europe. His mate Bluey Truscott was a Spitfire ace with No. 452 Squadron, the first Australian fighter unit in the RAF. He had shot down 14 German planes. Many friends from schooldays, sport and all walks of life were perishing or being debilitated by the war. Enough current or past players to make an XI from just his cricket club South Melbourne were killed, injured or taken prisoner.

The Japanese shocked the world by bombing Pearl Harbor on 7 December 1941. There were real threats that they were targeting Australian cities, which led to an unusual Christmas. At the height of the end-of-year shopping rush, the government brought in a black-out. Miller remembered the gloom in the city without neon signs. Japanese invasion seemed imminent. Digging squads began destroying parks and gardens to construct grotesque air raid shelters. The MCG, St Kilda, South Melbourne and Footscray grounds were to become service camps or depots. There was no interstate cricket in 1941–42 for Victoria, and the VFA was suspended. Geelong withdrew from the VFL, whose ranks would be severely depleted.

Miller was among those leaving all big competitive sport. In early 1942 he was sent to No. 4 Initial Training School, Victor Harbour, South Australia. Miller donned RAAF fatigue dress — loose-fitting overalls, buttoned at the front. It was a boring time for him, and he looked forward to weekend leave, once a month. But this precious break was dependent on not incurring the wrath of an aggressive, red-headed drill instructor, known as Sergeant Bluey. It was mid-morning on a Saturday. A train would take the lucky recruits to the bright lights of Adelaide at 2 p.m., if they escaped his sadistic whim on the dusty parade ground.

A drill error or even a whisper out of turn would see him cancel leave. After normal rifle drill, the sergeant began instruction with fixed bayonets. This was followed by lessons in unarmed combat, in which a trainee had to disarm the sergeant, who carried a rifle and fixed bayonet. The trainees were lined up in three rows. The sergeant called for a volunteer to come forward and relieve him of his rifle. But the inductees feared they might lose their leave if they managed to succeed. The sergeant protested that this was preposterous. He challenged them again.

One quiet voice from the rear said: 'I'll have a go, sergeant.'

It was Miller. He was asked to step forward. Miller reminded him that he had said leave would not be cancelled. The sergeant was adamant. He told Miller not to worry. He stepped up to the instructor, crouched, feigned a move left, right and left, then swung his right leg behind the instructor's right leg and tripped him. Miller pushed him down with his right hand while ripping the rifle from the instructor with his left hand. Sergeant Bluey went down hard on his back. His face was puce, matching his hair. He was fierce. He spluttered that Miller had tripped him, repeating the accusation as he scrambled to his feet.

'I disarmed you, didn't I, sergeant?' Miller responded.

Sergeant Bluey grabbed back his rifle. He challenged Miller to repeat the feat. Miller was reluctant. The instructor assured him again that he would not lose his weekend leave. Miller nodded an 'okay'. The two men circled each other again. Miller used the same technique, flattening the instructor and removing the rifle once more. This time he wiped his heavy-duty boot across the stunned sergeant's clean and ironed light-blue shirt. It was a gratuitous act of pure Millerism, appreciated by his browbeaten fellow recruits.

The instructor jumped to his feet and bellowed: 'Your weekend leave's cancelled, Miller! You're on guard duty!'

The recruits voiced their protest. The florid-faced Sergeant Bluey told them to shut up or they would all have their leave terminated. Miller insisted he wanted to see the camp adjutant. Minutes later, the sergeant, Miller and two witnesses were summoned to the adjutant's office. The adjutant was not at all concerned that Miller had tripped his opponent.

'I don't think it matters *how* you were disarmed, sergeant,' the adjutant observed dryly. He was not concerned that a boot had touched the sergeant's shirt. The adjutant gave the instructor a dressing down and put him on guard duty.

The four men left the office. Miller grinned. It was nice to score over authority. 'Come on,' he said to the two witnesses while eyeballing the sergeant, 'we've got a train to catch.'

Soon after that incident, Miller and all Australians were shocked to hear on 19 February 1942 that the Japanese had made devastating air raids on Darwin. Now Australia was really at war. Miller was next sent to an RAAF training station at Mallala, about 50 km north of Adelaide. Over the next nine months he gained his wings.

In May 1942 an overweight and unfit Bluey Truscott returned to Melbourne a war hero and cajoled his way into his old team for one last match. The Melbourne Football Club indulged him, aware of his courageous record defending the skies over Britain and France. Truscott put in a shocker against Jack Dyer's Richmond and was left standing by the game's pace. The war ace had dreamed of pulling on a Melbourne jumper just once more. Having survived his flying combat duties, he had to do it. He had diced with death so long that he didn't know whether he would ever play football again. His attitude was that there was no tomorrow. He was living each day as if it were his last. After fulfilling his wish, Truscott told his old schoolmaster Bill Woodfull that it was his last game. Soon afterwards he returned to active duty, at Milne Bay, on New Guinea's eastern tip, with No. 76 Squadron, fighting the advancing Japanese.

Miller was in touch with Truscott. His enthusiasm for playing one last game inspired Miller. He made time himself for a final indulgence in some local state final games. He was chosen at centre half-forward for the combined West Adelaide and Glenelg football team versus a combined Port Adelaide and West Torrens side. Miller starred in a match his team lost by 11 points. He would have wondered whether this was his last-ever game. Soon after it he was sent back to Melbourne where he was promoted on 17 December 1942 to the rank of flight sergeant. He enjoyed himself with family and friends through Christmas and New Year, then on 15 January 1943 he left Port Melbourne in the

38,000-tonne *West Point* bound for North America.

Keith Miller, who had only ever wanted to be a famous sportsman, had to forget his dreams. At the age of 23, Miller's world was turned upside down. He was to be trained for war.

PART 2

DUSTY'S WAR

CONFLICT AND CRICKET

It was snowing when Miller arrived at the Miles Standish training camp, south of Boston, in February 1943. Snow was a new experience for him, and some of his mates, who had come from dusty Outback towns. The roads were iced and the fields covered in a white crochet blanket. He used his leave to travel to Boston.

One night he was drinking with a mate, Bill Young from Broken Hill (nicknamed 'Pissy' by Miller), at the bar of the Boston Avery Hotel. He was standing next to a man with a dry martini. Miller and Young were intrigued. They had never had one. He asked the man about it. After explaining the intricacies of the soaked olive, the man noticed the Australian badges on their uniforms. Miller explained that he was in the RAAF and was en route to the UK. The man, Carl Wagner, a stock- and share-broker from a well-to-do Boston family, mentioned that his wife, Mamie, was from Hull in Yorkshire. The convivial education in sophisticated drinks ended with Wagner inviting Miller and his mate back to meet Mamie, at Beacon Hill, near the Boston State House. They lived on a stunning 27-acre property.

Miller was interested to meet the Wagner family, especially Carl's 25-year-old daughter, Peg, a beautiful brown-eyed brunette who worked as a secretary at the Massachusetts Institute of Technology and lived in her own apartment at 35 Beacon Street. She admired the tall, dark and square-jawed good looks of this young dasher who had befriended her father, which was an easy route to her affections. She was struck by the warmth and attention of his blue eyes and his easy, unaffected charm. It didn't hurt that he loved classical music just as she and her father did. Miller and Peg's first date of many was to a concert at which the Boston Symphony Orchestra played Beethoven's 5th Symphony at the Music Bowl on the Charles River. They had many a romantic night in front of a living room fire listening to Beethoven, Brahms and Tchaikovsky.

Like many unions during war, the uncertainty and urgency of time brought them close quickly. In the three weeks he was based at Miles Standish, Miller and Peggy fell in love. He proposed; she said, 'Yes.' He left, promising to return, and began writing to her on board the crowded, blacked-out *Queen Elizabeth* en route to Greenock, Scotland.

When he was not penning letters, Miller was acquiring a taste for gambling beyond his already established penchant for the racetrack love of the long shot, sure thing or tip from the horse's mouth. He joined a poker school and found he had some good bluffing skills, although his patience was limited. Miller played some other card games for the first time, including crown and anchor. He loved the bland, instant results of the traditional Aussie passion for two-up. It was all a useful distraction from the squalid, crowded sleeping accommodation below deck.

It was a relief to reach Scotland on 18 March 1943. He and his mates were herded onto a train, which took them on a 10-hour journey to the holiday resort of Bournemouth. The so-called 'gem' of England's south coast was a little tarnished by German air-raids, blackouts and the hustle and bustle of military traffic. Its 11 kilometres of beaches, parks and gardens now featured army patrols, camps and manned fortifications. The spirit of the English, who were handling the worst the Germans could throw at them without complaint, lifted him from the doldrums. 'The speed with which girls waiting on us [at the Bournemouth base], dished out food, together with their cheerful friendliness,' Miller wrote, 'gave our morale a tremendous boost. We had been told that people in England were creeping about looking miserable. What utter nonsense!'

He admired them more in the face of the assaults from German bombers. The Battle of Britain had been won in late 1941, but it was a prelude to continued and different kinds of attacks from the Luftwaffe. Just as Miller arrived in the south, 'hit and run' raids were beginning. German fighter-bombers would avoid radar by swooping in low over the Channel from their bases in France. They would drop their bombs, strafe the targeted town, then leave the area with alacrity before air defence could be mobilised. The courageous response of the British to these assaults gained Miller's admiration. It boosted his own desire to carry out any duty coming his way.

Eleven days after Miller arrived in the UK, he was shocked by the sad news that Squadron Leader Bluey Truscott, DFC and Bar (additionally Mentioned in Dispatches), had died in a plane accident on 28 March. He was piloting one of two Kittyhawks that were escorting a Catalina flying boat to Exmouth Gulf on the Western Australian coast. The two fighter-planes were larking about, looping and diving as they pretended to attack the Catalina. The water was still and clear below as Truscott dived close to the flying boat, not realising that it was dropping altitude to land. He misjudged the dive under the flying boat. When he attempted to pull out, a wing dipped in the ocean and the plane crashed into the sea. It was an ignoble end for a courageous larrikin, who had won many dogfights and survived the fighting over British and French skies. He had earned national fame with RAAF No. 452 and No. 76 Squadrons in the UK and New Guinea. Miller was stunned by the news. He cared little for the detail at that point, but could only dwell again on the swelling numbers of mates and acquaintances from all walks of life whom he was losing through war.

There was plenty of time off from training. Miller often attended the Bournemouth Orchestral Hall, where air-raid warnings sometimes formed a background to the main theme. Miller was in the audience for a recital by the renowned pianist Moiseiwitsch. His hands hovered over the keys to begin, but instead, he reached into the piano and took out a chamois duster. Moiseiwitsch inspected and shook it. Then, to a ripple of laughter in the audience, the maestro placed it on the floor next to the piano. He paused a moment, then went on with his recital.

Miller was enchanted with this and other performances. He took time to listen to a series of BBC radio talks called 'Appreciation of Music'. The passions drawn out in war were accentuating his sensitivity to the great composers and performers of the era. Whenever he heard that someone of note, such as the maestro, was playing he would go out of his way to see him. Miller had also been inspired to learn more by his love for Peg Wagner. Music was a common bond. It reminded him of those idyllic, romantic weeks just gone.

In April, when Miller had been in England only weeks, he was invited to play cricket for an RAAF side in London. He and Bill Young obtained permission to play over the weekend, and they travelled up to Dulwich College ground. There Miller met the team's skipper, Keith Carmody, a New South Wales cricketer with a gift for the game's strategies. While they were enjoying a relaxed leave on the Sunday after the Saturday game, a German bomber hit Bournemouth, knocking over a church spire, which crashed on to a pub. Miller would have lunched there on Sunday with seven friends, had he not been in London for the match. They were all killed. Miller was shattered to learn this from one survivor who ducked into the fireplace seconds before the pub was crushed. Miller went to bed in shock and with a sense of guilt that he had not been killed because he was away playing cricket.

Still stunned the next morning, Miller attended roll call. He was further unsettled to learn that three other men – apart from those killed – were missing. Their names were read out. 'Number 410608, Miller K. R., Sergeant,' was among them. Miller piped up that he was present. He had been given permission to take a weekend leave but had not been given an official pass. Because several of his mates had been killed at a pub, it had been assumed that Miller was among them. The fact that he was considered unaccounted for and perhaps dead accentuated his feelings of 'survivor's guilt', which psychologists today recognise as a specific condition. The emotion would stay with him.

There was plenty of time for recreation between training missions. The spring and summer of 1943 provided Miller with chances to play cricket often. There were scratch matches everywhere: a game for local county team Sussex one week; another against the county for a United Services team the next. The main venue was the Hove ground, not far from the sea. The Australians would wear drill shorts, army shirts and boots, often in Miller's case without socks. When asked if he ever got corns he replied: 'What are corns?'

Proper gear was in short supply. Bats were borrowed and balls worn colourless. The festival, or rather 'relief', atmosphere brought out a more attacking Miller than had been seen in the tight, sometimes grim competition of Shield matches in Australia. He did not always need to concern himself with building an innings based on defence and keeping the ball on the ground. The growing sense of living for the moment that his mate Bluey Truscott had exhibited was now Miller's way, too. After his narrow escapes, hearing about the deaths of so many friends, and the prospect of eventually flying bomber support missions into enemy territory, Miller was developing a certain outlook. Why potter around building a score? Why not go for big hits, take risks and bat explosively from the start? He was going in at first or second wicket down. With no sense of responsibility but to entertain, Miller was attempting bigger and bigger sixes. A pavilion roof, a clock tower, the tennis courts next to the Hove ground: they were all outrageous targets that the broad-shouldered Miller would aim to hit. More often than not, to the joy of the crowds flocking to see matches, he would reach 50 and get out to 'give someone else a go'. He was having a bowl, and taking the odd wicket without making a huge impression. Yet opposition players noticed that he could make a ball lift or skid through fast if he put his mind to it. His variable and whimsical run-up was often just six or eight steps, not much more than a spinner's approach.

Cricketer, commentator, poet and wine connoisseur John Arlott, who drank with Miller at the Seven Bells pub in Brighton in April 1943 ('there was no talk of cricket, but I can't say there was no action') had the impression that he was 'busy living life in case he ran out of it'. Arlott played against him in May. 'He bowled [for the RAAF] like fury and frightened the living daylights out of me on a mudheap wicket on the Parks at South-ampton,' Arlott said in his Hampshire burr in a BBC broadcast. 'He was bowling in shorts and [air force] issue socks. I'm a bit flattered, though, to say that at just about the same time he shook some much better players than me every bit as much.'

One of them was Jack Andrews, an opening bat for Hamp-shire. Miller, without a proper run-up, sauntered up to bowl the first ball of the innings. 'The ball pitched short,' Arlott recalled. 'Jack moved into a back defensive stroke, but not quickly enough or high enough. The ball lifted almost vertically, flicked his left elbow and cleared the long-leg boundary, a short one, but still a long carry off the funny bone.'

Up and coming Cambridge University all-rounder Trevor Bailey remembered Miller arriving for a game carrying a shirt and a pair of boots. 'That was all his cricket equipment at the time,' Bailey said. 'He borrowed a pair of trousers.' Apparently Miller forgot the issue socks that Arlott had noticed. Bailey agreed with Arlott: Miller was fast. 'He was certainly the quickest bowler to come on fifth change that I'd ever known in my life.'

The RAAF team was officially formed for the spring and summer of 1943 after hundreds of letters had been sent to bases all over England seeking players of senior grade standard. Many hopefuls puffed up their cricket histories in the hope of obtaining selection. The team had a respectable look about it with the flight officer Carmody as captain, supported by Sergeant Miller and the keeper Stan Sismey. It played some useful preliminary games in April and May, including the fateful match at Dulwich College. Then the competition stepped up on 5 June with the first main fixture, a one-dayer against an England team – Warner's XI – at Lord's.

The 69-year-old former England captain, Sir Pelham ('Plum') Warner, who had toured Australia 40 years earlier to play the 1903–04 Ashes, was acting secretary of the Marylebone Cricket Club. He was instrumental in keeping cricket going under almost all circumstances, including bombing raids, as a morale booster and a message to the enemy. Nothing could stop cricket at the game's headquarters. The son of a Trinidad governor, Warner felt that if the German propaganda minister Joseph Goebbels had been able to broadcast that the intensity of the German attacks had stopped cricket – particularly at Lord's – then it would have been valuable spin for the enemy.

Warner assumed that no matter what the Australian team looked like – none of them had played Test cricket – it would provide strong competition. There was also a little matter of Warner always enjoying victory over an Australian representative XI as a player, captain (of the first MCC-managed Ashes side to tour Australia in 1903–04), manager (in the Bodyline series of 1932–33) and selector. He had been steeped in the fierce combat between the two nations for half a century. With this embedded in his well-bred psyche, Warner scrambled together a respectable team that was first-class or county standard. It included two England captains: R. E. S. (Bob) Wyatt and Gubby Allen; the promising Bedser twins, Alec and Eric, who could already deliver top-class medium pace and spin respectively; Leslie Compton (Denis's older brother); and captain of Surrey, E. R. T. Holmes, who had led an MCC 'goodwill tour' of Australia in 1935–36.

There was also the all-rounder Trevor Bailey. *Wisden* had already earmarked him as 'a wartime discovery from Dulwich College and the Royal Marines'. There were high hopes that he would develop into a Test all-rounder.

Miller, based at RAF South Cerny in Gloucestershire, saw Lord's for the first time. It did not impress him. He viewed it initially as 'a crummy little ground'. He found the small capacity of 30,000 a disappointment when he compared it to the MCG with its crowds three times that, and huge stands. Miller didn't like the crowded dressing room used by both teams. He pushed someone hard out of the way to retrieve his gear with the request: 'Excuse me, sport, can you hop out of the way?' 'Sport' happened to be Sir Pelham. Miller was taken aside and told that such aggressive behaviour was not the done thing, which amused him. He was not happy with the huge communal baths on offer. He asked the room attendant Jack O'Shea for a shower and was taken to one at the back of the Members' Stand and told to keep quiet about it.

Despite the unprepossessing surrounds, Miller was aware of the great traditions at Lord's. Thomas Lord had built the ground between 1811 and 1814 on the site of a duck pond in St John's Wood. Miller and his Aussie mates were amused to learn that, having drained the pond, the builders had not bothered to level the ground, which was left with the famous slope. This seemed inappropriate for the home of cricket and the MCC, the guardian of the game's laws and spirit. But its imperfections became part of its quiet, dignified charm.

The RAAF won the toss and batted in front of thousands of dark-blue-uniformed RAAF personnel on one side of the ground. The Australians were soon 2 for 5, and Miller strode to the wicket. When he faced up there was silence. The RAF's red-headed quick, Dick Pollard, steamed in. He had claimed both wickets and wanted a third. His first ball was outside off stump. Miller late cut it through slips for four. The lads in blue roared with relief more than anything. Pollard didn't like the cheek of such a classy shot. He raced in and hurled down a bouncer. Miller could have been in the backyard at Mum's facing a tennis ball. He swivelled into position and hooked it for four. The RAAF supporters cheered.

Wickets tumbled around Miller as he launched into the bowling and scored a quickfire 45 (out of 56 in 62 minutes). The airmen managed to reach only 100 with Alec Bedser laying claims for future Test selection with 3 for 30. Warner's England XI batted and scored 201, and Bailey lived up to expectations with a patient 40. The RAAF had only 20 minutes to bat again, and reached 1 for 38. Miller, relishing every moment of his first gallop at Lord's, was 21 not out with a couple of audacious sixes. It was a useful start for him at the famous arena. He vowed to do better there.

The RAAF program included eight matches in the summer, with four won and lost. A highlight was Miller's 141 against Public School Wanderers at the end of July at Hove. It was a superb innings of controlled aggression at better than a run a minute, in which he hit just 1 six and 16 fours. He also lived up to his early reputation in England's south of being a somewhat lazy 'quick'. There was little science in his approach; no run-up to speak of and little accuracy. But when he bent his back and flung his right shoulder, he was a worry for any batsman. Yet Miller was never on long enough to give him a bag of five wickets, which might have made a deeper impression. His 3 for 29 return was good, but would not make headlines.

The 1943 season went well. Plum Warner decided on an England team (Sir Pelham Warner's XI) versus Dominions game at Lord's on 2 and 3 August, with proceeds going to charities for the war effort. Along with the in-form Miller, Carmody (captain) and Sismey, three other RAAF representatives were selected for the Dominions team: Pilot Officer Alan McDonald, a fine leg-spinner, whose claim to fame was bowling England's outstanding pre-World War II batsman Wally Hammond at Geelong in 1936–37; Flight Lieutenant A. W. 'Mick' Roper, a fast-medium bowler shouldering most of the airmen's bowling for the season; and Flight Sergeant Jimmy Allen, a tenacious opening bat. The other members of the strong Dominions line-up included the top-line New Zealand bat, Stewie Dempster, the talented South African all-rounder D. P. B. Morkel and three West Indian Test stars: Learie Constantine, Bertie Clarke and Mannie Martindale.

The squad, as a whole, was just below Test standard. Warner matched it with a near Test-level England team of Walter Robins, Les Ames, Trevor Bailey, Alec Bedser, the Compton brothers Denis and Leslie, Godfrey Evans, H. Gimblett, E. R. T. Holmes, A. W. H. Mallett and Jack Robertson.

The England side scraped in by eight runs, with Les Ames, the Test keeper/batsman, and Dempster each notching a century. The difference was the left-arm wrist spin of Denis Compton, who bamboozled all Dominions bats, taking 9 for 74 for the match. Miller was among his haul, caught by brother Leslie for 32 in a partnership of 69 with Carmody (43) out of Australia's meagre tally of 115. (Miller flicked at Alec Bedser in Australia's second innings run chase, and was out caught by keeper Evans for just 2.) Another to get scribes and selectors scribbling was Alec Bedser, who took 3 for 33, and 4 for 108. The big man's medium-pace swing was always a concern for Australian bats struggling under English conditions.

The game, entertaining enough to take many minds off German air raids, was memorable for the meeting of Compton and Miller. It happened when Compton and Ames, both experienced Test batsmen from the 1930s, were well 'set', with scores in their forties. 'I feel set for a big score,' Compton recalled as Carmody threw the ball to 'this very tall, slim chap with brushed-back hair, who had been racing round the boundary like a gazelle'. It was Miller, now the fifth-change bowler. Compton turned to keeper Sismey and asked, 'What does this chap bowl?'

'I've no idea,' Sismey replied, a touch disingenuously. 'He's not really a bowler. Probably wants the exercise.'

Another fielder close to the wicket added: 'He just runs up and lets the ball go. You might find him a bit quick, though.'

Compton watched Miller. He didn't mark his run. He didn't even roll his arm over for practice. 'So I am rather nonchalant when I take guard,' Compton said. Miller loped in from eight paces and heaved down the first delivery. 'When he lets the ball go,' Compton noted, 'my hair stands on end. This is the fastest ball I've faced since I played [Australia's] Ernie McCormick in 1938. The ball goes for four byes over my left shoulder and past Stan standing up to the wicket. So I do meet Keith Miller.'

Miller, too, was impressed by Compton, not just for his batting, which was ever outstanding, but the way he got out. There was a mix-up with his batting partner, who came charging through when Compton played a shot into the covers. Compton could have stood his ground and seen his partner run out, but he dashed for the bowler's end and was himself caught well short of his ground. He kept running towards the pavilion, without looking back or any sign of ill-feeling. Watching this, Miller knew he had a kindred spirit in the England champion. It was his attitude. Cricket was just a game, to be competed in 100 per cent, but it was not life or death. Miller was in the game as much for the competition as he was for the comradeship. That's the way he read Denis Compton from the start.

Miller's bowling capacities, noticed weeks earlier in lesser games by Arlott and Bailey, had now been on display at the home of cricket in a game that received plenty of newspaper coverage. Whether he liked it or not, Miller was recognised by his opponents as a bowler of potential who could zip the ball through when he wished. But he needed better figures than 0 for 25 to be thrown the ball earlier or more often.

By the end of that first game at Lord's, Miller had put aside his small-town prejudice of comparing it to the MCG and was already attached to it. He came to realise the value of its symbols. First there was a weathervane effigy on the grey roof above the scoreboard of a gaunt 'old father time' as he bent to inspect the bails on the stumps. Then there were the private boxes of the grandstand galleries, where some of England's ruling elite would invariably sit, and the Pavilion and its Long Room, where members turned to applaud a batsman passing through it to the dressing room if he had performed well or turned away in stony silence if he had failed.

Miller made up his mind to 'lift' for performances there if at all possible. He stepped on to the hallowed turf for the third and last time in the summer of 1943 on 11 September against the RAF. He had the British airmen hopping with that deceptively short run to the wicket and some zip off the mythical 'ridge' at one end. He took 3 for 23, and the RAF was reduced to just 9 for 105. Miller thumped 91 from the RAAF's 8 for 184 (Bedser 3 for 39). It was his best all-round performance since his schooldays. Yet despite the good crowd no one of authority in Australian cricket was there to take notice.

Miller would still be selected in any services representative games on his batting only. Cricket writer and historian Sir Home S. C. M. Gordon wrote of the 23-year-old Miller in Warner's magazine *The Cricketer*: 'My belief is that he has not yet attained his zenith as a bat, but that his bowling in the not too distant future will be regarded as more than a useful change.'

Miller was the batting 'discovery' of the 1943 summer in wartime England. Yet more than that, his exceptional character had come to the fore and charmed both men and women in and out of cricket across the south of England. 'He rises to the challenge,' Arlott commented, 'but gets fun out of cricket.' He reminded Arlott of 'the lady in Oscar Wilde who knew nothing at all about music but who was fond of musicians. Keith's not only fond of cricket but fond of cricketers. I never knew a man who had so many friends not only on his own side but on the other side as well.'

***

One night around midnight he was walking back along a dark country lane to his blacked-out Gloucestershire base. A car with its lights dimmed came up the lane and stopped. Miller thought the driver wished to ask the way. But it was his CO – a hard man, who made no secret of his dislike for Australians, whom he referred to as 'colonials'. He also had a distaste for non-commissioned men, such as Miller, who was still a sergeant. He was always riding him, picking him up for such things as dress code and lax drilling. The CO on this occasion looked him up and down in disgust and asked: 'Miller, why haven't you got your cap on?'

Miller detested being addressed this way. An altercation developed. Miller shaped as if to thump the officer, who drove off. The next day Miller was put on a charge of insubordination. He had to do a three-week 'refresher' or disciplinary course, which included some hard labour, at his RAF camp from 18 October to 9 November 1943.

The unpalatable experience reinforced his attitude to authority, and now a particular British kind he had yet to fully comprehend. The CO's riding him had brought back memories of his minor problems in Australia in the army. It also conjured hurtful recall about being picked on when small. Now he was a big man, he wanted to lash back, simply because he could. But he had to learn to bottle his tendency to 'square off', especially against a figure who had derided him over his 'colonial' background. Miller had never felt inferior over his nationality. But in England and in the military, where slights of any kind were part of the control mechanism, he took such references as insults. He carried much pent-up aggression, which was reinforced by the hard labour sentence. It simmered just below the surface. If he drank, it boiled over and found an outlet. Dusty Miller was ready to live up to his wartime sobriquet.

Despite the setback, Flight Sergeant Miller was taking the painstaking training steps necessary to become an officer himself. In mid-November 1943, he was posted to Ouston near Newcastle in England's north, which housed Anson and Oxford aircraft, flown to train navigators in the use of radar (which had been recently developed by Australian scientist Marcus Oliphant). The Ansons were equipped with Mark X air interception equipment. Miller flew with a navigator on rest from war missions, who instructed two trainee navigators. Planes went up in pairs during daylight for three and a half hours flying ('stooging'). Miller would fly according to instructions from the navigator, who kept his eyes on the so-called 'box' or 'fishbowl' – a collapsible radar screen pulled out from under the instrument panel in front of him. Metal objects could be detected in an arc of eight kilometres.

It wasn't unusual for humble trainees like Miller to secure a lift in a plane to other parts of England. Early in his stay at Ouston, Miller thumbed a ride from an RAF officer down to Northolt. 'Come on then, Aussie,' the RAF officer said. Miller did not know his aerial chauffeur by name or reputation. They had to circle for ages. The sky was full of planes, coming and going to and from the action across the Channel. Miller felt dizzy. The officer was given the order to land. They approached the runway. The undercarriage was down and the plane was heading in when a Spitfire whizzed in *underneath* them. Miller braced himself for a collision. But the skilled pilot managed to pull out of the landing and just miss a crash. Miller apologised for asking him for the Northolt ride, which nearly killed them both.

'That's okay,' the officer said with a grin, 'I've had worse moments.'

They found out soon afterwards that the Spitfire made an emergency landing because of an engine overheating following a glycol leak.

'You wouldn't know how to get to Ruislip,' Miller asked, 'would you?'

'I certainly do,' the officer said, 'I'll give you a lift.' He then commandeered a staff car and drove Miller to his destination.

The two men became good friends. Miller found out later that the officer – Wing Commander 'Laddie' Lucas – was a highly decorated airman. He had been posted to Malta in February of the previous year (1942) with No. 249 Squadron at the height of the battle for the island, flying Spitfires. He twice flew to Gibraltar for the reinforcement of Spitfires over Malta, flying off carriers. Lucas was one of the leading Malta aces. Earlier in 1943, he was posted to command No. 616 Squadron and later the fighter wing at Coltishall. (For the last six months of the war he led No. 613 Squadron Mosquitoes in support of the advancing Allied armies. He was one of Miller's heroes.)

Miller was quickly familiar with the seven other Australians at Ouston, including the lean, fit William Angus ('Gus') Glendinning, aged 20. When Miller discovered he was from Perth, his second question was: 'Do you play footy [Aussie Rules, which is the main football code in Western Australia]?'

Glendinning had played for East Perth, a top-level club. Miller suggested they draw a rugby ball from Stores and have a 'kick to kick'. They drew an interested crowd of Englishmen, New Zealanders and Canadians. Aussie Rules players put far more emphasis on kicking skills than other oval ball codes. The on-lookers were impressed by Miller's drop-kicks and place kicks, with which they were familiar. But they marvelled at his use of the 'torpedo', whereby the ball is kicked off the right side of the boot (if the player is a right-footer). It spins on its axis horizontally and can gain ten to twenty metres more distance than a normal punt.

Miller had plenty of time to develop skills in other sports. He was a believer in practice making perfect. Yet his innate hand–eye coordination gave him advantages. He would play Glendinning and others at table tennis, giving them 19 points start and beating them 21–20. No challenge was too big. Once world champion English snooker player Joe Davis turned up at Ouston to give an exhibition, and display trick shots. When he left, another trainee pilot bet Miller that he couldn't perform one of them. The white and red balls were lined up at the top of the table. The aim was to dribble the white ball to the near pocket. Before it reached it, the red balls had to be potted in the same pocket.

'Dusty had a dash,' Glendinning recalled. 'The last red ball kissed the white as it reached the pocket. He all but completed a really tough trick. He only needed practice.'

Glendinning witnessed something else that didn't need repetition to improve, just brilliant reflexes. He was playing snooker with Miller when a ball from a table tennis match two metres away flew towards their table. Miller was lining up to pot a red. He raised the cue, and with its tip hit the flying ball back to the other table, saying: 'Would you mind keeping the ball in your area, chaps?' He then potted the red without changing his stance.

The training at Ouston was interspersed with long periods of boredom, when the incoming mail was the most exciting moment of the week. Miller often received food parcels from Peg, which he shared with Glendinning and others. (She even remembered to send Bill Young a birthday cake when he turned 19.) Sometimes there were visits from wrestling troupes, which they found about as stimulating as kick to kick. This was the perfect outlet for Miller's latent aggression. He would take on the biggest man in the troupe. One evening he tackled a hefty bruiser, Ronnie James, and was thrown hard on to his back, injuring it. The injury was severe enough to stop him from carrying on. It would plague him, especially when playing cricket.

The only other steady entertainment came from the sergeants' mess. 'Whenever the amber fluid or "singing syrup" took over,' Glendinning recalled, 'Dusty would want me to sing "Amour, Amour". He liked to grab the microphone and give a commentary on the VRC [Victorian Racing Committee] Jockeys' Club autumn meeting. He always commenced with the Mia Mia Hurdle, Greensleeves No. 1 in the book, rider L. Meehan and carrying 12 stone 7 lb.'

Miller, by passion and instinct developed from his days as a kid at the Caulfield track, had a sharp recall for the horses, their breeding, the colours they carried, and their owners and trainers. 'I knew the name of just one Western Australian race horse,' Glendinning said, 'Gay Balken and jockey T. Unkovich. Whenever he insisted on me giving a phantom call to copy the great race commentators, the aforenamed horse and jockey always won.'

That amused Miller. In the true Aussie tradition of that generation, he had to find a nickname for Glendinning. He was christened 'Unky'. It was Miller's initial show of fondness for his new friend in the air force. They both liked a laugh, a bet, a drink and, as one writer once observed, their women thoroughbred and their horses attractive.

Glendinning, a man of medium height, was soon to learn about mateship, Miller style. One quiet afternoon with no flying, the mess was occupied by four aircrew members playing cards, reading books and drinking at the bar. One of the card players, a big man, was having the sort of losing streak which caused disgruntlement that not even several beers could soothe.

'Gus,' he yelled to Glendinning at the bar, 'go upstairs and get my pack of cards from the cupboard of my room.' The game went another round. The big man bawled out: 'If you don't get the cards I'll knock your block off!'

Miller walked into the mess at that moment. The big man rose from his chair. Miller walked straight to the card table. 'If you ever lay a hand on him,' he said, 'I'll break your bloody neck.' It's unlikely that Miller would have snapped the man's upper vertebrae. Yet he had a reputation for 'going on with it' if provoked. The big man went upstairs and retrieved his own cards. Glendinning was chuffed. 'I realised I had at least one mate [in the air force],' he said.

Miller had an opportunity to explore his love of music when the entertainment officer arranged a competition concerning the classics in the YMCA hut. About 80 contestants turned up to hear 50 gramophone records, played for a minute each. They had to write down the name of the symphony and its composer. Miller named 47 correctly and won the competition. An amazed Glendinning witnessed his musical knowledge, which was part of the more hidden side of his multifaceted character, and a complete contrast to the extrovert Miller, which was exhibited when gambling.

Miller had been saving up to buy a canteen of cutlery from Sheffield for his mother. But in late 1943 he had a justified concern that anything shipped in merchant vessels was likely to be end up at the bottom of the Atlantic. German submarines were doing great damage. For this reason, Miller had hesitated about buying the gift and sending it to Australia. The £130 he had set aside for the purchase taunted him to a point where he had to gamble with it. He told Glendinning and two English RAF friends that he had drawn the money to 'have a dash' when they went to a dog meeting at White City, Newcastle.

The four trainee flight officers sat in the bar at the track. 'We backed dogs because they stopped to have a "wee" during the parade,' Glendinning said, 'others because of their names or because they had unusual markings.' They lost on everything until a dog named Glenaars Idol was listed in a race.

Miller gave Glendinning £20. 'Go and back number 6, Unky,' he said, 'because *Glen*aars Idol sounds like you.'

Glendinning obliged. He went to a bookie and placed a £20 win bet on number 6 in the printed program booklet. Glenaars Idol won at 10 to 1, which meant a nice collect of £200. But there was a problem. Number 6 on the bookies' board was Slick Nick at 6 to 1. The bookies listed the dogs differently from the printed program.

The four men, who had been drinking steadily, protested, but to no avail. Miller said he had an idea. Why not exchange uniforms? They used the nearest toilet for a wardrobe change. The two RAF men wearing gray swapped with the two RAAF men in distinctive dark blue. Glendinning, now posing as an RAF flight sergeant, returned to argue again with the bookie. 'He and his tic-tac man were speechless,' Glendinning remembered.

The four disgruntled, inebriated punters displayed their displeasure at not being given a favourable hearing. The RAF service police at the dog meet were alerted. The senior policeman was only a corporal. He could not arrest a person senior in rank. While the police radioed for a staff sergeant or warrant officer, the four revellers changed back into their correct uniforms and walked out of the main gate.

Miller had blown his £130. He was staying in Newcastle and asked Glendinning for a loan. Glendinning gave him three shillings, leaving just a shilling for the bus ride back to Ouston. 'The loss didn't seem appear to worry him,' Glendinning noted. 'Perhaps taking a punt on the merchant shipping may have seen a better result. I was to learn that Dusty never "cried" when he suffered a loss.'

1944: LIVING DANGEROUSLY

The Allies made their biggest counter-offensive yet in World War II on 6 June 1944 – D-Day – when 156,000 troops were landed on the beaches of Normandy, France. Miller continued to gain experience as a pilot, particularly in the Mosquito, his fighter plane of choice, and waited to play his role in the fight-back against Nazi Germany.

In between training exercises, Miller found time for more cricket in the 1944 spring and summer. He began in April with warm-up games for Ouston in RAF station matches, with some at the quaint village of Clara Vale, about nine kilometres from his base. By May Miller was making an impact again, except that he was hardly ever called on to bowl in the more important matches representing the 2nd Australian Imperial Force (AIF). The back injury sustained in that wrestling match had curtailed his ability to roll his arm over. Miller's pace would have been an asset for both the AIF and the RAAF, even though the latter now included an influx of capable players, including the 24-year-old New South Wales leggie Bob Cristofani and South Australian left-arm orthodox (finger) spinner Reg Ellis. Both had important roles and would have been called on before Miller, even had he not been injured. He continued to develop with the bat for the RAAF or the AIF, which included players from the other arms of the Australian forces. But again, that back problem limited him.

One game – drawn – for the RAAF that would stay in Miller's mind forever occurred on 1 and 2 July. It was at Edgbaston against the West Indies. Miller had no influence on the match, but a good friend and team-mate, 21-year-old Clive Calvert, made a brilliant innings of 141. A few months later Calvert was flying near the Danish coast when he was shot down and killed. It was one of countless reminders that Miller could be the next victim of war anywhere and at any time. He was developing a kind of fatalism, whereby every game of cricket, every intimate moment with a woman, every concert and even every beer with a mate should be enjoyed with little or no thought for a future. For many of the people Miller knew and made contact with on any given day, there was no future.

He defied his back problem and played two outstanding innings in the summer of 1944. He batted with skill under wet conditions in a match against the British Civil Defence Services at Lord's on 15 July. He brought on all his shots straight and square of the wicket, reaching 96 with 8 fours and a further 9 threes, owing to the wet, slow outfield. An air-raid warning sounded. It was followed by the fearful low engine buzz of a German guided missile, or 'flying bomb'. The players remained on the field, waiting to see whether the missile passed overhead. If the noise were to stop, the players would duck for cover, knowing that the unpowered missile would go into a terminal dive and explode.

This one detonated south of them. Leg-spinner L. S. H. Summers delivered another ball. Another missile hummed overhead as Miller danced down the wicket and drove through mid-off to the boundary for his first century at Lord's. The second missile exploded not far from the ground just as Miller acknowledged the applause. A few seconds later, the All Clear was sounded. Summers bowled an over-spinner. Miller was trapped in front, lbw for an even 100. The nervous nineties would never be a problem for him after that experience.

His second prominent innings of 1944 came on 7 August,

Bank Holiday Monday, while batting for the RAAF against England at Lord's. England batted first and was soon in trouble against the variety of spin from Cristofani and Ellis. The airmen had them 7 for 118 and were set to clean up the tail when the magnificent Wally Hammond, 41 years old, eased into stride in the manner that had seen him become the greatest English batsman for most of the previous two decades. Hammond unleashed strokes which exhibited that he had lost nothing of his control of technique, and with little reduction in power. He stroked 12 fours in an innings of 105, taking 135 minutes. Acting skipper Sismey would have liked to call on Miller as the fifth change to see if he could stop Hammond. But his back would not allow it. Miller had to be content with fielding to a true batting master while he delivered a faultless display.

Miller could not wait to give an exhibition that might invite comparisons with one of the game's greats. His patience was not tested. Miller, batting at three, was in within 20 minutes. He wasted no time in moving on to the front foot. If anything his majestic 85, with the same number of fours (12) as Hammond, and created at a faster clip (100 minutes), was an even better knock. Miller was 17 years younger. Despite his painful injury, his strokes had more crunch; his technique, especially off the front foot, was just about as elegant and assured as that of the England champion. Miller's dominance of the crease was complete. Only another 34 were scored by his partners while he was in.

This performance put Australia on track to score the 227 required to win in 195 minutes. But leg-spinner Doug Wright took 6 for 62, including three tail-enders in five balls, and forced Miller to take risks. He was out caught and bowled by L. J. Todd. The RAAF fell 33 runs short.

After the match Hammond singled out Australia's spinners for praise, yet Miller had made the impression that would last. Warner, pleased that the exhibition game had produced such skill and that England had won, indulged in some generous circumlocution after the match: 'Bradman once said he'd like to give a million pounds for our young colts Hutton, Compton, Edrich and Wright. I wonder how much he'd like to ask for Miller.'

Bradman, in Adelaide suffering from severe tendonitis at the time, was in no position to donate anything. But he was reading the newspaper reports on the games in England. He would have been aware of Miller's blossoming batting skills consistently on display. (He scored a forceful 30 at Lord's again on 8 August playing for a Dominions team against England.) After what he witnessed at the MCG in the 1940–41 season, Bradman would have been wondering why Miller wasn't bowling more in the bigger games that were receiving a deal of newspaper coverage in Australia. Yet Miller was still rolling his arm over in the minor games where he would not be expected to bend that debilitating back so much. By the time of his last 1944 game, which was for the RAAF against the West of England at Clifton Close, Bristol, his injury was allowing him some leeway occasionally to bowl a bit quicker. He was dangerous on a slippery track, similar to the one that made John Arlott take notice at Southampton early in the previous season. His figures of 6 for 28 in the West's two innings did not tell the story of the concern his bowling caused. The opposition and conditions ensured that Miller once more did not receive rave notices for an impressive display with the ball.

***

After 10 months training at Ouston, Miller was offered a commission. But Glendinning missed out, which meant the two would be separated. A commission for Miller would see him posted elsewhere. The two wished to stay together.

'You must get a commission, Unky,' Miller said. 'I'll tee it up.'

Soon afterwards Miller instructed Glendinning: 'Apply straightaway for a 48-hour pass. Go down to Kodak House in London. I have spoken to a mate of mine, Flight Lieutenant Keith Johnson [Ian Johnson's father, a member of the Australian Board of Control], who will interview you there.'

Johnson recommended Glendinning for the rank of flight officer and told him the air officer commanding his area would soon interview him. 'He's a dear old soul, who wears World War I ribbons,' Johnson told him. 'He'll ask three questions: first: "What paper do you read?" You answer *The Times*. Second: "What does your father do?" Make your response as good as possible. Three: "Do you know Pythagoras' Theorem?" You answer, "The square of the hypotenuse is equal to the sum of the squares of the other two sides."'

Everything went as Johnson predicted. Miller and Glendinning were both commissioned. They were posted together to 12 Air Force Unit in Grantham, Lincolnshire, on 15 August 1944. They were trained in Blenheim Vs and were on the way to being chosen for an operational squadron.

They were given two weeks leave before the next stop in their training at Cranfield in Buckinghamshire. When in the Newcastle area, they couldn't resist going to Miller's favourite pub, nicknamed the Friggin' in the Riggin', back at Ouston. They met up with their sergeant mates and were smuggled into their old mess with flight sergeant RAF battle tunics covering their officers' gear.

The evening moved from conviviality to a night fuelled by a case of Bass beer. After demolishing the case, Miller and a Liverpool Irishman, 'Bluey' Dillon, decided on a snooker game, which Glendinning was woken to referee. At one point, Miller looked along his cue. 'Bloody thing's bent!' he slurred.

Dillon doubled up with laughter. Miller broke it over his knee. He examined the other five cues in the rack. He found them all 'bent' and proceeded to snap each one. He then played with the broken cues and ripped the pool table's cover.

'Caniva lenda yours?' Miller enquired of Dillon. The Liverpudlian refused to give up his cue, and then claimed the game. They left the games room. Miller was in a wilful mood. He set off a fire extinguisher and left it gushing foam on an anteroom floor.

He and Dillon headed upstairs to the sleeping quarters. Glendin-ning became enmeshed in the spirited moment. He picked up the extinguisher and followed them upstairs. He saw a light on in one bedroom. Assuming Miller was there, he began spraying the room through an open fanlight.

A person inside the room reached up to close the fanlight but, in his haste, smashed it and injured his hand. The extinguisher ran out of foam. The door opened. Expecting to see Miller and Dillon, Glendinning was stunned to see a New Zealander and an Englishman. The Kiwi threatened Glendinning with physical violence, but was distracted by the injury to his friend's hand. He had cut it badly when he tried to close the fanlight.

Glendinning called the station doctor. He was on the scene quickly. The Englishman had a severed tendon. His flying days were over, which made Glendinning remorseful. The next morning he and Miller were put under house arrest for, as one sergeant put it, 'Apart from all the damage, they were bleedin' officers as well! And sleeping in the sergeants' mess!'

Miller was hung over. 'Unky,' he said, 'you do all the talking.'

They were marched to the commanding officer, a decorated wing commander. He put them on eight charges and ordered them back to their station. Miller placed two hands on the table, eyeballed the CO, and said: 'You're a bit hard, aren't you, sport?' Glendinning froze.

'Get out and off my station immediately!' the CO bellowed.

The two revellers left and reported to Cranfield on 30 October 1944, and were paraded to meet the station adjutant. They were confronted with the eight charges. Their fates would be left to the station's commanding officer. They were left to fret over possible dishonourable discharges or demotion, which would end their chances of ever going on missions as war pilots.

'Having finally reached an OTU – (Combat/Fighter Support) Operations Training Unit – to familiarise ourselves with Beaufort [old coastal patrol aircraft], then Beaufighters and finally

Mosquito aircraft,' Glendinning noted ruefully, 'we appeared to have fluffed it.' While waiting for a decision, the course, which they should have been on, commenced without them.

They were paraded before Cranfield's CO. Miller and Glendinning were surprised. He had been their CO at Ouston. It seemed that Miller's luck was in. At first the CO said they would do a three-week 'disciplinary course'. This was a euphemism for more hard labour. But Miller pleaded with him. 'Give us a chance, sir,' he said, 'We've waited so long to reach this point in our flying careers.'

The CO reflected. 'I never had any problem with you at Ouston,' he said. 'I can't understand your behaviour.' After a few seconds silence, he asked, 'Miller, have you been on any disciplinary courses?'

The CO knew the answer. It was on Miller's record. 'Yes, sir.'

'How long?'

'Three weeks, sir.'

The CO looked at him long and quizzically. He might have wondered how Miller 'earned' this sentence, but did not ask. Glendinning was unsure himself. He had heard rumours that Miller had abused an officer while in army motor transport in Melbourne, and that he had been in a dispute with a British officer, which ended with Miller doing some hard labour, such as lugging heavy sandbags. Glendinning didn't wish to know. He did wonder whether these indiscretions had been provoked. Miller was never one for obeying the rules or being attacked verbally by his superiors.

Miller pleaded with the CO again, saying how they really wished to have a chance to tackle the enemy. The CO observed them for several seconds.

'Do you have 12 pounds 10 pence for the damage at Ouston?' the CO asked.

'Yes, sir,' Miller and Glendinning replied in chorus. The 'fine' was paid. They began their operations training course the next day.

Not long into it Miller had two doses of good fortune that might have made lesser men avoid real operational missions. The first was when he was receiving training in a Bristol Beaufighter. It was a heavy, long-range, two-engine plane. Once, on a practice run from Cranfield airfield, the oil-pressure gauge abruptly showed zero. Miller noted it, but was unconcerned. The instrument panel on this particular plane had been unreliable. Thirty minutes later another gauge was faulty. Two was one too many for Miller. He turned the plane and headed back to Cranfield. He ran into bad weather, which made the more demanding night flying worse. Pilots were trained to fly off the instruments and by sight of the terrain. With the panel more than faulty and vision impossible, he made a hazardous return to his base, and reported the aircraft as unserviceable. Mechanics worked on the faults and reported the problems rectified within an hour.

An acquaintance of Miller's, Jock Meek, wanted to go for a run in the suspect plane that same night. He was just airborne when he noticed that the instrument panel had gone haywire. Meek called up Control. It ordered him to return to base. He turned, attempted to land and crashed at one end of the airfield. Meek and his navigator were killed. It was a terrible shock to Miller, and a grim reminder of how precariously his fate was calibrated. It was the second time in little over a year that he felt a kind of shame for not being the one to be taken. It compounded a sensitivity over his 'survivor's guilt'. He called it 'Miller's Luck' in an attempt to put these incidents behind him. But they dogged him.

Weeks later, he had a second slice of fortune when he was gliding another Beaufighter in to land after a night training operation over Occupied France. He misjudged the runway in the darkness. The wheels hit the ground hard and the plane bounced. Miller revved the engines in the expectation of getting airborne again. But only one engine responded. A surge of power on one side of the aircraft caused it to veer to one side off the runway, heading for a hangar. Miller throttled back desperately, expecting to crash. The Beaufighter lifted centimetres over the building. He was able to wobble the plane in safely.

He had now had three brushes with death and had yet to fly on an official war mission. He drank more heavily than usual that night after scraping over the hangar.

Another non-flying incident occurred in London's Putney for a couple of days leave seeing a girlfriend, Christine, and her Cockney parents, who both worked on the buses. Miller was supposed to take Christine to the local theatre after drinking with friends at Flanagan's pub. He kept drinking to the point where he decided not to go to the theatre. While he was enjoying himself, a V1 missile hit the theatre and killed many inside.

His other favourite sport – cricket – had saved him earlier when he otherwise would have been in the pub that was crushed by a church spire at Bournemouth. Now he had been spared because he *had* been drinking in another pub. There seemed no rhyme or reason to all this. Miller decided there was nothing else to do but raise a glass to the lady of fortune, who seemed to be shadowing him everywhere. Yet he remained highly sensitive to the fact that her cousin, the grim reaper, was never any further away.

In October 1944 Miller was starved of classical music. He booked a £10 seat at a hall in London to hear violinist Yehudi Menuhin perform with the London Symphony Orchestra. The base refused his request for a 24-hour leave to see the concert. Miller walked out the main gate the next morning, and caught the train south. He was enthralled, and returned to Cranfield the next day invigorated. The furious CO threatened all sorts of punishment and dismissed Miller, saying he would soon hear of his decision.

Miller discussed the incident with Glendinning that night. 'Bugger 'em, Unk,' Miller said. 'It is possibly the only time in my life that I could see the great man in the flesh and listen to his mastery of the violin.' Later the CO compromised, ordering Miller to represent Cranfield in its next cricket match.

Miller displayed a hostile attitude to authority, pomposity, snobbery and pretentiousness. His answers to them varied from direct confrontation to a less than subtle response. Yet there were times when he was simply wilful and plain bloody-minded. Glendinning recalled an instance during their early training at Spitalgate, a paddock airfield near Cranfield from which they flew Blenheims. The trainees joined a table of eight British officers for breakfast in the officers' mess. On a whim, Miller took an instant dislike to one of their fellow diners. Just before food was served, the British officer motioned to Miller and said, 'Please pass the cruet, old boy.'

Glendinning thought this was a perfectly normal request. But Miller, in one of his feisty moods, nudged him and whispered, 'Listen to this, Unk.' Then he turned to the officer and said in a broad Aussie accent, 'Chuck us the pepper and salt, sport.'

Glendinning was stunned once more by Miller's confrontational style. 'I wished that I could disappear into a hole in the ground,' he said. 'But that was Dusty. He had a nervous tension in him. He was ready for anything and unpredictable. There was no need to give that fellow a "serve", but he did. A bit of inverted snobbery at times. I believe it was because of the [hard labour] sentence he served at the RAF Gloucestershire base.'

Glendinning became aware of Miller's prickly side, which could see him employing his 'in your face' style. But at no stage did Miller turn on his mate. 'The nearest I got [to being hit by Miller] was when he complained to me of having a cut lip that wouldn't heal. Miller wanted me to have a look at it.'

'You know, Dusty,' Glendinning said as he examined his lip, 'I think you may have a load [gonorrhea or syphilis].' Miller's eyes lit up. For a split second it seemed he would punch his wartime buddy. But Miller saw that his friend was only joking.

Late in 1944, when they were at the end of their pilot officer training, Miller and Glendinning were granted seven days' leave. At Miller's suggestion, they decided on a busman's holiday of sorts

– with the Royal Navy in action. The forces had agreed to let each other's officers observe how the other half operated. They travelled down to London en route to Portsmouth naval HQ and stayed a night at the home of Miller's Cockney friends in Putney.

'They were a terrific couple,' Glendinning recalled. 'They had two daughters. Miller fancied the pretty younger one, Christine, who was about 19, and he slept with her. He dated her several times. She was to come back into his life later in an extraordinary way.'

In the typical fashion of these two musketeers, they were ten hours late (after 'looking up a few mates') reporting to Portsmouth. 'The navy was not impressed,' Glendinning said, 'and asked whether the air force worked on a different system of time from the navy and army.'

These tardy flyers were told they would not be on the lead vessel. That privilege had gone to two Canadians. Instead they would be assigned to another Hunt Class destroyer. The penalty was sleeping in a 'real doss-house' overnight. Miller and Glendinning were customarily piped aboard. They saluted the bridge and were introduced to the captain and first mate. In the evening, they were given drinks with the captain and all the officers aboard. The last one to meet them was a South African sub-lieutenant, who had a bloodshot left eye. 'A couple of colonials, eh?' he remarked, patronisingly.

'You use that word again,' Miller said, 'and I'll close the other eye.'

Glendinning realised that Miller was sensitive to being addressed this way. Yet he was still embarrassed again at his mate's gratuitous remark, expecting a 'Dusty dust-up'. But the South African understood the strength of sentiment in Miller's reaction.

They sailed at noon the next day, escorting 30 merchant vessels across the English Channel to the port of Antwerp, Belgium. The Australians found the afternoon voyage pleasant. They were impressed by the way their vessel rounded up straggling ships, like a sheep dog. But it was a different story at night. They were hustled back to the wardroom, where temporary beds had been made up for them.

'Around midnight,' Glendinning recalled, 'all hell broke loose. Orders were flying everywhere. All guns were blazing. The ship vibrated violently.'

They had no idea what was happening. They asked to go up on deck to get a sense of the conflict, but were refused. The two intrepid airmen spent a helpless, 'bloody frightening' few hours, as a big gun and torpedo scrap ensued. At breakfast they learned that their destroyer had engaged a German U-boat, which had been sunk. The naval battle had been an even contest. In other words, there had been a 50:50 chance that their vessel, not the enemy's, would be now languishing on the bottom of the ocean. It was a sobering thought for the airmen as the convoy crawled into Antwerp harbour without the loss of a vessel.

The two diligent, punctual Canadians were given a night out in Antwerp, which had its night-life attractions. Miller and Glendinning were confined to the ship anchored outside the harbour, as further punishment for their late reporting and their previous misdemeanours, which would follow them wherever they were during the war. When they returned to Portsmouth the two airmen had a greater appreciation of their sister service. Yet they were not enamoured of navy life, preferring their attachment to the 'wide blue yonder'.

On 4 November 1944, soon after returning from their hair-raising adventure, both men were promoted from pilot officer (attained on 4 May) to flying officer. Their chances of seeing action were now high.

On a cold winter's morning one day early in 1945, Miller invited Glendinning to come on an outing after gaining a legitimate 24-hour leave. The destination was a church graveyard in the Buckinghamshire village of Stoke Poges. 'This is where Thomas Gray wrote one of England's best known poems, "Elegy

Written in a Country Churchyard",,' Miller informed an intrigued Glendinning. 'He's buried here, too.'

They found the grave and inscription on the headstone supporting Miller's claim. He could recite the poem's 32 verses, which his father had taught him. While not pretending to be a literary expert, Miller appreciated its importance to English literature. He was entranced by its depiction of the countryside, with which he had become fond and familiar from the ground and the air:

> The lowing herd wind slowly o'er the lea,
> The ploughman homeward plods his weary way . . .

More significantly, he appreciated it for himself. He was touched by the poem's dwelling on the solemn meaning, impact and human levelling of death, especially given his own enhanced sense of mortality after his many escapes from its clutches.

> The boast of heraldry, the pomp of power,
> And all that beauty, all that wealth e'er gave,
> Awaits alike th' inevitable hour: –
> The paths of glory lead but to the grave.

The sense that he had gone close to *th' inevitable hour* several times made Miller embrace life with increasing passion. He had seen the alternative, which had taken so many of his generation. From his school alone more than a hundred had died. Countless other mates and acquaintances had gone. Most deaths touched him deeply. Some left him speechless, including the fate of his good friend Bill Newton, who had flown Boston bombers in New Guinea and won the Victoria Cross for acts of conspicuous bravery. He was shot down, imprisoned and beheaded by the Japanese. Miller was haunted by a photograph that reminded him of his mate. The shot was of the Gunnedah-born Sergeant Len

Siffleet, who was kneeling blindfolded under the Japanese executioner's raised sword. In Miller's mind, Siffleet in that most graphic of all war photographs was Newton. (Much later in life, he would tell journalists that it was Newton in the photograph.) Deeper in Miller's psyche was the sense that there but for the grace of Miller's Luck went he. He would never forget the night that he got up to get the clock for winning the batting averages with the Colts. Newton was there to receive a mug for winning the bowling averages. 'He was a big, handsome strapping bloke,' Miller recalled, when in his mind he was describing himself. Newton's fate would never leave Miller. Nor would the apparent loss of Bill Young. He had gone missing on a non-operation flying run over France. Every day Miller had a painful sense of guilt that he, *especially he*, should have gone more quickly and certainly than any of them.

The visit to Stoke Poges on that chilly January day might well have been his way of putting into perspective the challenges ahead. He and Glendinning were now only weeks from joining war operations. Their training was nearly over. Whether they would see a premature *inevitable hour* would soon be known.

The visit left Miller in a pensive, no-nonsense mood as they took the bus back to Cranfield. They alighted with their greatcoat collars up and gloved hands in their pockets, and walked briskly along the road to the camp. An RAF official chauffeur-driven sedan drew up alongside them, travelling in their direction. A cultured voice from the rear seat yelled: 'Officers, take your hands out of your pockets immediately!'

Glendinning slowed his walk, apprehensive about Miller's reaction. Miller turned his head slightly towards the vehicle. 'Get stuffed!' he said.

The vehicle moved on. Glendinning was astonished. He caught up to a disgruntled Miller. 'That bloke was at least an air vice marshal,' Glendinning remarked, 'judging from the gold braid around the peak of his cap.'

'Yes,' Miller replied testily, 'and a shiny arse, I'll bet.' It was a graphic way of describing the air vice marshal as someone who sat on his backside, giving orders some distance from the action. Miller's growing antipathy towards authority would have been exacerbated by those churchyard contemplations. He would soon be aloft in combat conditions, not the vice marshal.

COMBAT

Miller's long, sometimes frustrating, training run ended in mid-March 1945 when he joined the RAF station of Great Massingham in Norfolk, East Anglia. He had made it to bombing and fighter support operations at last. He was greeted with snow and ice, which he and all the force members took turns in shovelling from the runways. Yet it was a different, more relaxed environment than that of the other bases. The station was really an extension of the town. There were no fences separating them, and personnel were free to come and go.

Miller and all the pilots and navigators slept in huts at the airfield. Within days he was familiar as a pilot by night and by day with the three runways created on the usual 'A' pattern. The longest was 1,800 metres; the other two were 1,300 metres. After his experiences in 1943, when he misjudged his approach more than once, Miller was determined to get it right. He knew he was not the best pilot in the RAF. He had not had time to accumulate hours in the pilot's seat. His nervous energy also made him a bit heavy-handed in anything with a steering wheel, as everyone who had driven or flown with him testified. When asked about 'Miller's Luck' and his sometimes fortunate landings, his navigator, Jim Brown, said: 'Every landing by Keith was a close shave.' Aware of his shortcomings, Miller wished to have everything going for him in this most critical moment of his flying career.

In his plentiful spare time, Miller kept up his correspondence with Peg Wagner in Boston and his family and friends in Australia, and played hard while waiting for squadron missions. At a base dance he met attractive Jean Slater, a driver, whose job it was to take the crews to their planes and pick them up after a flying assignment. She recalled his inability to dance, but a capacity to charm. That night when they went outside the hall to get some air, Miller collapsed either from too much to drink, or from one of his delayed shocks, or exhaustion, or all three. Slater helped get him into bed. He returned to base offices the next day to thank her. A relationship developed from there. Miller spent much of his free time with her on bicycle rides into Norfolk's inviting countryside. He often invited her to join him for his favourite relaxation at the Crown pub in nearby Little Snoring. They spent many a convivial lunch there. Slater became aware of Miller's softer, cultured side, including his love for music and poetry, which she shared with him.

His ability to hum and whistle Beethoven's *Eroica* Symphony impressed her, as did his knowledge of its background. Beethoven's lustiness when compared to earlier eighteenth-century classical trend-setters Haydn and Mozart appealed to him, especially the early piano sonatas, which he found more expressive. Miller was attracted to Beethoven's unconventional approach, sense of artistry and personal style in mixing with kings and nobles. Beethoven's hunger for women and unabashed love affairs with society matrons put them on a similar wavelength. Slater also recalled Miller's passion for Gray's 'Elegy' and how much it meant to him. She had great respect for Miller and all of the men she chauffeured to their deadly missions.

The time for more dangerous gambles aloft was fast approaching. By early 1945, as a member of the RAF's No. 169 Squadron (motto: 'Hunt and Destroy'), he was easing his angular frame more and more into his fighter plane of choice, the Mosquito. This was in preparation for his expected assignments: as a pathfinder for the heavy bombers – the Lancasters – marking targets in Germany by night; and himself dropping bombs on targets.

The Mosquito had 42 models, or 'marks', including one that could land on aircraft carriers. The fighter version flown by Miller and Glendinning carried four 20 mm cannons in its nose. Its top speed, retarded by extra tanks of fuel (crude bombs to be dropped on the enemy) was around 500 km/hr. The pilot and navigator sat side by side. The plane's range with extra fuel tanks was more than 2,700 km, or seven hours. The Mosquito was a war baby. It was designed, tested, built and put into extensive combat use within the years of the war. It was made of wood, which was the reason furniture makers were enlisted to build it.

The plane was versatile when it came to aerial combat. It carried two-ton bombs to Berlin, and shot down enemy planes night and day. It strafed shipping, rail and road traffic. A deed that endeared the plane to Miller was breaking down the walls of Amiens prison in northern France, which allowed French Resistance fighters to escape in February 1944. It also demolished Gestapo headquarters in Copenhagen. In short, this plane was a round-the-clock killing machine. The Mosquito could even destroy those guided missiles that nearly prevented Miller reaching a hundred at Lord's.

No. 169 Squadron took part in missions in the last weeks of the war (April–May 1945) that attacked V1 and V2 launch sites at the pine-clad island of Peenemunde in the North Sea. In 1935 Hitler had cleared the island of its inhabitants and transformed it into a huge research station for the production of the V missiles. He spent £50 million on the project. The RAF's raids on Peenemunde were part of its retaliatory low-run bombing to cut the production rate well below Hitler's 100,000-a-year target. This long-running counter-offensive helped save England from total destruction.

Miller took part in two dangerous missions. The first was on 19 April in an attack on a German stronghold at Flensburg in

Denmark. The fleet of Mosquitoes, which included Glendinning's plane, was to test the strength of the German night fighters.
The round trip from Great Massingham took 4 hours 5 minutes
across the North Sea. Mosquitoes flew under 1,000 feet (300
metres) to avoid German radar and to pass near the island of
Heligoland, a German base 80 kilometres from Denmark. Miller
and Glendinning negotiated this assignment without any major
dramas beyond scares that German fighters were on their tails,
which they managed to shake off. With so many planes in the air
in the darkness, they had to be careful that they did not mistake
other Mosquitoes for enemy planes.

On 2 May the war was all but over. Hitler had committed
suicide in his Berlin bunker, German forces were surrendering in
north-western Europe. It was only a matter of days before the war
would be finished officially. But this was the moment when the
commanding officer of RAF's Group 10, which included No. 169
Squadron, decided on a gratuitous attack laced with revenge.

This became Miller's second precarious mission, called Operation Fire Bash. It was to be directed at the Westerland Airfield on
the island of Sylt in the North Sea, off the coast of Denmark. It
was held by a garrison of 5,000 soldiers and a further 15,000
sailors. The Nazis had always feared that the Allies would try to
seize Sylt and cut off the Schleswig peninsula. They had fortified
it. The island contained more than 100,000 land mines. Five
thousand sea mines surrounded it. A squadron of fighter planes
based on Sylt had also protected German naval vessels throughout
the war. There were more than 800 artillery guns on the island,
half of which were flexible, mobile weapons, forming a strong
defence. They had huge supplies of ammunition. There was no
question that the Nazis would defend Sylt tenaciously whether or
not the war was declared 'over' and Germany had officially
surrendered.

The defence so far had led to 300 British and American airmen's
deaths. Now British commanders wanted to retaliate hard. Twenty-

four planes, 12 from No. 169 Squadron, including two piloted by Miller and Glendinning, and 12 (dropping 250-pound bombs) from a sister squadron at Little Snoring, were sent on this late mission. A couple of days before Miller and Glendinning took off, their squadron leader, Jimmy Wright, second-in-command to No. 169 Squadron's wing commander, Neville Reeves, asked Glendinning what operation he was going on.

'Sylt,' Glendinning replied.

Wright paused and said, 'What's your hut number? You've got some nice stuff in it.'

The next morning Wright apologised for the remark. But the point was made. It was likely that several planes would be lost on such a mission. It seemed an unnecessary assignment, so close to the end. The lives of brave pilots and navigators were going to be sacrificed needlessly.

The planes from No. 169 Squadron carried drop tanks beneath each wing. The tanks were loaded with an inflammatory compound (a form of napalm) and with Mills bombs. With such an inflammatory load, Miller and Glendinning felt the pressure after ten minutes of flying, when they were in enemy-occupied territory. If all went well, the round trip would take 3 hours 50 minutes. Pilots and navigators kept silent to avoid giving away their positions and 'Fire Bash' to the enemy. Miller's main job was to watch his altimeter. There was little chance of getting any bearings from positions below. He was flying over the sea in pitch black for most of the time.

Glendinning's Mosquito was hit by flak after he had dropped his bombs on Westerland airfield from just 400 feet (125 metres). One engine was hit and shut down. He was well versed in how to fly this way, indirectly because of Miller. He had been asleep one morning after a particularly heavy bout of drinking the night before and could not be roused. This caused them to miss the transport taking them from one flight training venue to another in 1944. They ended up arriving at the new place two days late.

Discipline was so tight that the tardiness was frowned upon. The two pilots guessed that when they were taken aloft for training, the examining officers would make the test so tough that they would both fail. One test was to shut down an engine without notice. The reaction to this became second nature to Glendinning and Miller.

Glendinning's major problem on the flight back from Sylt in the early hours of 3 May was the weather across 500 kilometres of the North Sea. He was forced to fly at 250 metres and in low cloud, a nerve-rackingly long experience. He caught some of Miller's Luck when he reached the English coast. The cloud lifted. He had a clear run home. As he began it, Glendinning noticed for the first time that he was sweating profusely.

Squadron Leader Wright, perhaps guilty because of his callous remark about pilfering his hut because he would not come back from the mission, flew along the coast in radio contact with Glendinning. There was concern about whether he had enough fuel to make it back to base. He did, just.

Miller too had been instructed to swoop low (at 125 metres) over Westerland airfield and release the drop tanks on buildings. When the Mills bombs went off, the tanks would ignite and cause a spectacular blast. He followed another plane in. It dropped its bombs and flew off without incident. The defences might have thought that the planes were on reconnaissance only. Those first bombs changed the ground forces' attitude. Miller's plane, the second one in, would not be so fortunate. As he approached his target at about 300 metres, he was impressed by the beauty of tracer bullets of different colours – green, blue, yellow, red – spraying like a garden hose in his direction. But when he heard the *whoosh* of the tracers, he became aware of their deadly intent. Miller's plane was caught in the searchlight beams. He veered and avoided the light for a few seconds. Then he made his low run on the field, watching the altimeter and then concentrating on looking through the target finder at the airfield. He pressed the bomb release. Only one of the tanks was dislodged. The other clung to a wing. The plane skewed to one side. Miller fought the controls. A hail of tracer flak shot up into what would have been his line of flight, had both tanks dropped as intended.

Miller looked back at the third No. 169 Squadron plane coming in to drop its bombs. It was hit and crashed. 'Miller's Luck,' he thought, and headed back over the North Sea to Great Massingham. But all the way home he was on edge about the remaining bomb stuck precariously to the underneath of the wing. What if it exploded? What if it dropped on an innocent village or town in England? Miller and navigator Jim Brown kept glancing at it, but could only make out a shape in the darkness. He tried jettisoning the tank over the North Sea, but it wouldn't budge. If anything, it was loosened and made even more unstable.

Miller called base. He told them of the problem. They instructed him to come in and land normally. It was the only choice. Miller was putting all his faith in his run of fortune and, if he had thought about it, the bomb itself. It had already saved his life over that target airfield by *not* releasing. Miller was in a sweat and so nervous that he was personally on autopilot when he landed the plane. He couldn't remember conversations with base, or directives from his navigator, or the approach or the touchdown. Nothing. He was in a state of shock when he made a pinpoint, perfect landing. The next thing he recalled was standing on the tarmac. Ground crew and a fire truck raced towards the Mosquito.

'I was shaking,' Miller said.

Someone asked him, 'Where's the tank?'

'On the plane,' Miller replied, jerking around to look at the offending wing and tank. It was not there. A few minutes later the ground crew found the tank 100 metres away. It had partly released when Miller pressed the firing button over the German airfield. The normal jolt of landing at Great Massingham had caused it to fall off. An officer said it was a miracle that it had not exploded. It was a mystery to everyone at the base.

Miller had delayed shock, which can cause the body to collapse some time later. Since he had arrived in England two years earlier he had survived purely by chance on six occasions: when he was playing cricket and the pub he should have been at was blown up; when at the Putney pub instead of being at the cinema; when the next man flying after him in a faulty plane crashed; when he slewed over the hangar; when that bomb under the wing didn't drop, thus preventing Miller's plane being struck by flak; and when the bomb fell off the plane on the tarmac without detonating. All these moments had their effect on Miller. He was disturbed in their aftermath.

He and Glendinning, and their navigators Jim Brown (who had been fighting with the 9th Division in the Middle East before joining the RAAF) and Bert Berriman (from Albury), made it back to base alive by luck, skill and courage. But five of those 24 planes, with ten British airmen, did not return that night of 2–3 May. It was to be No. 169 Squadron's last mission. The next few nights' weather was too poor for any more superfluous missions from Great Massingham on the vengeful whim of a safely grounded commanding officer. This was a blessing for the two squadrons. Miller's Luck had spread.

***

Miller stood on the edge of the Great Massingham airfield with a sense of despair. The place was desolate, and near-deserted; the sky overcast. The war in Europe had officially ended. It was early on 8 May. The Mosquitoes and Beaufighters of No. 169 Squadron sat dormant in the hangars. There would be no briefing that evening.

Unlike millions across Europe, Miller's immediate reaction was not elation. He was 20,000 kilometres from home. 'I simply stood there,' Miller said, 'and thought, "What the hell am I going to do now?" I'd never been so lonely.' He had known the day was coming, but with so much propaganda from both sides, no one accepted anything until it was official. A phase of his life was coming to an end. He felt at that fleeting moment as if all meaning and purpose had been snuffed out. Flying had been a well-defined existence for him. He had been a small cog in a huge machine, the broad aim of which was to defeat a fearsome enemy. This was clear, uncomplicated, stark, bloody and glorious. Now that the routine and purpose had been taken from him, he felt empty. VE (for Victory in Europe) Day, 8 May 1945, was a hollow experience for him.

Miller was 25. He was not qualified for anything, except flying. But after his experiences he was not about to make a career out of his good fortune in surviving. Besides, there was cricket. He wanted to prove himself at the highest level. He had yet to play a Test. Any job, just as before the war, would revolve around making time for top-level sport. But would he find work in Melbourne? The distant thought of sorting invoices at Vacuum Oil depressed him further.

Despite his initial feeling of uncertainty, Miller didn't have to worry about his future just then. He was still in the service. His duty on this momentous day was to play in an afternoon cricket match for the AIF against the North of England at Blackpool, Lancashire, 300 kilometres away from the base.

The highlight of the festive occasion was a century by Lindsay Hassett, which took 63 minutes. When Miller was batting, he took time at the fall of a wicket to quiz tall, lean and bald George Pope, the Derbyshire seamer, about his grip on the ball. Many likened him to the great Sydney Barnes. Pope, too, had a prodigious leg-cutter, which Alec Bedser and he had learnt from Pope's brother Alfred. Pope showed Miller the middle finger of his right hand. It had corns either side of it from the way the finger gripped the ball when he delivered those ripping cutters. Pope explained that the position of his hold on the seam depended on the wind's strength on the day. Miller, who had never given a thought to the way he held the ball, made a mental note to try different grips.

He also observed that when Pope took off his cap to begin an over, he would rub the ball on it, using the grease from his sweating scalp to keep the shine. Miller began to use cream on his hair to maintain a shine.

His bowling had been limited by his back injury, but he was aware of the speed he could deliver and the effect he was having on opposing batsmen. Should he be called on to do more with the ball, Miller wished to be better equipped in the hope that he could be recognised as a true all-rounder rather than a batsman who could bowl a bit.

He returned to Great Massingham to find that the base and the village had run out of celebratory beer. Miller had some leave owing to him, so he took off for London. He spent his time drinking, carousing with women, including Christine in Putney, betting wherever he could and hanging out with his mates. But he ran out of money fast, a common condition. This left him with no choice but to take the train back to his Norfolk base, which irked him. He still had a few days leave and was seconded by Commanding Officer Neville Reeves to fly ground staff personnel over the devastation wrought in Germany by aerial bombing. The flights were nicknamed 'Reeves' Ruhr Tours'.

Reeves was leading a formation of seven aircraft on the round trip of three and a half hours when Miller broke formation and disappeared. He returned to base 20 minutes after the last member of the formation landed. Reeves wanted to know why he had left. Miller replied that he wanted to fly over the 2,000-year-old city of Bonn in the Ruhr Valley.

'Why Bonn, Miller?' Reeves demanded.

'Because it's the birthplace of Beethoven, sir!'

Reeve didn't show it, but he was impressed. Miller was not put on a charge.

Nine days after his traumatic experience landing with the napalm tank, he was back at Lord's scoring a dashing 50 for the RAAF against a British Empire XI. It was a useful warm-up game to start the season, which would begin in earnest with the Victory Tests. These were hastily arranged to begin at Lord's just 11 days after the war in Europe finished. Once more in the twentieth century, cricket would be the symbol of British Empire dominance over its enemies. Warner had been instrumental in keeping the game alive at Lord's to demonstrate British defiance to the belting by German bombers. The national game would go on, regardless. Now it was a humane way of celebrating victory, lifting the national spirit and taking the collective mind off the destruction and deprivations in immediate post-war Britain.

The precedent for such England–Australia competition 26 years earlier was still well in the minds of Warner and others. In 1919 a team known as the 1st AIF Australian XI was selected from the 170,000 diggers in the process of being educated before returning to Australia after World War I. The Australians were happy to play official Tests, but the MCC, which controlled the game, was not. It pointed to just one available player with Test experience: 33-year-old all-rounder Charlie Kelleway. There was also one other established first-class player, the stolid 30-year-old batsman, Herbie Collins. The MCC would have been willing to play the series had big names such as Charlie Macartney been available. It didn't have access to a crystal ball, which could not have missed the serious talent among the servicemen, such as the dashing all-rounder Jack Gregory, the attacking batsman and outstanding cover field Johnny Taylor, the top-class keeper Bert Oldfield, the strong-driving C. E. 'Nip' Pellew, or the batsman/keeper Hampden 'Hammy' Love, and others. They all shone for the 1st AIF squad of 19 that in 1919 toured England, South Africa and Australia. It showed its strength by playing 47 matches, winning 25 and losing just 4. This success accelerated the return to cricket normality after the 1914–18 war.

In 1945 it was not the MCC but Australian cricket administrators who would not allow the four (eventually five) three-day matches set down to rank as official 'Tests'. The war might have finished in Europe, but there was still fierce fighting in the Pacific with Japan, which did not make it a propitious time for celebrating with the highest-level contest in cricket. Another factor was the inadequate number of recognised top-class players to choose from the 15,000 servicemen available in England. They were not representative of Australia's full talent.

The 2nd AIF and the RAAF fused in the interests of providing a contest for a near-complete England Test team. Even then, the Australians admitted to a sizeable inferiority complex to the old enemy, whose squad included Len Hutton, Cyril Washbrook, Wally Hammond, Les Ames, Bill Edrich, Walter Robins and Doug Wright. The RAAF provided six players in the Australian XI and the AIF five. The lowly ranked warrant officer class II Lindsay Hassett, who had played four Ashes Tests in England in 1938, was selected as captain despite some rumblings from Miller and others about the suitability of Keith Carmody for the job. Carmody, who was due back in England soon, had been shot down early in 1945 during an attack on four German ships off the Hook of Holland. He had been rescued by the enemy and put in solitary confinement at Venlo and Frankfurt. Weeks later he had been marched 240 kilometres to a concentration camp near Berlin. The Russians, advancing from the east on a crumbling Germany, released him when they overran Berlin late in March, but then held him throughout April for a possible prisoner exchange with the Allies. Carmody did not like the prospects of this arrangement and his chances of being shipped to Siberia. He escaped and managed to find an American force coming from the west. He was a hero in the eyes of Miller and his fellow airmen, as well as being a commissioned officer.

Yet Hassett was the only Test player available, and he was appointed. The fact that he had not lobbied for the position helped Miller and the other RAAF players accept him. The other personnel with first-class experience were Miller (Victoria, 9 matches), Sismey (New South Wales, 8 matches), Albert Cheetham (New South Wales, 18 matches) and Cecil Pepper (New South Wales, 10 matches). Pepper bowled leg-spin, but with variations, such as an excellent wrong 'un and a front-of-the-hand flipper, which he could deliver almost like an off-break. There was also medium-fast bowler Graham Williams (15 matches) and opening bat Dick Whitington (32 matches) from South Australia. Miller had come across them all in his one full season of Shield cricket in 1939–40.

Thousands of Australian (in dark blue), British and Canadian (in khaki) servicemen swelled the numbers at Lord's on 19 May 1945 for the first day of the First Victory Test. The usual crowd of members and notables, including Lord Mountbatten, filled the Long Room and private boxes. They broke open the champagne and chicken sandwiches. It might not have been an official Test, but it was an important match between two teams representing England and Australia. The weather was chilly and overcast; the feeling festive, yet with the suspense always associated with the first day of a big series. With the Union Jack and Southern Cross flags fluttering, the celebration of victory over European fascism within 11 days of VE Day created a palpably happy atmosphere. John Arlott described the emotion of the morning as 'a general euphoria generated by relief and nostalgia'.

The Tests were expected to mark a new post-war era of cricket. It had been seven years since the dour drawn Ashes of 1938, when opposing captains Hammond and Bradman refused to give an inch. There was now a hope that the competition would be more carefree and daring. There was all and nothing to play for. No little urn containing burnt bails was at stake. Hammond was playing, but Bradman, the winner's winner, was not. Both sides, particularly England, were expected to present new, dashing cricketers. The spectators were aware of an imbalance between the two old enemies, but were wistfully hoping for miracles. Those supporting England were expecting a special win.

Miller was the only Australian with a relaxed smile in the dressing room. After two seasons, he felt at home at Lord's. Besides that, he had found batting form in between flying missions with that 50 for the RAAF side against England and a dashing 52 against Lancashire. He was one of those whom Arlott recognised as 'relieved' simply to be alive and there at the home of the cricket.

Another was pilot Graham Williams, who had just been released after four years as a prisoner-of-war, where he had distinguished himself teaching Braille to blinded bombing victims – mostly children – in Germany. He had been shot down in the Western Desert during the Libyan Campaign. The 193 cm beanpole Williams looked emaciated, having lost much weight during his long ordeal. His last-minute act before taking the field was to swallow a cup of glucose in the hope of restoring energy to a body he was unsure would cope with physical exertion.

Hammond won the toss, and decided to bat. The tall, efficient medium-pacer Cheetham (who had been a Rat of Tobruk) had the honour of sending down the first ball in a new era to Hutton. But it was Williams who thrilled the Australians in the crowd next over when he had Hutton caught behind for 1. The recent POW would have pinched himself. Only a few weeks earlier he had been wondering whether he would escape Germany alive. Now he was being cheered at Lord's for dismissing cheaply the holder of the world record Test score (364 at the Oval in 1938). Later he got rid of Hammond for just 29, uprooting his off stump.

Miller came on as the usual fifth bowler, after Cheetham, Williams, Ellis and Pepper, and promptly bowled Bill Edrich (who had also been a pilot based at Great Massingham) for 45 just when he and Ames looked like taking the game away from Australia. Yet there had been no real thought of using Miller earlier. He took 1 for 11 off 9 overs. His economy rate was owing to his being both erratic and quick. On both counts he was tough to score off.

England reached 267. Australia was 2 for 82 at stumps on the Friday. On day two, a good crowd of more than 25,000 jammed into Lord's, demonstrating that Plum Warner's optimism about a series so soon after VE Day being a success was well placed. Miller loved the challenge of a big occasion and audience. He arrived at the crease at 3 for 136, and joined a subdued Hassett (77), who seemed to have lost his pre-war verve. This Miller innings would create no fireworks. He let technique override aggression as he took on two outstanding leg-spinners in Doug Wright and Walter Robins, who in his time had dealt blows to Bradman and Stan McCabe. On top of Miller's struggle with spin, which was still a problem for him, he was keen to make a good impression here. It could have some influence when real Tests returned.

Miller harvested rather than blasted until at 5 for 270 and, past England's score, his strokeplay blossomed. He unleashed shots that had electrified crowds in England in the past two summers. Urged on by the man mountain Cec ('The Ox') Pepper, who had a sound defence but loved to attack, Miller drew applause from some of the most critical observers in the Long Room. Comparisons were made with Victor Trumper, Archie Jackson and McCabe.

At one point Colonel John Stephenson (later to become MCC secretary and a good Miller mate) bowled Miller a late-outswinger, which just missed hitting the off stump. Miller strolled down the pitch and patted the spot where the ball had landed, tossed back his mane and glared at the colonel. 'I bowled Miller an identical ball,' he said 'He drove it into the stand for six.'

Miller again strode down the pitch towards the bowler. 'A better ball,' Miller called to the colonel, 'but the better the ball, the bigger the six.'

Miller made 105 in 210 minutes. He struggled in the nineties for 40 minutes. Yet it had the required effect. Spectators – particularly the Australians – seemed pleased enough. They drank the ground's beer supply and applauded all the Australian performances.

One memory of that rapturous day at Lord's would stay in Miller's mind forever. It was not that brilliant straight drive off Stephenson, or raising his bat when he reached his initial first-class century at Lord's. It was the reception for lanky Graham Williams as he emerged from the Long Room to bat. 'I have heard touching applause at Lord's, in fact all around the world,' Miller said, 'but this was hand-clapping with a difference. I have never heard it before or since . . . magical, heart-felt hand-clapping. It is a scene I will never forget.' There 'had been press reports on Williams' plight as a POW, and he was being warmly welcomed back 'home' and to freedom. But the response would have had a deeper effect on Miller. His gentle tears for Williams were for himself, too. Miller's last dice with death when he limped home from Sylt was just two weeks ago. He could not explain – indeed no one could explain – why some survived and some did not.

Williams, not known for his batting, celebrated with a delightful 53. He was living a fantasy and could do no wrong with ball or bat.

Miller's 'notices' were good. *The Times* thought his knock 'as good a century as has been seen at Lord's in many a long day'. *Wisden* liked his 'elegant, emphatic style'. The London *Daily Telegraph* looked ahead and would have pleased Miller: 'It proves how valuable he will be to Australia in future official Tests.'

His sterling effort at the crease helped Australia (along with Hassett's 77 and contributions of 35 or more from six other batsmen) to a healthy 455. England's second innings of 294 was a fraction better than the first. It left Australia 77 minutes to reach a target of 107. Hassett's men took up the challenge. The impetuous Pepper led the way with his usual attacking approach. He hit one prodigious six into the top deck of the grandstand. It was the strike that symbolised Australia's intent, which at certain moments led to panic and two run-outs. Anyone thinking that the game would be played to the finish in an atmosphere of total generosity, or that the spirit of the game counted more than winning, would have raised eyebrows at England captain Hammond's placing of eight on the boundary. It slowed the run rate, caused frustration and helped England to a point where it could force a draw.

At 4 for 76, Australia needed 31 in 12 minutes for victory. Pepper was in everything. He thumped a straight four off Gover, then followed it with a cover drive. Lieutenant Colonel Griffith, wearing a cream cravat, moved around the boundary to cut it off, but the ball evaded his ungainly lunge and slipped over the boundary rope. The Australians needed 23 from 18 deliveries.

'What's that around neck?' a Yorkshireman called. 'Cravat or noose?' Griffith nodded a rueful acknowledgment of his error in the tense final minutes. 'Why don't you tighten it, guv'nor?' the spectator yelled.

The finish soon boiled down to six deliveries and 5 runs to get.

England's 'affable Alf' Gover, an England Surrey medium-pacer, was thrown the ball for the final over. He put the first one in the blockhole. Pepper's partner Charles Price just dug it out. No run. The second ball was pushed to mid-off for a scampered single. Four balls to make 4 runs. Hammond fiddled with the field, bringing two of his eight boundary riders closer in. Everyone, including Pepper himself, knew that he would swing at the next ball, no matter what was delivered. The big, talented all-rounder proved far more predictable as a batsman than as a wily spinner. He launched into an on-drive but mistimed it. The ball flew high, but directly above Doug Wright at mid-wicket. The fielder ran forward, then back, reached up with his left hand, lost his balance and clutched at his second attempt. Wright had it at a third attempt, but it was a juggle too much as he toppled to ground. The ball spilled free. Wright accidentally kicked it away in his fall. Pepper called Price through for a second run. Three balls remained; 2 runs were required.

Hammond held up play again, moving everyone in to cut off the single. The crowd of 17,000 was hushed and expectant. Gover delivered his fourth ball on middle stump. Pepper, who would never die wondering about anything, went on to the back foot and cross-batted the ball. It squeezed through mid-wicket, running down towards the boundary rope in front of the seats where the Australian servicemen were predominant. They were on their feet cheering as the batsmen ran two. Australia had scraped in with two balls to spare and six wickets in hand. *The Times* noted that Hassett's men had beaten the fieldsmen, the clock and expectations. Miller, Pepper, Hassett and co. celebrated long into the London spring night.

The competitive but fine spirit of the game, marred only slightly by Hammond's defensive field placements in the last half hour, was outstanding, and drew comparisons with the dour 1938 Ashes series. Commentators spoke with authority rather than hope now for 'a new post-war era'. The three days drew 67,660 spectators, who paid a shilling each to pack Lord's. The total gate for the game was £3,383. After tax and expenses, £1,935 went to the Red Cross and five Australian charities.

The game had been a spectacular success. Warner and Keith Carmody, two prime movers over the years in setting up the series, were pleased. England showed that it was taking the competition most seriously by making changes for the second Victory Test more in keeping with an Ashes contest than a peace celebration. They dumped Test players Gover, Ames and Robins and replaced them with Pope, Pollard and batsman Maurice Leyland, whose last outing against Australia in the 1938 Oval Test produced a thumping 187. But Leyland withdrew unfit, as did Stephenson. England and Surrey batsman Errol Holmes and Lancashire's left-arm spinner, W. B. Roberts, replaced them. Australia brought in Carmody, who was back in England after his escape adventure. He replaced the battler batsman Ross Stanford.

In the run-up to the second of the Victory series, Miller gained wider experience under the peculiarly Mancunian conditions of grey skies and plenty of rain interruptions. It was in a two-day county match beginning 6 June for the RAAF against Lancashire at Manchester. Fast swingers such as Pollard were demon bowlers under these conditions. Miller made good use of his opportunity, scoring 52 from 109 – the only fifty in the match – in a fine display on a slow, muddy track so affected by rain that an emergency pitch was prepared in order to save the Test wicket.

In the following week, he turned in another fine performance for the RAAF against the RAF at Lord's on a Saturday, which assured another full house and a good gate for charities. RAF captain Bill Edrich sent the Australians in on a lively wicket but, after an early collapse, Miller, coming in at number three (63 in 90 minutes), supported by all-rounder Flying Officer Jack Pettiford (57), pulled the side around to reach 7 for 243 and an easy 81-run victory.

Miller and Pettiford enjoyed their 'sweet' partnership, which Miller described as 'more Mozart than Wagner'. The two airmen had a lot in common. They were born a day apart (Pettiford on 29 November 1919), they were both all-rounders (Pettiford was a leg-spinner) and they both loved their classical music, with Beethoven being their shared favourite. During the fall of wickets, other players were bemused to hear them talk more about symphonies than the state of play.

The Second Test began on 23 June at Sheffield's Bramall Lane. It had been hammered by the Luftwaffe. Areas of the grandstands were charred and dented. The ground was pockmarked.

Hassett won the toss and pleased the Yorkshire crowd by sending England in. The local hero, Len Hutton, didn't get going, but the crowd was content with a domineering even century by Hammond. Warner classed it as one of his best ever, and raved about a strong 63 by Cyril Washbrook. Miller was thrown the ball as fifth change to hold up an end. He was quick but too erratic to cause other than the occasional discomfort, returning 0 for 19 off 11 overs.

Hammond singled out Pepper for special praise, saying that his bowling 'was some of the finest spin I have ever faced'. Considering Clarrie Grimmett had won his tussle with Hammond during the 1930 Ashes in England, and that he had also faced O'Reilly at his best, this was a high accolade indeed.

Miller, not always the best runner, found himself batting in the second innings with someone less reliable in Carmody (42), who ran him out for 17 when he looked set for another big innings. Australia struggled to 147. Pope, living up to S. F. Barnes standards, took 5 for 58.

England's openers reached 41 without loss in its second innings, when Hassett, for no apparent reason beyond using the surprise element, threw the ball to Miller to replace Williams. Miller's back still had its moments, but if he did not overwork it, he could generate the speed he demonstrated before the wrestling incident in late 1943. It was a challenge to be given a chance first change rather than fifth and with some shine still on the ball. Taking the role a fraction more seriously, he raced in from nine paces instead of a leisurely six. He was off-line and didn't trouble Washbrook. The next over, Ellis was on in another change, and he tied up Hutton.

Miller's second over was quicker and shorter. He hit Washbrook a painful blow on the thigh. The batsman hobbled for a bye, leaving Hutton to face. He ducked a very quick head-high bumper. Miller, nostrils flaring and hair flopping, looked back at the batsman, as he returned to his mark, more or less. In what was becoming a Miller trademark, he flicked his hair, running a small concealed comb through it, and then charged in. Hutton was hit on the left forearm, the one he had injured in 1940 in a gymnasium accident while training to be a commando. He stumbled a bye and dropped his bat at the bowler's end. Miller examined the hit and rubbed the welt.

The Yorkshire crowd reacted to its champion being struck. There were yells of 'Larwood! Go off, Larwood!' in reference to Nottinghamshire's pace demon of the 1930s who had terrorised Yorkshire in county games.

Miller now had both batsmen uncertain. When Hutton was ready but still sore, he walked back to his mark, shoved back his mane and steamed in. More in reaction to the crowd than out of any desire to do further damage, Miller tore in this time at the hapless Washbrook. The ball was another head-high bouncer. Washbrook ducked, but into the ball, which cannoned into his crown.

The crowd roared. The ball flew clear. Hutton set off for another bye, but seeing that Washbrook was dazed and in trouble, he returned to his crease. Miller was catcalled and booed. Play was held up as the hardy Washbrook took some moments to clear his head, which fielders, Hutton, Miller and the umpires examined as if it were a damaged bowling ball.

Miller's third over was better-mannered. Each ball was of good length. The crowd settled down and watched as Washbrook flicked at a very quick delivery outside the off stump. The ball flew straight to keeper Sismey. It popped out of his gloves as Pepper dived from slip and just failed to snaffle it. Miller stood mid-pitch, hands on hips. But instead of snarling, he pushed back his hair with his left hand and that comb, and waved to Sismey with his right. The bowler knew that both batsmen had been softened to the point of vulnerability.

Miller's fourth over was his best so far. He kept a good length with three deliveries. Then he released another dangerous short one at Washbrook, which would have arched his nerves. The crowd was temperate in its response, perhaps sensing that Miller was now bowling with some science. The next ball was a quick away-swinger. It had the nervous batsman pushing again. The edge went to Sismey, who held it. Hammond came in. Miller delivered a variety of pace and bump at the super-batsman, who looked uncomfortable.

There was a tea break. Ellis removed Hutton (46), and Miller beat Jack Robertson with sheer speed, trapping him lbw for 1. Hammond (38) never looked happy against Miller's pace or the spin of Pepper and Ellis, and was bowled by the latter. England stumbled to 190.

The more astute observers of this game felt it was the turning point for Miller as a bowler. But most of the press still regarded him as a batsman, who was brought on to rest the four main bowlers. One scribe who thought otherwise was the aptly named South African former speedster Bob Crisp, writing in the *Daily Express*. He advised Miller to lengthen and mark his run to 15 paces, a novelty for the bowler on two counts: distance and calibration. Crisp also notified Hassett that he should open the bowling with Miller. More than Washbrook's head, it seemed, had been struck by Miller's effort.

Australia was set 330 to win in 360 minutes on the final day. Whitington (61) and Workman (living up to his name, with a dogged, yeoman-like 63) gave the servicemen a fine start and fair chance. But Miller was bowled by Pollard for just 8, and while many players managed starts, Australia fell 41 runs short in another thriller. The series was square. The result caused Hassett to consider using Miller more proactively with the ball.

MOSQUITO DOWN; ALL-ROUNDER UP

There were rumours in June 1945 that No. 169 Squadron would be sent to Burma to join the fight against the Japanese. But not even wing commanders really knew. The missions were now peaceful formation flying, which could be done only by day; low-level cross-country flying; and the testing of planes for their night-flying capabilities. The squadron was filling in time, without any real sense of what would happen in the future.

The lads were getting bored and frisky. One afternoon after a bout of lunch-time drinking, Miller and Glendinning flew in separate planes with their navigators down to Epsom racetrack. They fooled about flying low over the main stretch and cutting each other off, covering several circuits of the field. No race meeting was on, but a few startled strappers stopped training to watch the daredevil display.

On another afternoon after a similarly convivial lunch, the two pilots were asked to test a plane together. They didn't need a navigator. The test would be done in daylight, and they would fly no further than the coast, which was about 150 kilometres away. Neither of them wished the other to act as pilot, given the number of beers they had consumed. They tossed for the pilot's seat. Glendinning won.

With Miller urging him on, Glendinning flew along the coast at about 100 feet (30 metres) over a beach near Great Yarmouth, causing sunbathers to run for cover. After several low swoops they returned to Great Massingham. In the mess that night, Squadron Leader Wright confronted several pilots and asked if any of them had flown low over the coast. Glendinning and Miller said they had not. Wright himself had been at the beach.

'We couldn't get the markings,' Wright said, 'but the plane did look like one of ours.' He paused and asked, 'You're sure it wasn't you, Glendinning?' Glendinning was sure it had not been him. 'Well, don't do it again!' Wright said, before turning on his heel and leaving the mess.

When he wasn't doing routine flights or larking about in the air, Miller now had much more time to play cricket. As long as he was representing Great Massingham station or the Australian services teams, he could get time off, and anything now was better than being stuck at the airbase.

Miller even managed to secure a game for Glendinning representing the station after persuading Neville Reeves, who captained the side, that his mate was a 'useful off-spinner' when he had hardly ever played the game, even at school. Reeves gave Glendinning a chance in an inter-station game one afternoon. His first ball was whacked over the fence. Miller in slips clapped his hands: 'Good ball, Unk; it was a very lucky shot!' Glendinning was hit for runs each ball. After each dispatch, Miller would clap his hands and call encouragement with a comment, such as: 'Nearly got through, Unk; he didn't know much about that one.' Glendinning went for 22 runs in the over and never bowled again.

On 28 June Miller was detailed to fly on another Ruhr Tour for ground staff at Great Massingham. His passenger was his corporal mechanic. On the way from the huts to the planes, Miller whispered to Glendinning: 'I don't want to fly today, Unky. I'm going to call in sick.' That excuse didn't work. Miller's next ploy was to try four Mosquitoes and pretend that each one was 'unserviceable'. Wing Commander Neville Reeves, once more leading the tour formation, was over Germany when he heard of Miller's 'game'. His report that each plane had a fault meant that ground crew members were rushing around trying to service them for more than two hours. It was a huge waste of time, money and effort. Despite Reeves's fondness for Miller, his behaviour angered him. He was compelled to maintain discipline. Reeves had been the only pilot to fly a brand new Mosquito, which was in perfect order. He radioed base: 'Put him [Miller] in my new aircraft and see if he can mark that unserviceable. Then tell him to complete an hour's flying.' Miller took off in the Mosquito with the mechanic. Meanwhile Reeves returned from the tour and took some of the others in the flying tour group to a cricket practice area just off the end of the main runway.

Up in the clouds, Miller had been flying for 45 minutes when there was a surge on one side of the starboard wing. For a second he felt he had lost control and that the plane would plough into a field below. He managed to gain some height. A split second later there was a flash of flame from the starboard engine. It caught fire. The wing, made of English ash, would soon burn. Miller radioed base with his problem. He pressed the fire extinguisher and prayed for 'Miller's Luck'.

Down at the practice nets, Reeves was bowling his off-spinners when a vehicle approached at speed. The driver informed him that Miller's starboard engine was on fire. 'There's bugger-all I can do about that!' Reeves snapped back, perhaps miffed that his new plane would definitely be unserviceable soon. He continued bowling his off-spinners.

Glendinning was in the cricket practice area. He scanned the skies. 'The Mossie appeared with the starboard prop feathered [whereby the engine is shut down and the propellers lined up with the body of the aircraft to prevent drag],' he said, 'and no smoke coming from the aircraft. It was at 2,000 feet [600 metres].'

Miller was on one engine. Normally he could be relied on to land such a disabled plane. A standard practice drill was to kill one engine and land. But Miller didn't have his navigator, Jim Brown, with him. It was a tougher assignment without him.

In the minutes it took to prepare for an attempted landing, stomach-tightening thoughts were on his mind. Miller was aware that an Australian squadron leader had been killed at Ford, Brighton, when he crashed his Mosquito after undershooting the airfield. In that incident, the squadron leader had lost one engine. When he circled and was preparing to come in for a fourth attempted landing, the other engine failed. The Mosquito plummeted to earth. Another problem was overshooting the runway. It had its own perils. If Miller did so and wished to pull out, the Mosquito tended to rear or pitch skyward because the trim for landing was aft of centre. The pilot had to push the 'stick' forward very hard at the same time as opening up the throttle. A mishandling of this action had seen Mosquitoes stall on the climb and crash.

A further concern that might have flashed across his mind was the way his good mate Bluey Truscott had died larking about in the air. Might his own life end so inappropriately and anticlimactically on a joy ride for a member of the ground crew?

With the runway in sight, the way the Australian squadron leader had met his death at Brighton loomed as Miller's main fear. If that second engine failed he would die. He made up his mind to go in once, and once only, whatever the consequences. He could see Reeves, Glendinning and several mates at the practice nets. Miller wished he were with them.

'It's now or never,' he thought as he began his descent. Miller was conscious of forcing the tail down quickly in a changing wind. But it wouldn't oblige. He was at the point of no return. 'Button up!' he yelled. 'I'm down,' he thought, 'and I'm staying down!' As the wheels touched, he still had flying speed.

'We could see on the approach that he had plenty of height,' Glendinning said. 'Having taken up half the runway, the aircraft was still "ballooning" [kangaroo-hopping] when he tried to land her . . .'

The tail was elevated and the nose down. He was forced to bellyland. The Mosquito careered off the end of the runway. Its starboard wing hit a gun emplacement and sheered off. It bumped across a road. The plane's port wing was ripped off when it hit a fence post and gutter. The fuselage entered a paddock and slithered to a halt, its back broken. Within seconds thousands of litres of high-octane fuel had spilt around the Mosquito.

'I stood frozen to the spot,' Glendinning said, 'where I watched the whole performance.'

Reeves stopped delivering his offies. He and the others abandoned their net and rushed towards the plane. Fire trucks and an ambulance hurried to the scene. Miller and the mechanic climbed out gingerly. Both were still in one piece with no apparent or obvious injuries. As the cricketers reached them, Miller quipped: 'Nearly stumps drawn that time, gents.'

The plane was a write-off. Miller cracked hardy. He went to his hut. Glendinning entered it. 'What time does the soccer match start, Unky?' Miller asked. He played in the game soon afterwards, even though in the back of his mind he knew he should have seen a doctor, especially after so many experiences of delayed shock following other incidents. The trauma, far worse than on any other occasion, hit him during the match. He collapsed and had to be carried to a medical officer.

The crash had other ramifications. Reeves was under instructions to maintain discipline at the base in the months after the end of the war in Europe. His fondness for Miller made the situation difficult for the wing commander. Yet he couldn't be seen to be playing favourites, which led him to consider putting Miller on a charge for his reporting those four aircraft inoperable when they were not. The severity of his misdemeanours and the fact that he had crashed a brand-new plane meant that a court martial was possible.

Miller had a night's rest after his delayed shock, but on 30 June he was on a train to London for a one-day match for the RAAF against the South of England at Lord's. Just 48 hours after his ordeal in the Mosquito he was performing with ball and bat. He had only a few undemanding overs (0 for 7) after Ellis had done most of the damage capturing half the wickets to fall (4 for 52) by normal bowler-accredited means. In his short stint with the ball, Miller demonstrated his agility by soccering the ball 15 metres to miss a run out by centimetres. The journalists covering the game were aware of his lucky escape at Great Massingham. On seeing his deft footwork, one senior reporter remarked, 'I'll bet he is a wonderful dancer, too.' Jean Slater, who had been to a few base dances with Miller, would have disagreed. But it was the thought that counted.

Edrich was run out for 43. The former England skipper Gubby Allen was out in a contentious, unusual manner. He played a dead bat to a ball from Mick Roper. The ball rolled back and came to rest at the base of the stumps, knocking them and causing a bail to jump out of its groove. It came to rest on the top of the stumps. Allen picked the ball up and tossed it back to the bowler. Roper saw that the ball had broken the wicket. He appealed, for bowled. The umpire, Archie Fowler, had no choice but to give Allen out, not bowled but *handled the ball*. It was the first such decision at Lord's since 1857.

Allen stormed off, muttering about Australian sportsmanship, which had a fine irony given that he was Australian by birth. The Lord's crowd booed. RAAF captain Keith Carmody told Miller to call Allen back. Miller hastened after Allen, and informed him he could return to the wicket. 'I will not!' Allen fumed.

South of England managed 208 in 250 minutes. Miller, who seemed to have recovered from his shocking crash, drove the ball fiercely in, compiling a beautiful cameo of 78 not out in 95 minutes. It should have ensured an easy win for the RAAF but for the rain, which cut the innings short at 3 for 184.

Miller's courage in coming down to Lord's to play a game of cricket and in performing so admirably so soon after such an incident was sure to become part of the folklore already building around him. He was fit to play at Lord's in the Third Victory Test, which began on 14 July. The series had captured the nation's imagination, and Miller was the star of the season. He had impressed and thrilled crowds for three summers in England. Now his stage was national and he was very much the pin-up boy of the media and spectators. Miller's skills, athleticism and sporting demeanour appealed to just about everyone. His all-round strokeplay, especially his front-foot driving on the off, had the connoisseurs salivating and making flattering comparisons with Victor Trumper. He oozed more sex appeal for women than any film star, which is not surprising. Miller was real. Women could go to a cricket ground and see this tall, broad-shouldered, lean and handsome showman perform in the flesh. Then there was the mop of hair. It was unfashionably long on top, and he rarely wore a cap in the field. Along with sending him letters, notes and chewing gum, women were enamoured of his mannerisms in attempting to keep order with his locks. They were unaware of the concealed comb. He was sent hair clips, which were meant to mock him. Yet the knockers were outnumbered by thousands as he entered the fantasy or heart of many an English fan.

Lord's was now his favourite ground. He had played there as many times as he had the MCG and was familiar with it and with the Lord's regulars, members and staff. They too were impressed by him. Lord's had been starved of good cricket. The flamboyant Miller was feeding them on brilliance and creating more than a sense of hope now for the future.

Australia made one change for the Test. RAAF match-winner Bob Cristofani replaced injured spinner Price. England's veterans came under criticism, and the selectors swung the axe, dropping Errol Holmes and Robertson. Pope, further in the tradition of Barnes, withdrew to play a professional Lancashire League match. One way or another, the selectors decided on infusing the team with a deal of class. In came Donald Bryce Carr (aged 18), the captain of a leading public school, Repton; the Honourable Luke Robert White, the 5th Baron Annaly (17), in his first year at Cambridge University; and John Gordon Dewes (18), a Portsmouth naval cadet. The selectors thought that this was the time to blood promising youngsters. The thought had merit, given the likely resumption of official Tests in 1946.

Bob Crisp in the *Daily Express* on the morning of the match maintained his campaign to have Miller opening the bowling. He had a different view of England's injection of well-bred teenagers. What better time to give Miller the new ball, Crisp suggested, 'than against this cavalcade of youth'?

Hammond won the toss and batted despite a rainstorm, which held up the start on a Saturday for 40 minutes. The weather did not stop spectators pouring in and packing the stands. Hutton opened the batting with Washbrook. Hassett ignored the newspaperman's crisp advice and let Williams and Albert Cheetham have the new ball. Williams had Washbrook caught behind for 8, but Hutton was his usual immovable self. When bowling changes were due, the Australian skipper once more demonstrated that he thought Miller's form at Bramall Lane was a fluke by choosing the spinners Ellis, Pepper and Cristofani before him. Miller was thrown the ball as the sixth option. England was 2 for 100. Hutton was set. New left-hander Dewes was looking the part.

Miller paced out a 12-step run-up. It wasn't the 15 recommended by Crisp, but the fact that it was longer and marked with a swipe of his boot indicated that he had accepted the gratuitous advice. He tore in faster than ever before. The Long Room members, near-fossils and younger observers alike, held their breath. Miller made the ball zip and rear off a good length. He was relying on speed, causing Dewes, who said he had never faced anything like it, and Hutton, who was too experienced to comment, to play, miss and edge. Miller hit Dewes before cartwheeling his off stump for 27. England was 3 for 107.

After tea, a refreshed Miller sprinted in again. He uprooted young Carr's middle stump for 4, and then Hutton's prized middle and off stumps for 104. Miller was nearly unplayable and accurate enough to bowl all his three victims. The buzz at Bramall Lane, which brought back unpleasant memories of Larwood for Yorkshire supporters, was transmitted to cricket headquarters. Yet the observers here mumbled 'Larwood' more in awe than anger. Miller, the batsman who was being compared to the great Wally Hammond, could also bowl like the man who was responsible for England's last Ashes victory, now in the dimming past of 1932–33.

Miller ended with 3 for 44 off 18 overs, a dent in England's youth policy and a few concerns for Hutton, despite his typical century made in 209 minutes. The shrewd old pro was not about to praise Miller, knowing that he was likely to face him in the future. Yet he had never experienced express and unpredictable bowling like this, not even from Ernie McCormick.

England made 254, and Australia responded with just 194, which it would have been lucky to reach but for Hassett's best innings (68) of the season. Pollard overshadowed Miller's efforts with 6 for 75 and bowled him cheaply (for 7 with one that kept low) for the second innings in succession.

The question now was whether Hassett would open the bowling with Miller in the second innings. Williams and Cheetham had toiled hard but for a return of 1 for 92 between them during the first innings. Crisp once more pushed for Miller to open. This time Hassett obliged, and with little to lose. England was without Hammond, who had a severe attack of lumbago, which not even a valiant effort by Australia's physiotherapist, Larry Maddison, could remedy. Washbrook, with an injured thumb, wisely dropped himself down the list. This left England's new chum Dewes more vulnerable to speed. He coped with Williams well enough. But Miller with a new ball was something else. Now the speedster could employ swing with pace.

A blur of a late-outswinger knocked back Dewes' middle stump for 0. Hutton scraped through Miller's opening burst with courage, luck and skill, in about equal measure. The bowler came back in a second spell to bowl the in-form and gritty Edrich (58), then later had delight in flattening Pollard's stumps for 9. England was reduced to just 164 (with Cristofani taking 5 for 49, giving him 9 for 92 for the match). Miller returned 3 for 42 off 16 overs, giving him 6 for 86 for the game. All his victims were clean-bowled, which was testimony to his accuracy and pace. Crisp in the press box could be forgiven for saying 'I told you so'.

Miller was suddenly a paceman to be reckoned with. There were consequences for the effort. His back was in spasm and pain during England's second innings. Miller was in no doubt that it was caused by the injury sustained in his foolhardy wrestling match in late 1943. Yet it would take more than this to stop him batting. Australia was set 225 to win in 300 minutes. Miller came to the wicket with the Australians at 3 for 104 after three hours of stubborn batting. He had two hours to secure victory, and batted accordingly with a crafted innings (71 not out) of controlled drives, giving Australia victory by four wickets. Miller had provided the best performance with bat and ball in a single match of his cricket career. By 16 July 1945 at Lord's, an all-rounder of enormous skill and capacity had been born.

His extended purple patch with the bat continued in a two-day services match, beginning on 23 July, this time against Yorkshire back at Sheffield on a greentop where he plundered 111, including 3 sixes when none of his team-mates passed 30. His strokes off the front foot had all the power and majesty of earlier innings. But he demonstrated he was on his way to mastering all conditions by his superb placement and power off the back foot. His season-long tussle with Hutton continued. The Yorkshireman also scored the Nelson, 111, in a drawn game. A day later, Miller fronted for the RAAF in a one-dayer at Sunderland against Durham in front of 10,000 fans, where he performed another exciting cameo – 75 (7 fours) in 83 minutes – in a comfortable win for the airmen.

This kind of dashing batting, with inherent risks, could not go on in the crowded program of games for both the services and the RAAF, and he hit a down patch in several matches before the Fourth Test beginning on 5 August, which was again at Lord's. Australia was weakened by the loss of Cheetham, who had gone back to Australia, and Carmody, who was rested. Stanford returned and was joined by Jack Pettiford, a leg-spinning all-rounder.

Miller had put paid to England's youth policy. The three youngsters were dropped and replaced with a more traditional, mature look of Pope (aged 34) and Robertson (28), and a seemingly retrograde step of adding to the list Surrey left-hander Laurie Fishlock, who was 38.

Australia led 2–1. England needed to win or draw to keep the series alive. Hassett won the toss and batted, and the Australian plan was apparent early. One player would hold up an end, and his partners would keep the scoreboard moving. The designated 'stayers' were opener Workman and Sismey, batting at three. The latter did the job when Workman was out for 6 at 15. Sismey saw Whitington (46) and Hassett (20) go before Miller got up from his seat on the Pavilion balcony with the score at 3 for 108. He emerged from the dressing room through the Long Room along the silent rubber mat and down the pavilion steps to strong applause from the August Bank Holiday crowd of 34,000. The buzz of 'Miller's in' had become synonymous with brilliance, class and a fast-changing scoreboard.

He had to counter the swing of Pope, who had already seen off Whitington and Hassett. In earlier games, Pope had been a mystery. No one in Australia bowled like him. He caused Miller to push and probe at balls which swung either way or came straight on. By luck and his good eye, Miller squeezed through an early examination and settled down. His cover-driving was a dream. It was used to collect 8 of his 10 fours as he piled on another century. It took him 170 minutes, which, as planned, made up for the slow rate generated by Sismey, who scratched together 59 in 4 hours, injuring his thumb in the retarded process. Pope eventually bowled Miller for 118 in a 200-minute exhibition of grace and power. Pepper rubbed salt into English wounds with a quickfire, six-laden 57. Australia reached 388 in 420 minutes at a respectable rate of 55.43 runs an hour.

But the English press, reverting to a negative, nationalistic style now that the series looked like going Australia's way, criticised the batting approach and run rate. Miller's magnificence received minor status. Sismey's doggedness was attacked instead. *Wisden* didn't like the scoring rate. It accused Australia of playing to avoid defeat, which was harsh given Miller's performance. Whitington, a wordsmith, was driven to write to the *Daily Telegraph* and explain that there had been no Aussie plan to play for a draw. But he shouldn't have bothered. His excuse that his side set out to put England in a position where it had to take risks to win seemed to give credence to the whingeing.

Rain and bad light delayed play until after lunch on day two. Miller opened the bowling. He delivered with fire, pace and accuracy. Although he didn't take a wicket, he was unlucky with two catches being put down by keeper Workman, who was standing in for Sismey. The 30,000-plus crowd was impressed by Miller's application and the confirmation that he was an opening bowler of distinction. None of the top England batsmen were comfortable against him.

Workman's struggle behind the stumps saw extras take on the proportion of a good batting score for England. He let through 51 by the end of the day. Hammond, who was batting, allowed Hassett to use twelfth man Carmody as a keeper the next morning. 'There is only one thing stopping you from using Carmody behind the wicket,' Hammond told Hassett. 'That is my permission, and you have it.' It was an act of sporting generosity rarely seen at the top level of the sport. Commentators dived for the records to find that this had been done just once in England/Australia Tests at the Oval in 1905. Then Australian skipper Joe Darling allowed England's twelfth man Arthur Jones to stand in for injured Arthur 'Dick' Lilley.

Hammond had encouraged and enjoyed the fraternising of the two teams each evening in the shared dressing room and else-where. The change was welcome after the grimly fought Ashes Tests that culminated in the sporting disaster of Bodyline, when ill-feeling between the teams was at its peak. The irony of this largesse was that it prevented Hammond from scoring a century. He was in sparkling form on 83 when he cut a ball from Ellis. Workman, happily replaced as keeper, flew horizontally and held a one-handed 'blinder'. Hammond had been in a strong partnership of 157 with Washbrook (112 in 4 hours).

England went on after tea on the last day to 7 for 468 declared – a lead of 80, which meant it had no serious intention of striving for a win. The folly of not declaring earlier seemed apparent when Australia collapsed in its second innings, losing 4 wickets before it had wiped off the deficit. But Miller held the side together in a textbook example of sensible batting, remaining 35 not out from Australia's 4 for 140 at the close. This gave him 153 runs for once out for the game. His bowling figures of 0 for 49 off 23 overs with five maidens did not reflect his impact with the ball.

The run rates for the two first innings (Australia 1 run for every 2 balls; England, 1 every 1.9) were similar enough to support Australia's argument that the onus was on England to fight harder for a win. The inherent competitive nature of games between the two countries had turned exhibition three-day games into well-fought scraps, albeit in good spirit, that could only be resolved by five-day contests. Australia's tactic of forcing a draw or a desperate response from England had worked. It led 2–1 with one Test to play.

A record attendance for a three-day match at Lord's of 93,000 demonstrated the huge public appeal of the series, which led to a Fifth Test being tacked on at Old Trafford, Manchester.

The Lord's game finished on 8 August, two days after an atomic bomb, carried from the Marianas in a US B-29 plane, was dropped on Hiroshima, Japan, killing 80,000 people and injuring another 70,000. On 9 August a second bomb was dropped on Nagasaki, killing 40,000. By the next day, the Japanese government understood the impact of these horrific new weapons of mass destruction. It began moves to surrender. The Pacific War was over.

Miller's No. 169 Squadron disbanded that day. His days of flying Tiger, Oxford, Blenheim, Beaufighter, Beaufort, Anson and his beloved Mosquito aircraft, were over. He had spent about 550 hours in the air on assignment for the RAF, while officially always with the RAAF. Miller would go home with honours and awards: 1939–45 Star, France and Germany Star, Defence Medal, War medal 1939–45, Australia Service Medal 1939–45 and Returned From Active Service Badge. The last award meant much to Miller. He had survived against very long odds in the air and on the ground, on training drills and in combat. He would not care if he never slipped into another pilot's seat as long as he lived.

Miller was buoyed by the knowledge that his war had ended. He could now enjoy the rest of the 1945 season without any concerns about being shipped to the Pacific for more combat. He was the spectators' favourite of the summer. The fans at Lord's were the most generous to opposition players in the world. But Miller had generated an extra dimension on the basis of his war effort for England in the RAF, his outstanding batting and his glamour. In the electric, immediate post-war era, he had substance and a certain charisma when it meant something beyond the plastic smiles of packaged politicians and film-stars. Miller was being greeted with as much feeling and expectation as any England star. He was feeding off the positive energy generated by and for him. Most of all he was celebrating life. Miller was simply thankful to be out there and entertaining full houses in a way that he had never dared dream of during the war. The much larger theatre of war dwarfed the sports arena. To Miller now, cricket was just a game to be treated as such, and not as a full-scale conflict between nations. He had experienced *real* international combat. He would never again regard sport as serious.

When asked by a reporter before a Victory Test about the pressures on the cricket field, Miller responded: 'I'll tell you what pressure is. Pressure is a Messerschmitt up your arse. Cricket is not.' He could have said that pressure was 'landing a plane carrying a partly dislodged napalm bomb', or 'crash-landing a charred plane on one engine', or 'dodging machine-gun fire when flying low over a well-armed enemy airfield' or any number of other incidents when he had been in an instant life-or-death situation as a wartime pilot. They all amounted to forming an attitude to everything after his wartime experiences. Everything else pretty well was a stroll in the park by comparison. War would be his yardstick for every day for the rest of his life. Memories of what happened in the heat of competition on the pitch would be forgotten, perhaps forever. He hardly remembered details of innings or bowling stints that were outstanding by anyone's standards. But Miller would recall until his last days the far too many mates who died in battle, how they died and where their graves were. And if he didn't know where they were buried he would track them down even if it took years, and visit them, leave flowers and pay his respects to those far less fortunate than him. These memories occasionally made him weep because of that lingering unjustified sense of guilt for being alive. He never again would have much time for reflection unless it had to do with what happened to him and others in service from April 1943 to June 1945.

In that halcyon summer of 1945 his 'Test' and first-class average was an important topic of conversation for mere mortals and cricket fans. It just happened to be superior to that of Hammond and Hutton, the best two batsmen in the world after Bradman.

His bowling, which he had always liked because it kept him in the game, but which he had never taken seriously since his days a decade earlier at Melbourne High, was an unexpected bonus. He even surprised himself. His shoulders and chest had filled out in the war years and he was now tall *and* stronger. He weighed 82 kg without a milligram of fat. Only Cec Pepper could wallop a ball as hard, but he didn't have Miller's eye or skill. If Miller latched on to a ball he felt he could now put it out of any arena except perhaps the MCG, surrounded as it was by steepling grandstands set well back. Yet he was holding back this latent aggression and confidence. There would be a time to unleash and experiment, but not just yet when a series, which England if anything was taking more seriously than the Australians, was at stake.

For the moment, he mixed restraint and responsibility with force and fours, but not sizzle and sixes. Miller was aware that on his record already in this season of 1945, he could well slot into the Australian Test side. He might have lost four full seasons from 1941–42 to 1944–45 at home because of war, but now he sensed an opportunity to cement a Test spot. He had the running, the form and a spot in a competitive, if not quite Test standard, national team that was making headlines back home and in England. Don Bradman and his fellow selectors were taking notice. Miller's attitude was to celebrate his chances, enjoy himself and be carefree without being careless. It was paying off.

He celebrated the end of his career in the RAF in the final Victory Test at Old Trafford beginning 20 August. Hassett again won the toss and batted under fair skies. The crowd of 28,000 was a sell-out. Another 10,000 unlucky cricket fans swarmed around the gates and tried to gain admittance as play began.

After a fair start, a mini collapse saw Miller at the wicket with the score at 4 for 66. New man Eddie Phillipson (who replaced William Roberts) joined Pollard, his opening bowling partner at Lancashire, to give England a decided home ground advantage. There was no Manchester black cloud to assist, yet still they were a formidable combination, especially when backed up by the brilliant Pope, who could swing the ball in any atmosphere. The wicket was soft. The bowlers' boots were cutting it up, which assisted the three professionals, who managed swing and cut, and a swathe of wickets. Yet Miller began his innings with intent, slamming 14 off the first over he faced, from Phillipson. Miller showed that he was a quick learner and becoming a master of all conditions by conquering the three specialist bowlers. He proceeded to dominate the Australian innings as wickets fell steadily, reaching 77 not out (7 fours) in 115 minutes in the team's meagre tally of 173. Square cuts and strong drives were a feature of his batting. Given the state of the wicket and the opposition, this was Miller's finest innings yet. He never seemed to be in trouble, and used his excellent eye and reflexes to counter Pope's prodigious swing late off the back and swiftly off the front foot in a manner few in the history of the game could have matched.

Invigorated by his batting, Miller came on to the field revved up to blast England out. It seemed the only option. He smashed through Fishlock (9), but Hutton (64) and Hammond (57) demonstrated why they too were class acts by defying Miller's tearaway tactics.

England stumbled to 243 (Cristofani 5 for 55), a lead of 70, which on a responsive wicket and with the permanent threat of rain, was strong. Half of day two was lost when Australia limped to 3 for 37 at stumps, drawn 20 minutes early because of rain and bad light. Miller, much to his chagrin the next morning, made just 4, caught behind off a big away-swinger from Phillipson. It was the first time he had failed at a critical moment in an important international.

Australia fell apart and was 8 for 105 when Cristofani, who had starred with the ball, took charge. His method was to stand a stride forward of the crease, forcing the three swingers to bowl short and lose their length. The tactic worked. Cristofani hooked with short-arm jabs, cut off the front and back foot, and reached the pitch of the ball to off-drive. Inspired by previous innings by Miller and Pepper, the young spinner played the shot of the match by hooking Pope for six into the terraces. Cristofani remained 110 not out in Australia's 210.

His gallant effort was not enough. England mopped up the 141 required, losing 4 wickets in the 150 minutes left. This drew the magnificent and evenly fought series, which was watched by 367,000 people. 'This is cricket as it should be,' Hassett wrote after the match. 'These games have shown that international cricket can be played as between real friends – so let's have no more talk of "war" in cricket.'

Miller was undoubtedly 'player of the series'. He topped the batting averages with 443 runs at 63.28, well ahead in aggregate and average of Test batsmen Edrich (331 at 47.28), Washbrook (329 at 47.00), Hammond (369 at 46.12), Hutton (380 at 42.22) and Hassett (277 at 27.70). Hassett summed up Miller's efforts with the bat, saying: 'In our team Miller stands out. He hasn't Hutton's solidity yet, but as a strokeplayer he is second to none in the world today.' Miller's returns with the ball (fourth on the Australian list with 10 wickets at 27.70 each) were more modest, yet they masked his imprint as a real all-rounder.

There were still some big games to play in the seemingly endless summer of 1945. The first, much to Miller's pleasure, was another match at Lord's, between England and a Dominions team. Proceeds would go to King George's Fund for Sailors, the Australian services charities and the New Zealand Sports Fund. Australia, with eight representatives, dominated the Dominions team. Hassett was expected to lead the team, but when he learned that the dynamic 43-year-old West Indian Learie Constantine would make his final first-class appearance, he sportingly withdrew, citing ill-health. This paved the way for the inspiring all-rounder to captain the side, which he accepted as a great honour. The West Indian, a lawyer who had done welfare work among black communities in London during the war, played his last Test at the Oval in 1939. Then Constantine showed his skills, scoring a zestful 79 and taking 5 for 75 – including the wickets of Hammond and Joe Hardstaff Jr – in England's first innings.

On Saturday 25 August, Constantine won the toss and batted. New Zealand's Donnelly dominated with a dashing 133 (2 sixes and 18 fours), while Miller managed a start before the crafty Hollies trapped him lbw with a wrong 'un for 26. The Dominions team reached 307. England responded with 287, with Hammond delivering another immaculate display for the summer with 121 in 160 minutes, but without having to contend with Miller's disturbing pace. He sent down one over before retiring from the crease holding his back. He kept fielding, but in slips where he would not have to run.

After treatment from the physiotherapist Miller was able to bat on the second afternoon of the match. He had something to beat when he arrived at the wicket. Hammond had been his main rival for the season, and so far Miller had matched or bettered his performances on most occasions. The challenge had been laid down. Miller's response was to attack from the first ball but without throwing the bat. He restrained himself from 'having a go' until he was well set. Then he had some sweet revenge against Hollies, belting him for 2 sixes just before stumps. The next morning he brought up his century in 115 minutes, thus improving on Hammond's speed by 20 minutes. Miller swung another 5 sixes in that pre-lunch session, and inspired Constantine (2 sixes) to follow suit. One of them would stay forever in Larry Maddison's mind. 'It was a slog-sweep over the square leg fence,' he said, 'but it was a more graceful sweep than slog.'

In one 35-minute stanza they added 91 runs. Constantine fell to Hollies for a sparkling 40, and soon after Miller was on his way for 185 in a 165-minute display of calibrated mayhem. Each six and lofted four was struck with head down and correct technique. Interspersed with the mighty strikes were shots of perfect execution in defence, drives along the ground and finely honed late cuts. The latter stroke reminded onlookers that he was not always intent on sending balls into orbit.

As he walked up the steps towards the Long Room, he grinned at Glendinning, sitting in front of the pavilion: 'Come in, Unk,' Miller called. Glendinning followed him through the Long Room, where members turned to Miller and applauded, and into the dressing room. On Miller's instruction, Glendinning had put six bottles of Bass beer in a Gladstone bag in the room.

'He had not even taken off his pads,' Glendinning recalled, 'when the door of the players' room opened and in walked a gentleman with a bowler [hat] in hand, followed by four other gents.' It was Plum Warner.

'Congratulations, Keith, on a marvellous innings,' Warner said. 'My word, we are going to hear from you in the future.'

Miller was still high and hot from his performance and not in the mood for visitors, no matter who they were. 'Couldn't knock my girl over,' Miller said, hardly acknowledging Warner. His dismissive remark was about the capacity of the bowlers, whom writer Denzil Batchelor reckoned were 'pretty well the best in England'. Miller seemed more intent on his thirst than praise. 'Give us a Bass, Unk,' he said to Glendinning, who rummaged in the Gladstone bag.

Miller's attitude caused Warner to turn on his heel and leave with his entourage. Next in to congratulate Miller was Gubby Allen, now recovered from the 'handled the ball' incident earlier in the summer. He wrung Miller's hand. 'Well done,' he said, 'but tell me, how do you belt those sixes?'

'Gubby,' Miller replied, 'you just shut your eyes and swing.'

Whatever the method behind those 20 boundaries, the innings brought comment from all the leading English experts. 'From the moment he takes guard he plays each ball just that much below its supposed merits that scratches a bowler's pride,' R. C. Robertson-Glasgow wrote. 'It is dignity with the brakes off.'

Miller's domination of the home of cricket was complete. He

had batted eight times at Lord's this summer, scoring 568 runs
and three centuries and averaging 94.68. The returns were Brad-
manesque but had a most unBradman-like lust for the lofted shot.

After a few drinks in the Lord's dressing-room, Miller and
Glendinning went on to the Boomerang Club, a West End hang-
out frequented by Australian servicemen. When they arrived,
there was an Australian flight lieutenant, with a DFC (Distinguished Flying Cross), sitting at the bar. He greeted them with
a handshake. 'Looks like you've had a big day,' Miller said to
the man.

'Have I what!' the man said. 'Been drinking with Keith Miller
all day.'

'Have you really?' Miller said. 'What's he like?'

'Oh, a great bloke. A really great bloke.'

'Well, have a good night,' Miller said.

'The man to this day would not know he had shaken hands
with Keith Miller,' Glendinning said. 'Keith would not have
given him a serve, mainly because he was a DFC winner.'

Miller's back again curtailed his bowling the next day in the
Lord's Dominions match. In the second innings, he managed just
five overs in two spells and was hit for 28 runs. Hammond had
less to worry about again, and could concentrate on countering
Australia's four spinners. On 102, he fell stumped by Colin
Bremner (in his initial first-class appearance) for the second time
in the match. In the first innings Pepper lured him out of his
crease, and in the second, Cristofani tempted him further.
Hammond's sensational double did not prevent the Dominions
winning by 45 runs. *Wisden* described the game as 'one of the
finest ever seen'.

Media attention paid to Miller for his performances with bat
and ball in the eight weeks after he crashed the Mosquito would
not have hurt his earlier off-field problem of threats of a court
martial. Just after Miller's game for the Dominions at Lord's,
Neville Reeves was heard to say of him at a London dinner: 'He

was one of my finest [pilots]; perhaps the bravest and most willing I had under my command. He wouldn't be alive today but for what we came to call "Miller's Luck". He kept taking the most fantastic risks. And they all came off.' These did not seem like the words of someone about to press on with parading Miller before a military court. If doing so had been ever seriously considered, the idea would now most certainly be dropped. In this instance, Miller's timing was more helpful than his luck.

Three days after his triumph at Lord's, Miller travelled to Nottingham and hammered 81 not out in a win for the AIF against a strong Nottinghamshire on a dewy pitch. He was the only batsman to handle Harold Larwood's Bodyline partner, 36-year-old left-arm paceman Bill Voce, who had everyone else in trouble while taking 11 for 113 for the match. Once more Miller didn't get a bowl in a game dominated by spinners Cristofani and Pepper, who had been supreme all summer, and who together took thirteen wickets.

Miller's form was a continuation of his performance at Lord's. He and his slashing blade rolled on to the final 1945 summer match of significance for him, beginning 5 September. It was played at the Scarborough Festival between the Australian services team and H. D. G. Leveson-Gower's XI. In the tradition of these festival matches to end the season, England selected a Test side, in the hope of sending off the old enemy with a loss. In effect, it was the seventh major contest of 1945 between an England XI and an essentially Australian XI, made up of services personnel.

The AIF clobbered 506. Pepper, in his finest ever batting performance, smashed 168 (6 sixes and 18 fours), which for sheer power came close to Miller's 185 a week earlier at Lord's. One of Pepper's smashes cleared the ground above the sightscreen and sailed on over a row of high-gabled houses. Miller himself, although overshadowed in front of the overflowing marquees, produced a clean-hit, speedy 71 in just over an hour, slamming 3 sixes and 5 fours. No matter what England's intent in this game,

Pepper and Miller turned it festive, with balls intermittently bouncing into the surrounding streets or thudding onto the marquees.

The England squad intended to match this electric hitting but could only muster 258 (L. B. Fishlock 95) and 140. Miller opened the bowling and was spirited and accurate without taking a wicket. It was the spinners Ellis and Pepper who did the damage again. Pepper's all-round performance prompted Miller, with typical generosity, to regard him after the 1945 summer in England as the best all-rounder in the world. His own efforts ranked him high too, and placed him as the best performer with the bat for the season. In games given official first-class status by the MCC, Miller scored 725 at 72.5 from 13 innings with 3 not outs. This placed him second only to Hutton in the aggregates (782 from 16 matches) and second in the averages to Donnelly (348 in 4 innings at 87).

His domination of the season established him, at 25, as an international cricketer of the highest order. An English journalist called him the 'Golden Boy' of the summer. The description was mangled by Australian observers, not content with such an effete, immodest epithet. They referred to the 'Golden Nugget'. By season's end Miller's new enhanced image had earned him the truncated nickname 'Nugget'. 'Dusty' Miller, that feisty, relative nonentity of the war years, hidden from public view, had disappeared. He had matured. His success had salved some of his more aggressive tendencies, especially towards authority. In England, authority or the Establishment had embraced him and softened his often 'chippy' outlook. The replacement nickname was still rustic but more mature and solid. Friends, cricketers and journalists would know Keith Miller as 'Nugget' from then on, except for mates from the war, like Glendinning, Brown and Berriman. They would forever refer to him as 'Dusty', remembering that at times tightly coiled character and loyal friend.

Miller and the rest of the AIF squad would have loved to travel directly back to Australia for demobilisation. But its matches had generated excellent money for charities in tough times, which prompted the Australian Labor Government's foreign affairs minister Dr Evatt to direct that the team return via India and Ceylon and play matches in aid of the Red Cross and local hospitals. Cricket was once more the vehicle for helping to re-establish the status quo of a now-shaky British Empire. Under these terms, Miller had little choice but to accept the offer to tour the long way home.

He said goodbye to many friends made in England after his nearly 30 months of RAF service and three seasons of playing cricket in all conditions, in front of packed houses, purely for the joy of it. Some, like Glendinning, would be lifelong mates he would see again in Australia, even if they lived on the other side of the vast continent. Others in the UK were promised a return. Miller said he would be back. He was thinking seriously about taking up an offer to play professionally in England. If that didn't happen, he might return as an Australian Test player.

Miller's love for England and the English was cemented forever. He had changed in the three years, and had learned from the best the country could offer. Miller had experienced the nation's collective courage and traditions. He had revelled in its culture from the Albert Hall to Lord's; its music, poetry, humour, history, grandeur; its glamorous events like Ascot; its own brand of 'mateship' and its women. For a brief period, he had been at or near the centre of the victorious nation's public attention. Miller loved it all, and took it in his stride. He wanted more.

INDIAN SUMMER

'Where's Nugget?' Lindsay Hassett enquired, as the time for the train to leave London for Liverpool approached. None of the other 13 players and four managers knew. It would become the most common refrain for the next six weeks. Miller was late more often than not. If he wasn't saying a lingering goodbye to a woman, he might be sleeping off a heavy night. Without a reliable room-mate such as Glendinning or Roper, there was a fair chance he would miss an appointment.

Miller just clambered aboard the train as it began to move off. He carried a suitcase and no 'coffin' for his cricket gear. He had borrowed bats, gloves, box and pads from Hove to Edinburgh. The only hint that he was a sportsman was a worn pair of old, white boots. Miller liked to travel light. This way he didn't forget things on the trip aboard His Majesty's Troop Ship *Stirling Castle* from Liverpool to the first stop at the Suez Canal. If he was lacking equipment for the matches later in India and Ceylon, there was always a mate like Pepper, who would lend him anything, and Whitington, who carried a full kit with several bats.

En route to Suez, Miller rested his weary body after about 40 matches, major and minor, for the 1945 season. The ship, with thousands of services personnel on board, was hardly a luxury liner. Yet he took time to catch up on some reading. Glendinning, travelling with Miller to Suez, took a photo of him lying on the deck reading an expurgated version of D. H. Lawrence's *Lady Chatterley's Lover*. This book, Lawrence's last novel, was controversial for the depiction of a sexual relationship between the lady of a grand English estate and its fit young gardener. 'I'm sure Dusty related to Mellors [the gardener],' Glendinning said.

At Suez, Glendinning went on to his home in Perth while Miller and the cricket squad travelled to Bombay. Despite his tardiness, he, more than many on the tour, was conscious that this was the first official Australian group to visit India. Miller was vice-captain of the squad, and was prepared to live up to that responsibility, at least on the field and at official functions. Hassett set the tone well by informing Bombay journalists when he arrived that the Australian servicemen had come to play cricket, 'not win trophies'. They would play to win, but winning was not everything. They wished to enjoy the visit. They would have fun. So far, Miller would have thought, it was his kind of tour.

Their host in Bombay was the England-educated Test batsman Kumar Shri Duleepsinhji, known as 'Duleep'. He and Miller struck up an immediate friendship. He showed them the sights, although not the brothels of Fort Road, where Miller, Roper and Whitington ended up by mistake. A day later they took the rough Frontier Mail train on the 2,000-kilometre, 44-hour journey to Lahore, in North-West Frontier Province, leaving the depressing slums of Bombay and entering stunning countryside featuring green hills and deep river valleys. This scenery was interspersed with village squalor, made fascinating to Miller by the hordes of boys playing hockey. The train meandered on, late because of extended stops at crowded stations, towards Peshawar and the Khyber Pass.

When the squad arrived in Lahore, they had little time to rest before being guests of honour at the local Gymkhana Club. The next day, 28 October, the Australians were playing North Zone, in a match attended by 30,000 spectators. Conditions were bizarre. Vultures circled above as if waiting for one of the visitors to fall in front of the English-style red-gabled pavilion. A Sikh military band played Scottish medleys. 'Auld Lang Syne' was a favourite. So were 'We'll Meet Again' and 'Lilli Marlene', which amused the Australians and gave them a strange sense of nostalgia, enhanced by their war experiences and their being so far from home.

The local team batted, and was still there on day two thanks to some more than doubtful umpiring decisions. The most outrageous was a thick edge to second slip by keeper/batsman Imtiaz Ahmed off Cristofani with the score at 4 for 186. It was an obvious catch, but the batsman stood his ground. The Australians appealed belatedly. The umpire said, 'Not out.'

Miller was not impressed. He had a clear attitude to walking. If you felt you were out, you walked. If there was doubt in your mind over a catch, you asked the fielder if he had caught it. If he nodded, you were off. If there were any further doubts, you left the decision to the umpire. That system of goodwill and trust between competitors evaporated if a player cheated or an umpire let him. Ahmed's attitude disappointed Miller. It soured the start of the tour, at least for on-field events. Cristofani was from the same sporting college as Miller. The spinner marched off the ground in disgust at the end of the over. He had two of the four wickets to fall. He wanted to return to the field in the evening when a light dew would have made the pitch conditions a little more to his liking. Hassett refused him.

The next morning, pacemen Miller and Roper were ill. Miller's condition was not improved by a swarm of wasps that took a liking to him. 'They're probably female,' Hassett commented. Cristofani was back in favour, and the wickets. It was left to him and Pepper to tackle the batsmen, umpires, heat and flies and to make sure that the vultures kept wheeling high. North Zone scored 451. Australia's reply was 100 short in a drawn game. Miller batted with some discomfort, down an order decided by the need for runs to the toilet, rather than just runs. He made 46. But Pepper once more was the star. He took 5 for 45 in the second innings, and top-scored for the tourists with 77.

The team took the train to India's capital, New Delhi, Miller suffering all the way with 'Delhi Belly' and an enthusiastic driver, who insisted on sounding his whistle every few minutes to avoid killing sacred cows that might have wandered on to the track. Vic Richardson, the former Australian captain, who was an RAAF welfare officer in India, hosted them this time.

The New Delhi match was against a strong Prince's XI, led by the young 199 cm Maharaja of Patiala. His potency, in more than one sense, was noted by the tourists in a story about his portly father, who played and adored the game. The old man, who died in 1938, had allegedly sired nearly 200 offspring. When hearing this, Hassett remarked dryly: 'If he reached 200, would he receive a new ball?'

Miller was not well enough to play, but took the field. The Maharaja won the toss and batted under a scorching sun. The upright Vijay Singh, hard-hitting Lala Amarnath and gifted Mushtaq Ali all carved out centuries on the first day. Miller was in no state to bowl. When the tourists batted he was out for a duck. Luckily for them, Hassett was fit and in touch, scoring 187 and 124 not out, which was enough to allow Australia to compete well in another drawn match.

The tourists were honoured by the appearance of the light-blue-turbaned prince fielding at point, while one of his 93 brothers, Rai Singh, wearing a pink turban, acted as his personal backstop.

Miller did recover enough for a Bombay game against West Zone a week after his illness began. Hassett took a well-earned break, and Miller captained the servicemen for the first time. He was determined to lead from the front and top-scored for the Australians with 106 in 3 hours in a third successive draw. This effort was testimony to his constitution as much as to his batting skills. The game allowed the beanpole Rudi Sheriyar ('Rusi') Modi to display his patience and sound defence in collecting a slow 168 in the West Zone's score of 9 for 500. This stick figure signalled a major problem for the Australians if they could not remove him early.

Modi was not the only batting obstacle for the tourists in the international games, or unofficial Tests known as 'Representative Matches'. They would be confronting a line-up of fine Indian batsmen. There was also the dynamic duo encountered at New Delhi: Amarnath and Mushtaq; there was Vijay Merchant, Vijay Hazare, and M. H. Mankad, not to forget the two centurions at Lahore, Abdul Hafeez Kardar and Imtiaz Ahmed.

Hassett delayed that problem by winning the toss at Bombay on 10 November in the first Representative match, and batting and batting . . . Carmody (113), Pettiford (124) and Pepper (95) did enough to engender Miller's (lbw to Nayudu for 1) disinterest in Australia's heavy score of 531 in a four-day match. India's response was 339 and, when forced to follow on, 304. Miller toiled hard in conditions not conducive to pacemen, taking two prize wickets: Modi in the first innings and Kardar in the second. The tough-minded Indian skipper Merchant was never going to make a generous declaration, whether or not Hassett had declared earlier in Australia's first innings.

Australia was given half an hour to make 103. Hassett opened with Miller, and placed Pepper at three, in a desire to get the runs. Merchant further showed his colours by putting five men on the boundary from third man to mid-off. All nine fielders apart from the bowler and the keeper were placed on the off. This extreme setting meant the bowlers had to put the ball well outside the off. They obliged by aiming at a spot more than half a metre wide of the wicket. Miller made his thoughts known to Merchant. Hassett began bravely, taking 11 off the first over, but he dragged a ball on to his stumps in the second over.

Pepper came in. He exposed Merchant's folly by taking block a metre outside off stump and asking for 'middle to off'. The umpire was dumbfounded at the geometrically impossible directive to line up the middle stump at the umpire's end with Pepper's off stump. But Pepper insisted on going on with the farce, even though the umpire could not assist him. He took some time scratching his mark, looking at Merchant as he did it. At the end of the over, Miller strolled up the wicket. 'No use going for it, Cec,' he told Pepper. 'Let's shut up shop.' Australia crawled to 1 for 31. The game ended in a miserable draw.

An incensed Duleep was in the members' section of the Cricket Club of India. He yelled at Merchant loud enough for many members and all the cricketers to hear: 'Merchant, you have brought eternal shame upon the name of Indian cricket!' There was no need to say why. The field placements were not in the spirit of the game. The approach angered Miller, especially after the spirit in which the Victory Tests had been played. The worst moment in that series was Hammond's placement of a ring of players on the boundary in the First Test at Lord's. But Hammond did not employ extreme or absurd off-side theory when Australia had an even money chance and won. The England captain had been generous and led the way in attacking play. By contrast, Merchant upset the start of the series.

None of the Australian squad had played in the Bodyline series in 1932–33, but they all recalled the bad spirit engendered between Australia and England. A year after the Bodyline series finished Miller was at Melbourne High. The school was sensitive to Bodyline's impact because of Woodfull. Miller attended the Melbourne Test of that series. He was very aware of the negative atmosphere caused by the England skipper Douglas Jardine, who intermittently stacked the leg side, especially close to the wicket, and had his bowlers direct their deliveries on the leg stump rising up into the rib cage. Then only the genius of Bradman had managed to challenge the tactic by changing his batting technique. But even he was reduced to the standards of the next rank of the world's best batsmen, having his average halved to 57. Merchant's attitude made Jardine pale by comparison. Not even Bradman would attempt to counter such bowling and field placements. The Indian skipper had stretched the rules to an unacceptable point.

All but three of the Australians had a form of dysentery on the trip. They were all fed up with train travel, especially as the majority of the squad, including the senior manager, Keith Johnson, was made up of RAAF men. A disgruntled Mick Roper attempted a mid-tour coup. He suggested to Johnson and Hassett that they all travel by air. When his suggestion was ignored, he organised a meeting of the airmen at the team hotel at Poona during a game against Combined Universities. Roper was upset. The students had taken to his bowling in amassing 4 for 600, in what was certain to be the fifth successive draw of the tour. He felt that all the Australian bowlers were not as fit as they could be if they travelled by air. If they wanted to do their best and win the series, he claimed, planes had to be the best option. He put to the meeting that if the management did not agree to travel the rest of the tour by plane, then it should be abandoned. Alternatively, Hassett should be dumped in favour of Carmody or Miller as skipper. Both of them were airmen. They agreed with Roper that planes were a better proposition on such an arduous tour.

If Hassett were dumped it was thought that Johnson would agree to move about the vast subcontinent by air. Johnson was in a difficult position. He was suffering with the rest of the squad. He could see that the team was struggling. Air travel would be a better proposition. But as the person representing the Australian Board of Control, he did not wish to dispose of the skipper.

The squad split roughly between the airmen and big drinkers on one side, and the AIF men and the more moderate drinkers and non-imbibers on the other. At one point, Miller, the most popular character on tour for both his personality and his on-field leadership, looked likely to replace Hassett as captain. If this had eventuated, it would have had repercussions for the coming 1945–46 Test tour of New Zealand. Bradman, known to be recovering slowly from severe fibrositis, was not expected to play

Test cricket, or any other form of the game, again. Should Miller take over, and perform well on this tour and in Australia, when the services squad was expected to play games against the states, he could well lead the Test squad to New Zealand.

Miller himself remained out of the feud. He preferred the plane alternative, but would not lead the rebels. In the end Squadron Leader Stan Sismey broke the impasse by arranging for the Australian air force based in India to provide a plane for the cricketers. It would take them from Bombay to the next stop, Calcutta, for three games, then Madras for two and finally on to Colombo, Ceylon, for one match. The coup was averted. Hassett remained skipper. He, not Miller, was most likely to captain Australia in the post-war, post-Bradman era.

All ten airmen, except Miller, began to regret the choice of plane travel on a precarious trip on a bulky RAAF freighter plane to Calcutta. On 23 November they encountered electrical storms that made flying dangerous, especially over mountains. The airmen knew the frail nature of planes during the war. Their knowledge made them fine pilots but fretting passengers. Only Miller stayed calm as the aircraft rocked and pitched, and more than once dropped altitude alarmingly. While the others held on to the sides of their seats with white knuckles, he seemed to enjoy the bucking bronco, and was the only one not to poke his head into the cabin to observe the overworked pilot and troubled navigator.

Miller's cool display was based on a philosophical outlook. He reckoned always that his 'luck' would mean nothing would happen to him. If it did, well, that was explicable, too. He knew he should not have survived the war. No one he knew had made it through so many death-defying moments. If his time was up now, it was up. No use worrying about it. Best to sit back and enjoy a beer.

They touched down in Calcutta low on petrol and two hours late. There was barely time to put their bags down at the hotel before they were whisked off to a civic reception in their honour given by the Governor of Bengal, Australian R. G. 'Dick' Casey, followed by dinner at Government House. Miller was seated next to Mrs Casey and His Highness the Maharaja of Cooch Behar, who was captain of the Bengal cricket team. The Maharaja loved his cricket and his horseracing. He gave Miller a tip for a coming Calcutta meeting.

The hot topic over dinner was India's situation in the last throes of British rule. Protests for Indian independence were leading to riots in the city. The services team management and some players were concerned they would be targeted. Casey urged the players to go on with their game against East Zone beginning the next morning at Eden Gardens. They would be given a military escort to and from the ground and at the arena itself. Miller was again nonchalant about events even when riots in Calcutta on the first day of the game on 21 November led to 23 deaths. It was not the best playing condition, but he admired the impressive, courageous Casey, who addressed the anti-British rioters in an attempt to calm them. He suggested two minutes silence be observed by both teams before play began on the second day. It did not prevent thousands of protesters invading the pitch. Play was interrupted for an hour as the military cleared the arena. The game went on. It was a tight, hard-fought contest.

That night Hassett and Miller ventured out of their hotel for a walk. They turned a corner and were caught up in another riot. They ducked into a cinema to avoid the violence coming their way. The film showing was *Lost Weekend*, starring American Ray Milland as a drunk. It depressed both men, who could relate at least to Milland's hangovers. Half-way through the film, Hassett got up to leave. 'Let's get out of here,' he said, 'I'd rather face the riot.'

By the third and final day, the match was on a knife-edge. Denis Compton, who had reacquainted himself with his good mate Miller, was on army service in India and playing for East Zone. He had reached 88 not out in a typically dashing display. East Zone was 8 for 268 and needed 13 runs for victory.

Demonstrations had been going on in the streets outside Eden Gardens. Protesters began lighting fires in the stands. The military moved in, but showed restraint. Rioters broke the military cordon and invaded the pitch for the second time, marching in two long lines. The Indian leader of the demonstrators literally knew the score and how close East Zone was to victory. Or perhaps he feared a loss. He approached Compton. 'You play a very good innings for us, Mr Compton,' he said, 'and you very good player. But you must stop.' Compton argued with him. 'Five of our friends have been shot by the British police . . .' the leader added emphatically and repeated: 'You very good player, but you must stop!'

'You'd better speak to Mr Hassett,' Compton said, pointing his bat at the Australian skipper. 'He is a captain. He is in charge on the field.'

Hassett was talking to the Australians' masseur, Larry Maddison, who had come on to the field to add his muscular support. Maddison was a tough character partial to displaying his amateur wrestling skills. Big Cec Pepper had experienced them in one altercation in the dressing room. 'What are you doing?' Hassett asked.

'Just thought I'd lend a hand,' Maddison replied.

Hassett motioned him off the field just as the protest leader approached followed by other rioters. Miller, Pepper and Roper, the three biggest members of the team, closed ranks behind their skipper, with the same intention as Maddison. This was not a team to cut and run. When the leader stopped in front of him, Hassett smiled and asked: 'You wouldn't happen to have a cigarette, would you, old boy?'

His pleasant, calm attitude disarmed the rioters. They fumbled in their pockets in search of a smoke. It was in their interests to close off the game without causing more violence and death. Moments later, Panjak Gupta, secretary of the Indian Cricket Board of Control, arrived on the scene and began negotiating for the game to continue. The players waited while the

Indians debated. Meanwhile, the police managed to lead the bulk of the protesters off the arena. After an hour, the game resumed.

Compton farmed the strike until the scores were level. He was on 97. He attempted to cover-drive Cristofani, but managed a snick for four between keeper Sismey and Pepper at slip. It gave Compton his century and East Zone victory. The ball was swallowed by more invaders, this time fans celebrating an Indian win. Hassett's nerve, Compton's skill and an Indian win had allowed the game to finish without further rioting. Miller shook hands with Compton as he approached the players' gate, flanked by police. 'You very good batsman, Mr Compton,' Miller said in a mock Indian accent, 'but you must stop.' From then on it would be a catchphrase whenever these two greeted each other.

***

Compton and Miller went to a race meeting in Calcutta during the two-day break before the Second Representative Match. Both loved to gamble and bet heavily on the horse tipped to Miller by the Maharaja of Cooch Behar. When asked by Hassett on the morning of the Representative game how the horse had gone, Miller replied: 'It's still running.'

The loss didn't affect his cricket. He strained his back, but was able to bat and put in his best performance of the series. Miller came to the wicket with the score at 2 for 250 in response to India's 386. He joined opener Whitington, who noticed that his new partner was twirling one of his new bats. Whitington complained, suggesting that Miller get his own blade.

'There won't be a mark on it,' Miller said, 'you'll see.'

He was in an aggressive mood. He hoicked the left-handed Vinoo Mankad for 4 straight sixes over a temporary marquee. They sailed out of the ground and into a water-lily pond. At the end of the over, Whitington said, 'I thought you said you'd be careful with my bat?'

'I am! Take a look. Every one came out of the middle.'

Whitington inspected his bat. It was a smudge of bullseyes right in the bat's sweet spot.

Miller collected a bludgeoning 82 before Mankad had him caught and a little revenge. But Miller's back was aggravated, and he couldn't bowl more than seven overs in India's second innings.

Once more the Australians were annoyed by the antics of the smallish, talented Merchant, this time in apparent collusion with the umpires. There was no doubting his wonderful footwork and strokeplay. But they estimated that he was lbw at least five times and caught behind four or even five times. This added up to a possible nine dismissals as he flaunted his way towards a century of sorts. His nine lives earned him the sobriquet for the match of 'Cat'.

Not just lusty maharajas, it seemed, but other wealthy members of the elite such as Merchant were favoured with decisions. He moved imperviously to 99 not out. Then came the biggest insult to the opposition and the game's principles. Mick Roper was bowling and making sure his front foot was planted more than a boot's length behind the bowling crease to avoid a pot-hole. The umpire no-balled him when there was no question that it was a legitimate delivery. Merchant's back-foot movement into position to hook for four seemed premeditated. Had there been collusion between umpire and batsman to ensure his century? It seemed so to the Australians. But perhaps they were just weary and dispirited by the unsporting play.

Merchant secured his nine or ten innings century and went on to 155 not out. He declared at 4 for 355. Miller, Roper and the other bowlers were disgusted. The only way to avoid such cheating was to run Merchant out, but it seemed that he would have to be stranded and clearly metres out – as he was in the first innings for 12 – before an umpire would raise a finger in anger against him.

The game dawdled towards another depressing draw on Miller's twenty-sixth birthday in the second devalued contest of the series. Nevertheless, he answered skipper Hassett's call for a bowl when many in the squad were ailing in the Australians' next match against East Zone at Madras. Miller put in his best effort with the ball, taking 3 for 19, helping to secure the tourists' only win – by six wickets – in India. He failed with the bat in the final Representative Match at Madras, making just 2 and 7, when a Miller special in just one innings might have swung the game Australia's way. Instead it was the wristy, elegant Modi's 203 (319 minutes, 24 fours) and the dashing Amarnath's 113 that determined the game and series in India's favour. A minor consolation for the team was Pepper's trapping of Merchant lbw with a flipper. It skidded on and trapped him back on his stumps, low down and heading for the middle of middle stump. He made just 11 in the first innings and was again run out by metres for 35 in the second.

Miller rarely failed to deliver something in a game, and he again put in for his team with the ball, sending down 22 overs for 2 for 60 in India's first knock of 525, and 3 overs in its second innings, when it stumbled to 4 for 52 and a six-wicket win.

Miller's batting figures in the international games – 107 runs at 26.25 – were matched by his unflattering bowling numbers: 4 wickets at 40.5. The bowling conditions in India, against a strong list of top-class bats, were more suited to spinners. If Miller was uninjured, there was a pattern through his career of his efforts being commensurate with his enthusiasm for matches. Had India played the series in the spirit that England did, his performances would have lifted. Illness and the strenuous tour didn't help. But the early tone of play made him listless, and caused him to think ahead rather than in the present.

There was some consolation for him and the team in Colombo for the final match against 'All Ceylon'. He smashed 132 in a score of 306 and the Australians won by an innings and 44 runs.

After playing above themselves in the five Victory Tests in England and drawing the series 2-all, it was disappointing for this brave services team to go down 0–1 in India, even though the Australians believed they had been cheated. In the interest of diplomacy, Hassett and his men would not complain, especially as the tour was one of goodwill following the war. But unfairly for them their record would be tarnished at a moment when several of the squad would be expecting to have a chance to step into the Australian Test team. Hassett would continue his Test career. Miller headed the list of those who had yet to play at the highest level. All-rounder Pepper, spinners Ellis, Cristofani and Pettiford, and keeper Sismey made up the list of those most likely to come under consideration.

They still had to make it home. The squad could wait well into the New Year for a ship, which would mean a further trip of a couple of weeks and arriving home sometime in March. Miller had met an Australian pilot in a Colombo bar. He agreed to squeeze the squad aboard a tired old twin-engine York bomber, which had bullet holes on the fuselage and wings after four years active service against the Japanese. It was carrying a spare engine back to Australia. The pilot already had 14 friends scheduled to make the trip. There were no seats. The servicemen had to sit along a ledge for the 5,000-kilometre journey to Perth. Yet the inducement of being home for Christmas was too much for the squad. Members and management agreed to go.

Miller alarmed them by turning up at the airport on the morning of 16 December with six black elephant-hide trunks. Whitington complained that weight would be a big problem on the plane. 'You'll have to leave that lot behind,' he said.

Miller pointed to Whitington's suitcase and 'coffin'. 'Weigh them,' he said. They came to 23 kg. Miller placed his bags on the scales. They came in at 17 kg. They were empty. He had bought them as gifts for friends.

The plane chugged and strained its way skyward. Suddenly the pilot decided to turn back to the airport. 'What's wrong?' Hassett asked the pilot.

'Nothing serious. A little engine trouble.'

'Good thing we have a spare on board.'

After some hours delay they were on their way again over the Indian Ocean and the mountains of Papua and New Guinea. It stopped one night in the Cocos Islands before bumping down to Perth on 17 December.

Miller was wistful for home, family and friends he had not seen for approaching three years. Yet in the back of his mind were thoughts of an uncertain future. He hoped to play Test cricket. But that would not give him a living if he wished to marry his lovely fiancée, who was waiting for news in Boston. The talk among the players through India had been what they would do for employment and the possibility of playing professional cricket in England. Pepper for one was likely to take up an offer if things didn't work out in Australia. Miller had been approached by a Lancashire League club. His long-held dream of playing Test cricket for Australia was tempered by reality. If he did settle down in Australia, he wanted to concentrate on his batting. Miller made this clear on arrival back in Australia. He did not wish to be known as a 'bowler thundering in' all the time. 'If they like to throw the ball to me as a change bowler I'll oblige,' he told reporters in Perth. 'But I don't want to jeopardise my career.' Miller wished to make his name as one of the greatest batsmen of all time. It carried, too, more prestige than being a top bowler. As Arthur Mailey observed, the last bowler to have been knighted was Sir Francis Drake.

PART 3

STAR IN THE TEST ARENA

TURMOIL AND FIRST TEST

Miller had to put his life on hold. There were still six services matches that he had to play against the states in less than five weeks. The order to do so came jointly from the armed services and the Board of Control. Although he was fed up with cricket and needed a break, he had to perform. The games were meant to revive cricket in Australia after the war. They were also the trials for Test selection for one Test against New Zealand in three months time in March 1946 and, more importantly, for the expected full Ashes tour by England in the following 1946–47 season. There were protests from team members and a petition to lessen the burden to just a couple of matches. But the board and the services commanders were adamant. Despite the two long 'tours' of England and India, the players would have to endure a third trek across Australia.

Miller would have to wait two weeks before he would be in Melbourne. In the meantime, he played in Perth against Western Australia and put in the best batting performance with a scintillating 80 in a drawn game. It was the start he needed. After catching up with Glendinning, Miller and the weary services caravan moved on to South Australia for a game over the New Year. It had been agreed before the tour started that Miller would be rested for this game to allow Graham Williams and Bert Cheetham, both stationed in South Australia, to play. Miller happily watched the game from the dressing room.

It was an important event in Australian cricket history. Bradman, now 37 years old, was making a tentative comeback. He had played for South Australia against Queensland in a game that finished two days before the services match, scoring 68 and 52 not out. Bradman himself described his performances as 'painstaking'. Yet the 50 in his first innings took just 54 minutes. Miller had played in Bradman's previous first-class match at the MCG early in 1941, when he scored 0 and 12. That was five years of debilitating illness ago. Bradman had been discharged from the army in mid-1941, after being hospitalised with fibrositis, an ailment that affected nerves in the back muscles and spine, and was incapacitated by it periodically. In 1943 he began swinging a golf club and playing tennis, but did not touch a cricket bat. In mid-1945 the share-broking firm he worked for collapsed in scandal. He was persuaded by the Adelaide Exchange to set up his own operations, taking some of the clients from the collapsed firm. He and wife Jessie were building the operation and working long hours. Bradman's illness and workload made it unlikely that he would return to the demands of full-time first-class and Test cricket.

The services game was billed as Bradman's personal 'test'. If he did well, he might go on. If he were hopelessly out of touch, he would not attempt to go further. This gave the contest an edge. All the services bowlers wanted to claim the biggest scalp in the history of cricket and go down in the sport's annals as 'the bowler who ended Bradman's career'.

Pepper, 27, was the player most keyed up for the contest. He informed the press on the morning of the match that he had turned down an offer to play professional cricket for Rochdale in the Lancashire League. He wished to represent Australia.

Bradman began cautiously. Early in his innings he played forward to Pepper and was struck low on the front pad by a top-spinner, according to Whitington at first slip, and a flipper, according to Miller in the pavilion. Pepper, seeking immortality, let out an air-splitting appeal for lbw. Umpire Jack Scott shook his head. Pepper threw his arms in the air, clasped his massive hands to his head, and called, 'What do you have to do?' He continued to complain loudly.

Bradman scored a single and was close to Scott at the end of the over. Pepper was still complaining. According to Whitington, Bradman said to Scott: 'Do we have to put up with this sort of thing?'

Scott lodged a report to the South Australian Cricket Association. It was forwarded to the Board of Control. Two months earlier Bradman had for the first time been appointed to the board as one of three representatives from South Australia. He was a national selector along with Victorian and former Test captain Jack Ryder and New South Wales administrator Chappie Dwyer, who would choose the team to tour New Zealand.

No action was taken against Pepper, who was advised to write an apology to the board. It did not receive a letter. When told he had written one, the board advised him to send another. Pepper stubbornly refused. The entire incident would not have helped his chances of gaining national selection, given that he would be fighting with Miller for the all-rounder's spot. The selectors favoured choosing just one leg-spinner and an off-spinner for variety, if they were good enough. They had chosen two leg-spinners more than a decade earlier when O'Reilly and Clarrie Grimmett were the best in the world, but it was rare. Those two spinning spots were expected to be taken by Bill O'Reilly and Ian Johnson respectively, unless Pepper impressed the selectors as an all-rounder so much that he could not be ignored. Even then, he was not going to replace Miller, who was being tipped to open the bowling. The selectors wanted pacemen as a priority. There was no Shield competition in 1945–46. They had only a handful of first-class games and the services matches on which to make their judgements. It was unfortunate for the AIF players that they were losing touch at the end of their three continuous tours.

Bradman went on to a chanceless 112 in 95 minutes against the servicemen, throwing his wicket away to Williams. He was in scintillating touch. He punished Williams and Cheetham and relished dancing to the spinners, especially in dispatching Pepper to the cover boundary. Whitington writing in the Sydney *Sun* said, 'Bradman making 112 batted better than anyone I have seen since I last saw Bradman. That word "anyone" includes Hammond, Hutton, Compton and Amarnath. Bradman is still in a class of his own. It would take a Harley Street specialist's certificate to convince me he is not fit enough to score hundreds in Tests.'

Bradman did not believe the services bowling was a true test, yet was satisfied with his physical reaction to the game. He refused to commit himself or rule himself out of the tour of New Zealand. He would not make a final decision on his future until the next season when first-class cricket resumed and England was on tour. His thoughts in the drawn game about the bowling did not augur well for chances of national selection for Pepper (4 for 100, and a good innings of 63), Ellis (5 for 88) and Cristofani (who didn't take a wicket in the first innings). A major problem for the two leg-spinners was Bill O'Reilly. He and Grimmett, who had retired, were Bradman's yardsticks.

Miller arrived home on 2 January 1946 and did not have a day's break before he was scheduled to play against a strong Victoria. He stayed with his parents at his Elsternwick home, catching up with his siblings and their families, and friends. Miller felt good to be home at last, but unsettled. After his experiences Melbourne seemed to have shrunk. Compared to Boston and London, it now seemed to be a small provincial town. Miller wasn't sure he could adjust. He had loved England and the English, sharing their trials through unprecedented attack and their success in vanquishing a powerful enemy. Miller was idolised in England for deeper reasons than the hero worship that would develop around him at home. In Australia, it was all about sport, not war. Miller also simply appreciated life in Europe more.

England's easy access to so many countries was appealing. For him it meant opera houses, concert halls, racetracks, vacations and history. By contrast, Australia, except for the Japanese bombing of Darwin, had been left unscarred by the direct physical damage of war. Miller felt remote – a little alienated – from those who had not been through the intensity he had experienced. He gravitated to ex-servicemen, especially those who had been to Europe. They understood. The cultural life in Melbourne, too, was limited. There was a straitlaced atmosphere of which he had not been quite aware before he went away.

For the moment, he would put those sentiments aside to concentrate on earning a living. He could still draw a salary from the RAAF, and he could always earn a few quid in the nearby delicatessen run by brother Ray and his wife Molly. His old job at Vacuum Oil was still open and to be considered. They presented options, but not tempting ones from a longer-term perspective.

He still had the whole of January to complete his commitments to the services team, which was jaded. It was thrashed by an innings by Victoria. Miller, in boots borrowed from Pepper, maintained his batting form, top-scoring in both innings with 37 and 59. Ian Johnson sealed his place in the Test squad with a 10-wicket haul for the match while the services bowlers took a pasting. There was some resolve to do better a few days later against New South Wales, using resentment towards players who had not served in the armed forces – which included most cricketers in the state teams they were encountering – as a motivation. The colourful, quirky batsman Sid Barnes was the key target. Miller was the striker who would attack the opener with bumpers. He set out to intimidate, marking out a longer run than normal. He bowled faster than he had since the Victory Tests. But Barnes, after giving an early chance, made a superb century in New South Wales's massive 7 for 551 declared. Miller didn't take a wicket. Pepper was dealt with harshly, taking Ron Saggers' wicket for 137.

It was a further blow to his immediate prospects of representing Australia.

Miller then faced his biggest test yet with the bat against O'Reilly, the square-shouldered new speedster Ray Lindwall and the tall, left-arm, fast-medium Ernie Toshack. Miller restrained the desire to obliterate the opposition, realising that this would be folly against O'Reilly, who could not be treated lightly on his home ground. Miller opted for drives along the carpet and late cuts. He was 62 not out when the eighth wicket fell at 159. Ellis joined him. Miller farmed 12 runs before Ellis ran himself out trying to give the strike to Miller. The score was 9 for 171. Miller was on 74. Jack Pettiford had been taken to hospital with appendicitis and could not bat. This meant technically that the innings was over. But O'Reilly sportingly allowed twelfth man Workman to bat in a gesture aimed at giving Miller a chance to secure a century. Yet it was not going to be handed to him on a platter, especially with Lindwall tearing in with short deliveries. He had attacked bowlers Williams, who in ducking a bumper had dislodged a bail, and Ellis. Lindwall had lifted his performance in this match, knowing he would be compared with Miller, the other new speed demon. Whitington, who had only faced Miller in the nets, reckoned Lindwall was the fastest bowler he had faced since everybody's yardstick for speed, Ernie McCormick (who had been the measure for Compton and Hutton too, when they judged Miller as exceptionally quick).

Writing in the Sydney *Sun*, Whitington observed: 'When he [Lindwall] bowls a bumper, he directs it at the right objective – the batsman's head and shoulders – not a point feet over his head.' Lindwall's short delivery was rarely wasted and mostly lethal. He could drop his right shoulder, and deliver the ball more round-arm, causing it to rear at the batsman's throat.

Miller took up the challenge. He accelerated his hitting, taking 31 of the last 33 runs scored. His unbeaten 105 (out of the team's 204) included 11 fours, took 172 minutes and drew rave reviews from past stars of the game. He had met the challenge of facing O'Reilly, Lindwall and Toshack. O'Reilly was still a tough competitor despite being beyond his best. A knee injury was taking its toll and slowing him down.

'Australia has unearthed a new champion,' stylish former Test bat Alan Kippax announced. 'Miller is probably a greater cricketer even than Jack Gregory, who had emerged from the AIF team of 1919. Very few batsmen I have watched have had his ability to blend beauty with power.' Kippax added, perhaps portentously, that he and [former Australian Test captain] Herbie Collins agreed that Miller should always be given 'a free hand so he can be himself'.

It was the first time O'Reilly had bowled to Miller post-war. In the 1939–40 and 1940–41 seasons, he had picked him up cheaply twice in seven encounters, when Miller did not once reach 30. The astute judge had no opinion of him then, which meant he was unimpressed. Five years on it was different. O'Reilly now assessed him as having the makings of a great batsman. This century was 'one of the best hundreds ever got against me'. He wished, however, that Miller would give up bowling.

New South Wales forced the services team to follow on. Miller maintained his form with a fine 46 before receiving a fast leg-break from O'Reilly, which pitched outside leg and clipped his off bail. The spinner and Lindwall (seven wickets apiece for the match) proved a touch of class too much for the tourists. They went down to their second successive innings defeat. By the end of the game, they were being written off and judged an ordinary cricket team. The cruel conclusion was that England must have been weak in the Victory Tests.

The AIF's run of matches ended in an even draw against Queensland, where Miller bent his back in the state's second innings, taking 4 for 49, and domination of Tasmania, in which he scored two fifties.

Before the last match against the weakest state, the statistics for the AIF's tour of Australia were revealing. Reg Ellis from South Australia, with his slow, left-arm orthodox spinners, had 17 wickets at 26.41 runs. These figures were consistent with his overall numbers for the AIF on three tours – 73 wickets at 25.48 – that would have impressed the selectors. But rheumatism of the chest finished his first-class career (but for one disappointing game against Victoria at the end of the 1945–46 season). Miller was second with 6 wickets at 31.83. His batting kept him prominent and a near-certainty for a higher cricket calling, averaging 58. Pepper, Cristofani and Williams all suffered on home soil for a tour too far. Pepper, before the Tasmanian game when he took 9 for 142, had just 10 wickets at a costly 80.40. Regardless of his dispute with the board, he was unlikely to be chosen for Australia on those figures. Unlike Miller, he had not done enough with the bat (195 runs at 27.85) to justify selection on that part of his game alone. Cristofani's statistics (5 wickets at 76.66, and 89 runs at 12.71) were against him too. The selectors would not be interested in his good numbers in 15 first-class matches for the AIF (39 wickets at 30.54 and 648 runs at 29.45). The leg-spinner had played one game for New South Wales before the war. His form in India and Australia, along with a knee injury, went some way towards finishing his first-class career (except for two lacklustre performances for New South Wales in 1946–47). Williams retired after the AIF games.

Eighteen months of touring and more than 60 games had taken its toll on an efficient unit. It had peaked at Lord's in the third of the Victory Tests half a year ago. Miller proved to be its best and most consistent performer with the bat and its finest paceman. The AIF experience had been fun while it lasted. How Miller would react to a sterner, less carefree examination in Test cricket remained to be seen.

In February 1946 he was at last allowed to attend to such issues as employment and marriage. His parents and family were concerned for him. The war had changed him. Apart from being exhausted after the extended journey, which had made him feel like a nomad, he was mentally drained. His nerves were frayed. He was suffering a kind of delayed nervous breakdown. The family found that he couldn't sit still. He always had a tennis ball or something to throw or toss around. Miller was also uncertain about what to do about Peg in the US. Should he follow through or abandon the plans for marriage? It was three years since they had been together. He had no money or prospects. What could he offer a woman from an upmarket Boston background? How could he even approach the lifestyle to which she was accustomed? He had not written to her for months, although letters had come from her.

Les Sr, without Miller's knowledge, rang Carl Wagner in Boston to discuss issues. Wagner was unsure about his daughter travelling so far to an uncertain future. But he did acknowledge that Peg wanted to marry Miller, and was willing to partner him under any circumstances. Wagner would have been aware of another significant factor that was not mentioned to Les Sr: Peg did not have a good relationship with her mother and was keen to leave Boston to be away from her orbit of influence. Les Sr felt from what Wagner said that Peg was a wonderful woman, and that Miller should go through with the marriage. But it was up to him. Les Sr would have said something had he believed his son should not go through with it. But he and wife Edie now quietly encouraged their son. They were supportive and wished him to stay in their Elsternwick home until he had settled back into Australia.

That solved Miller's accommodation problem for the moment. He was happy to help out Ray and Molly at their delicatessen, but slicing ham and weighing cheese were not him. Nor was sifting the dreaded invoices at Vacuum Oil. But a job was still there for him. He could delay facing that until after he was discharged from the RAAF. He would stay with the air force until problems with his skin and back – the lingering wrestling injury – were given treatment and hopefully cured. The issue of his long-term security and employment remained unresolved. Apart from Vacuum Oil, a possible job option still was a professional cricket career in England, for which he already had a little nostalgia.

Miller hardly had time to draw breath when he was selected for the New Zealand tour, beginning mid-March. Only he and Hassett made the squad from the services team. Pepper, predictably, missed out. He felt his Australian form and the incident at Adelaide had ended his prospects of ever playing for his country. This caused him to take up the offer from Rochdale to commence with it in April, which he had recently rejected. The impractibility of playing six months in England and six months at home meant that Pepper, potentially a great Test all-rounder, would be lost forever to international cricket. His priority, like most servicemen after years of war disruption, was to gain the best possible employment and settle down. Test and Shield payments were a pittance. Players had to have jobs. The option of patiently waiting for the possibility of playing Test cricket was unrealistic, unless the individual was Job-like and prepared to take an ordinary job. Even then any position had to have not flexible hours but flexible half-years. Pepper, for one, was not ready to wait. A nice professional contract in England beckoned.

Bradman also ruled himself out of the team, which was to be captained by Bill Brown, another surprise. Most observers thought the leadership would go to Hassett after his experience captaining the AIF side. Had it won one or both of the big games against New South Wales and Victoria he might well have been skipper. But the poor showing of the servicemen in Melbourne and Sydney had a negative influence. He wasn't even given the deputy's job. That fell to ageing Bill O'Reilly. Hassett would have to bide his time.

The team's players with Test experience were Brown (Queensland, captain), O'Reilly (New South Wales, vice-captain), Hassett (Victoria) and Barnes (New South Wales). The newcomers were

Bruce Dooland (South Australia), Ron Hamence (South Austra-
lia), Ian Johnson (Victoria), Ray Lindwall (New South Wales),
Colin McCool (Queensland), Ken Meuleman (Victoria), Miller
(Victoria), Don Tallon (Queensland) and Ernie Toshack (New
South Wales.)

Miller was disappointed that Pepper missed out, suggesting
that had the selection panel and the board been made up of ex-
servicemen, and if they had seen the Victory Tests, he would have
been selected. Hassett, too, Miller believed, would have been
captain.

Miller began the tour well, as was becoming his habit, as if he
were following the dictum that *first impressions are lasting impressions.* He top-scored with 139 against Auckland while Barnes and
Hassett also hit centuries and O'Reilly took 9 for 103. Miller had
now made centuries in five countries in 11 months, and he had
yet to play a Test.

In the hotel one night, he was drinking with Ian Johnson when
he mentioned Peg, 'the girl I intend to marry'. 'Are you in touch
with her?' Johnson asked.

'Haven't written since India,' Miller responded, glumly.

'Why not?'

'Don't know. Since we arrived back home I kept putting it off;
waiting for something important to say . . .'

'If you want to marry her, you'd better call her, right now.'

Miller tried making the call, but couldn't get through. The line
was too bad. He began writing to Peg on 16 March, apologising
profusely for his lapse in not communicating for five months.
What he did not say was that he had been mentally and physically
drained after his war experiences, the excitement of the Victory
Tests and the non-stop touring. He was still uncertain about the
situation with Peg and whether or not he could provide a secure
home for her.

Miller mentioned catching up with his brother Les Jr, who was
married with a newborn baby and lived in Dunedin. Two days

later, he got through to Peg by phone. Hearing her relaxed, honeyed voice, and her mock anger at his writing lapse, rekindled Miller's affections. Resuming his letter begun on the 16th, he wrote:

> My dearest, I've just finished talking to you on the phone, and honestly I'm shaking all over after talking and hearing your voice again. Honestly sweetheart, I feel so lovely and content just to hear you again . . .
> Gee, I am so excited I just want to go back home, get out of the RAAF and get a ship over immediately to you.

Peg's genuine warmth and understanding had dissolved all his concerns. He was determined now to marry her.

But before he could fulfil his desires, there was an international match (the game did not receive official recognition as a Test until 1948), his first, to negotiate. It was at the Basin Reserve, Wellington. New Zealand won the toss and opted to bat on a rain-affected pitch. Brown decided on a right-arm, left-arm opening bowling combination of Lindwall and Toshack that had been working well for New South Wales. After 15 overs he kept Toshack (4 for 12) on, and replaced Lindwall with O'Reilly.

New Zealand's number three, Verdun Scott was slowing Australian progress. Miller thought him well named. His motto was the same as the town of Verdun on the Western Front in World War I: *Thou Shalt Not Pass*. Miller likened him to the snore-inducing defensive skills of England's Trevor Bailey. After one over to him, O'Reilly was irritated. 'How can you bowl to this fellow?' he said to Miller. 'He doesn't play a shot.' A few overs later, O'Reilly appealed for lbw against Scott. It was turned down. O'Reilly took his cap from the umpire, put it on vigorously and said, 'I always thought you knew bugger all about this game. Now I'm certain.'

After a painfully slow, single-by-single innings, O'Reilly had

Scott caught by Barnes for 14, which signalled the end of the home team's defiance. Only one other player reached double figures. Miller was not needed as New Zealand crumbled to all out for 42. Australia declared at 8 for 199, Brown leading the way with 67, supported by Barnes, 57, and Miller, 30.

The Australian skipper had an embarrassment of riches in the bowling department. In New Zealand's second innings, he decided to share the spoils. He tossed the ball to Miller, thus beginning the brilliant speed combination of Lindwall and Miller. They were already becoming friends off the field. In some ways they were opposites. Miller had developed volatility during the war. Lindwall very rarely lost his cool on or off the field.

Lindwall did not view Miller as the flamboyant character he had been painted by the press and observers. He told *Cricketer* magazine:

Nugget is a fairly nervous sort of bloke. He waves his arms around when he talks and a lot of his mannerisms on the field were an expression of nervous energy. In fact, if you grabbed Nugget's arms I'm sure he would be speechless.

I heard once that he was forced to go on television with his hands tied simply so that he would not be waving them around in front of the camera. I often wondered how he got on.

Miller didn't mind a bit of verbal interplay, often good-humoured, sometimes less so, with opposition batsmen. Lindwall rarely spoke to the 'enemy'. Instead, he would ignore them to make them feel uneasy. He also instigated the team breaking up after a huddle and ignoring a new batsman when he came to the wicket. 'We would break up, turn our backs and walk away,' Lindwall said. 'It didn't help him.'

They also had things in common. They were both ex-servicemen. Lindwall had served in New Guinea in the army's

Anti-aircraft and Fortress Signals Unit. He, like Miller, reckoned he was lucky to live through the war. His unit was bombed near Port Moresby. Lindwall was also conscious of surviving when others did not.

They were both rugged men, good at contact football. Lindwall had been a first-grade Rugby League player. They liked a beer and a bet, and took their fame in their stride. There was a special greeting between them. Lindwall saw plenty of the American forces during the war and was taken by the number of black servicemen with the name 'Jackson'. Once he told Miller about this, it was 'Hello, Jackson' from then on.

Despite his earlier protestations that he wished only to be a change bowler, Miller was raring for the opportunity to take the new ball against New Zealand. He obliged Brown by taking 2 for 6 off six overs before that recalcitrant back of his 'went'. It had failed him in England when he bowled fast, and again on his return to Australia. This was the third mishap. But it did not have a bearing on the mismatch. New Zealand, without the outstanding Martin Donnelly, who was still stationed overseas, did not provide a contest. Toshack, Lindwall, O'Reilly and McCool lined up for the kill. New Zealand reached 54, giving Australia a massive win, and setting back trans-Tasman contests nearly three decades.

O'Reilly, who had the bowling figures for the match with 8 for 33, tossed his boots out of the dressing room window, declaring his career was over. His knees couldn't take the grind any more. They would be big boots to fill after a mighty Test and first-class career. Unfortunately for Australian cricket, the leg-spinner best equipped to do so, Cec Pepper, was already on a boat to England and first-class obscurity, never to return. He began a trend. Bill Alley, Bruce Dooland, Fred Freer, Jack Pettiford, George Tribe and others would follow.

O'Reilly's retirement meant further changes to the new-look post-war Australian line-up. For various reasons, Stan McCabe,

Jack Badcock, Jack Fingleton, Alan Chipperfield, 'Chuck' Fleetwood-Smith, Ernie McCormick, Barry Scott, Frank Ward and Clarrie Grimmett had also moved on from the game. Ross Gregory, Charlie Walker, Glen Baker and Ken Ridings had been lost as a direct result of war and combat. Whichever way it was viewed, Miller would be part of a rejuvenated side that would take Australia into the post-war era.

The day after the squad left New Zealand in early April, a tsunami hit from New Zealand to Hawaii, causing much destruction. Miller put down the timing of the team's departure to his perpetual luck in avoiding death and disaster. On return to Melbourne, he was looking to some more fortune rubbing off in other matters, such as money. He and the other tourists had been paid a pound a day expenses for the New Zealand trip, which had drawn large crowds and revenue. New Zealand administrators were prepared to play the tourists a bonus. The 13-man Australian Board of Control lived up to its restrictive, domineering name. It refused the offer, wishing to maintain a 25-year tradition of treating players like second-rate amateurs. The attitude of keeping the game as a sport was fine at face-value, but mean-spirited and backward-thinking in reality, especially with cricket being an increasingly international sport that attracted huge crowds and earned revenue.

The result was Miller being out-of-pocket on his return to Melbourne. He was also betting at racetracks whenever possible, in the hope of a bonanza. Like most returned servicemen, Miller felt the pressure to play 'catch-up' for those 'lost' years. He was a typical 'mug-punter'. They were legion among ex-servicemen. They lost much more than they won. Bookies literally saw them coming. Miller wanted a post-war jump start in the tradition of servicemen from two world wars. They resented those who had stayed behind and made money while they were away fighting for their country. The lack of preferential treatment and public appreciation for their sacrifices, and the absence of counselling or constructive schemes to get them suitable employment, created embitterment, even hostility, in ex-servicemen. Miller vented his feelings about the people at Vacuum Oil who had advanced their positions while he was away. When ex-servicemen discussed others they would often start an assessment with 'did he serve?' If not, there was an immediate question mark over a person's character, which by implication cast doubt on the individual's courage.

Despite distractions and drawbacks in those early months at home, Miller's single-minded, determined character came to the fore. He was inspired to go through with his plans to return to Boston and marry Peg. He told Ray's wife Molly that Peg was a cut above all the other women he had met in England and Australia. 'I want her to be the mother of my children,' he said. There was also another aspect that appealed to Miller, perhaps because it was something he lacked. She had a deep spiritual side, of which her regular church-going was only a part.

He was frustrated by his injuries and by the endless red-tape over his passport, taxation and acquiring US dollars. Bureaucratic interference seemed to be the rule rather than the exception, not to mention the problem of finding a suitable boat in the chaos and uncertainty of post-war international shipping. It was tough for him. He was presenting a good image in letters to Peg of staying with his parents and not drinking much. There was little mention of gambling and repeated reassurances that 'all would be well'. Miller's letters were now frequent. They made several references to their common love of music, and listening to it in front of a cosy log fire, which would have conjured pleasant memories for both of the atmosphere when they first met in the middle of a North American winter.

'At the moment I'm with Mum and Dad listening to our good friend Arthur Schnabel playing Beethoven's 2nd Piano Concerto,' he wrote on 9 April. 'I don't think I've heard it before, but being Beethoven, it's extra good.' Then again on Sunday 15 April, he told her that he was in front of a fire, feeling the bruising effects of his return to big-time football with St Kilda after four years out of the game. 'I'm listening to the NBC Orchestra under [English conductor] Malcolm Sargent playing Sibelius' 1st Symphony,' he said, 'but I'm not impressed.' On 23 April Miller had 'the radio on. It's playing Mozart's Piano Concerto with Arthur Rubinstein as soloist and John Barbirolli conducting.'

Miller showed his gallantry when faced with trouble obtaining a US visa from the American Consulate. He had to deal with 'a dumb Yank', who asked him why his fiancée didn't simply come to Australia. Miller explained that it was unfair to ask a woman to do this. He told the consular official: 'If you had read the papers recently you would have seen that many Australian girls had travelled to the US and found that their [prospective] husbands were already married. It would not be nice for a girl to travel all that way on her own to find out things like that.'

After 'a lot of arguing with him' the official wanted a letter from the bank 'saying whether or not they could allow me sufficient dollars to release for my travel'. 'Is she coming back with you?' the official asked.

'Yes,' Miller replied.

'But how do we know that?'

'Just because I'm telling you!'

'Did you find out if your wife would be allowed into the country?'

'Yes, and she is allowed.'

'Can you provide a document that makes it clear that your fiancée intends to marry you?'

Miller fought to restrain his temper. 'What?'

'Can you get her to write a letter . . . ?'

'I can show you portions of her letters to me that make it clear.'

'That will do, Mr Miller.'

Miller's natural instinct, he told Peg jokingly, 'was to rip his [the official's] leg off and beat him over the head with it'. Instead he said 'thanks' and 'left in a hurry'.

When he went to his bank to obtain dollars, he was asked the same questions about why Peg shouldn't make her own way to Australia. 'I got a bit hostile,' Miller wrote to Peg, 'and told him politely to mind his own business.'

The weeks were slipping by. His frustration with obstacles grew. 'It's remarkable that in wartime they just load them [military personnel] on to ships like animals, no passports, no nothing,' he wrote on 1 May, 'but now all the rubbish you have to go through, makes you wonder if we are civilised or just plain stupid.'

Three days later he received his final promotion in the RAAF to flight lieutenant, which carried a pay rise, and he was asked to do some clerical work. It irritated him. He had little choice but to obey the directive. He wanted to keep getting back and skin treatment while drawing what he described now as 'pretty good' pay. 'When that [his back] is fixed,' he told Peg in a letter dated 9 May, 'I shall be right finished with the RAAF. I reckon they did a great job for me as I have seen the world at their expense. Above all, had it not been for them, I'd never have met you Peg dear. So we have something to be grateful for.' Miller's sensitivity to the many mates, friends and acquaintances who died in service was always close to the surface when he reflected on his time as a pilot. 'But for many of the less fortunate ones, the RAAF was their downfall. It's just a trial and error sort of outfit to be in.'

The day Miller stepped off the plane from Auckland after playing several weeks of cricket, he pulled on borrowed footy boots for a practice run at the St Kilda Junction Oval. The selectors at his old club took one look at him and placed him straight into the team for the first Australian Rules game of the season. It was against North Melbourne. Miller played on Syd Dyer. Miller felt a kick in the ankle the first time the ball came their way. He ignored it. The second time it was an attempt to trip him. Miller turned to him. 'Look, Syd,' he said, 'in the war we were taught how to kill. Do you want me to revert?' Dyer might not have known what 'revert' meant, but the look on Miller's face said a lot more. Dyer kept well clear of his opponent for the rest of the game.

Miller enjoyed those St Kilda matches, and performed even better than he had done in 1940 and 1941. Miller never lacked toughness. He always had a touch of aggression in him. Yet now he had a body language and attitude that caused other players to take short steps when he attacked the ball. A few bruises, a broken nose, a corked thigh and a strained hamstring were not going to stop him. Nor would any opposition player. Pain and injury were trivial compared to what he had faced in the war years. Miller carried his back injury when most would have given in due to the demands of Rules, where that part of the anatomy was constantly being pushed, hit, shoved, kneed and thumped in packs.

Miller stood out for the lowly Saints, who wallowed at second bottom, just below Geelong and a game above Hawthorn, where they had been when Miller played before. His drop-kicks were still prodigious; his high marks were now supreme against all-comers. It was no surprise that he was chosen for the Victorian state team mid-season for a spectacular drawn game against South Australia at the Carlton ground. He played alongside some of the greatest names in the history of the game, including Dick Reynolds, Jack Dyer, Norm Smith, Bob Chitty and Des Fothergill (who also represented Victoria at cricket). Miller, at 26, had now achieved the rare double of playing at the highest level: representing Australia at cricket and football at the top, for his state.

He arranged to have discussions with Vacuum Oil after he was discharged from the RAAF on 26 June. While waiting in the head office for an interview with the management, he nodded and chatted to some employees he knew from pre-war days. Miller noted that they had all used the war to move up into less laborious positions with fatter salaries. He didn't express it then, but it annoyed him, especially when his bosses wanted to send him to a dead-end job in the Melbourne industrial suburb of Yarraville. He objected. His bosses said he would be sacked if he did not take what was on offer. Miller had no choice. He took the job. Yet he was resentful of what he saw as the injustice of his being offered so little after risking his life in war, while some of his contemporaries had risked nothing for their country and had advanced up the managerial ladder. The trouble was that his bosses had not been to war either, and they were not going to penalise their loyal underlings who were just like them.

More than that, Miller, through cricket, had had a taste of mixing with the elite in England. During that glorious summer in 1945 he hob-nobbed with lords, leading politicians and captains of British industry, and he had been appreciated, not just for his cricket. Miller's service for the RAF had made him an honorary 'Pom'. By comparison the Yarraville installation at which he worked was depressing. The menial work was demeaning. During June, he often thought wistfully of where he had been a year ago. He had no 'work' in the usual sense as he drew his RAAF salary in 1945. He played cricket every other day after the war ended on 8 May, followed the races, met and mixed with mates like Glendinning and the cream of British society.

Miller appreciated that those circumstances could never be repeated, but he could return to the scenes of his triumphs if he took up an offer from Lancashire League professional club Rawtenstall. It was for three years at £1,000 a year. Miller was told he could triple that salary each year with advertising and commercial 'tie-ups'. Three thousand pounds a year was nearly ten times what he would earn playing Test and Shield cricket. It was a tempting offer and would mean a security he had never experienced, especially as he was ever conscious of providing a good life for Peg. Miller said many times, 'She's too good for me', but it was not a comment in jest. Her father, Miller knew, was concerned about his daughter leaving to live in Australia with a relative stranger. (Peg's brother was in England later and only then realised how famous Miller was when he happened to mention to some friends in London he knew him.) Although he would see a lot more of Old Trafford in Manchester than Lord's in London, he would be thereabouts, and who knows what would happen in that three years? Something else more to his liking might bob up. Rawtenstall also was talking to him about what he might do in the British winter. A bloke of his size and power could play professional rugby and earn more good money.

Miller weighed the cons as well. Miller loved his cricket, but appreciated that playing the game day in and day out could kill his enthusiasm. He knew his quixotic, mercurial character well. He had enormous all-round skill, perhaps more than any player who had ever played the game. But he relied on inspiration and a good stage – liked a packed Lord's in a tight game. There was a fear that professional cricket would crush spontaneity and quell desire to strike out, take risks and achieve great deeds. Even if Miller did slash a brilliant century, who would know about it, except for the Manchester locals? He knew too that, like Pepper, he would be lost to Australian cricket for good. Miller would be 27 in a few months. That three-year contract would take him to age 30, the time when many cricketers in Australia thought about retirement. One three-year extension of that Rawtenstall contract would reduce his options in sport to one thing: playing more professional cricket.

The dream of regularly playing for Australia, which was tantalisingly close, would be snuffed out with the suddenness of a first-ball duck. It would mean missing the fun of playing Aussie Rules in the southern winter. But he had been there and done that. Besides, if he played cricket for Australia those footy days were numbered anyway. And if he took the Rawtenstall offer, and wanted football so badly, he could always explore the rugby option.

After a few days, the futility of his being stuck at that Yarraville oil installation got the better of his reasoning, especially as the Rawtenstall club chap doing the negotiation was solid, pleasant and polite. He painted a rosy picture that not even thoughts of Manchester's weather could blight. Miller signed the contract. There was always the thought in the back of his mind that he could opt out of the Rawtenstall deal. He would at least have a chance at one home Test series against England in 1946–47 before meeting his obligations in England by April 1947.

Soon afterwards he was told he could get a boat – the *Marine Falcon* – to San Francisco. Miller approached his Vacuum Oil bosses and requested two months leave without pay to go to the US and be married. They refused, telling him he had been 'away long enough'. It was time he 'settled down and did some work'. Miller again considered his options. He would be in the US two months and then play cricket through the Australian summer. He had enough finance to live on until he took off for Rawtenstall in April. Miller didn't need Vacuum Oil or Yarraville or boring invoices any more. He resigned. On 8 August 1946 he wrote to Peg:

> I don't know if I told you but I signed the contract with the cricket team in England for 3 years, and we have to be there by April. Incidentally it's another place you'll love especially in summer time, although around the parts where we shall be the weather is very unreliable – you ask Mammy (Peg's mother). It's around Manchester, but we'll have fun, and as I keep saying, you shall see the world.

Miller was able to play out the season with St Kilda before he boarded the *Marine Falcon* on 24 August. Through no fault of his, the club ended up in its comfortable second-bottom spot. The team, family friends and a couple of curious reporters were at Spencer Street railway station to see him off to Sydney where he would catch the boat. There was some mystery for the press in Miller's trip. It was discreetly reported that he was going to see 'American friends' he had met during the war. But newspaper editors were more concerned with when he would return. Would the dashing Miller line up in the Ashes series that would commence in late November? Would he back by then? Would he be ready to play against England? Miller would only say that it was his intention to return in time.

The boat crossed the Pacific in 22 days and docked in San Francisco on 16 September, where Miller ran into more problems. A zealous US immigration official, ignoring the paperwork of his counterpart in Australia, blocked his disembarkation. He wanted to know why Miller had come to the US and when he intended to leave.

'I'll be here only a few week,' he said.

'What proof have you got?'

'Australia is my home,' Miller replied.

'Saying that is not proof,' the immigration man said. 'We have millions of illegal immigrants. If we catch them, they all promise they're leaving for their "homes".'

'But Australia *is* my home,' Miller repeated, lamely in the face of the challenge.

'I'm afraid you'll have to return to the ship, sir.'

Miller's heart sank. Then he remembered he had a letter from a Victorian government official to a high-ranking counterpart in the US State Department asking for assistance in making sure he was flown back to Australia quickly. The compelling reason of playing international cricket for Australia against England was good enough to convince the immigration man.

Miller flew on to Boston to meet Peg after three and a half years. They picked up naturally and sweetly where they had left off. If anything their love had been accentuated by being apart. It had been tested and survived, while many more such relationships in war failed than succeeded. She admired his compassion, manliness, warmth, humour and strong personality. He admired her femininity, warmth, charm and character. Their physical attraction for each other was strong. Her mellifluous voice appealed.

His expressive, authoritative speech had become softer and more modulated after living in England. There were none of the vowel-crushing sounds that Americans expected from this, in many ways, typical Australian character. Miller saw no change in Peg at all. But she did in him. His handsome face was now even more attractive and mature for his 26 years, without having lost anything of its healthy outdoor look. The accelerated life he had lived over 36 months, and more than flirtations with ending it, had set into his features. The strength she saw now had a kind of indestructibility.

She and Miller, who wore his air force uniform, were married at Milton, Massachusetts, on 21 September 1946. They had time for a little sight-seeing honeymoon in the US and attendance at Boston Symphony Orchestra concerts beside the Charles River, where their romance had begun. Among the many telegrams received was one from Manchester. It read: 'Rawtenstall Cricket Committee and members send hearty congratulations to you and your fiancée on forthcoming marriage[.] If successful in returning to Australia and playing in Tests we wish you every success and will follow your performances with great interest.'

The news of his signing with Rawtenstall made the papers in the UK and Australia. A Victorian member of the Board of Control, Dr D. L. Morton, told reporters: 'Once a man plays for the English League he cannot play for Australia again. He would automatically forgo selection for any future Test. That's the only penalty we can impose.' This rule was in place to stop stars from making the move to England and therefore weakening Australian cricket.

With wife Peg coming by boat and joining him later, Miller took the Skymaster plane alone from Vancouver to Melbourne, arriving on 23 October. He had very little money and no job. This put Miller under pressure to make final career-determining decisions.

ASHES AND CLASHES

The ball sped towards Miller in the covers. He positioned himself to cut it off but it rifled through his hands and legs for four. A roar went up. This was a lapse for a man with superb skills and reflexes. After the crowd reaction, a barracker called: 'Miller, you're not on your honeymoon now.'

His response was a rueful grin and a small wave of acknowledgement. The sharp, informed comment was more accurate than its author would ever realise. Miller had not played cricket for more than half a year and was out of touch. Yet he had not lost his sense of humour. Moments after the fielding mishap, off-spinner Ian Johnson bowled Hutton for 15, bringing Compton to the wicket. He passed Miller at cover, took block and surveyed the field. At that moment, Miller clapped his hands and said in his mock Indian accent: 'You very good batsman, Mr Compton, but you must stop!' Compton laughed. Miller grinned.

The batsman couldn't have been more relaxed and went on, the *Argus* noted, to a 'wonderful batting exhibition' marked by quick, decisive footwork against two good spinners in Johnson and George Tribe (leg-spin). Compton's 143 inspired Miller to attempt emulating the performance, as he often did in 1945, when Hammond, Hutton and Compton set the pace. This time, however, his timing was out. He struggled to 32 when his Victory Test adversary, fast leg-spinner Doug Wright, had him caught.

Left-arm spinner James Langridge bowled him for 8 in the second innings. Hassett didn't bother throwing him the ball, despite Victoria's sending down nearly 90 overs in England's first innings and 60 in the second. A week's preparation before performing against this strong visiting team was not enough. Miller could have stood down and played a couple of district innings with South Melbourne. But he opted to play, not the least reason being that he would be reacquainting himself with many friends, who made up half the England team.

Playing took Miller's mind off other matters that were preoccupying him. The press wanted to know whether he was going to play professional cricket in Lancashire. Miller was saying, 'No comment.' But his instinct was to say, 'I wish I knew.' Rawtenstall wished for confirmation that Miller would fulfil his contract and play for it next April. He was not responding to their communications. Victorian cricket officials were making public pleas for someone to employ him so he would continue to play for the state and not leave. Miller was waiting to see whether something attractive would emerge. Peg was not keen on moving to England when she had just made the transition from Boston to Melbourne. Yet in private she was leaving every decision to Miller.

Meanwhile there was a lot of cricket to be played, and he had to perform well. He wished to secure a Test spot. He also wanted to attract possible employers. A scintillating century or two in the heightened atmosphere of the first Ashes season in Australia in a decade would help. Miller felt the squeeze and lack of practice. He was chosen for an Australian XI to play England (represented as the MCC) in a rain-reduced game, which began on day two, 9 November. He failed with just 5, and had no penetration with the ball, sending down just four overs.

Bradman in this game, according to *Wisden*, 'showed that he remained a master (with a strong 106), and he inspired the young left-hander [Arthur] Morris, who hit a century in his first appearance against the MCC'. This century caused Bradman to make himself available for the Tests. Two weeks earlier he had looked frail and not on song, making 76 and 3 for South Australia. England had scored 5 for 506 declared, with Hutton acquiring 136. This brought back nightmares for the Don. England had amassed 7 for 903 declared in the Fifth Test of the 1938 Ashes at the Oval. Hutton had then scored 364. Hammond had been captain of England in both games. His attitude was to produce huge scores. He had a long experience of chasing big Bradman-dominated Australian tallies. The responses formed a vicious cycle. Now Bradman was forced to respond in a similar manner or see Australia swamped in the Tests. The only way to break the cycle was to have bowlers who could restrict this rash of mammoth accumulation.

Bradman and his fellow selectors were looking keenly at pacemen first and spinners second. There would be a new front-line attack in the Australian team, with Lindwall being the first choice to open the bowling. Bradman had a chance to assess Miller as a bowler at close range for the second time after viewing him as no more than a prospect when he last saw him in 1941. Bradman liked the post-war Miller look, and was more than conscious of the England batsmen's unease when facing him. But Bradman would need to see more of his bowling before he would be convinced that Miller should open for Australia. The press concentrated on the performance of Queensland's Colin McCool, who stole the limelight with 7 for 106, which ensured that he would take O'Reilly's place in front of Miller's symphony-whistling mate, Jack Pettiford, who had been chosen in the Australian XI.

All games now were trial matches, if players were in front of selectors, as Miller was mid-November in Adelaide performing this time against Bradman and his South Australians. It was thought that any bowler, and to a lesser extent any batsman, in stand-out form would have a chance of Test selection. Miller cracked the standard he expected from himself three weeks after returning from his honeymoon. He scored, according to the Adelaide *Advertiser*, a 'dashing and colourful' 188 (run out), regaining all the form of 1945, with drives, cuts, deflections and the odd lofted shot. Knowing that he was under examination, Miller was more conscious of looking like a responsible bat than producing fireworks in about a day at the wicket. Miller was more impressive with the ball, too. He tore in at the South Australian openers, bowling V. R. Gibson with sheer pace. Bradman faced a little of him, which was good for Miller, who had everyone's respect, taking 2 for 32 from two spells of 6 and 5 overs.

This all-round performance began setting possible solutions to Bradman's main concern about curtailing England's mighty batting strength of Hutton, Washbrook, Edrich, Compton and Hammond – a formidable line-up in any era. Bradman's logical mind was ready to break the convention of choosing six specialist batsmen, if he had five who could do the job well enough. In this case there was an added thought. Bradman knew he himself was worth *two* batsmen. His average of about a hundred in Tests was roughly twice that of the rest of the best in the world. If he needed only five batsmen (really six, given he was worth two), he could bring in an extra bowler.

What tantalised Bradman's fertile selectorial mind even further were the exciting prospects Miller brought to the team. He could be chosen as the fifth specialist batsman. He would also bowl, giving Bradman at least *six* strong options with the ball. In effect, Miller's all-round skills gave the team 12 specialists when most teams only had 10 – if the keeper was excluded as an all-rounder.

It was enough to make the calculating Bradman drool. Miller himself was ambivalent about being used as a front-line, or even first-change, bowler. He regarded himself as a batsman first and foremost. But he wanted to play for his country. Once he was in, he would do his best for captain and nation. If that meant bowling a lot too, then he would perform. Despite his flamboyant nature, Miller was selfless, and self-disciplined when it came

Weedy's way: Fourteen-year-old Miller (standing, far right) in Melbourne High's First XI, 1934. Team captain Bluey Truscott (seated, with shield) was an early Miller mentor who went on to be an air ace in the European and Pacific theatres of war.

Copybook drive: Miller, at 18 years, shows his driving style.

Nash's dash: Speed demon Laurie Nash lets one rip. Nash was one of the great footballers of the 1930s and also opened the bowling for Australia. He inspired Miller and was at the South Melbourne Cricket Club with him, along with Ian Johnson and Lindsay Hassett.

Snowmen, airmen: Miller (left), with his navigator Jim Brown, clearing snow from the Great Massingham RAF bomber base in Norfolk when they first arrived in March 1945 to join 169 Squadron.

War mission: Miller (left), with navigator Jim Brown, about to take off in a Mosquito from Great Massingham, Norfolk, in May 1945.

Crashlanding: Miller (left, half-hidden) and navigator Jim Brown with Miller's plane. He crashed it on 28 June 1945 – seven weeks after the end of World War II. The Mosquito caught fire and one of its two engines went down. A mechanic from Great Massingham was with Miller. Both walked from the plane shaken but uninjured. Two days later Miller was at Lord's making a half-century.

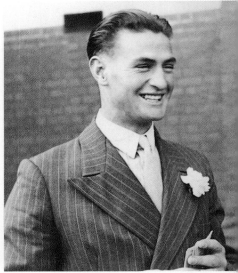

Dream girl: Peg Wagner and Miller fell in love in Boston early in 1943. Peg sent food parcels to him in England.

Suitably attired: Miller, aged 23, in a pinstripe suit Suits were a Miller feature, especially during his cricket career when he was in the limelight.

Keeping in touch: Miller kept up his correspondence, especially with fiancée Peg Wagner in Boston, during his war years in England from 1943 to 1945.

Style and elegance: Miller with Peg outside her family's beautiful estate home at Beacon Hill, Boston, in late September 1946.

Together at last: Miller overcame many obstacles to marry Peg in Boston in September 1946.

First impressions: This portrait of Peg was taken when she got off the boat at Melbourne's Station Pier – her first day of a new life in Australia with Miller.

Miller's favourite team: Miller enjoyed playing with the Australian
Servicemen's Team of 1945 in the Victory 'Tests' more than any other.
The following squad played the first 'Test' of the series at Lord's:
Top row, left to right: Bob Christofani, Dick Whitington, Graham Williams,
Bert Cheetham, Cec Pepper, Keith Miller.
Middle row, left to right: Jim Workman, Lindsay Hassett (captain),
Ron Stanford, Stan Sismey.
Front row, left to right: Reg Ellis, Charlie Price.

Fêted in Colombo: The Australian servicemen in Ceylon in December 1945. Miller
is third from the right in the back row. The weary squad was looking forward to
the ride home to Perth on a York Bomber.

Nugget strikes out: Miller shows his batting style, with head steady, balanced stance and high back lift. He often used the long handle in lofting the ball and always liked to hit sixes.

Miller magnificent: Miller leaves the field after his finest ever batting display – 185 at Lord's for the 'Dominions' side (made up of 8 Australians) versus England in August 1945.

C. P. S. Boyer, Wellington

W. Watts   D. Tallon   K. R. Miller   W. J. O'Reilly   E. Toshack   B. Dooland   R. A. Hamence   F. C. Yeomans
(Vice-Captain)   (Manager)
I. W. Johnson   C. V. McCool   A. L. Hassett   W. A. Brown   S. G. Barnes   K. Meuleman   R. Lindwall
(Captain)

First Test team: Miller (back row, third from left) in the Test squad that toured New Zealand early in 1946. Miller played his first Test at the Basin Reserve, Wellington.

Padding up: Miller hurries to prepare to bat.
Many times, especially later in his career, he
was expected to bat early in a Test innings
after an exhausting performance bowling.
His batting suffered.

The Saint: Miller (in vertical stripes) playing Australian Rules for the St Kilda Club in 1946. He also represented Victoria and New South Wales. He was a brilliant high mark and long kick. Good judges considered him an outstanding player who would rank with the best of any era.

Battered but unbowed: Miller with scars on his nose and forehead during a torrid Australian Rules state game in 1947.

Coming and going: Miller and Bill Johnston coming off the ground after batting in the 1948 Ashes series in England.

The eyes have it: Princess Margaret in 1948, when Miller first met her. They had an instant rapport. Miller said the three most beautiful sights in England were the hills of Derbyshire, the leg sweep of Denis Compton and Princess Margaret.

Beautiful body language: Miller (centre) walking with Princess Margaret at Balmoral Castle, 1948.

The corkscrew: Miller winds himself up for a big slog-sweep. He could play this most powerful shot with his left hand only on the bat.

Too wet for practice: Miller and Ron Hamence leave cricket practice during the 1948 Ashes tour.

Relaxed and upright: Miller's stance at the wicket was classically natural and still.

Top reception: Miller (left) with British Prime Minister Clement Atlee (centre) at a reception during the 1948 Ashes.

Love that blazer: Once he grew too tall to win the Melbourne Cup as a jockey, Miller's greatest dream was to play for Australia. He enjoyed wearing the team jacket, but rarely put on the baggy green.

Royal contact: Miller shakes hands with King George VI at Balmoral in September 1948.

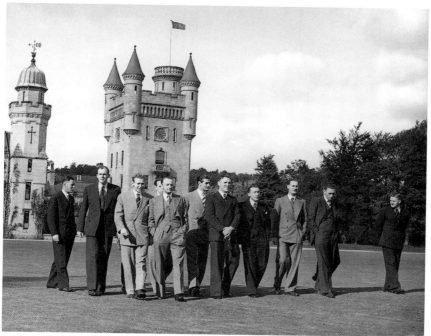

The Invincibles at Balmoral: Don Bradman (hands in pockets) with his squad at Balmoral Castle, Scotland, in September 1948. That week Australia got through their 34th match on tour without defeat. This unparalleled feat earned them the Invincibles tag.

Classic square-cut: Prime Minister Robert Menzies had this photograph of Miller on his office wall, saying it was 'a beautiful piece of sculpture'. Ross Freeman of Sydney's *Daily Telegraph* took the photograph in November 1950.

to team matters. He was very much an independent thinker, yet he would subjugate his individualism for the sake of a well-oiled unit. If Bradman wanted him to open the batting he would do it. If Bradman wished him to bowl into the wind, there would be no argument, knowing that Lindwall would receive preferential treatment when it came to the breeze at his back.

Bradman was further salivating during the Victoria versus South Australia match at the thought of the bowling combinations and permutations he might have in his charge. Victoria's all-rounder George Tribe had come from nowhere with his left-arm spinners – both orthodox and Chinamen (left-hander's leg-breaks) – taking 13 wickets for 153 for the match, and embedding himself into the consciousness of Bradman batting against him and Jack Ryder watching. Tribe's snaring of Bradman, stumped for 119 in his second dig when he was in full flight, would have helped the bowler's cause. Then there was right-hand off-spinner Ian Johnson, not forgetting McCool, giving Bradman four spinning options, if Miller was included as a part-time tweaker. The skipper would have all possible variations of left-hand and right-hand off (orthodox finger) spinners and leg (or wrist) spinners. On top of that there was the likelihood of three pacemen, with one, Toshack, being a medium-fast left-armer.

With England's batting power fresh in Bradman's mind, he felt he needed all options. Another Australian advantage, even if the selectors chose only five specialists bats, was the batting depth. McCool, Johnson, Don Tallon, the keeper, Lindwall and Tribe could all bat well on their day. Only Toshack could be regarded as a 'bunny' at number eleven. Yet above and beyond that in Bradman's thinking was how to target the top England bats. A major key was to have men who could force their way through with the new ball. Real pace seemed the most obvious answer.

Miller celebrated his twenty-seventh birthday on the eve of his first Ashes Test, beginning 29 November. The celebration was a low-key affair with Lindwall, Hassett, Johnson and English wartime pals Compton, Edrich and Godfrey Evans joining him for a quiet hotel-room drink. Bradman and Hammond, the two long-term rivals, who had never relaxed in each other's company, were absent, preparing for the next day's activities.

Gone was the convivial mixer Hammond from the Victory Tests, who shared a Lord's dressing room and drink after the game with Miller and all the Australian servicemen. Not even his own players were well disposed towards him now, mainly because he kept to himself, or away from the team, sometimes preferring to travel and mix with Australian friends. Bradman, and the combative nature of Ashes competition, seemed to be pressing hard on him. This was on top of a personal problem following Hammond's divorce from his wife Dorothy in 1945 and his intention to marry a Durban beauty queen, Sybil Ness-Harvey, with whom he had an affair during the war.

Miller, by contrast, was relaxed. He was among friends on both sides. He carried no pre-war baggage. He had only terrific memories from playing against England. The competition had been tough, but played in an infectious spirit of goodwill. Reflection on the Victory Tests caused Miller to be loose. Besides that, he was not in the spotlight. All eyes and talk, among players, press and fans, were on Bradman. How would he go in Tests? In the build-up he had shown fair form by Test standards but not by his own. Bradman was guided by his own inner clock and no one else's. He was a perfectionist, and had been unhappy with his build-up. It was thought by those close enough to gauge his mood that if he failed in the First Test he might bow out of the game. He was working long hours on building up his broking firm with Jessie. At the age of 38, making a living was his priority, not sport.

Australia batted first at the Woolloongabba ground with the line-up Bradman had wanted: Barnes, Morris, Bradman, Hassett, Miller, McCool, Johnson, Tallon, Lindwall, Tribe and Toshack. It was a most flexible and imaginative combination. Bradman came to the wicket at 1 for 9 after Morris had been dismissed by Bedser. The tension arced considerably. A nation stopped and listened to its radios. Would Bradman lift, or would he fail? He began in a most mortal fashion, seeming tentative against good, tight bowling.

With Bradman on 28 runs, Voce over-pitched an away-swinger outside off stump. Bradman chopped down on it, expecting to guide it through the gully. The ball flew chest high to Jack Ikin at second slip. He tossed the ball in the air. Bradman thought it was a bump ball. There was no anxious look to the catcher. No one appealed. The fielders expected Bradman to walk. When he stood his ground, Ikin, a fair-minded player, held the ball up and enquired, 'How's that?' Umpire Borwick said, 'Not out', without a blink. Hassett, batting with Bradman, was adamant that it was not out. So was square-leg umpire Scott.

In almost any other circumstance, the incident would have been forgotten. But not when Bradman was involved. There was consternation in the British media contingent, and among those Australian pressmen, such as O'Reilly and former Test opener Jack Fingleton, who disliked Bradman. They were in no doubt some distance away in the press box that he was out. Miller, sitting in the dressing room and waiting to bat, thought it was out, too, although he had mixed feelings. He saw the eagerness of his English mates, who knew how vital it was to knock off Bradman early. He heard later that Hammond had said to Bradman at the end of the over, 'Fine way to start a bloody series!'

The incident was like a traffic accident. Some swore that they had seen a clean catch. Others claimed that the ball squeezed out. Miller recalled the moment at the MCG late in 1939 when he stood his ground after Bradman had 'caught' him off Grimmett and might have bluffed the umpire. Miller was given out. He, like Bradman, had left the decision to the umpire.

Miller, batting at five, had to keep the pads on until stumps. Australia was 2 for 292, with Bradman on 162 not out and Hassett 81 not out. After the Ikin 'catch', Bradman reverted to his old self. Perhaps it was Hammond's stinging remark. Maybe he thought the cricket gods were with him. Whatever it was, much to the chagrin of his detractors and those with a vested interest in his demise, Bradman was back. With such form, the fate of the series seemed sealed.

Yet he was fallible. Bill Edrich bowled him the next morning for 187, bringing Miller to the Ashes arena for the first time. The score was 3 for 322; the wicket was good, if slow; the weather was fine; the pattern of play was set. He would be expected not to take risks. Bradman would be happy to bat all through day two and post one of those killer scores that would push England out of the competition.

Miller, making a virtue of being laid-back before the word was in vogue, was dozing when Bradman's wicket fell. He was woken up by the crowd reaction. Then the nerves set in. He began his innings in an adventurous mood, reaching 50 in just 80 minutes of polish before lunch. He let his instincts go with one mighty drive over long-on for six on to the roof of the members' stand. No one had ever seen a bigger hit at the 'Gabba'. Those who knew Miller well waited in vain for him to break loose, especially as the score touched 400. But he might have ingested a Test bug at the interval. Emerging cautiously after lunch, he treated Bedser and Wright as if they were delivering hand grenades. The second half of the innings in a further 80 minutes yielded just 29 uncharacteristic runs. *Bacillus Testi*, which caused batsmen to experience the gravity of history and bog down, gripped Miller until Wright cornered him lbw for 79. Still, most batsmen would take that in their first-ever Ashes knock, not least among them Bradman, who had managed 18 and 1 in the Brisbane First Test 18 years earlier.

Australia was 5 for 595 at the end of day two, which seemed like more than enough runs. But Bradman pushed on into day three, much to the distaste of the English camp. Any thought that this series would emulate the Victory Tests was swept away. Australia reached 645. The weather forecast was for a tropical storm on day three, and it looked likely as England began its innings.

Bradman threw the new ball first to Lindwall, then Miller, ignoring Toshack. The difference from Bill Brown doing it in the second innings of the New Zealand 'Test' was that Bradman was anointing the combination for a series. He had a plan. They would be used to put speed pressure on the grand array of English batsmen.

The storm put the tourists at a considerable disadvantage. Miller was quick. He sent down several bouncers at Hutton. When the Yorkshireman was up the bowler's end he recalled a dinner he and his wife had with Miller in 1945. Miller had told Hutton he had a 'very nice wife'. Hutton said to Miller as he walked past: 'My wife sends you her love.' Miller's face broke into a fleeting grin, but he said nothing.

Hutton faced him an over later, and he kept up the barrage of bumpers. Not even an ice-breaker remark meant in half-jest and half-salutation was going to placate Miller. In the next over he broke through Hutton with sheer pace, bowling him for 7. England was 1 for 21 at stumps.

The hot sun baked the surface into a dreaded Australian 'sticky'. Miller mixed pace with medium-pace off-breaks, causing the ball to fly through at varying heights off a good length. The medium pace gave him more control. By keeping the ball up and straight, he forced batting errors and uncertainty. Intermingled with this were fast bumpers, which Jack Fingleton, among several commentators, was counting. He reckoned that Miller and Lindwall delivered more than Larwood and Voce had during the Bodyline series. Given that the former Test opening bat was numerate and had faced them, it made a nice headline for his newspaper column. Yet there was a major difference. The Australians did not bowl anything like Bodyline, which by its nature was both restrictive and intimidatory. There was more stacking of the slips with Lindwall and Miller bowling than the on side close to the wicket. Batsmen facing Bodyline were cornered or battered into false strokes. The Lindwall and Miller offering was just as intimidatory, but left open the option of a batsman hooking his way out of trouble, if he were inclined to do it or had the courage.

They were not the first combination with an inclination to scare and hurt batsmen. The best and most dangerous pacemen had hunted in pairs, leaving batsmen nowhere to hide. In Miller's case, his threat of damage, and occasional strikes, let out some of the pent-up aggression that had simmered just below the surface during the war years. He had let it out with bat on ball. Since finding he had real ability with the ball in the past two years, he was ready to dissipate his inner tensions with some hard leather on bone.

Hutton was a challenging target. He was technically a superior bat with a lot of grit. Yet he was not prepared to spar with the Australian speedster, preferring to stand his ground and duck and weave. Often more courage was shown in staying at the wicket, being hit and batting on, rather than the swashbuckling 20 – usually out caught in the deep. This did little for the team's tally and even less for morale when the bladesman ended up back in the pavilion looking on after the adrenalin rush to nowhere.

Hutton's wicket any time gave Miller satisfaction. He liked taking him on more than any English bat. The dour Yorkshire-man was ranked at the top above Hammond and Compton, which caused Miller to lift against him for combative reasons. Yet there was a personal element. He had never evoked what he considered any emotion from Hutton, off or on the field, even when he hit him. Until he did that, Miller would not ease off.

Compton offered a different target. He was a hooker, and if he could counter-attack, he would. The same applied to Hammond. But at 43 years of age, he was more circumspect than in his impetuous youth, or his adventurous years as England's greatest bat after Jack Hobbs.

All the leading English bats showed courage. They were hit repeatedly. Edrich was struck on the arms, legs and upper body.

Miller, in the middle of his torture, said (later) he felt sorry for his pilot co-tenant from those Great Massingham days, claiming that he eased up on him after he had been struck about 40 times, despite Bradman, he said, urging him on. Yet Miller didn't let his compassion interfere with taking Edrich's wicket for a defiant 16 in 90 minutes, along with that of Washbrook, Compton and Ikin, giving him all five wickets to fall, and reducing England to 5 for 56.

Hammond (32) held Miller up with some dashing counterplay, including several drives, and England's tail wagged its way to 141. Miller ended with 7 for 60, giving him a remarkable Ashes debut with the ball. But there was more to come. He had Hutton caught for a duck first ball of England's second innings. Picking up this prize wicket twice was special for Miller.

There was no discernible dropping off in his intensity against mates Edrich and Compton. Miller enjoyed bowling against those he considered were in his class as a cricketer. Collecting Washbrook (13) a second time, he put England at 2 for 13.

Toshack was bowling in place of Lindwall, who was ill. Before England's second innings, Bradman had taken Toshack to the wicket to show him where to pitch the ball. The left-armer had listened after being wayward in the first innings. He kept the ball in the right zone and collected 6 for 82 in England's second innings of 172, which was again interrupted by rain which produced a second 'sticky'.

Miller's match figures of 9 for 77, along with his 79 with the bat, ranked high as an entry to Ashes cricket. This success accelerated speculation about his future. Rawtenstall was now asking Miller whether he intended to honour his contract. He was still not answering them, while saying 'no comment' to the press. He was stalling, and hoping someone would make him an offer that would allow him to refuse the professional England club. Yet it was Christmas. Australia shut down from mid-December until the end of January. There were unlikely to be serious offers until the end of the month. If he were going to catch a boat to start a professional season in England, he would have to be packed and ready to go soon after the Fifth Test in Melbourne, which was due to end on 5 March.

Even then, he would miss Rawtenstall's opening game in April 1947. He knew he would have to make a decision soon. In the meantime he played in the Second Test at Sydney, in mid-December, where he was hardly needed. Miller made 40 in an innings dominated again by Bradman, and this time Barnes, who each made 234 in Australia's score of 8 declared for 659, which was then the highest Test score made in Australia. This was in response on a slow, turning wicket to 255 by England. Miller played second fiddle to spinners Johnson and McCool, who both took 8 wickets for the match. His sole wicket was that of Hutton, who was out hit-wicket for an explosive, all too short 37 in just 24 minutes.

Some critics were annoyed by Bradman's tactics of again batting England out of the match, especially in his record stand with Barnes of 405 for the fifth wicket. They had something more 'sporting' in mind to keep the series alive in the interests of 'goodwill' and a vaguely defined 'new era' – perhaps a declaration when Australia was 100 ahead, instead of 400. But Bradman was programmed to win, not make festival occasions out of Ashes Tests. There would be no even breaks for Hammond and England, just as there had been no even breaks for Bradman and Australia in his experience of 1928–29, 1930, 1932–33, 1934, 1936–37 or 1938. It didn't stop huge crowds of 40,000 and 50,000 turning up to watch the Don do his thing at the batting crease, which was to crush the opposition.

A legitimate excuse for England's inept display in the first innings was Hammond's negative instruction to play the high-looping spinners Johnson, McCool and Tribe from the crease. It was not always his way. Certainly Edrich and Compton liked to use their feet. They were curtailed by their skipper's directive. In the second innings, Hammond seemed to reverse his tactic.

Hutton came out firing uncharacteristically. Edrich was defiant with 119 in 314 minutes, and Compton in touch with 54 in 119 minutes. England did better, reaching 371. But Bradman's decision to bat on and on for the second successive Test was, in terms of winning, the right one. England fell 33 short of forcing Australia to bat again.

This second massive innings win demonstrated that the two sides were mismatched in all departments. Miller and several of the hopeful tourists, who thought that the Victory Tests were the start of less fiercely fought contests, were by now disillusioned. There had been much talk about playing 'cricket, not war', as first outlined by Hassett in 1945, but that glorious season now seemed to have been a false dawn in the wake of the euphoria of war's end. This meant bright batting all the time, early declarations to keep games alive, and less concern for winning and losing. Yet unless no player who had participated before the war, and indeed only players who had been to war, were allowed to begin the new era, then history and tradition would always be dominant. The two countries had provided fierce competition since 1877, making carnival Ashes cricket an impossible dream and nothing more than a hopeful platitude. No skipper on either side going back 70 years (or forward 60 years) wished to be known as the sweet fool who threw away an Ashes series. That little urn of burnt bails, created in jest, and forever a bitter object of victory and theoretical acquisition, or at least not defeat, had much to answer for.

Miller had to be content with a Shield match to let his natural inclinations flow. He chose the big four-day game of the calendar: Victoria versus New South Wales at the MCG, beginning on Boxing Day. New South Wales batted first, scoring a modest 205. Miller came to the wicket at 1 for 31. He was on 3 when Toshack came on from the Richmond end. His medium-pace left-armers looked delicious to Miller. He used the first couple of balls as 'sighters', then hooked the third over the fine-leg fence. The crowd had read and heard much about the 'new Miller'. He had been seen just about everywhere except his home ground of the MCG. Now it was his patient local fans' time to rejoice in his batting brilliance. He heaved Toshack's sixth ball deep into the stand at square leg, then belted the seventh back at the astonished bowler. The ball was too hot to handle and bounced several metres out of Toshack's hands. Perhaps this 'life' would have curtailed any other hitter. But Miller ignored his reprieve. A dropped chance was hardly going to unsettle him. He leapt into Toshack's last ball, blasting it over long-on, much to Bay 13's delight. The crowd was in continuous voice of support.

Three sixes in an over in a tight contest against the biggest state. This was not expected or the norm. But Miller had never conformed in any form of the game. He crunched his way to 50 in 41 minutes and 79 not out at stumps with Merv Harvey 63 not out. Miller hammered on to 153 in 186 minutes the next morning in a 271-run partnership with Harvey (136).

Bill Ponsford was in the cigar-smoking Members' Stand, loving Miller's show. It was the hardest hitting he had seen. Miller was flattered to learn that his hero appreciated him. It didn't seem like an eternity to Miller since he had sat with his father and brothers in the outer at the MCG receiving a long batting lesson from Ponsford.

Toshack (0 for 133) was obliterated, and Lindwall (1 for 100) thought he might have come back too early after getting over chickenpox. Miller produced with the ball, too, taking 2 for 22 and 1 for 41, when used sparingly by Hassett, who knew more about this bowling commodity than any other captain. Victoria ran out winners by an innings and 114 runs – a most satisfying result for Victorians. They had seen the main rival humiliated and Miller in full batting flight.

It was enough to make fans celebrate after the game finished on 30 December. The next day many New Year's Eve revellers joined the crowds around the Town Hall and the Post Office, then went straight to the MCG at about 1 a.m. to add to the queue for the first day of the Third Test, which would see in 1947. They were hopeful of seeing Australia wrap up the Ashes, with expectations that Bradman would turn on one of his outstanding MCG performances. The last time Melburnians had seen a New Year Test was 1937, when Australia, not England, was down 0–2. Bradman produced the finest fighting innings ever seen in a Test, making 270. Australia went on to win the game and the 1936–37 Ashes in the greatest comeback in Test history. The MCG fans were sanguine of similarly spectacular performances in a six-day match.

Those New Year revellers were expecting something at the MCG to keep them celebrating, and interested, or even just awake. The 66,000-plus spectators – a strong crowd even by the standards of Australian Rules Football – were thrilled to see Bradman come to the wicket with the score at 32 and stay for 169 minutes for 79 runs. It would not have been sufficient or at the right pace for the tired and hung-over who had stayed overnight. But for many of the rest it was perhaps a last taste of Bradman in an Ashes Test. It was a cameo, not the innings of a colossus, yet a performance of some satisfaction.

Miller, the man capable of enthralling such an audience more than anyone else, batted and seemed out of sorts. He was picked up for 34 by England captain Norman Yardley, whom he would normally delight in dispatching over the fence with menacing regularity, and caught behind off Wright for 33. His medium-pace was just right for belting. Yet Miller delivered mediocre performances that matched his attitude. He was not quite fired up enough to be influential. Nor was the packed colosseum to his liking. After Lord's and countless quaint little grounds from Hove to Clara Vale in England, Miller was now more favourably disposed towards Adelaide and Sydney than his famous home-town stadium. In spite of his recent successful outing against New South Wales in front of smallish crowds, the MCG was now far from being his favourite arena, although it had been in his youth when he had no comparisons. 'Too much a sense of the Christians being thrown to the lions,' Miller said. 'Fine for footy, but not cricket.'

More important than the venue, he needed either a convivial atmosphere of exhibition or the fiercest of competitions to bring out the best in him. Neither was in operation in the Third Test at Melbourne, where he watched McCool score a useful century in the first innings and Morris pull out of a slump with 155 in the second. He enjoyed the smash-and-grab raid on injury-depleted, tired, ordinary opposition bowling in Australia's second innings by Tallon (92 in 105 minutes) and Lindwall (100 in 113). That was fun, although he was not so amused by Bradman again shoving England out of the game for the third successive time by letting his charges run up the third huge total (536) until near the last session of the fifth and second-last day. Australia had gone on perhaps a session too long. England was left the near-impossible task of scoring 551 in four sessions.

According to Miller's future co-author, Dick Whitington, Miller was in a careless, listless mood during the Test. He spent part of the second hot night of the game drinking in Whitington's room at the Australia Hotel. He would not talk cricket, indicating to Whitington that he was not interested in the proceedings at the colosseum. Instead they amused themselves by flirting with two attractive lift attendants. Schooners of iced beer were handed to the women every 15 minutes as they arrived at their eighth-floor level. After an hour their piloting skills were impaired.

Despite his apparent lethargy early in the match, the competitor in Miller re-emerged on the final day, when England could have been beaten. He took 2 for 41 after going wicketless in England's first innings and had a hand in a run-out to remove his mate Compton for 14. (Compton tallied just 25 for the match after receiving a woeful lbw decision in the first innings. His remonstration with umpire Jack Scott brought boos from the parochial fans.) England was on the ropes at 7 for 310, some 240 short of Australia and the game was drawn. With two games to go, life had not quite been extinguished from the series, if England could lift its morale and win in Adelaide.

Rawtenstall began expressing its annoyance that press reports were saying Miller would not be playing in the Lancashire League in 1947. 'It is not cricket if he does not honour the contract,' the club's president, Mr G. Whittaker, told England's *Daily Mail*. Miller was receiving feelers from Australian companies and employers, but not the sort he could contemplate seriously, including an offer to work as a barman, and a couple that involved work as a travelling salesman for a soap maker and a hair brush manufacturer. Peg was settling in to Melbourne and was not enamoured of the thought of moving again. Miller had written off the Rawtenstall contract, although he still refused to inform the club.

His continued good form with the bat, and consistency with the ball, kept him in the headlines in January 1947 between the Tests. His batting gripped public attention. Ron Eaton, the head of a liquor supplies company, and manager of North Sydney club, was impressed enough to offer Miller a sales job. There would be time off for sport. The salary package seemed attractive, but he would be based in Sydney. Peg was happy with the less demanding move to a more metropolitan city but still in Australia. Miller accepted the offer, but decided not to make it public until after the Tests.

That major problem solved, he was in the right frame of mind for the Fourth Test at Adelaide, beginning on 31 January. The usual good batting wicket in the city of churches ensured that England, in first, would have its best chance yet to build a sizeable innings. It compiled 460 with Compton at his concentrating and defiant best scoring 147. Miller and the other pacemen received no help. His only wicket was Joe Hardstaff Jr, who hooked a short one into his stumps.

Australia had a nasty little session to negotiate at the end of the second day and lost Harvey (12) and Bradman (0), to be 2 for 24 at stumps. Morris (122) and Hassett (78) put Australia back in the game with a 189-run partnership. Miller came to the wicket at 3 for 207, which normally would not be called a crisis. But with a deficit of 253 runs, it was a tense time. A wicket or two now would swing the game England's way. Miller's competitive urges were now flowing more than at any time in the series so far. He was still there at stumps on 33 not out. The next morning, day three, he hooked the first delivery, a no ball, over square leg. It soared over spectators still settling into the seats and landed just short of the vice-regal box where the Governor and special guests were juggling cups of tea. The early clout indicated an alertness of mind, which was always his state in a Test, although not always in lesser games. It brought him to 39. Then he added 61 in the next 71 minutes to reach his first century in Tests. The crowd expected Miller to cut loose but, conscious of the run shortfall and the clatter of wickets around him, he had little choice but to become defensive. Yardley was employing a 'silly season' negative field placing of six players spread on the leg side, while bowlers 'attacked' the leg stump.

As the tail dissolved, Miller accelerated again, taking on four fielders parked on the northern boundary. The crowd laughed at the farce as the out-fielder ran around trying to catch his high hits. He went on to 141 not out in 270 minutes off 198 balls, in an uneven yet responsible performance of three parts: attack, forced defence, and hit and giggle. Seven wickets fell as he more than held up one end. Australia climbed to 487 – 27 ahead. It was the right time to make his first Test century, which ranked as one of the best – if not the best and most watchable – innings of the series. Miller had answered the first real challenge from England and Compton, yet the game was still more in the tourists' favour. Compton, in turn, responded again, when his country needed him, making 52 not out by stumps on day five, from England's 8 for 274. Evans, who faced 44 balls without scoring, was not out with him. England was 250 ahead.

On the last day Compton and Evans hung on through the

morning session. Compton was on 103 not out, and Evans, who broke a world record of 95 minutes to avoid his duck, was on a painful 10 not out.

Hammond's mien for the tour had worsened with each match. He became the first, and possibly only person ever, to refuse a lunch invitation at Don Bradman's Adelaide home. The Don might have been obsessed with winning on the field, yet he was willing to go more than half-way off it to create some harmony with the troubled England skipper. It didn't work. Hammond confirmed his mood by waiting for the first ball after lunch to declare at 8 for 340, leaving Australia 314 to make in 195 minutes. He was still fearful that Bradman would upstage him. He knew too from experience that Miller was capable of challenging such a tough target. Then there were Lindwall and Tallon if the chase were taken up.

Bradman was open-minded about going for the runs, which would incur big risks. But he took one look at Bedser's leg-theory bowling with five on the on side and knew where Hammond stood. He was going to make the challenge too hard from the start. Had there been a reasonable field and the England skipper had gone for a win, Bradman would have responded. But Hammond made no effort. The game fell away to a draw, with Morris emulating Compton's feat of a century in each innings of the match. Bradman's determination and England's lack of enterprise had handed the Australians first the Ashes, then the series.

Miller, playing for Victoria, had one more tilt at England in mid-February at the MCG before the dead fifth match of the series. He knew it would be his last of 18 matches for the state. It took the combined brilliant skills of keeper Evans, standing up to the stumps, and the swinging Bedser, to see him stumped for just 6 in front of nearly 24,000 fans. Such a failure was not good enough for Miller on this occasion. He bowled with hostility and took 4 for 65 in MCC's first innings – his best haul since the Brisbane Test. By dismissing Compton caught and bowled for 93, he stopped the England champion from completing a fifth successive century. That was something to remember on his final appearance as a Victorian. He felt no sadness. Miller would rather look forward than reflect.

He thought the Fifth Test at Sydney in early March had a rather stale and morbid feel to it. The selectors dumped Hammond, thus bringing one of the greatest cricketers to an ignominious end in Tests. Hammond had brought his demise upon himself, partly because of his obsession with Bradman. Miller's mind was elsewhere. He had been making the move with Peg to Sydney, although it was still not public knowledge. Accommodation had to be found. Yet he bowled with force and hostility, giving support to the in-form Lindwall, who took seven of the nine wickets to fall. The combination was relentless. If one wasn't taking wickets, he was putting so much pressure on batsmen that there was no respite over after over. Only brave Hutton resisted, but he fell to tonsillitis when on 122, and took no further part in the match. The weather reduced it to a tight affair, with Australia needing 214 to win with two days to get them. A wearing wicket, not time, was the issue.

Any total higher than 200 was a niggling, nerve-racking target on the fifth day (really a sixth, with a rest on Sunday). Bradman (63) led the way towards victory, and was replaced by Miller at 3 for 149. He travelled well enough in the tight situation until Hassett (47) was removed, making the score 4 for 173. Then Hamence was caught off Wright for just 1. The top half was now back in the pavilion for just 180. McCool joined Miller. The required 34 extra runs looked much harder than such a small number would normally seem. England was on top and fighting hard. Wright was bowling at his best. He delivered three booming leg-breaks and left Miller floundering each time. Australia was bogged down. Miller, on 11, was defending grimly. If the trend continued, Australia could be spun to defeat. Bradman considered the line-up still to come. Tallon and Lindwall could both hit the team to victory. The captain sent out a message for Miller. It was just one word: *attack*.

This was all Miller needed. He tried to hit Bedser for six over mid-off, and managed four. Next ball, Miller swung again, belting the ball straight over the bowler's head for another boundary. These were head-down shots, not panicky head-up attempts, dealt against good deliveries that were hittable if the batsman had the reach, skill and courage. The tally was down to just 26 needed. He had broken the shackles. Miller's nerve held. He batted commandingly from that moment on, going on to 34 not out. When his partner McCool made the winning stroke for three, an exuberant Miller grabbed a stump before charging for the final run. He playfully ran away from Compton, who had been promised the souvenir, then gave it to him. Australia won by five wickets and took the series 3–0.

Miller had done better with both bat and ball, at least statistically, in the 1946–47 Ashes than in the much-lauded Victory Tests. His batting average of 76.80 from 384 runs was second only to Bradman (97.14 from 680). He was second only to Lindwall, and then by half a run per wicket, in bowling, taking 16 wickets at 20.88. How much better would his batting figures have been had he not bowled at all? He was hardly ever fresh at the beginning of an Australian innings, and while he was not always called upon to bat early, he was often 'flat' when he had to bat. There is no doubt that he would have been freer of mind and body without the stresses and pressures of matching Lindwall and taking on England's strong batting line-up.

There had been few great all-rounders in the first seven decades of Test cricket (and even fewer in the following nearly six decades). The concentrated energy needed to deliver the way Miller did, along with the stresses on feet, leg joints and muscles, shoulders and, in Miller's case, the back, sapped the all-rounder's strength, will and capacity to bat with calm, precision and stamina. Mental and bodily tiredness were the enemies. A bowler could make plenty of errors, get hit for 100 and still come back to take a few wickets to improve his statistics. But a batsman was often allowed not even one error before he was out of the game. Any little lapse in concentration caused by fatigue was often fatal. Tiredness of muscle, even when a batsman was set, could see him out for 20 or 30 that, when fresh, might have ended in a century.

Many times in history, the batsman who bowled would accumulate ordinary batting performances or efforts that were well below his capacities. This would become a pattern and the norm. The strong batting display would become the exception. In Miller's case, observers were noting a tendency to big on-side hitting, whereby a less gainly swing of the bat collected the lofted four or six. This was opposed to his capacity to show polish in drives all round the wicket and refinement in glances and late cuts.

Miller was in danger of never again performing the way he did in the Victory Tests and in 1946–47. A clue to what he might have done in the 1946–47 Tests as just a batsman was seen from the results of his visits to the crease for Victoria. In four Shield games (as opposed to five Tests), Hassett used him in short bursts. Miller sent down only 65.4 overs (taking 10 wickets at 23), a little over half the number he had to deliver in the longer, more demanding Tests. The results with the bat – six innings for an aggregate of 667 runs at an average of 133.40 – approaching twice his batting figures in seven Test innings perhaps revealed a story that because of the heavy demands of fast bowling might now never unfold. Miller's success with the ball, especially in combination with Lindwall, would mean that his bowling would take on a new and *essential* imperative in terms of his nation's cricket status and success, whether he liked it or not.

***

Miller had bowled flat-out in the heat near the end of the fifth day of the 1946–47 Adelaide Test for the reward of just Bedser's second-innings wicket. He was relaxing in the dressing room when team manager Bill Jeanes, secretary of the Australian Board of Control, urged him to hurry for a taxi that would take him and others back to the team hotel. Miller wouldn't budge. An argument ensued. Jeanes reported him to Bradman, who sent a message for Miller to come to his broking office before play the next day. Bradman would reach his desk at 7 a.m., squeeze in as much work as possible and then walk to the ground, ready for the morning session. Bradman had not intended it to be a summons. It was more convenient to meet Miller at his office. It was also away from the team hotel and the ground, which would allow the minor issue to be settled in private.

Miller reluctantly obeyed the directive. He found Bradman buried in paperwork in his office on Grenfell Street. Bradman explained that Jeanes had been ill recently. He agreed that the board secretary might have erred in rushing Miller when all he wanted to do was relax after some hard work at the bowling crease. Bradman suggested he forget the incident. Miller left the meeting still unhappy. 'Here I am just back from the war,' he thought to himself, 'a war which had been dangerous for me in parts, and I am sent for like an erring schoolboy called to the head's study.'

Given that the complaint had come from the board's secretary and team manager, Bradman had to show some authority, although there was no penalty or even a reprimand. He was conscious of not imposing too many rules on his charges, especially the ex-servicemen. His only directive was that they turn up fit to play when they had to. But Miller resented any show of authority at all. He was still haunted by the harshness of the sentence he received after the altercation with his commanding officer at the RAF Gloucestershire base.

The incident also contributed to a festering attitude towards Bradman, for whom he had mixed feelings. It had begun back in early 1939 when Bradman had caught him off Grimmett, in what Miller suspected was gamesmanship after hitting a bump ball. It offended Miller's sporting sensibilities. That incident had been accentuated by Bradman's approach to winning the Ashes, when Miller had so much wanted to be part of a repeat of the spirit engendered in the Victory Tests. He didn't like Bradman's attitude of driving the opposition into the turf at every chance. Nor did he appreciate or care about the history of fiercely fought Ashes contests in decades before the war.

Both sportsmen had the 'killer instinct'. The difference was that Bradman had it all the time, in whatever level of the game, or any contest in which he participated, from squash and tennis to billiards and tiddlywinks. Miller reserved his desire to beat an opponent for certain occasions, and did not believe in one-sided contests. As a batsman, Bradman treated every bowling opponent the same from country and club to state and Test cricket. He wanted to accumulate a winning score as fast as possible. Miller often didn't care for more than a cameo performance – a 70 in 80 minutes was good enough even in first-class games. If he were bowling, he wanted to be at the crease only if there were a worthy batsman facing him.

Bradman planned his cricket with an obsessive attention to detail. His style fitted that of ancient Chinese philosopher, Sun Tzu, who said: '*Those who triumph, compute at their headquarters a great number of factors prior to a challenge.*' Like the great general of World War I, Sir John Monash, Bradman always thought it better to have a plan than no plan at all. Miller, by contrast, went by the maxim in the Koran: '*Man makes plans, God laughs.*'

Bradman calculated with the sharpest of minds how to beat an opponent before a game began and how to destroy him when it was on. Miller was more instinctive. He had to have the right atmosphere and mood to let his gifts loose. He was more the artist whereas Bradman was more the artistic technician. Neither man was enslaved by technique, but Miller had allowed himself the luxury of letting power dominate technique more often than Bradman. The evidence for this was Bradman's utter control of his six-hitting, especially in Tests. He dispatched only a handful in his career, and went by the dictate that you can't be out if you keep the ball along the carpet. That was part of his success in accumulation.

Miller always had his eye on hitting at least one six an innings. Along with that, he liked to loft the ball to all points of the compass. The 'along the carpet' directive had been drilled into him since his youth, and even then it irritated him. English critic Neville Cardus wrote:

> Strictly and austerely speaking, his [Miller's] technique is sometimes not above suspicion. It works less by reason than by instinct. You might as well refer to the technique of a young panther on the 'kill' or in repose! Miller is a cricketer of reflex action. I don't intend to suggest that he puts no intelligence into his play, but only that at his best he is swayed rather by the logic of the heart than by the logic of the head.

By contrast Bradman was unerringly logical in everything he did. No sportsman ever entered any contest better prepared than him. The force of his will to achieve what he set out to do is unmatched in the annals of sport.

Bradman performed to the beat of his own drum, not that of the spectator. It mattered not a jot to him what fans thought when he batted. Yet he was an entertainer. He was the fastest accumulator of the huge run-making batsmen of the late nineteenth century and the first half of the twentieth century. His dexterity with the blade, and uncanny precision in piercing the field rather than going over it, enchanted those with a fair knowledge of the game. The connoisseurs loved his all-round stroke-making skills. They were copybook and second to none. Bradman was also appreciated as an innovator with his shots, which demonstrated a certain flexibility of mind and body. His genius was evident and somewhat exposed with Bodyline, when he changed his batting style and had more success than any other batsman against that difficult, potentially lethal form of bowling.

Australians loved a winner, and Bradman was the winner's winner. He could program and discipline himself for the massive score, which cricket lovers enjoyed. It was part of cricket's peculiarity to keep going at the crease, when dehydrated or with aching muscles or when the brain was tired. Stamina, patience, hunger, even greed for runs and occupying the crease, were essential to reach 100, let alone 150, 200, 300 (Bradman did it nine times in all cricket, with one 299 not out in a Test) and once, 400.

Miller didn't just satisfy spectators, he excited them. He performed according to the way he felt on the day. He was a crowd pleaser. According to the Melbourne *Herald*'s Percy Millard and Whitington, he needed to feel 'liked', despite the fact that he was uncomfortable with applause, which indicated that too much focus was on him. This was perhaps an over-statement, even of his early years (and was certainly not symptomatic of his later years after 1946–47 when he riled and baited crowds with his hostile bowling). Yet both observers had seen him go out of his way, in those formative years from the ages of 16 to 27, to the extent of taking risks in manoeuvring the baying mob to support him. It had often seen him lose his wicket. When bowling at Lord's in 1945, the Australian servicemen in the crowd urged him to bowl bumpers and he obliged. He responded when fans at Sydney or Bramall Lane bellowed for big-hitting.

Miller cared little for averages and record-breaking. He was not enchanted with those who did, although his boyhood hero, Ponsford, like Bradman, was keen on lifting the bar to the outer limits. Bradman had been miffed early in 1930 when his skipper, Alan Kippax, had declared a New South Wales innings closed while Bradman was on 452 not out. It was then the highest ever first-class score. He had wanted to go on to 600 and shut out all challengers for a few hundred years. Miller, when in the right frame of mind, would hit a double hundred, but never felt the urge to go on for a record. Cricket was to be played more for enjoyment and camaraderie. He also lacked the consistency needed to conquer and annihilate that featured in Bradman's play.

Like Bradman, who loved taking on the greatest bowlers of spin and speed in history, such as O'Reilly and Larwood, Miller was the competitor's competitor. He loved the one-on-one challenge within a contest. Even in his years with perennial VFL losers St Kilda, he was the stand-out performer in a defeated team. Miller feasted on the greatest opponents. The formidable and powerful Bob Pratt was a foe to be reckoned with. The wily Norm Smith at Melbourne was to be out-thought. But that was where the similarity ended. Winning as comprehensively as possible within the rules was always Bradman's over-riding desire. Miller loved the personal battle within a war, and cared less for the outcome of the conflict as a whole.

Bradman didn't drink alcohol (although when he retired he enjoyed catching up on lost opportunities), and was a 'Melbourne Cup Day mug punter'. His battle to earn a living in the 1920s and the Depression made him frugal. He didn't 'mix with the boys' in the traditional Aussie sense, preferring to be at home with his family or working. Miller and others found Bradman a good travelling companion, but he was more at ease with his own company and often sought it on tour. He found solace in music, playing the piano, reading and letter-writing. In many ways, he was a sports professional more in keeping with the twenty-first century than the twentieth. He kept his body in top condition in order to perform at his best.

Miller loved a drink and a bet. He was generous with gifts and money, even when he didn't have it. He was restless for the convivial company of both sexes. Even an oddball stranger could phone Miller and interest him in a good time. Miller would behave spontaneously. Bradman would never accept such an offer. There were so many invitations that he went the other way and could be blunt in turning them down. He never felt the need or urge to be spontaneous. He liked his life ordered. Chances were that there was always something planned each evening.

Miller loved classical music, especially in grand settings at the opera and concert halls. Bradman, a self-taught, proficient piano player, had less highbrow, more catholic tastes in music.

Miller made a virtue of having a good time no matter what the occasion the next day. He was known often to turn up hung-over for a match, but he had a strong constitution. His sodden condition did not appear to ever spoil a performance. His conviviality was a characteristic. There have been few players as popular with both his team-mates and any opposition, at home or abroad.

Their private lives were vastly different. They had both chosen warm, loving life partners. Bradman was a family man and devoted to wife Jessie and their two children. Miller was a 'player', who loved women and womanising. Unsettled by war, and his uneasiness with what 'fame' meant, Miller would never be faithful in the conventional sense. He had chosen and pursued Peg across the world when scores of attractive women in London during the war, or in Melbourne when he returned home, would have settled for the dashing sportsman. It was as if he were driven by what selfish – in the true sense of the word – life he desired in the future for himself. Peg was from a family that was socially above his own. She would bring refinement and strong values to the marriage and tender care to their children. Peg would always represent the right mother image that Miller desired in a wife, in what his psychotherapist niece Jan Beames described as 'the Madonna/whore complex'. Peg was the idealised mother and wife figure. He would play with many other women, who were not 'whores' as such but simply play-objects for fun-loving Miller. He would always return home to the earth mother Peg. In his own way he was committed only to his wife and to whatever family was to come.

Miller had tasted real fame in the summer of 1945, and the adulation and easy access to admiring women, which it, his matinée idol good looks and great charm brought him. In the mid-1940s Keith Miller was compared to that other Australian Lothario, Errol Flynn. Elvis Presley and Marlon Brando would follow in the next decade. Instead of giving up a Peter Pan or playboy existence for married life, Miller would take on both almost on a seasonal basis.

Miller and Bradman, then, were men of two different temperaments and outlooks. They were bound often not to see eye to eye. The minor encounters on the field, Miller's disagreement with Bradman's approach to the 1946–47 series and now the reprimand-that-wasn't rankled with Miller, who had long hated authority, or even posturing that affected authority.

Whitington and Millard, who followed Miller's early playing career (from 1936 to 1946) more closely than any other observers, put this rebellious nature and 'chip on his shoulder' down to his being underdeveloped for so long as a kid. Right through those formative years as 'Weedy', he was bullied and picked on. It wasn't until he left school and joined the workforce that he fully transformed from runt to rugged six-footer who would rarely, if ever, be challenged. Millard also thought setbacks when trying to break into first district, then state cricket added to his being at odds with authority. Miller was a relatively late achiever, and had not cemented his place in the Victorian team in 1940–41 at the age of 21. It wasn't until he was 27 in 1946–47 that he was just about the first player selected in the state team. The war forced him to miss several seasons. Yet he never felt appreciated by state administrators. It was suggested, too, that this was the reason Miller often sided with the underdog. This was all consistent with his reputation on the football field if anyone dared challenged him physically. He had had more than enough of that sort of intimidation when a junior. The aggressors would always receive a response. Sometimes it would be brutal.

Gus Glendinning's experiences as Miller's closest mate over two years of war fitted a pattern. Miller tended to be a hell-raiser and confrontational. He disdained taking orders, or anyone in any capacity standing over him. It provoked reaction whatever the consequences. He was indeed a rebel without a pause until the end of the war when he had 'grown up'. Yet still his incapacity to take orders at times remained. Hence those mixed feeling towards Bradman. He appreciated his skipper both for his greatness as a cricketer and for his importance to the nation in historical terms. But as a character, Bradman was not to his liking. Miller would never be a 'yes' man or keep an opinion to himself. It was in his nature and would not change. This gained respect from many, including those without the courage to be their own men. Miller was not easy to lead, which is a characteristic of rebels and sometimes natural leaders.

IN OLD
SYDNEY TOWN

The move to Sydney left a wake of grudges, threats of recrimination and general ill-feeling in Victoria and Lancashire. Some sensitivity from Miller's forsaken state was understandable, although unfair. He had to live. He had a wife to support. If he wished to play for Australia he had to be employed. There was an angry attitude to him at district club South Melbourne. It was a few weeks from the finals in which it had an opportunity for its first premiership in 30 years. Miller's departure reduced its chances. An apocryphal story developed that Hassett had led South on to the field in a final only to find that Miller was not there. He had, the false tale went, failed to inform the club of his move to Sydney. More accurately, South members believed that Miller's absence from the club was *as bad as if* he had been picked and not turned up to play. The feeling ran deep. Miller would never again feel welcome at the club, which had nurtured, coached and developed him after St Kilda had rejected him.

There was even more hostility from Rawtenstall. It made sure that Miller was forever banned from the Lancashire League. He had dishonoured their contract and would be pursued for compensation.

Miller, meanwhile, began to settle into Sydney. He had felt stifled in Melbourne. The harbourside city, the most beautiful in the world geographically, was very much to his liking. The place seemed more relaxed than his strait-laced, flat home town. Sydney was more curvaceous. Its topography had more appeal. 'More Sophia Loren than Audrey Hepburn' was the way Miller saw it. The climate was better, too, if you preferred to wear fewer clothes. And the fact that the women did, and were less fashion conscious than in Melbourne, meant that more sensual flesh was exposed. This would always appeal to Miller. It gave the town, which only seven generations earlier had begun with convicts and whores, a more licentious air, even if it were myth. That crude start had left its mark, although generations of freedom had refined the Sydney character into something approaching the international sophistication that Melbourne lacked in 1947. There were little cultural advances, too, that he liked. Sydney sidestepped draconian drinking laws that prevented pubs serving alcohol after 6 p.m. by allowing endless liquor supply with meals taken *before* six. If you kept ordering food, the booze could come with it.

Being able to swim nearly all year round on Sydney's close surf beaches was a further attraction. Miller's main physical exercise, apart from golf, cricket and footy, was swimming. It kept his aerobic conditioning high and soothed those many more than niggling injuries within bounds of control. The surf, too, was therapeutic for that chronic back problem.

Miller lacked nothing except for family and friends. Yet he had never had trouble making new acquaintances. He could carry his classical music everywhere. There were racetracks, such as Randwick, which had been a favourite long before the move 800 kilometres north. He could always return to Melbourne for the Cup. That left only footy, and he could play that in Sydney, albeit in a reduced standard of competition. An early move was to notify the Sydney club that he would be a starter in their XVIII. But not before he fulfilled a promise to play for his new employer's cricket club, North Sydney, in a final against Northern Districts on Saturday, 21 March. Miller didn't let anyone down, scoring a dashing 56, and blasting through the opposition with 5 for 56.

There was only one major hitch in this adventurous move to Sin City. Miller was having difficulty with the job. It entailed driving around the grand metropolis selling spirits and liqueurs to bottle-shops and pubs. It was the most sociable of work. Every pub owner and barman in town, it seemed, wanted to have a drink with the legend Keith Miller. The salesman insisted on his wares being sampled. It led to many a hazy afternoon, even the occasion forenoon, imbibing Cointreau and crème de menthe. Female liquor store proprietors favoured Gilbey's Gin. Males seemed to go for the Vat 69 Scotch. Before long Miller was imbibing more than he was selling, and enjoying it less. It was a sea change for a strictly beer man. Peg became unhappy with his perpetual state of intoxication. So did he, especially in the morning. After three weeks it was all too much. He resigned.

The Melbourne *Argus* heard about his departure from his wobbly trek around Sydney's hotels and wondered on 26 April if he might just return south, especially in light of the VFL's failure to clear Miller to play footy in the New South Wales league. But he was determined to stay. He had already been appointed vice-captain of Sydney, he told the paper unconvincingly.

Employment was once again Miller's problem. It was solved by Eric Kennedy, chief executive of Australian Associated Newspapers, who introduced Miller to former Australian cricketer A. G. 'Johnnie' Moyes, a close friend of Bradman. Moyes was just starting a new magazine, *Sporting Life*. Miller became a sports journalist, which suited him. He could write about cricket, as long as his writing did not run contrary to the board's directives. There was also football, racing and golf.

Now that he had a pay packet, he could spend more time at Randwick, and the dog track too, supplementing his income, on a hope, a prayer and, for a while, more than the odd hot tip. It began in the office. Nothing escaped Miller when it came to the horses. He noticed that coded messages were passed to editor

Moyes on days of interstate race meetings. Miller was on good enough terms with his boss. He asked him if there were a connection. Moyes, a fraction coyly, admitted there was a link. Trusting his new charge, he admitted he was receiving more than useful tips from bookies, owners, trainers and jockeys, in exchange for favourable bites of publicity. Miller asked if he could put bets on the tips. Moyes, swearing his new employee to secrecy, agreed. A two-man syndicate was formed. Miller began winning much more often than he had ever experienced before.

Sydney began looking more beautiful every day. Miller received his football clearance and began earning a few extra quid playing for Sydney in the local league. He dominated games when he wished, his performance often depending on the night before. It was no surprise that he made the New South Wales state team to play in the national 'Carnival' at Hobart in June. This gave him the unique double of playing interstate football for two states. Miller played outstanding games against Canberra and Queensland, despite carrying a leg injury. He was given three votes in the Tassie Medal for the Best and Fairest at the Carnival. Good judges said he was one of the event's outstanding players.

In those first few months in Sydney, Miller built a friendship with Neville Cardus, who had been based there since 1939 to avoid what he feared would be a Nazi victory. He had been the *Manchester Guardian*'s music critic from 1926 to 1939. Cardus was also a vivid cricket writer, which meant he had three things in common with Miller, the journalist neophyte. They lived for a time in the same block of flats when Miller first arrived. He would ask the respected professional to comment on pieces he was writing. Cardus would correct Miller's punctuation, which tended to be sloppy or non-existent. The Englishman had a reputation as a perfectionist. He sent his dispatches to English papers and magazines by cable and would put in words such as 'comma' and 'semicolon'. Telegraph companies charged for every word and punctuation, and editors worried about the cost. One of them once sent him a cable saying: 'Please send story we'll fix punctuation.' Cardus responded snappily: 'I'll send punctuation. You fill in words.' That editor would perhaps have appreciated Miller's style of economy more.

Cardus admired Miller's carefree spirit on and off the field. But they talked more music than cricket. An Australian journalist observed them at a party. Miller was whistling a classic piece for the expert to identify. 'That's a Rossini overture, Keith.'

'No, Neville, that's Beethoven's *Eroica*.'

'But Keith, you are whistling up with the violins. That piece comes down with cellos.' Cardus made his point by sawing with an imaginary bow.

They attended Sydney concerts together. Miller borrowed music from Cardus' collection and spent many hours in his flat listening to it. Miller's favourite was the *Emperor* Concerto.

Cardus saw Miller as a welcome antidote to trepidation in batting. He appreciated Bradman's greatness, but disdained his domination of cricket and the legacy it had left England: a team of cautious accumulators so exemplified in the just-finished Ashes series. 'There is about him [Miller] and his cricket the style and flavour of the picaresque,' Cardus said. 'He has swagger – and it is fervently to be hoped that the solemn, humourless, kill-joy atmosphere of contemporary Test matches will never quieten his ardours.'

As well as this roguish impression, he saw Miller as a throwback to another universe of Victor Trumper, Charlie Macartney, Stan McCabe and Wally Hammond in his prime. 'It is a world capable of wonder,' Cardus wrote without mentioning Bradman's name but with him clearly in mind, 'a world unstaled by too much achievement, by too much abnormal skill cultivated by neglect of imagination and relish of risk.'

Cardus had never got over Bradman's force of will in 1934. The night before the Leeds Ashes Test, he had invited Bradman to dinner. The Don declined, saying he had to rest. It was important he made 200 the next day.

'You won't do it, Don,' Cardus said, clearly in need of a dinner companion.

'Why?' Bradman asked.

'You scored a triple century at Leeds in the [corresponding Ashes] 1930 Test. It's against the law of averages to get near that again.'

'I don't believe in the law of averages,' Bradman said matter-of-factly and without bombast. He batted the next day with the Australian score at 3 for 39. His first two scoring strokes split the field with a surgeon's precision and reached the boundary. He proceeded to 304, more or less in this fashion, defying Cardus, England and the law of averages, as only he could do.

It was too much for the English critic. He didn't want either the colossal scoring or the slather and whack of park cricket. Cardus disliked the signal of will and determination that Bradman sent to opposition teams when he took block again at 100, 150, 200, 250 and sometimes 300. Nor did he desire to watch the village idiot who put no brain into his cricket at all. But he did want his flawed cameos, with lofted drives, sixes over long-on and general batting brilliance. Miller and Compton provided hope.

Miller fascinated Cardus. This was in part because their common interests made him accessible and comprehensible. Typical Australian or Sydney types might have been too one-dimensional for his liking. Whereas Miller could mix with them in any pub, the English writer in his long sojourn Down Under would have found little in common with the average bloke beyond a beer and a superficial chat. He was mesmerised when he first observed Miller – without his being aware – in a pub arguing with a fellow drinker he had just met, about the circumstances of a Miller innings. There was a dispute about how many sixes he had hit and where it had been. The man bet Miller he was correct, then suggested they go to a newspaper office to verify the facts. Miller then revealed who he was. Cardus was stunned. He could not think of the same thing happening quite the same way in any other country. Miller's humility and utter lack of pretension and arrogance left an impression on the Englishman.

On a later occasion, a post-party, badly hung-over Miller, wearing a tuxedo, drove the writer to the SCG for a New South Wales game. Miller apologised, telling Cardus he would not see much sparkle from him before lunch. New South Wales won the toss and batted. Miller, who had overdosed on aspirin, came to the wicket to join Arthur Morris before lunch, and struggled. He was still in at lunch, where he overcame his retarded condition with a meal and a cold shower. After lunch Cardus was delighted to report that he played 'wonderfully, all gay and cavalier'.

The capacity to hell-raise all night, then hours later turn on a matchless batting display, or even crash a plane and slash a 50 the next day at Lord's, was the macho stuff of the growing Miller legend. Yet much of it was true. For these and other reasons, Cardus, like many a commentator from England and Australia, idealised Miller. For countless Australian boys, and even men, he was what they all wanted to be. For eloquent observers such as Cardus, and many others to follow, the Miller character was the myth writ large to which they thought the best of the Australians should aspire.

Cardus, for once forsaking his concern for punctuation, particularly the full-stop, wrote of the post-war Miller:

He is a magnificent and typical example of Australian man-hood. Tall, with good loose shoulders, handsome in a sun-tanned, wind-swept way, aquiline of face, long eyelashes, brown hair that is not so much unruly as rhetorical in its falling disarray, long legs firm to the ground and astraddle as he stands in the slips, probably as he does looking straight into the sun and blue sky to identify a plane on the way from Sydney to London – you would swear that he is the incarnation of the spirit of young masculine life in Sydney, as much the product of surf and sea as of turf and willow.

Cardus believed that Miller was a natural Sydney-sider. 'There is evidence of his birth certificate that he was born in or around Melbourne,' he wrote, 'which is Australia more or less on its dignity, with rolled umbrella and top hat. New South Wales and Sydney have assimilated Miller.'

The integration into the new city was just about complete when the Millers moved to a flat in Manly, on Sydney's northern beaches. Even its name seemed right. The surf-side suburb was only a ferry ride away from the city across the harbour with the mighty steel coat-hanger of a bridge in view. The only feature lacking for them was an opera house. It wasn't yet a twinkle in an architect's eye. Manly had a strong cricket club, however, with history to rival South Melbourne's. Miller's residency meant he could abort the short-lived connection with North Sydney and join it. He was settled in for the 1947–48 season, which would feature his initial games for New South Wales and a visit to Australia by an Indian team for the first time. This tour had been brought about by the servicemen touring the subcontinent in 1945. The Australian board felt an obligation to invite the Indians to visit.

The tourists, led by Lala Amarnath and escorted by the popular Duleepsinhji, were missing Vijay Merchant, which did not draw crocodile tears from Miller or Hassett. They had vivid memories of his negativity on the field in India. Yet he would be missed as a batsman, as would Mushtaq Ali and Rusi Modi. Without these three, the Indians had little hope of competing, especially as they would be in unfamiliar territory. The visitors hoped Bradman would play because they thought it an honour and that they would learn from him. This was a big change from Hammond's form of Bradmania, but did not augur well for a competitive series.

Bradman decided to play in the Tests after scoring two early-season centuries – one against India, which brought his first-class tally to 99. He led an Australian XI versus India in mid-November 1947 in Sydney. Miller joined him at the wicket at

2 for 31 after lunch on day two in front of a Saturday afternoon crowd of 32,000 at the SCG. Bradman was in striking, typical form, although he laboured for a while en route to a big innings, for which he had set himself. Miller began to match him but back-pedalled when he realised that the Don was careering towards his hundredth century. He turned over the strike to Bradman near tea, allowing him to reach his milestone in 130 minutes. Miller was first to shake hands with him.

After tea, he let his skipper roll on at twice his rate in a 252-run stand. Both men threw their wickets away, Miller for 86, half Bradman's 172 – his last 72 taking just 47 minutes. This was not an act by Miller to ingratiate himself with the leader. It was an appreciation of the event and what it meant to the crowd. The thoughtful, selfless act gave the day over to the Don.

Australia was set 251 in 150 minutes on the last day. It might have made them but for the left-arm spin of M. H. 'Vinoo' Mankad, who stole the show in more ways than one, taking 8 for 84, which won the game for India by 47 runs. Early in the chase, Bill Brown was backing up more than usual in the search for quick runs. Mankad did the right thing and warned Brown he would lift the bails while coming in to bowl if Brown continued to move out of his crease at the bowler's end. Brown cribbed again. Mankad lifted the bails and himself into cricket's minor league of immortality when he repeated the act against Brown in the Second Test, but without a warning. Any dismissal this way, more common in the backyards of suburban Australia than first-class cricket, was known thereafter as being 'Mankaded'.

Bradman did not let the Indians down, amassing 715 runs in the Tests at a blistering average of 178.75, in Australia's 4–0 thrashing of the visitors. Miller seemed out of sorts in the Tests, with so many one-sided contests and four of the batsmen above him in the order – Bradman, Hassett, Morris and Barnes – all doing well and far better than him. He scraped together 185 at an average of 37.00 with two fifties.

This series, Bradman did not over-bowl him. Miller sent down just 72 overs for 9 wickets at 24.78 each. The reverse was the case in the Shield matches. New South Wales skipper Arthur Morris used him for twice his Test overs – 143.2 in the same number of matches (five). It was not surprising that he took just 15 wickets at 36 apiece. He was further used in three other first-class matches, two against India and for an Australian XI versus Western Australia, where he sent down another 67.3 overs, again as less of a shock bowler. Miller's strength would always come in bursts, not in stock-bowling endurance examinations, which his nearly 211 overs in eight games outside the Tests represented.

Thirteen first-class games of bowling reduced his effectiveness with the blade. His batting figures in Shield cricket were saved by a last New South Wales game for the season at the SCG against newcomers to the competition, Western Australia, led by Keith Carmody. Miller hammered 170 in 181 with 3 sixes, in an exhilarating display of power hitting. His fans, particularly on the Sydney Hill, where big things were expected of him, had missed this kind of effort. The match boosted his average for the season from 31 to a respectable 49, but could not hide the let-down in his overall season performance. The most telling statistic of all was his placement at number 10 in the 1947–48 season's first-class batting averages with 46.52. This was a far cry from his dream and expectation to rival even Bradman for the world's number one spot.

The heaviest season of bowling in his career had taken a serious toll on Miller's batting capacities, and perhaps even his aspirations. At the end of a not-so-memorable season, he was conflicted by the thought that he would be soon on a boat back to the birthplace of his heroism and international superstardom. The 1948 Ashes tour of England beckoned. There was just one regret. Peg had given birth to their first child, William, soon after the Fifth Test against India. He was named after Miller's mate, William (Bill) Young, who went missing on a training run over France in 1944.

Miller would have liked more time with his extended family. His sister 'Snow' was there to support Peg, who then decided to return to Boston to be with the Wagner family while her husband was on tour until much later in the year. The Millers had been used to being separated since first meeting in early 1943. First it was war, now it was sport that kept them apart. Peg faced life as a cricketing widow. But she had come to terms with her position. She ignored Miller's philandering, which was non-existent or inconspicuous in Sydney. Despite everything, there was a strong bond between them. On top of that, she was determined, if she could, to stay in the marriage in Australia because she did not wish to return permanently to Boston and her mother.

ON THE ROAD TO IMMORTALITY: 1948

Miller was thrilled to be back. Arriving at Southampton on SS *Strathaird* early in April 1948, he was looking forward to seeing old friends from the RAF, girlfriends, mates in high places, parties, races whenever he could make it, Wimbledon and even Paris. And in between, here and there, he would play a lot of cricket. The prospect enticed him less than it did in 1945. He would be asked to bowl more. Miller, in tandem with Lindwall, would be vital to Australia's success as planned with military precision by Bradman. They would have the front-line duty of stopping England's key batsman Len Hutton. All other players in the squad were happy to have direction in broad strategy and match-by-match tactics from their leader. Miller was the odd man out.

Bradman's not-so-secret aim was that his squad would go through the scheduled 34 games undefeated. His men would play bright, sometimes brilliant cricket at every chance. Miller agreed with the attacking play, but didn't care much for winning every game. He would prefer a close contest in which the winner was not preordained; in which Australia lost a few in the interests of entertainment. Most annoying of all for him was the knowledge that he would be just a cog in the Bradman machine driving forward with a growing sense of invincibility. Whereas Miller would love to bat at four, and not bowl at all, he would have to bat four or five and open the bowling. From Miller's perspective this would restrict his batting. Bradman's view was to use the players he had in the best possible combination that would win a five-match Test series. He also had two very good left-armers in Bill Johnston and Toshack, who could also partner Lindwall or open the bowling together in their own right. Yet his first choice was the Lindwall–Miller team. They would put fear into all the opposition batsmen. They were most likely to break through England's strong line-up.

There was another technical factor, which was probably the most important of all in terms of deciding Miller's fate as a bowler and a batsman. A rule had been brought in to make the new ball available after 55 overs. It played right into the hands of the side with the best fast attack. In theory, Bradman could rotate his other quicks and ignore Miller. But it was never really a consideration. No one could seriously imagine opening with Lindwall and Toshack, or Johnston, and leaving Miller to wallow in slips while England's openers were allowed to settle in. If England didn't lose a wicket, would Miller still be left languishing in the field? Not likely. Coming on as third, fourth or even fifth change would see him used more as a stock bowler, which would be even less to Miller's liking.

These options in the end were simply theory. Bradman had never failed to see the value of one of the greatest speed combinations in history opening his attack. Bradman, too, in his logical way, knew that Miller was of more use to him as a bowler than a batsman. There was a surfeit of Australian quality in the top order with Brown, Barnes, Morris, Bradman, Hassett, and Harvey all vying with Miller for five spots. He didn't need Miller with the blade, but he wanted him with the ball.

Miller had brought his little black book and called friends from 1945. One of them was the pretty Christine from Putney. Miller was shocked to learn she was in a psychiatric ward suffering from a form of schizophrenia. He visited her there.

Then the tour began in earnest and with promise. Miller didn't open the bowling in the wet and wintry conditions in the traditional opening against Worcester under the 1,300-year-old cathedral, yet he did send down 20 overs in two innings. He came in at number nine on day three, 30 April, and belted 50 not out, including 5 fours and 3 sixes, one of which sent watchers scattering from a huge red-and-white-striped marquee. It proved a nice warm-up for the next day, when Bradman put him in when the first wicket fell against Leicester.

Hundreds of spectators hurried across to the pavilion. Cameras were prepared to capture Bradman. 'Everybody wanted to see the Don,' Miller said in his autobiography. 'They had come from everywhere to watch him. The crowd went crazy trying to get the first glimpse of Bradman walking down the race. You should have heard the hoots and groans when Muggins Miller walked out. Blimey! Do you reckon I was the most unpopular man in the land? I forced my way through the crowd, saying Bradman would be out in a minute . . .'

Miller was in a different mood from the day before. Batting at three, especially after not bowling in the game, he was spirited and determined. He partnered Barnes for 111, then Bradman came to the wicket to sustained applause. He was the Australian who had captured the public's imagination all over the country in 1930, 1934 and 1938, and they were willing him to do it again. He pleased the crowd with 81 runs before, according to Miller, 'getting a bum [caught behind] decision' after a 159 partnership. Miller went on for 325 minutes and reached 202 not out. One of his sixes hit a 16-year-old youth on the head. The groggy lad was taken to a local hospital but released after observation. It was a wonder that Miller's big hitting had not done more damage over the years.

Despite being missed three times, his innings was a fine, telling performance so early in a tour. A first-game double hundred had been the Bradman trademark. Now it was Miller who had stamped his authority in the second game. Much to his pleasure he was not asked to bowl when tired in Leicester's first innings.

That kept Miller's mercurial mood strong for the next day, the first of the important game against Yorkshire, always a tough contest for the tourists. Bradman returned to the bunker in the team's London hotel and let Hassett captain the side at a dank Bradford with its uninspiring backdrop of brickworks. He won the toss and sent the home side in on a wet wicket unfit for cricket. Miller was eager to get the ball, recalling his success in Brisbane in the First Test of the 1946–47 series. He delivered his medium-paced off-breaks and was again effective. Hutton laboured hard for 5 before Miller had him caught by Harvey. He took 6 for 42 off 23.3 overs. Proud Yorkshire tumbled for 71.

No less proud Australia was bundled out for 101. It was able to pass the county because of Miller's batting. He straight-drove the first ball he received. It rattled the metal sightscreen, signalling that, instead of letting bowlers dictate, he would hoe into them. He hit 2 sixes and 2 fours in his 34 – the highest score of the match. It was equivalent to a dashing hundred in normal conditions. Yorkshire collapsed again for 89, Miller taking 3 for 49 off 16 overs. Bill Johnston took 6 for 18, giving him 10 wickets for the match. Australia lost 6 for 31, which was really 7 down since injured Sam Loxton could not bat. Young Neil Harvey, 19 years old, was dropped early but from thereon batted with aplomb, scoring 18 not out and bringing Australia a four-wicket win with a towering straight drive for six.

It was Miller's kind of game. He batted with belligerence in a crisis, bowled with venom, and fought always to win. Yet he could not care less whether Australia won or lost. The result of a beer after the game with mates was the one he was after. Not so Bradman back in his hotel room sorting out his 600 letters a day. He kept in touch with Hassett by phone every half-hour and was relieved at the win. His dream of going through the season undefeated had had its first challenge.

Miller missed the next game against Surrey and returned to do his bit to help Bradman's reverie come true by taking seven wickets against Cambridge University. The game was on Fenner's Field with its velvet-like alternate light and dark green strips. Students and fans watched the game near chestnut trees and a marquee on one boundary, and beech trees on another. It was a pretty sight, but not so 21-year-old John Dewes, the left-hander, who had been terrorised by Miller during the Victory Tests. He looked portly and misshapen wearing a thick towel under his shirt. The former Portsmouth naval cadet turned student was willing to sacrifice aesthetic appeal for protection. This was a red rag to Miller the bull. He delivered Dewes a short one that had him ducking, then bowled him with a yorker that had him propping at the crease.

The contest began, as usual, the day after the previous match. The rigours of such a tour forced Bradman to rotate his team as best he could without weakening it too much against the stronger counties. The tourists were formidable, scoring massively and dismissing oppositions for low totals. Crowds were turning up to see the massacres and enjoying them. The Australians were entertaining. The sixth game began on Saturday, 15 May at Southend versus Essex. There was a carnival atmosphere with the early celebrations of the Whitsuntide holiday as the Australians were on their way to compiling another big score. Brown and Bradman put on 219 runs in just 90 minutes. It was wholesale slaughter. Everyone at the packed ground – except for the county players – appreciated and enjoyed the mid-May show. Then medium-pacer Trevor Bailey, on a secret trial for a Test spot after scoring 66 not out for Cambridge against the Australians, removed Brown. Expectations were high. The conditions were now festive.

Big-hitting would be Miller's opportunity when he was due at the wicket with the score at 2 for 364. He had been having a siesta an hour after lunch, and didn't really want to bat when woken. But he had to. He smoothed back his mane and put on his cap. He took block. Trevor Bailey couldn't believe it when Miller seemed to let a straight one hit his wicket. Miller turned to the keeper, said, 'Thank God that's over', and walked off.

Bradman said to Bailey, 'He'll learn.'

'He just surrendered his wicket,' Bailey remarked afterwards. Lindwall and other Australians in the dressing room thought that Miller must have lost sight of the ball. It was not unusual for a batsman who had been waiting for a long time to bat to be unsighted. But whatever happened, Bailey was pleased. He had two good wickets – Brown and Miller – in two balls that boosted his figures.

Miller's explanation for his first-ball duck was that he had been making a protest. He had let the ball hit the wicket. Bradman, he said, could have used batsmen like Brown and Ron Hamence in such games 'to build their form and confidence'. But in that game, Brown was the man out before him for 153, following a double century against the students a few days earlier. Hamence batted after Miller's duck and made 46. He had made 92 against Cambridge. (Brown would play in 22 games for the season, the same number as Miller, and have as many chances – 26 – to bat. Hamence would play in 19 and get 22 knocks.) Miller maintained, however, that he preferred a fight or no involvement at all. This game in front of a packed house on a sunny day was no contest. He had, he claimed, deliberately missed the ball.

The festive seaside crowd had no such quarrel with the tourists. It was seeing fireworks as never before in this history-making team effort. The other Australians had a different attitude from Miller, especially Bradman (top score with 187 in just over two hours with 32 fours), Barnes (79), Sam Loxton (120) and Ron Saggers (104). Australia went on to 721 (including 87 boundaries), the highest first-class score ever recorded in one day. Miller's effort with the ball the next day gave no hint of slackening off to continue the alleged protest. He bowled with fire and competitive intent in Essex's first innings, taking 3 for 14 off 8 overs. Australia won its sixth successive match in just 19 days.

Bradman left himself and Miller out of the next fixture, against Oxford University. The captain brought Miller back for the following game, versus the MCC at Lord's. This was a near full-dress rehearsal for the Tests, and one of the most prestigious matches of the summer. It was the game that Miller had looked forward to since the tourists' ship docked, being a welcome return to his sporting 'home' after nearly three years absence. The Lord's spectators gave him a strong reception, second only to Bradman. Many of them had Miller's 1945 performances fresh in their minds.

This time, when he came to the wicket with Hassett after waiting for another long partnership (160 between Bradman 98 and Barnes 81), he took block. He marked the crease with his boot, making a rough reverse 'V'. There would be no show of indifference today. Miller's first 50 took 85 minutes; his second 80 minutes. Another century at Lord's took away all the irritation of being classed as an all-rounder, for the moment at least. He went on to 163 before having a go at off-spinner Jim Laker and being caught. The innings consisted of 250 minutes of high-class batting, with driving all round the wicket and strong lofts to leg. He hit 20 fours and 3 sixes, one of which, Cardus observed, was 'one great blow square from the shoulders to the upper and non-alcoholic regions of the Tavern'. It was just like old times for Miller and the fans. It rekindled the bond he had felt with all at Lord's in three seasons from 1943 to 1945. The only difference from those years was the composition of the crowd. Miller missed the sea of blue RAAF uniforms supporting him. Yet the fans today were behind him, while being less boisterous, in keeping with the no-nonsense traditions of the ground.

It was a great day for the South Melbourne club. Apart from its deserting star, Hassett managed 51 and Johnson, in partnership with Miller, a hard-hitting 80. Australia climbed again to an orbital score of 552. The talented Jim Laker had been a main target. He went for 10 sixes in all, which would be a character test and stretch the selectors' faith. Yet he plugged away with a tenacity that suggested he would survive and prosper, taking 3 for 127.

The season's stakes were higher now. Miller, who had gained an ascendancy against Hutton at Yorkshire on a bowler-friendly pitch, tore in at the MCC captain, as did Lindwall. Hutton used his considerable technique to keep the pace in check. But the others were not up to it. Miller dismissed his two other old foes from the Victory Tests, Edrich and Robertson. Lindwall and Toshack (6 for 51) supported him and reduced MCC to 189 all out and following on. Hutton's efforts (52 and 64) were not enough. A second-innings score of 205 could not avoid the seventh innings defeat of an opposition on the tour and the eighth successive Australian win.

Miller's removal of Robertson for a duck put paid to the plucky, dignified Middlesex opener's chances of opening for England in the Ashes. He was casualty number one, but not the main target. Hutton's guts and skills saw him on better than even terms with his adversaries. But he was concerned with the pace of Lindwall and Miller. If anything, they were quicker than in 1946–47. Lindwall was always a problem, but Hutton found Miller the greater threat. He could do alarming, unpredictable things. Lindwall was dubbed 'Killer'. But the word in Hutton's mind rhymed with Miller, although he would never let anyone know it, not even his closest Yorkshire pals. Hutton would disclose that emotion of concern only after he had retired. It would have done him no good at all to give Miller an inch of a psychological advantage. Hutton's granite face would remain stubbornly shut off from hints of feelings, or any communication at all with Australia's pace demons, on or off the field. Lugubrious Lindwall couldn't care less. Gregarious Miller would have loved to make contact. When it was not forthcoming, it pushed him to bowl with even greater intensity at the England champion.

Miller's high profile brought a variety of responses. Not so palatable was Rawtenstall's pursuit of him over his breach of contract. The club had solicitors' letters delivered to the team hotel. In the Long Room during the MCC game Miller told Plum

Warner about his problem. 'I wouldn't worry too much about that, Keith,' Warner said, waving his hand at the members sitting in front of the pavilion. 'We have judges, KCs and solicitors sitting out there. Which do you prefer?'

'A good solicitor might be handy,' Miller replied.

'We have no bad ones,' Warner said with a smile. 'Let me see what I can do.'

With the exception of one or two others, Warner and cricket headquarters would avoid such a dispute and tell the cricketer concerned to look after his own problems. But Miller was Miller, and this was a classic case of the maxim *it's not what you know, but who you know.* Warner talked to MCC secretary Rait Kerr, who went out of his way to help, suggesting a solicitor, who did not charge for his advice. This was to make Rawtenstall a one-time offer of £50 to settle the matter. The club accepted it.

The settlement put Miller in a good frame of mind at the end of the MCC match. As usual, he was taking his time in the dressing room and was the last in there when a well-dressed gentleman approached him.

'Mr Miller?'

'Yes?' he replied, while still looking in the mirror, combing his hair.

The man said something he didn't quite hear. Miller only absorbed: 'Margaret would like you to join her at the Embassy Club.'

'Margaret who?' Miller asked, still brushing.

'*Princess* Margaret.'

Miller stopped brushing. He eyed the man, assessing his unwritten royal credentials.

'I'm the Princess's equerry.'

'Really? What club was that again?'

'The Embassy in Bond Street, at 8 p.m. tonight.'

Miller thanked the equerry and said he would be there.

That night at the team hotel, Miller, dressed in a sports jacket and louche cravat, was about to catch a taxi when he bumped into Bradman, in a dinner suit. 'Where are you off to, Braddles?'

'Dinner at Buckingham Palace. And where are you headed, Nugget?'

'Well,' Miller began a trifle coyly, 'Princess Margaret has asked me out.' Miller glanced at his watch. 'And I'm late!'

'Good to know you don't make an exception with royalty, Nugget,' the Don said with a grin.

Miller met the Princess at the Embassy Club and was introduced to some of her aristocratic and social 'set'. They got on well. She was a very attractive, petite and big-eyed teenager, with an hourglass figure. Margaret was in her prime. As the second daughter of King George VI, she had enough royal duties to justify her support from the public purse and was a popular royal. The most photogenic of women was the darling of Fleet Street. She represented limited but good copy with lots of photo opportunities. It was an age when having a good time, simply because she could afford to, was not considered offensive to a public content to pay for her indulgent largesse, as long as it remained discreet.

Margaret was often surrounded by a bevy of eligible – and a few ineligible – young men. Miller, 28, equally photogenic and in the newspapers and magazines as frequently as she was, was invited to join her set. He had even been given the highest stamp of approval by *Debrett's Peerage*, which named his strokeplay as 'one out of Debrett'. He, like her, accompanied the most attractive partners of the opposite sex because he could.

Margaret felt an affinity with Hollywood and its stars, who were fun, famous and fatuous. Miller had all that, with substance when required as well. He was already being dubbed 'sport's Errol Flynn' after the Tasmanian actor who had made it in Hollywood in the 1940s on the strength of his good looks, mellifluous voice and other tangible assets. She was known to be attracted to certain men in uniform, or those who had been. Margaret had been smitten since she was 14 with an unattainable man, Group Captain Peter

Townsend, a handsome Battle of Britain fighter pilot, who was equerry to her father. Townsend was married and not of royal 'stock', which was regarded then as undesirable. In-breeding was still more fashionable than out-breeding. Yet Margaret's fecundity, for the moment, was not on her mind. Townsend was side-lined and she was having a good time. Miller, also married, a 'commoner' and a former war pilot, was now part of it.

He was able to sleep in the next morning and miss the train to Manchester for the game against Lancashire, the first draw for the tourists. He was active again against Nottingham, scoring a breezy 51 and keeping in touch at the bowling crease with a wicket in each innings, while Lindwall in the first innings and the spinners in the second scythed through the opposition, which scrambled to the second successive draw. At the tree-bound, pretty Southampton ground against Hampshire, Miller lifted for the fight he had missed at Southend when, in response to the county's 195, Australia stumbled once more on a damp surface and without Bradman's leadership.

Hassett seemed to be having the worst of the weather when Bradman let him take the reins, and Miller seemed always the man to pull Australia back into the game. This time he took on Hampshire's most damaging bowler, C. J. Knott, and almost ruined his excellent figures (5 for 57) by hoisting him high out of the ground for 3 successive sixes. At one point Australia was 8 for 63. Miller's top score of 39 helped Australia to a modest 117.

It was the second time that a spanking 30-odd from him had saved the tourists. Miller's attitude was unusual for a top-line batsman. In a way, he had a park bowler's mentality to run-scoring. There was little concern for topping the aggregates or averages. Most leading batsmen would take the opportunity to make a useful not out score when a game was heading for a draw. It was human nature and acceptable to put runs in the bank for a rainy day and a wet pitch such as Bradford or in this game against Hampshire. But Miller had a sort of couldn't-care-less sporting nobility about him that was above normal desires for run acquisition for its sake, or maintaining an average. The 77-run deficit in Hampshire would magnify if Australia could not restrict the county. Miller, loving the challenge, did better than hold them. He took 5 for 25 and, with Johnston's dynamic support (5 for 43 after 6 for 74 in the first innings), spiflicated the opposition for just 103. Australia mopped up the 182 runs required with eight wickets to spare, thanks in large measure to Miller's all-round genius in a contest.

He was rested again from the next match at Hove against Sussex, in which Lindwall (11 for 59), Morris (184), Bradman (109) and Harvey (100 not out) all ran into top form. This enabled Miller and Ron Saggers, Australia's reserve keeper to Don Tallon, to visit Paris for a few days. They took a taxi to Vincennes for a trotting meeting. When they arrived the taxi driver, a brave or foolish man, seemed to be charging them an 'exorbitant' fare. Miller refused to pay it. The driver gesticulated wildly. Miller called over a gendarme. A bit of pidgin French flew around as Miller and Saggers complained. The gendarme looked at the *English* foreigners in smart suits, then the fare. He judged the visitors' grievance was correct. The gendarme told off the taxi driver and sent him away – without any fare.

When they arrived at the course a tout pestered them and gave them a tip. Miller was just cooling down after the near-altercation with the taxi driver. He had experienced 'urgers' on courses in several countries, which made him dismissive of the tout. He told Saggers to have a look at the horses in the race and the tout's recommendation while he bet on something else. He returned to Saggers. 'How are they travelling?' Miller asked.

'They're just trotting around for the start.'

Miller looked through binoculars. 'No, they're not!' he said. 'They're racing!'

The tout's tip won.

Miller had the gambler's disease of the 'if onlys'. If only he had taken the tout's tip when experience at race meets from Caulfield to Colombo had taught him to ignore them. If only that taxi driver hadn't made the two visitors suspicious of strangers' intentions . . . Like all gamblers, he believed that with a little wriggle of fortune here and a squeeze there, he could win much more often. 'Miller's Luck' would bring him consistent wins and money. The problem was that once he found pots at the end of the rainbow, he would always go in search of more. Yet the uncertainty of the bet was one more thing that gave Miller a thrill. He needed life's little rushes to make him feel alive. The pump or the let-down could make or break his mood, which would be fuelled, either way, with a drink or three.

On return to London, Miller was invited for more partying with Princess Margaret, again at the Embassy Club and later at Kensington Palace. Miller later somehow acquired the Princess's own royal standard, a flag she had been given by the King, along with her own coat-of-arms, on her eighteenth birthday. The standard had been prepared by the Royal College of Arms. It was composed of her coat-of-arms without the supporters and coronet.

Lindsay Hassett and Ian Johnson spotted it in Miller's hotel room. When Miller would not say how it happened to be in his possession, Hassett remarked: 'Seems you have raised your standard in more ways than one.'

Did the Princess give it to Miller for services rendered, which he would later tell friends and family, or did he haul it down from a flagpole in a convivial moment at the palace? Whatever way it was obtained, it did not travel with Miller for long but was shipped to his parents' house in Melbourne. He and Peg had vacated their Manly flat and would be looking for a new place at Dee Why when she returned from the US and he returned from the tour of England. The flag's storage in Melbourne would avoid embarrassing questions about how such an item could fall into Miller's possession.

Any disgruntlement he might have felt about opening the bowling on the first day of the First Test at Trent Bridge would have been partially appeased by his spearing through Hutton to clean bowl him for 3. The bowler had been assisted by a downpour pre-lunch, which caused the ball to skid through. Miller triggered England's resignation by also bowling Compton for 19. He ended with 3 for 38 and took a brilliant catch. Lindwall broke down with a groin injury. Bill Johnston, who had such a low profile he could have been called Bradman's secret weapon, stepped in and did the rest, taking 5 for 36. England reached a disappointing 165. Miller, who liked batting to Jim Laker, was caught off him for a duck, but Australia's powerful batting line-up could afford the usual two or three failures. It still reached 509 (Bradman 138, Hassett 137).

Combative Miller was at it again in England's second innings, this time bumping Washbrook in his second over. The batsman tried a hook and was caught behind for 1. Hutton recovered England's position in a partnership with Compton, reaching 50 with two successive fours off Miller, who was trying his off-spinners. The one over cost him 14 runs. The bowler was riled and unforgiving in the next over. He gesticulated to the fielders, then bent forward, head down like a charging bull, and gathered momentum for a certain bouncer. The Notts crowd reacted with catcalls and booing. Nottingham had been the county of Bodyline's great disciples, Larwood and Voce. They had long memories of how Larwood had been drummed out of the game for its use, and Voce had been reprimanded and stripped of the weapon. The Notts supporters, not surprisingly, were hostile.

Miller, the former crowd pleaser, turned crowd tormentor and let go five bumpers in his last eight balls. His third-last ball cannoned into Hutton's shoulder. The Yorkshireman was in pain. Miller, throwing back his hair, steamed in again. Hutton defended. He leg-glanced a four to end the day. Miller, tired after carrying the bowling with Johnston, was last player off the field.

He could have been back at the MCG after flattening Percy Beames as the Notts members vented their feelings at him. He slung his pullover over his shoulder and straggled off, unfazed by the angry noise about him. Although Miller had not been there in 1934, this was the way the members reacted after Woodfull had objected to Voce's bumpers. This was nothing to football crowds in Melbourne, where umbrellas were crunched on players' heads by elderly women and intoxicated young men hurled abuse, as footballers moved down races to the sanctuary of dressing rooms under pavilions.

If he wasn't concerned, the Notts secretary, Captain H. A. Brown, was. On Monday morning he deplored the barracking of Miller on Saturday and appealed to the crowd to leave the conduct of the game to the umpires.

> Let us keep Nottingham a place where Test matches can continue to be played [he said]. On Saturday the Australian, Miller, was booed and there was much subsequent publicity in the press. These Australians are great sportsmen. They stood by the Empire in the war and we should be pleased to greet them. Let us show them how really pleased we are and give them a warm-hearted greeting this morning.

The plea worked. The Australians were applauded when they came on to the field. But the undercurrent of attitude remained. Miller was the 'bad boy'. The crowd would give him plenty of abuse and curt advice at every opportunity. It worked against England's interests. Miller was determined now to win this for his country. After thunderstorm interruptions, he again bowled Hutton, this time for 74. After Hutton had looked solid in the MCC match, he now seemed vulnerable to Miller's cold fire. It was the prize wicket but for Compton, who was batting with courage, defiance and beauty.

At one point, Miller was bowling steadily to Evans, who was

patting the ball back. After four balls, Miller let go a sizzling short ball, which caught the batsman by surprise and nearly knocked his cap off.

'What the hell are you doing?' a shocked Evans called down the wicket.

'Sorry, old boy,' Miller responded. 'Things were getting a bit dull. Had to liven it up a bit.'

At the end of the fourth day, Evans was 10 not out and Compton 154 not out. England was one run ahead with four wickets in hand. These two carried on stubbornly the next morning before Miller let go a surprise, thunderous bumper – keeper Tallon said it was the fastest all tour – at his good mate. Compton, on 184, shaped to hook, changed his mind and turned his head. His evasive action caused him to overbalance and fall on his wicket. Compton stood up, dusted himself off and called, 'You bastard!' to Miller. The bowler threw his head back and laughed.

It was a sad end to a brave performance. His innings of 10 minutes less than 7 hours gave England hope. It climbed to 441, about a hundred short of pushing Australia.

The players trudged off the field. Members forming a human lane pressed towards Miller, who was again bringing up the rear. More angry comments and abuse came his way. One spectator threatened to do Miller bodily harm. It was a gesture too far. The Australian grabbed him by the coat collar and turned him towards the dressing room door. 'Are you coming with me?' Miller asked.

The spectator went white, fearing what might happen to him in the tourists' inner sanctum. Miller released the man, grinning (or was it a grimace?) at him. The jellied spectator disappeared into the crowd, chastened by the experience.

The tourists polished off the 98 with eight wickets to spare.

If Player-of-the-Match had been awarded it would have been line ball between Miller (7 for 163) and Johnston (9 for 183). Miller might have just pipped the lanky Victorian for dismissing

Hutton and Compton in both innings and taking two terrific catches. Once more Miller had his adrenalin flowing, just as he had over the German-held island of Sylt. He had taken on the role of Bradman's top jousting knight even if he had been reluctant about it. Miller sent down 44 overs in England's second innings, which was by far the most exhaustive bowling effort of his career to that point.

He would dearly have loved a dashing century with the bat to his name rather than a duck in his first Test on England's soil. But with Lindwall injured, Miller wanted the ball for combat with the opposition's best, not to mention the Notts crowd. He couldn't help himself. Cardus called Miller an Australian *in excelsis*. At Trent Bridge in mid-June 1948, he was Miller *in excelsis*.

***

Bradman wanted to preserve Miller for the Lord's Test after his long bowling spell at Trent Bridge. The all-rounder was rested for the Northampton game but came back for the drawn second match against Yorkshire, to keep the pressure on Hutton. Miller's presence would unsettle the England batsman, even if Lindwall's groin prevented him from adding to the opener's torment.

Miller's bowling duties would be limited, so Bradman let him open the batting. He failed with 19 in the first innings, but scored an excellent 113 in the second. At the same time he made a point: if he didn't have to bowl and tire himself out, he could perform fine deeds with the bat. But the pattern for the summer had been set and confirmed with his outstanding effort with the ball in the First Test. Miller would be called on to open the bowling for Australia when fit.

He did so against Hutton in Yorkshire's first innings, sending down six overs and conceding only 4 runs before being replaced by Toshack, who took 7 for 81. Perhaps the relief of seeing Miller off caused Hutton's downfall. He fell to Toshack for 39. In Yorkshire's second innings, Bradman did not ask Miller, whose back was playing up, or Toshack, who had leg soreness, to bowl. It was the moment for Hutton to gain some confidence. But Ron Hamence, just a net trundler, bowled him for 10. Hutton was jaded.

Fans began queuing the night before the Lord's Test. The next morning – 24 June – there was an expectant atmosphere as long lines of hopefuls snaked into St John's Wood Road. Not long after Bradman put Lindwall through a morning test in the nets, which the canny sportsman passed, the gates around the ground were shut. Many more people were in the streets around the ground than inside. The lure of an Ashes Test, and Bradman's last appearance in one at Lord's, assured a full house, even on a Thursday. Spectators were allowed to spill on to the ground behind a white line in front of the pavilion. This added to the appearance of a reduction in the size of the arena, especially on the Tavern side, where there was a short boundary.

Before the toss, Miller told Bradman that he would be unfit to bowl, which was useful information if the Australian skipper wished to send England in under grey skies. He won the toss and decided to bat, which pleased Miller. His main energy could go into his batting.

Morris was caught late in the second session after a glorious 105. The score was 3 for 166. Miller was sitting on the balcony to the dressing room on the first floor. He uncoiled himself from a chair, and began the walk that he loved so much, down the stairs to the Long Room. Members, sitting on high stools at the back and low stools at the front, turned their heads. There were a few calls of 'Good luck, Keith', even 'Good luck, Dusty' from an Australian in the Lord's members' nest, who must have known Miller in his RAF days. A sprinkling of applause for him fused with clapping for Morris as Miller made his way along the linoleum, through the pavilion door and down the steps to the little gate that led to the ground.

There was strong applause. Perhaps the moment got to him. Miller was often a nervous, tentative starter. He was lunging at balls that he would, if in touch, jump to or go on to the back foot to clip away. Another tell-tale sign of uncertainty was his back leg dragging across the crease as a second line of defence. He also over-balanced and had to stop himself from sprawling on the pitch by using the bat as a prop. Bedser was alerted. He probed Miller on 4 with three away-swingers, then an in-swinger. Miller didn't play at it and was trapped lbw. He trudged back, swinging his bat carelessly, and had to traverse the Long Room's linoleum in silence through the members, who, in a morbid tradition, ignored the failed batsman. Only a throaty 'Bad luck, Dusty mate' from that loyal Australian supporter penetrated the gloom.

Australia was 7 for 258 at stumps, which made it very much England's day. Dashing Don Tallon (53) waggled the score up to 350 the next morning.

Lindwall opened the bowling and felt a nasty twinge in his groin. Bradman noticed but did not let on. He knew that ex-rugby star Lindwall could carry an injury. The bowler finished his over. Bradman moved towards Miller and tossed the ball to him in the unsaid hope that he might follow Lindwall's lead. But Miller knew his dodgy back. It had been playing up ever since his stint at Trent Bridge. He could not deliver. He tossed the ball back, with a little gesture to say he was not up to it. It was a simple non-event. But the press, looking for any headline, turned it into an 'incident'. Miller had defied Bradman. It was big news.

The game continued. Lindwall stepped up and mesmerised England with his pace, removing half the side for 70 runs. Johnston and Johnson (who bowled Hutton for 20) supported him in keeping England down to 215. Miller could not be kept out of the game. He took two thrilling catches in slips.

This put him in good spirits waiting to bat in Australia's second innings on Saturday afternoon, day three, in front of another packed crowd. At 2 for 296, Barnes was dismissed after a strong, bit-hitting 141. Miller was padded up and would follow Hassett, who had been watching Australia's John Bromwich play at Wimbledon on the TV set in the dressing room.

England captain Norman Yardley caused Hassett to play on for a first-ball duck. Two wickets in a row, and Miller striding to the crease. The Lord's crowd, who had been watching Barnes in destructive mode, and Bradman moving steadily towards a century, was alive. Yardley rapped Miller on the pads. The bowler, the keeper and every English supporter went up for lbw. The umpire said, 'Not out.' Miller shook his head and gestured humorously to the crowd, who laughed at their own impetuous appealing.

Up in the dressing room, Hassett resumed his seat in front of the TV. 'Well,' he said, 'at least I didn't miss any of the tennis.'

Miller was just the player to keep everyone engaged. He heaved a mighty six into the grandstand. Bradman, on 89, nicked a catch to Edrich off Bedser, who had now snared him four successive times in Tests. Bradman marched off the Lord's ground for the last time in a Test to a standing, cheering ovation.

Australia resumed on Monday morning, with Miller powering on. At one point, Edrich threatened to throw his wicket down after picking up the ball on the follow through. Miller put up his hand like a traffic cop. Edrich held on to the ball and grinned. Miller went on to 74 before Laker had him caught. Bradman closed at 7 for 460, with Australia 595 ahead.

Hutton's relief at not facing Miller was short-lived. He looked out of sorts. Lindwall in slips dropped him on 0 off Johnston. Lindwall rolled in with that smoothest of run-ups and made up for his error by having Hutton caught for just 13.

Miller still couldn't bowl, yet he was in the game, taking another great catch. This time Compton went for his favourite shot: the square cut. Miller dived at first slip, got a hand to it and, as he fell back, grabbed it. Catches win matches, the cliché goes, and this one was special. Miller knew it. He drop-kicked the ball to Tallon in delight. Compton must have wondered how he could avoid Miller. If he wasn't at him with the ball, he was catching him.

England crumbled for 186 and was beaten by 409 runs. Australia now had a strong grip on the Ashes.

Miller, wearing a tuxedo, went to a concert on the last night of the Test's final day, 29 June, and a party afterwards. He did not straggle into the hotel until breakfast time. He bumped into Bradman coming out of his room. Miller thought he might have been in trouble because Bradman said, 'Good morning, Keith,' whereas he usually called him by the more matey 'Nugget'.

Miller was in the side for the Surrey match at the Oval that day. Bradman won the toss and put the county in. He placed Miller at fine leg and opened the bowling with Loxton and Toshack. At the end of each over, Miller had to trudge from fine leg at one end to fine leg at the other. Miller chatted to spectators, who were amused by his plight, which was Bradman's minor punishment for disobeying his only rule for the players of turning up in a fit state to play whenever selected.

'I can lend you my bike,' one spectator close to the boundary said.

'That's a good idea,' Miller replied.

A few minutes later, the bike was handed over the fence to Miller at the end of an over. He cycled to the opposite fine leg position, much to the amusement of the crowd and the cricketers. Bradman could not help laughing, and soon after brought Miller to a position closer to the wicket.

He was not up to bowling, and Bradman spared him but for one over. Miller scored just 9 in the ten-wicket thrashing of the county. It was the beginning of a lean first three weeks in July for Miller, who seemed more interested in partying, the major race events and concerts at Albert Hall than the cricket. Morris with 290 at Bristol against Gloucester commencing 3 July overshadowed Miller (51) and everyone else (including Loxton, who smashed a six-laden 159) in the most masterly performance of the entire summer.

Miller's impact in the psychological stakes played a major part in the England selectors' dumping Hutton, which, to many observers, including the Australians, seemed premature and wrong. In essence, Bradman's broad plan of using his speed attack to pressure the number one opposition bat had worked.

During a long rain delay in the Third Test at Manchester in England's first innings, Miller went to the England dressing room for a game of poker with Edrich, Evans and Compton. A large pot built up after an hour. Hassett stuck his head in the door and said: 'C'mon, Nugget, we're on.'

'Go on without me,' Miller called back, 'I'll follow you out.'

The poker game went on as Bradman led his team out without Miller. The players began to move to their positions just as Miller won the pot. He stuffed the money in his pockets and hurried on to the ground. When he was 20 metres on to the arena, he pulled out some of the notes from his pockets and waved them at the English dressing room.

'Hey boys, I've got it all!' he yelled back to the England players, 'all your money!'

His prowess at poker outweighed his on-field performances with a score of 31 in his only innings. A bright spot, at least in terms of his fitness, was his return to the bowling crease. He didn't take a wicket but sent down 14 overs, conceding just 15 runs. In one spell, Edrich on-drove Miller for four, spoiling his figures. The bowler reacted predictably with a vicious bouncer. But there was more to it than mere retaliation for a boundary. In Australia's first innings Edrich had bowled several good bouncers at Lindwall, hitting him on the hand once. This was an evening up after Lindwall had rapped Edrich on the hand in England's first innings. Lindwall put on a brave face, but he was uncomfortable.

Now Miller was sticking up for his bowling partner in what was becoming a mini bouncer war. His second short one thudded into Edrich's elbow. Hand-rapping was moving up the arm. Any former on-field sympathy Miller might have had for his old pilot friend had evaporated. He let him have another two bouncers. The Old Trafford crowd booed. Miller was again the bad boy.

Bradman intervened. He spoke some words of apparent comfort to a battered Edrich, and then had a word to Miller, who did not deliver a bouncer in his next over.

These moments of spice and spite were short-lived in the rain-interrupted drawn game that prevented any chance of an England victory. Incidents remained on the field, and didn't interfere with those keenly fought but friendly poker games.

The Australian squad was on a mission but its members had not forgotten to enjoy themselves. After a black-tie dinner outside London, Miller was driving Hassett, Johnston and Johnson back to their hotel after midnight when, at Hassett's request, he veered down the driveway of a country estate. Miller pulled up outside a two-storey mansion.

'Who lives here, Lindsay?' Miller asked.

Hassett didn't reply. He got out of the car, walked up to the front entrance and pushed the bell. Miller followed. A window on the top storey was thrown up. The estate's owner enquired, 'What the hell are you doing?'

'Just thought we'd pop in,' Hassett said, looking up.

'Are you Lindsay Hassett?' the man asked, eyeing their attire and squinting at him, then at Miller.

'Indeed I am,' Hassett replied.

'Good God! That's Miller . . . !' Miller waved. 'Wait there.' The owner hurried to let them in.

'Do you know him?' Miller asked Hassett.

'Never seen the old boy before in my life.' Hassett had gambled that they would be welcomed, even at that late hour.

The Australians had made an impact in England throughout the summer, and most people knew them by sight from TV news, cinema newsreels and the papers. A butler was roused to let the four revellers in. Port and cigars were offered. The host, who happened to be a cricket fan, entertained them for two hours. Miller and Hassett heard later that their host dined out on the unscheduled visit for years afterwards.

The team visited Windsor Castle and was shown around by Lord Gowrie, VC, Lieutenant Governor of Windsor and a former Governor General of Australia. Lord Tedder, the former deputy to General Eisenhower in World War II, and the man in charge of all air operations in Western Europe, joined the tourists for tea. He fooled around with Miller, whom he had befriended during the summer of 1945, by pretending to be a waiter. With a full tray in his hand, he approached Miller. 'Excuse me, sir,' Tedder said. 'Your tea, sir.'

'Thank you, boy,' Miller replied in an exaggerated pompous English voice to the astonishment of others in the tour group who recognised the illustrious servant. 'Here you are, lad.' Miller gave him a penny.

'Thank you very much, sir,' Tedder said with a deferential tug of his cap as he backed away.

Back on the playing arena, it took a Leeds Fourth Test upheaval for Miller to galvanise his mind for a lifted effort after several weeks of distractions. England, who had much the better of the Third Test, continued their revival with Hutton back opening in front of a full house. His 81 set the foundations for a big innings, and Washbrook (143), Edrich (111) and Bedser (79) all contributed to a healthy 496.

Events were again overshadowed by emotion from the Leeds crowd for Bradman. In his last three Tests here he scored two great triple centuries and a century. He was a legend in his last appearance, and the Yorkshire spectators greeted him with a human tunnel and cheering. He was 31 not out and Hassett 13 not out at stumps. Australia was 1 for 63 and poised to challenge England's tally. But Dick Pollard removed them both early. This brought Miller, then 19-year-old Harvey, in his first Ashes Test, to the wicket at 3 for 68.

Harvey's words: 'Let's get stuck into 'em' inspired Miller. This was a crisis. Australia was more than 400 behind. Another wicket or two at this juncture and England would be in a position to win.

Miller had a dual role. First he had to bat Australia into the game. At the same time, he had to protect Harvey early.

Miller started to play shots, all of them. Laker came on. Miller lifted his first ball, a long hop, over the square leg fence. But the off-spinner, turning away from the left-hander, caused him trouble. Miller decided to control the strike against Laker, keeping Harvey up the other end. But he went further and launched into the bowler. First there was a stunning Miller off drive, which had been so prevalent when his batting was at its best. Two balls later he belted a low, explosive straight six that sent spectators ducking as it skimmed like a missile at them. Miller strolled down the wicket to Harvey between overs. 'Feel better?' he asked Harvey with a grin.

The teenager was already over his nerves. 'Those two shots and his comradeship paved the way,' Harvey said. He, too, went after the off-spinner with two successive scintillating fours.

Miller was in such an aggressive mood that the crowd was alert to his potential for causing grievous bodily harm. He wound up for a terrific hit that went so high it was in serious danger of going into orbit. Hutton, on the long-off boundary, thought he was hovering under it, which he was, vaguely. When the ball succumbed to gravity it was well clear of the boundary, striking a blonde girl in a green dress. Ambulance men arrived on the scene and led the limping, distressed victim away. She was the second casualty from Miller monstering for the summer . . . so far.

No one in the ground, or outside, was safe. Miller now hurled his bat at one from Yardley, which sailed high over long-on for another six. He was 58 when Yardley enticed him for one lunge too many. Miller, off balance, edged the ball. It bounced off Evans' head. Edrich took a finger-tip, diving catch at short-fine leg.

Such an expert observer as John Arlott judged this as one of the most memorable innings – long or short – of all time. This was the real Miller, hidden from view until needed when the team was in its most vulnerable position in the series. 'Miller played like an emperor,' Arlott wrote. '. . . Every stroke would have been memorable but each one had bettered its predecessor. Miller's was not merely a great innings, but I cannot believe it possible for a cricket brain to conceive of an innings that would be greater.' Arlott said that the performance would remain in his mind even if all others were forgotten. It had raised cricket 'to a point of aesthetic beauty'.

Harvey went on to a magnificent 112. Loxton (93) then took up the cudgel against Laker, whose deliveries turned in to the right-hander with just enough pace to be hit with the natural swing. In this period, the off-spinner was hoisted for 5 sixes. Lindwall followed with 77 and helped Australia to 458 on day four – Monday. It was in striking distance of England.

But the home team was still far better placed. It batted evenly in the second innings, with five players scoring between 47 and 66. Yardley did not declare England's second innings closed until two overs into the final morning. This allowed him to use the heavy roller in the morning in order to help break up the wicket and make it conducive to spin.

Australia was set 404 to win – in less than a day. Thanks to some final Bradman brilliance (this turned out to be the last time he scored in a Test) with 173 not out, and Morris magic of 182 (their partnership was 301), Australia was able to secure a win with 15 minutes to spare. The tourists, with a 3–0 lead, held the Ashes and won the series. Miller had contributed strongly in all but one of the Tests.

Bradman's main goal of going through the season undefeated was now a chance and the squad's main aim. Only Miller did not care for it, although anyone watching the next county game – against Derbyshire – would not have been aware of his contrary view. He scored a 50, very much in the vein of his effort in the Test. Then he ripped into Derbyshire's openers, taking 3 for 31, thus doing more than his bit in another innings win.

Perhaps it was a full house, maybe he just liked Welsh singing.

Miller at Swansea against Glamorgan a day later repeated his all-round skills for the 50,000 August Bank Holiday spectators who turned up on the one and a half days that the inclement weather allowed. He took a couple of wickets and dampened the hopes of the opposition, which was favoured to win the County Championship. Glamorgan managed 197. Ten-year-old Tony Lewis, a future county star and England batsman, watched the match. He had queued from daybreak outside the walls of the St Helens ground in Swansea to watch both days' play.

> I sat halfway down the rugby stand, straining without the benefit of binoculars, to see the great Australians [he wrote]. S. G. Barnes (31) was lbw to Allan Watkins and then there was a roar. Down the long run of steps came Keith Miller, flicking back his hair, striding out to the middle. The game was transformed as he crashed the ball all over Swansea, playing some strokes from nearer the bowler than the wicketkeeper.

Miller cannoned 5 sixes and 7 fours. One of the sixes had him in his coiled position as he hit the ball over square leg with his left hand only on the bat. It landed 20 rows back into the crowd. 'Dal ati, Keith y Melinydd!' spectators called. 'Keep at it, Keith Miller!' He did, for a rapidfire 84 before torrential rain ruined the match with Australia at 3 for 215. Yet drenched young Lewis and the crowd left the ground happy.

The juggernaut rolled on. Miller missed the low-scoring nine-wicket win against Warwickshire at Birmingham. The main interest centred on leg-spinner Eric Hollies, who took 8 for 107 and troubled Bradman, whom he bowled for 31. His form earned him a place, along with Glamorgan's Watkins, in England's Fifth Test.

Miller returned against Lancashire and supported Lindwall, who appeared to be winding up to his best pace for the season. He had taken wickets but could not remove the stubborn, gutsy Jack Ikin, who had received several blows on the body on the last day. Ikin reached 99 as the county fought a rearguard action to avoid being just another team thrashed by the tourists. The new ball was due. Bradman threw it to Miller, who had been having an easy time, sending down just 5 overs. Miller tossed it back.

'That guy deserves a century,' he said, in one of his unpredictable moods. 'I don't want to be responsible for getting him out now.'

Bradman then called back Lindwall into the attack. He had no compunction about bowling the batsman one short of a deserved century.

Miller turned up for the final game, also drawn because of the rain, before the Fifth Test, versus Durham at Sunderland. He performed his usual trick of pulling Australia out of a slump with an aggressive 55 in 51 minutes.

Miller, a man of passions, hates and loves about people and places, detested the Oval as a cricket venue. He preferred a sense of enclosure at grounds, and not the feeling of being watched by people in 'a crescent of barrack-like flats'. He had a phobia about spectators, who had not paid to get in, peering out of their living room windows 'while having lunch or afternoon tea'. Even the buses going by on Harleyford Road and giant cranes put him off. Miller was further bothered by the black smoke coiling from the factory behind the Vauxhall Stand. He reserved a special negative passion for the ugly gasometer, which dominated the area.

The bleak prospect of rain, the tourists' constant companion, did not help his demeanour as he arrived at the arena on 14 August. The weather delayed England's decision to bat first. That was Yardley's first mistake. His second was to send in John Dewes to open. The young left-hander was chosen to start the innings in place of the injured Washbrook. It seemed foolhardy given his history versus Miller, whose mood brightened at the prospect of bowling to his favourite 'rabbit'. Dewes had shown gifts when a teenager, but not surprisingly they deserted him in 1945, when he first faced Miller. The thick towel under his shirt had not helped at Cambridge earlier in the year when he had been dealt with quickly. Now it was asking a lot to face his living nightmare on a sodden track under grey skies.

Dewes took a single off Lindwall and was forced to face his tormentor. Miller bowled a skidding delivery and was unhappy with his footwork. He laid more sawdust, taking his time and building tension. Then his second ball scattered Dewes' stumps. England was 1 for 1. Miller soon dismissed Jack Crapp for a duck, leaving England 4 for 23.

He had 2 for 3. The smoke belching from the factory had turned golden, the gasometer overshadowing the ground wasn't so unattractive, and the people hanging out their washing on the flat balconies were friendly. Lindwall did the rest, taking 6 for 20, which Bradman described as the most devastating spell of speed bowling he had witnessed. Miller took 2 for 5 off 8 overs.

England was dismissed for 52. Bradman's memory of the last time he played at the Oval, when England scored 7 for 903, would never be erased. Yet such a vanquishing of the opposition was more than satisfying.

Bradman came to the wicket at 1 for 117 and was bowled by Hollies' second ball. It became the most famous duck in history and robbed Arthur Morris of due recognition for his 196, one of the finest innings ever played in a Test. But where Morris might have been miffed by Bradman's misfortune, Miller might have been happier. He was stumped by Evans off Hollies for 5, after overbalancing and ending up doing a press-up, his toes clear of the crease. Miller's ungainly lapse was forgotten but for a photo of his press-up. It made the walk back to the pavilion, with those prying eyes in the flats watching, a fraction easier to take.

Australia reached 389. Rain again softened up the pitch for England. Hutton, who had batted magnificently for a top score of 30, repeated the feat in the second innings before Miller had him caught behind for 64. It was perhaps fitting that Miller was the man to dismiss Hutton in his last innings of the series. Lindwall had troubled him. He was an outstanding quick who would worry anyone in history on his day, or most days. But Miller was the one who bothered Hutton more. He also bowled Crapp. That is to say, he removed this batsman for the second time in the Test, taking 2 for 22. Lindwall's 3 for 50 and Johnston's 4 for 40 ensured the inevitable as England was all out for 188.

Australia won by an innings and 149 runs, giving it a 4–0 series victory.

The Test statistics were published the next day in the papers. Morris (87.00), Barnes (82.25) and Bradman (72.57) were at the top in the batting. Miller languished at tenth spot with 184 runs at 26.28. This was once more a clear reflection of his bowling workload, not just in the Tests, when he sent down a modest 138.10 overs, taking 13 wickets at 23.15, but through the season. The Lindwall–Miller–Johnston–Toshack combinations took 78 of the 91 wickets to fall in the Tests. Primarily it was the shock of Lindwall (27 wickets at 19.62) and Miller that did the early damage, especially against England's top order, which was never allowed to settle. Bradman was fortunate to have the left-armers Johnston (27 at 23.33) and Toshack (11 at 33.09) as first and second change. In several instances when the top two were injured, Johnston was an outstanding opening bowler, who did at least as well as Lindwall and Miller. Johnston and Toshack provided superb back-up and variety and allowed Bradman to take full advantage of the 55-over new-ball rule.

Miller had contributed strongly in four of the five Tests, and was a match-winner in the First, which set the tourists up. In the Fourth his batting at least turned the match. In three Tests his slips catching helped change the course of the game.

Bradman's would-be Invincibles accounted for Kent without Miller, but he was selected for the final game at Lord's for the summer, versus the Gentlemen of England. It was a season of finales for Bradman, and this would be his last appearance at cricket's headquarters. The 'Old Boy' – he was a few days away from his fortieth birthday – left everyone with 150 reminders why he was still the top batsman in the world, despite his powers having declined. He threw his innings away after hitting 19 fours, but not the team innings. Bill Brown displayed his best form for the season with his eighth century, and Hassett looked intent on a double hundred as Australia reached 3 for 478.

Miller, 59 not out at stumps, believed the score was enough in a three-day match, but Bradman sent him and Hassett back out to the middle on day two. Miller's decision, if captain, would have been to declare an hour before stumps for a crack at the Gentlemen. Bradman, on the other hand, now had his sights set on remaining undefeated. There would no compromise, no 'fair go' for the opposition. There were still six games to go, including this one. Bradman would continue the relentless method of batting the other team out of the game, then going for a win.

Miller was going to try to make runs but at a pace more suited to the event. He did his corkscrew swivel and hooked the first ball he faced for four. He repeated the shot next ball, and it sailed over square leg for six. Yardley placed a third man in the deep. The bowler, W. Wooller, delivered a good bouncer. Miller took it on and was caught deep on the square leg fence for 69.

Hassett reached his 200 in the last over before lunch. Bradman declared at lunch at 5 for 610. This was surely overkill in a three-day match. But Bradman was rarely criticised. More often than not when his team had batted beyond any chance of being beaten, they would dismiss the opposition twice and win the contest easily by an innings. This happened with the Gentlemen. It was hard to argue against perpetual success and the wonderful but brutal, attacking cricket the Australians were playing with bat and ball. Not only that. The crowds were loving it all and unconcerned about the thrashings. The gate takings each match were big, often records, regardless of the weather. On several occasions, the proceeds from the Australian matches were the difference between a profit and loss for the season for a county.

Bradman, who would have loved a break, was forced to play more than anyone else. County administrators begged him to turn up. He was the big draw that sucked the fans through the gates. In more ways than E. W. Swanton's description of him, Bradman was a victim of his own success.

The season was taking on his character, with emphasis on attacking play, winning with a minimum of risk and not losing at all costs. How different would a Miller captaincy and style have been? Australia would not win everything. There would be no talk of invincibility; no winning for winning's sake. Instead there would be declarations and uncontrived or contrived tight finishes, which would have made the season markedly different. But no captain would scheme to play down his team's overwhelming strengths or boost those of the opposition. The plain fact was clear by season's end. This touring team was superior to any opposition team it met on any ground in the UK.

Miller would have thought that his day as skipper would come. If so, he would strut his stuff then. For now, Bradman's machine drove on with maximum planning and efficiency. Somerset went down by an innings without Bradman. The South of England, a strong line-up that included Edrich and Compton, was also on the way to being typically crushed when the rain stopped the slaughter. Then came the so-called festival match at Scarborough against Leveson-Gower's XI, beginning 8 September.

Once more Bradman displayed his sensitivity to recent history. He recalled that the tourists had been beaten in this game in 1938 when he was injured and Stan McCabe was deputising. England then chose almost a Sixth Test team. Bradman insisted this time that only six of the opposition team should have Test experience. He asked all his team to attend the ground on the morning of the match, then chose a full-strength Test team.

Miller loved these games. He was hostile in private about

Bradman's approach. He told Jim Laker not to think that 'all the Australians were as prim as this little man'. Miller wanted no part of it. 'This is no way to play festival cricket,' he said. 'I'm buggered if I'm going to support this "head down" idea.'

When the Leveson-Gower team batted, Miller rolled his arm over without venom or intent. Lindwall, on a roll, took up the slack, bowling Hutton for a duck and ripping through the opposition, taking 6 for 59. Leveson-Gower's team managed 177. Bradman, calm and cheerful, was playing his kind of festival match in his role as the smiling assassin. He joined Barnes at 1 for 102. They put on 225, taking the game out of the opposition's reach once more. After 275 minutes batting, Barnes was out caught on the boundary for 151. Bradman powered on to 153, top score, and threw his wicket away. He had entertained, taking only 190 minutes while hitting 19 fours. He also lifted 2 sixes late in his knock, a major concession to 'festivity'.

Miller had been dropped down the order. True to his word, he went on the attack from the start, slashing at Bedser. He was caught behind for just 1. He too had thrown his wicket away, but for different reasons from Bradman and Barnes.

Bradman declared at 8 for 489 after tea on the third and final day, making the event pointless, although there was a bit of levity when Harvey, Hassett, Morris and he bowled out the match. Bradman was smiling even more at the finish. The potential danger game had fizzled to a draw.

The last two games of the season were against Scotland at Edinburgh and Aberdeen. They were not first-class matches, but the team still played them as if they were, winning both by an innings. On the afternoon of 14 September, after the win at Edinburgh, Miller played a round of golf with Bradman and Lindwall. He had a poor game, then rushed off to the team hotel to change into a brown suit. He wanted to be at Edinburgh's Usher Hall to hear the Glasgow Orpheus Choir give the final concert of the Edinburgh Festival.

But he turned up without a ticket. The door attendants didn't know him but responded to his charming plea – that he was an Australian of Scottish descent and wished to experience the best of his cultural heritage. 'You can sit on the stairs,' he was told. 'It's a full house.' Miller was thrilled. He sat on the red-carpeted stair and remained enraptured by the performances of 60 voices.

A *Scottish Daily Express* representative spotted him. 'He smiled at the rollicking "Bonnie Dundee", leaned forward with others in the international audience to catch the lilt of songs from the [Hebrides] Islands,' the reporter noted. 'He applauded his favourite "Jesu, Joy of Man's Desiring". When offered a seat he hushed the Good Samaritan to silence.' At the close as he rose to leave 'a flaxen-haired lass took his hand'. Miller might have thought his luck was in, but he was linked up with 2,000 others singing 'Auld Lang Syne'.

The reporter approached him as he left the hall and asked for a reaction. 'I didn't know half the words,' he said, 'but what lovely melodies come from the Hebrides. And that funny little man with the white beard – [the conductor] Sir Hugh Robertson – is a magician with his hands.' Miller made his way towards the festival crowds. 'I'll get back now,' he said to the reporter. 'We're playing Scotland tomorrow. I missed my dinner for that concert. But it was worth it!'

Bradman's dream was fulfilled after the thirty-fourth and final match at Aberdeen. Australia had gone through the entire season without a loss, winning 25 and drawing 9. It had never been done before by any touring squad. Shorter seasons in the modern era meant it would never be done again. It was a record for the ages. Because of Bradman's obsession, the 1948 team would forever be known as the Invincibles.

He praised Miller for his dangerous bowling with the new ball and his capacity to swing it both ways at nearly Lindwall's speed. The captain also judged him as the best slips catch in the world. But he criticised him for his six-hitting (26 in 22 matches), saying he would have been a better batsman had he shown better judgement in his stroke-making. Bradman thought him limited by his inability to concentrate.

This was the master judging another by his own standards and approach. Had Bradman calculated who did most to avoid defeat on tour, as opposed to causing crashing victories, and so did most to maintain the unbeaten streak, Miller would have been high on his list. Above him would have been Morris, who dominated the Tests and the entire 1948 season. So would Bradman for his batting, planning and leadership, both tactically and strategically. If due weight was given to influence on wins, Miller's all-round skills would rank with Lindwall (27 wickets at 19.62 and 191 runs at 31.83) and Johnston (27 wickets at 23.33 and 60 runs at 20.66). Miller's batting had put the team back on even keel at least six times. His bowling bursts, especially at the beginning of games – in and out of the Test series – put paid to any chances of any opposition mounting a winning score.

Miller's tour figures did more to reflect his influence on the season. He ranked eighth in batting with a more than respectable average of 47.30, and had an aggregate of 2088 – which was second only to 2428 by Bradman, who had five more innings and generally went in before Miller. Factor in Miller's capacity to hit Australia out of trouble and his value went beyond the indications of raw numbers. Miller ranked third in the bowling, taking 56 wickets at 17.58, behind Johnston (102 at 16.42) and Lindwall (86 at 15.68). Again, Miller's impact with the ball against opposition top orders must be factored and once more increase his true value. Put together his all-round performances from these perspectives and add his 20 catches (with due regard to their degree of difficulty), and there is a strong case for ranking Miller as the tourists' most important player for the entire 1948 season after Morris and Bradman.

The irony was that the man who later alleged he disdained the concept of winning simply for winning's sake, or not losing at all, did as much as anyone to make sure that the Australians did not lose a game. Next to Bradman and Morris, it could be argued that Miller was the most vital player in making a legend of the 1948 touring team.

On 19 September, the happy, fatigued squad members were content to end the tour with a stroll in the grounds of Balmoral Castle, about 80 kilometres from Aberdeen, after meeting the royal family. Miller was perhaps happiest of all. He was able to chat with the two princesses, Elizabeth and Margaret. He walked with Princess Margaret on the lawn in front of the castle. While wandering around the castle, he spotted a radiogram with a pile of records beside it. Beethoven, Bach and Mozart came to mind. He glanced at the top record, and was surprised to see it was a current hit. On reflection, Miller said he was aware that the royals 'shared many of the tastes of their subjects'.

Later he and Princess Margaret took tea with the others in the banquet hall. Those in the party aware of body language – especially conversation of the eyes – no matter how discreet, suggested it might not have been their last meeting.

Just before boarding the boat home, Miller was asked what he considered were the three most attractive sights in England. He replied: 'The hills of Derbyshire, the leg sweep of Denis Compton, and Princess Margaret.'

PART 4

NUGGET'S NIRVANA

13

THE SOUTH AFRICAN BEAT

Miller wheeled around. Bradman, on 49 not out in an hour at his farewell appearance at Sydney, waited. Miller decided to bowl a bouncer. The master batsman swivelled into position. He hit the ball forward of square, which was the highlight of the whole Bradman knock – a perfectly executed hook stroke for four.

Miller, as ever, was riled. He clapped the shot, flicked his hair, then called for the ball to be sent back to him quickly. He recalled Bradman asking him, just for the fun of it, to give his (Bradman's) good friend Walter Robins a bumper in the Australia versus Gentlemen of England game at Lord's in the previous year. Miller remembered Bradman's own lust for short-pitch bowling (except during the Bodyline series) and how he was such a strong hooker and believer in the shot. Why not liven up the game and give the Don one more? Miller thought. Next delivery, he bent his back for a searing head-high bumper. Bradman was not amused. 'He looked daggers at me,' Miller recalled, 'so for sheer devilment, I decided to give him a third bumper.' Bradman anticipated it, took it on and hooked it again. But this time it sailed straight to Ken Meuleman at mid-on, and he was out caught for 53.

This mini-barrage was hardly reported in the press. Fans expressed their disappointment that Bradman didn't get a hundred in his farewell to Sydney. Yet his cameo was a fine innings that pleased the 41,575 spectators and helped fill the coffers for the joint testimonial for former test stars Alan Kippax and Bert Oldfield. The late February 1949 game was also a Test trial for the tour of South Africa, which would commence the following October.

Miller's typical whimsy and temerity in bouncing the Don would have been forgotten but for the events of a week later when the team to tour South Africa was announced. Miller went to Sydney's Cricketers Club for a drink and spotted one of the selectors, Chappie Dwyer, and the new captain of Australia, Lindsay Hassett. Dwyer ignored Miller, and an hour later Miller knew why. The Australian squad was posted on the club's notice board. The name *Keith Miller* was not the list.

He said he expected it, but *not* seeing it typed on official Board of Control paper was a shock. The omission was the most amazing selectorial bombshell since Bradman's dumping from the 1928–29 Second Ashes Test at Sydney. Yet this was bigger. Bradman had been dropped after one Test in which he scored 18 and 1. That omission proved to be a retrospective blunder. Bradman soon after began his 20-year dominance of Test match cricket. But Miller was established as the best all-rounder in the world. There seemed no credible form or cricketing reason for leaving him out. Journalists at first fumbled for a rational reason and some logic in the thinking of the selectors, Dwyer, Jack Ryder and Bradman. Commentators looked at the figures and noted Miller's ordinary season with bat and ball. In 13 innings he had scored 400 at 33.33. He had taken just 11 wickets at 24.09. Eleven batsmen, including keepers Tallon and Gil Langley, had made more runs. A dozen bowlers – many of them with no hope of Test selection – had taken more wickets.

As ever, the story behind the batting figures made them misleading. Miller played several dominant innings, including, according to the *Sydney Morning Herald*, a 'magnificent display of aggressive batting' in a century to start the 1948–49 season against Queensland; a patient 52 versus Western Australia; a rearguard 52 not out when suffering from conjunctivitis, which was an innings that saved his state in the return game against Queensland; and the top score of the SCG game versus Victoria – 99 – on a difficult, fast wicket. The best ball of the match by H. F. Lambert dismissed him. Had he managed a second century for the season, he might well have been selected. Miller failed with the bat in games against South Australia when the Don was watching, and again in his presence during two testimonials. During the earlier one at the MCG, which raised £5,185 for Bradman, Miller had flung the bat for just 2 and 14. Miller claimed Bradman had given him 'a filthy look' for this 'couldn't care less' approach to such games.

There was a persistent rumour that the selectors had taken Miller at his word, repeated during the 1948–49 season, that he did not wish to bowl. This was reflected in his first-class season in which he sent down just 77 overs, compared with 429.4 overs in England in 1948. Miller wanted to concentrate on his batting. If that were the case, then perhaps the selectors had ranked him below the specialist batsmen chosen. Maybe they had noticed his lacklustre performance in the trial match in which he had scored 15 and 6. Many statistical excuses were flung about. But none was credible. Individual motives were considered. Had the old problem of 'horse-trading' between the states – whereby selectors supported favourites from their states – been in play at the selectors' table? It was likely that Jack Ryder voted against Miller. His leaving Victoria had caused some ill-feeling in that state administration's hierarchy. That left two votes from Dwyer and Bradman. At least one of them had to be against Miller.

Analysis reached fever pitch, especially among those who supported Miller or had long-standing grudges against the Don. There was even speculation that Bradman was annoyed that Miller had bowled bouncers at him during the Test trial-cum-testimonial in the previous week and that this had led to his dumping. Considering that a fair percentage of the thousand or so bowlers who delivered to the Don in his 338 innings had sent down bumpers, and he relished the challenge, this was unlikely.

Soon after the South African tour Whitington (in collaboration with Miller) wrote:

Scores of newspaper columns have tried to find the true culprits (there must have been at least two) to blame for his [Miller's] omission . . . After spending months travelling through South Africa, scheming and applying tricks to trap Dwyer [the tour manager] into clarifying the position, I am still as much in the dark as to which two selectors voted against Miller's inclusion as ever I was.

One of those 'tricks' was to present Dwyer with a letter from Bradman to Johnnie Moyes, which had a postscript. It said: 'I hope Keith doesn't think I had anything to do with his omission from the team to South Africa.' If Bradman was to be believed, this left Dwyer as the other one who voted against Miller. Contrary to popular opinion, Bradman did not always get his way at the selection table. The selectors had a long-standing agreement not to disclose their votes or their reasons for selections or non-selections. The three men responsible remained mute, except for Bradman's private letter to his friend Johnnie Moyes, which turned out to be an indiscretion for both of them. Whatever the real reason for Miller's exclusion, the selectors were collectively responsible for the non-selection.

Miller took his rejection well, although he thought, and many observers suspected, that it could not have been done on merit. Angry reaction from the media and experts galvanised support for him during the off-season. Apart from getting on with his career as a sports journalist, he found time to flirt with a late career in baseball, which he had not played since Melbourne High days more than a decade ago. Friends had urged him to consider try-outs in the US, where his outstanding athletic skills would have been valuable. Training and instruction might well have seen him develop as a batter. His capacity for six-hitting ensured this. His strong arm would have been suitable for pitching, and he would have had few peers among fielders even in the US. Even his speed was exceptional. Miller was found to be second in circling the bases in New South Wales field games. He was timed at 14.8 seconds, which was only 0.6 seconds outside the Australian record. It made news. Miller received satisfaction from it. He might have wondered what those selectors at Elsternwick club, who dumped him for being tardy, would think when they learned how fleet of foot and athletic he had become.

There was some talk about enticing Miller to have a run with the Boston Red Sox, but he declined knowing that such a move, like his near-deal with the Lancashire League, would end his Test career. Miller was still under 30, just. He had played only three international Test series. His shock non-selection had made him determined to get back in the national team. If he could manage injuries, he could play on until his mid-thirties as long as the enjoyment was there.

***

Miller at this time received a letter from his Cockney bus conductor friend in Putney, with whom he and Glendinning had stayed en route to their naval adventure in late 1944. The information in it shook Miller. Christine, the friend's daughter, when on a break from her psychiatric hospital, had decapitated her mother.

Miller wrote back a compassionate letter, promising he would see his friend and Christine on his next trip to London.

***

While his Test team-mates toured South Africa, Miller started the 1949–50 domestic season as captain of New South Wales, his first experience of leadership since the Servicemen's Indian tour in 1945 and his first captaincy in the Shield competition. The responsibility, if anything, saw him lift his all-round performance in making a solid 80 with the bat and bowling with speed and penetration for three wickets in each Queensland innings. New South Wales won. He led his team to a second successive victory against Western Australia before hearing from the Australian Board of Control.

Would Miller be able to get leave from his employer to tour South Africa? He was needed as a replacement for Bill Johnston, who had been injured in a car accident in Durban. Ernie Toshack, also playing for New South Wales, had been in excellent form before injuring his back and knee. He was approached first by the board. When he reported unfit, it turned to Miller. Pressure had come from South Africa for his inclusion. Hassett and selector/manager Dwyer had cabled the board asking for him. The request was supported by a concerted effort from touring journalists, who wrote articles pushing for him.

Miller had 48 hours to make up his mind. Peg was expecting their second child at least six weeks before he would return from South Africa. The board offered him £400 for the trip. He would need to take extra cash to pay for his drinks, bets and partying. He was in two minds about going. Once more there would be disruption at home. Peg was now used to the term 'cricket widow'. Even when her husband wasn't on tour, she missed him for weeks at a time when he played Test and Shield cricket interstate. Even when he was in Sydney, Manly cricket, mates, pubs, functions, the races and work took precedence over the family. Miller was not alone in his neglect of wife and children, even for those who didn't rush about the world and interstate. The 1940s and 1950s was an era of male domination in white, bourgeois Australia. The man was the breadwinner; the woman, the housekeeper and nurturer. Miller was archetypal in some ways and an extreme version in others.

He got away with a lot because of the character he was. Many men and women appreciated in him what English painter Walter Sickert saw as 'the delicious mixture of grace and gaucherie that touches the heart and clings to the memory'. Much closer up, Peg loved him without condition or complaint. She saw that he wanted to tour South Africa. She gave his four-month adventure – her four months of further emptiness – her blessing. At least she would have the ever-supportive Snow coming from Melbourne to help out.

Miller came to an arrangement with his editor and made a public statement: 'I am going to South Africa because it seems that the selectors and the team feel that I can help Australia at this time. My wife agrees with me that it is my duty to go. Actually it would suit me better to stay in Sydney. But if the boys think I can help, I'll be with them.' Miller took the opportunity to comment on his non-selection in March: 'At that time the selectors may have been right. They may have been wrong. But I did not then, and do not now, query their good faith.' This was magnanimous, especially given that his omission rankled with him in private. It reinforced his long-standing feelings about authority and its attitude to him.

By making it clear he held no grudge, Miller was smoothing the way for harmony with manager Dwyer on the trip. Miller also now had to set aside his desire to do less bowling. He was going to South Africa to strengthen this department first. Not only was Johnston injured but also pacemen Lindwall and left-armer Alan Walker lacked form. Miller had set a realistic pattern by throwing himself at the opposing state batsmen in his two Shield games and for Manly in club games in October. He was in touch with ball and bat, and ready.

Miller made his way to Perth to catch the ship, the *Dominion Monarch*. After a bout of drinking at a hotel with Glendinning, Miller slept soundly. Glendinning, recalling the days at Ouston and Great Massingham, arrived in his Austin A40 the next morning at Miller's hotel to drive him and masseur Charlie O'Brien, who was also joining the team in South Africa, to the ship for an 8 a.m. departure on 21 November. O'Brien was ready, bags packed. Miller, as ever, was difficult to rouse. His gear was not packed. Glendinning and the masseur helped him get ready.

There would be embarrassment and some explaining to do if Miller missed the ship. The next boat for South Africa would not be for several weeks, which would mean he would miss the First Test.

Glendinning and his passengers made a dash for the dock. They arrived at 8 a.m. Glendinning sped to the wharf, ignoring workers who yelled that he could not take his car there. He pulled up at the gangplank. Wharfies again tried to block him.

'It's Keith Miller!' Glendinning cried. 'He's late!'

The wharfies changed their attitude and helped Miller with his bags.

Five young women at the top of the gangplank were waiting and waving. 'Mr Miller! Mr Miller!' they called.

Miller, badly hung-over, perked up. 'I'll buy you all a drink after dinner tonight, girls,' he called with a smile and a wave, and a wink to Glendinning.

The *Dominion Monarch* arrived at Table Bay, Cape Town, in time for Miller to attend a Kenilworth race meeting with Bill Johnston, who would room with him on the trip, and local race-horse owner Freddy Burmeister. Johnston, sporting a deep gash in his head and other injuries, had recovered remarkably from his car crash and would play on during the tour. Miller had an extra-ordinary day's betting. He backed four winners and two seconds. This always placed him in a good mood as opposed to the high dudgeon more recently if he lost. It augured well for room-mate Johnston and the tour.

Soon after the races, Miller was in a two-day game 80 kilo-metres north-east at attractive Wellington. He hit the ground running between wickets – making a slashing 49 – and rushing in at the Western Province Country Districts batsmen to take 2 for 9. Miller thought for a moment that he might be back on the 1948 tour of England. Morris made 146, and the relentless team crunched its way to an innings win. It then took the Blue Train 1,700 kilometres through stunning country in the heart of South

Africa. There was a stop at Kimberley to see the diamond mines. Miller did some 'hush-hush' negotiations with a manager and acquired some diamonds before the tour ploughed on to Johannesburg.

Miller wasn't ready for the examination against Transvaal on a soggy pitch. Off-spinner Athol Rowan, a large man's Jim Laker, took his wicket after he had struggled to 7 in one of the most remarkable hauls ever against an Australian XI. Rowan took 9 for 19 and destroyed the tourists, who scraped together just 84. This was the kind of wake-up challenge Miller needed. He reverted quickly to his form for New South Wales and sent back an opener for 0. Transvaal slipped and skidded its way to 9 for 125 on the atrocious wicket, Miller taking 2 for 48. Australia was sent in again and once more fell apart to spin, tallying a pitiful 109. Rowan bowled Miller for 1 and again was the butcher, taking 6 for 49.

The home team needed just 69 to win and create history. No South African team had yet beaten Australia in four tours led by Joe Darling (1902–03), Herbie Collins (1921–22), Vic Richardson (1935–36) and now Hassett.

'We are going to do something to you that not even a [South African] Test side has done,' the affable Transvaal skipper Eric Rowan told Miller the night before the final day. 'We're going to thrash you hollow.'

'We'll see, Eric,' Miller replied with a grin, 'we'll see.'

Miller's targets the next morning were Rowan and arguably South Africa's finest batsman, Bruce Mitchell, whom he sent back for 4. Rowan was made to regret his cockiness. Miller delivered some brutal balls that jumped off a good length in a torrid spell. He stood mid-pitch, hands on hips, waiting to catch the Springbok's eye after each delivery spat nastily at his torso. Wisely, the batsman never quite lifted his head. That charming Aussie bloke Rowan had met and had a drink with the night before was nowhere to be seen. The intent in Miller's body language was intimidating. After he had shaken and softened Rowan, stand-in captain Morris brought Johnson on early. The relief for the batsmen was palpable, but it was the Springboks' undoing. The spinner dismissed Eric Rowan for just 11, leaving the opposition at 3 for 22. Johnson then took another three wickets for nothing. That 69 now looked very much like a difficult, if not an unattainable, object of desire.

Transvaal crumbled to be all out 53, giving Australia a very satisfying win by 15 runs. The last wicket to fall was that of Athol Rowan, whose triumph of wickets turned to tragedy when he reinjured a war wound while trying to avoid being run out. McCool first and then Ken Archer came to his aid while the others rushed to the dressing room to celebrate. The breakdown meant Athol Rowan would miss the series. (It later ended his career.)

Miller struggled in the drawn pre-Test warm up against a South African XI at Durban, making just 6. But his form with the ball (a dogged 22 overs and 2 for 63) was going to be more important for the team. The batsmen were all in touch, and Jack Moroney, the cautious opener, Neil Harvey, Hassett and Loxton were all making runs. Or so it seemed.

Back in Johannesburg and rugby's Ellis Park for the First Test, Australia received an early shock when both openers were back in the pavilion for just 2 runs. Miller, batting at three to allow Hassett more time to rest with tonsillitis, scratched around for 21. Hassett played the innings of his life, considering his illness. He hit a century, as did Loxton, in his only three-figure score in a Test. Australia's recovery was a serious team effort – with partnerships of 69, 92, 37, 83, 37, 52, 36 and 5 – after the woeful start. It reached 413.

Miller bent his back and broke the spine of the home team's batting by taking 5 for 40. South Africa caved in to be dismissed for 137. It was over to Johnston, who, showing that the car accident had not weakened his resolve, gave Hassett a brilliant extra option. The lanky left-armer took 6 for 44 in the Springboks' second dig of 191. Hassett the Brave walked away thankful for Miller's match-clinching performance. It played an important part in his first Test win as captain by a healthy innings and 85 runs.

Miller's removal from the Test scene was already an aberration. Miller had time to celebrate and recover for the start of the Second Test just three days later on 31 December. It was at Cape Town, where his trip had begun a month earlier. His bowling had acclimatised easily from the beginning, but his batting had been ordinary for him, especially since he had been asked to take the hot seat of number three when Hassett was ill. Miller was placed better in this Test, again batting at first drop because of the skipper's lingering illness. Moroney and Morris opened with 68, after Hassett won the toss again, and Miller didn't have the added pressure of a crisis and fresh opening bowlers. He set his own pace and did the job expected with a diligent 58. Hassett, faced with having his tonsils removed or battling on below par, managed another gutsy half century, while Neil Harvey stole the show, batting fluently and with command of all the bowlers en route to 178. Hassett, who in many ways seemed to be emulating Bradman in approach, competency, courage and leading from the front, put South Africa out of the game by declaring at 7 for 526.

Miller was again stunning with the ball. He unsettled the early batting with pace and skill on an unhelpful, slow wicket, leaving the home team 3 for 169 and vulnerable at the end of day two. Resistance had come from the strongest vertebra in the backbone of South African batting, Dudley Nourse, on 65 not out. He used his woodchopper's forearms for powerful backfoot play, especially cutting and hooking. His form looked good for a double hundred. Nourse stood between Australia and victory.

The next morning Miller was late for the start of play at the Newlands ground. Showing the same questionable skills at the car wheel as he did as a pilot, he had driven his old hire car into a deep gutter. He arrived at the ground as Hassett led his men on to the field. The skipper was informed that his bowler was reporting for duty at last. Hassett was the coolest of men in any crisis. He seemed to be debating fielding places with Morris. Players were swapped either side of the wicket and changed from long-on to deep third man. The captain made some play of positioning Johnston at silly mid-on.

Miller emerged from the pavilion in a state of undress that would have embarrassed a homeless derelict. While fumbling with the last button of his fly, Hassett strolled to him and tossed him the ball. 'See if you can avoid detention,' Hassett said, still poker-faced. Miller grinned and ran in to bowl. His first delivery was well wide of stump, but reared like a bucking bronco. The second was straight. Nourse played back and defensively. The third delivery, in line with leg stump, kicked off that tired pitch and speared for the batsman's ribcage. Nourse fended it off. The ball popped softly into Johnston's hands.

In the huddle that followed, Miller apologised to Hassett for being late. 'Just don't do it again,' Hassett said with mock admonishment, 'unless you can be assured of picking up Nourse's wicket.'

Miller collected 3 for 54, allowing McCool to pick up the pieces in the lower order with 5 for 41. Hassett consulted his bowlers after South Africa had been dismissed for 278. They all voted to make the home team follow on. It was hard work for all, but Lindwall (5 for 32), missing in action on the tour so far, found some touch after Johnston (3 for 70) enfeebled the top order. Only Nourse with 114 held up the bowlers. His team struggled to 333. Australia was untroubled in winning by eight wickets.

Miller's all-round results were key factors in winning in the second successive Test and putting Australia in an almost unassailable position. He was batting in the position that Bradman had enshrined as the most important spot in the order. Miller had done more than his share of bowling and sent shock waves through the opposition from which they did not fully recover. Miller's capacity to challenge, if not defeat, the opposition's top performers with bat and ball was unmatched to that point in history. No other all-rounder had taken on so much responsibility in a Test and succeeded. Miller's return to the national side had vindicated critics and embarrassed selectors.

The team travelled by road round the picturesque south coast 700 kilometres to Port Elizabeth. It was a happy, united group feeling very much the Invincibles still. Miller revelled in his return to form with the blade with a bludgeoning 131 against Eastern Province on a wet pitch. The freewheeling knock included 7 fours and 6 sixes. His thumps electrified the crowd and had them ducking. It was the cricket fans' method of self-preservation and a form of homage to such power.

Hassett sagely didn't bowl his greatest asset, but threw the ball to Walker and Lindwall. The latter kept his form running with another five-wicket haul. Winning by an innings was becoming the norm on tour. Border, further up the coast from Port Elizabeth, did not have to face a revived Miller but suffered the same fate as Eastern Province with a thrashing from the visitors.

The gregarious group kept rolling up the east coast, this time by train through the Transkei Bantustan and down through the Drakensberg Mountains to Durban, its favourite city. Hassett's main problem was to keep his players' minds on the right job mid-tour, especially with the distractions such as hospitality, always a hidden weapon in South Africa, and women. Miller the magnet was the perpetual personality of the tour, to whom women were attracted. But he was not the only one. There was even a competition between the more priapic tourists to see who could accomplish the most off the field. Unlike his hosts, Miller did not discriminate on the basis of race. Blacks and Indians in Durban were forbidden fruit for veldt whites. But the Australians continually flouted the law. Hassett, like Bradman, turned a blind eye to any excesses. He did ask his men to turn up on time, in a sober state and with their energies focused on representing their country. The captain's unruffled style and dry wit were factors that would sustain the team at this time when concentrations could lapse.

The squad members needed all their collective faculties for the challenge in the Third Test on Durban's Old Kingsmead Ground, especially when it was South Africa's turn to win the toss and bat first on Friday, 20 January. The weather was fine; the wicket good for batting. The Springboks reached 2 for 240, Eric Rowan on 133 not out and Nourse on 65 not out.

After his boast in the game against Transvaal the outspoken Rowan was again full of bombast. He would score 200. This time the visitors would be crushed. The latter half of his prediction seemed likely as rain crashed down on Durban in the early hours of Saturday morning. Later, a hot sun baked the muddy pitch as play resumed at 12 o'clock. It was High Noon for this game and the series. South Africa already had more than enough runs in the bank on such a treacherous 'sticky'. If it declared before going out to bat it could even wrap up the Test by stumps on day two, before the rest day and the sun restored the wicket.

Egos and national characteristics would come to the fore. The tight-knit, self-effacing brilliant Australian team worked as one. The South Africans had individuals like Rowan, who continually criticised the captain, Nourse. Rowan wanted that double hundred against those bloody Australians. He would fight his skipper if he mentioned the 'd' word – for declaration. Rowan would counsel against a premature closure. He would prefer a mountainous score like 500 on the board, with himself hitting a double hundred. The Aussies' faces could then be rubbed in Durban's wicket of caked mud.

Shrewd Hassett, Morris and Miller discussed the situation on the field when they examined the wicket. It dawned on them that keeping the Springboks batting might well be a priority. They all remembered Bradman's delaying tactics during the vital Melbourne Third Test in the 1936–37 Ashes. Bradman instructed his attack to bowl innocuously to keep England batting on a gluepot. Gubby Allen realised the cunning move too late. He declared at 9 for 76 (after Australia had scored 200). Bradman then reversed his batting order, sending in 'rabbits' Fleetwood-Smith and O'Reilly to open. The aim was to allow the sticky to dry out and improve by the time Bradman batted at seven. It worked. Bradman's 270 was ranked as one of the greatest Test innings ever. Australia reached 564 and won easily.

To achieve a similar result at Durban, Australia would have to bowl so badly that the pitch would look good. This was a bigger challenge than the normal desire to bowl well and dismiss the opposition, especially on a juicy track that would yield up tempting bags full of wickets. The main aim was to keep the South Africans batting in the hope that there would be enough time left on Saturday to dismiss Australia once only by stumps. The Sunday rest day would, hopefully, allow the pitch to improve by Monday, when it was expected that the Australians would be forced to follow on.

Miller began proceedings, sending down off-spin, which would be expected, but not the gentle lollipops he was directing wide of the off stump. A couple of balls in the first over bit and spun, despite Miller's intention for them not to. Such was the deviousness of the track. But because the batsmen were not rushed, they were not bothered. At the end of the over, Miller wanted to confirm to his skipper that the wicket was a shocker without alerting the batsmen. Nourse and Rowan would know by instinct and experience, no matter how selfish they might be in the lust for runs and big scores, if the Australians showed 'concern'.

Hassett and Miller stopped as they were about to pass each other at the end from which Miller had been bowling. Without a look or a glance, they knew they had to perform a bluff. Miller dropped to one knee, playing with his shoe-lace. Hassett, an even better poker-player and bluffer than Miller, took a white handkerchief from his pocket and feigned interest in the wind's direction as they spoke to each other. They agreed that Johnston, cutting his pace as he often did, could deliver the most accurate, innocuous trundling from the other end. Miller stopped at his place in slips. Hassett motioned to Johnston. The captain pretended to point at the flags on the pavilion, which were limp, as he said to Johnston: 'Need to bowl rubbish, Bill. The best rubbish you've ever delivered. We don't want wickets. We want time.'

Johnston obeyed his leader. But the wicket was too rotten. He sent a flat, boring delivery outside off stump. Nourse flicked at it and was out for 66. The saving grace for the Australian plan was that Nourse reproached himself for such an awful shot. He did not blame his dismissal on the state of the pitch. If he had stayed, he might have realised the tourists' ploy. But the Springbok captain was back in the dressing room in a black mood about getting out.

South Africa crawled to 3 for 254 at lunch, having added just 14. After the break, Miller, in a performance that would make Edward G. Robinson or any thespian applaud, groaned and flicked and glared after each awful bowl. Rowan, concentrating on his accumulation, was unaware of what was transpiring. Keeper Billy Wade, the new bat at the other end, was thinking only about staying. He was not under orders to take the long handle. The Hassett–Miller ruse seemed to be working as the field was changed after each over. Players were moved into positions that suggested containment, but were meant to make catches less likely. But it didn't quite work. Rowan drove at a ball and was caught by Johnston off Miller. It was such a simple catch that had it been dropped, the Australian ploy might have been exposed. Rowan trudged off the field, preoccupied by his defeat at Miller's hands and his score ending 57 short of his aim of a double hundred, and 13 below his highest Test score.

Fifty minutes later, the runs had dried up. The Australian game to stay out there under the guise of defensive tactics was working.

Then Wade nicked a ball from Johnston. It sailed at shin-level straight into the hands of a crouching Miller. He bobbled the ball, snatched at it and went down like a rookie TV wrestler as the ball hit the ground. Miller waved a 'sorry' to Johnston, who didn't react. No one could recall Miller dropping anything, let alone a sitter. Some observers were alerted but not Nourse or the South African team hierarchy.

After 80 minutes, the wicket was baked and doing such irrational things that neither W. G. Grace nor any batsman since could have handled it. South Africa stumbled and slipped, losing 7 for 57 between lunch and tea to be all out 311, despite the Australians' deception.

The trickery gave the tourists the slimmest of chances. Hassett decided to half-follow Bradman's example with the batting order reversal. Morris and Moroney would open. Ian Johnson would bat three, Miller, who was fatigued after his bowling and histrionics, four, and Hassett five. Saggers, McCool and Lindwall would come in before Harvey at nine and Loxton ten. Johnston would stay at eleven.

Leaving Morris at the top of the order was the only move that worked. He made 25, but the jumbled line-up seemed confused even before individuals reached the wicket. Australia was rolled for just 75 – 236 behind. Off-spinner Hugh Tayfield had a habit of deliberately stubbing his toe before bowling. This 'tic' became more pronounced with each of the 7 wickets he took (for 23).

The Australians had managed to hang on until 5.50 p.m. – 10 minutes before stumps. Those precious minutes were standard for an innings change, which meant stumps were drawn. Hassett and his team, by shrewd management and luck, despite the failure to rejig the batting order effectively, had achieved their aims. They were in good spirits that evening, believing they had been successful despite the scoreboard indicating that they were in a terrible position. Journalists who interviewed Miller were surprised by his optimism. He laid bets that Australia would win. Strangely, no one took him on. They had heard too much about the myth of Miller's Luck. They had not learned so much about his big losses, which were not discussed as readily as the wins. 'We are going to win,' Miller told one journalist, 'and you'd better say so.'

The weather held until Monday. Nourse inspected the pock-marked, gashed wicket and decided to bat again. Johnston and Johnson shared the wickets and ran through South Africa for just 99. Australia needed 336 for a win, which no one countenanced on such a dreadful strip, especially when it was 3 for 80 at stumps. Miller (10 after his 2 in the first innings), like Moroney and Hassett, was out lbw playing back.

The next morning Australia lost the efficient, dependable Morris for 44 and the tourists slipped to 4 for 95. South Africa and its media salivated at the prospect of seeing Australia defeated. But against all odds Neil Harvey grafted a dogged, patient style on to his exceptional skills and accumulated the runs on the drip. He was supported by first Loxton (54) then McCool (39). He reached 151 not out, and Australia won by five wickets. South Africa had to swallow its feverish desire to gloat and wait for another time. The tourists had locked away the series 3–0.

Miller's mini-slump with the bat continued in the return match with Transvaal. But he worked hard with the ball, taking 4 for 25 in the home team's first innings of 122. He steamed in again in the second innings, bowling Eric Rowan for 22. When J. Pickerill hit him for 2 fours, Miller retaliated with a series of bumpers. The batsman approached Morris, who was captain, and complained. Morris then moved close to Miller and said, 'This chap doesn't like bumpers.'

'I can see that,' Miller muttered.

Miller then bowled Pickerill a very slow delivery and smiled. Next ball was a searing bouncer. Medium-pacer Geff Noblet trapped him lbw soon after.

Transvaal was dismissed for 161. Australia was left 61 to get in the last session. Miller approached the watching Hassett. 'I'll slip off now Lindsay, if that's okay,' Miller said. 'Want to play a few holes with Bobby Locke [South Africa's British Open champion].'

'No, it's not okay, Keith,' Hassett said firmly but with a smile. 'You're in the middle of a cricket match and you'll stay here.'

Miller felt he had done his job and was disappointed. But he knew Hassett was right on principle. If he let Miller go, others would be asking for leave during games. Miller didn't complain. It was a reminder of his responsibility, especially as a team leader. He missed the next provincial game, played a round with Locke, and turned up fit against North-Eastern Transvaal, picking up another four-wicket haul. Miller failed again with the blade, but would have been judged superhuman to bat brilliantly in every game when he was doing his share of the bowling.

The Fourth Test at Johannesburg was set up for him to do better with the bat. Australia was in first. Centuries by Morris and Moroney saw Miller in at 1 for 214. He batted attractively for 84. Hassett closed the first innings at 8 for 465. South Africa replied grimly with 352, and Miller returned the best figures of 3 for 75 and, as usual on this tour, exhausted himself at the bowling crease with 28 overs. Australia was 2 for 259 when the game ended in an uninteresting draw.

In a situation where it was important that he bowled, his batting suffered, especially when he did not have to perform. Those around him were doing the job. Morris was consistent and nearly up to the high standard he set himself in England. Hassett was in touch with a 50, and Harvey was unstoppable with 56 not out and an even 100. Moroney scored hundreds in both innings, thanks to Miller, who reminded the dawdler at the end of the second innings that he could be the first Australian to hit centuries in both innings versus South Africa and only the fourth (after Bardsley, Morris and Bradman) to do it at all. School-teacher Moroney liked the idea of creating history. He accelerated from 75 to 101 not out while Miller (33 not out) and he added an entertaining 61 unbroken for the third wicket.

Miller's next game was at Ladysmith in Natal against Natal Country Districts. He was looking forward to a relaxing game in a quaint bush setting at an oval surrounded by willows and near a gentle river. But once more he had to heave his bowling shoulder into action after the local farmers demolished Australia for 74 on another wet track. After performing so well in the Tests he did not want to be humiliated in the bush by a bunch of part-timers. The rustic men of Natal experienced the full wrath of Miller, who was near-unplayable.

By mid-afternoon of the first day, Miller had taken three quick wickets on a quagmire. He sent down two consecutive deliveries that appeared to catch the batsman plumb in front. A diminutive umpire in a white floppy hat rejected Miller's two vociferous appeals. After the second plea for an lbw, Miller stopped at the umpire, lifted the turned-down hat brim and bent down to eyeball him. 'Which stump would they have missed, ump,' Miller asked with a smile, 'the off or the leg?'

The next ball was similar to the previous deliveries. It skidded off the batsman's pads and into the wicket. Miller appealed unnecessarily. The umpire signalled 'out'. Miller walked over to him again and this time turned down the brim.

There was always room for a bit of fun, even when the team was in a dire position. He brought the tourists back into the match by taking 6 for 21. The farmers, inclined towards up-country 'hoicking', were all out for 88. Australia went on to win by 129 runs.

The team travelled south to Pietermaritzburg for a three-day drawn game against Natal beginning 24 February. There Miller learned of the birth of his second son. In a phone call to Peg in Sydney, there was a debate over the baby's name. Peg wanted 'John'. Miller favoured 'Ashley'. There were a few other suggestions, but the parents couldn't agree. Miller broke the impasse by coming up with 'Peter' in honour of the town he was in. The news of a successful birth was an inspiration. He went out and celebrated by scoring a dashing 54 and taking 6 for 35.

In the Port Elizabeth Fifth Test, four days after the Natal game, he scored just 22 while Morris, Hassett and Harvey got big hundreds in another massive innings of 7 for 549. It once more shut the opposition out of a contest. South Africa crumbled twice, giving the tourists their fourth Test win – by an innings and 259. Miller shook the top order, taking 4 for 42 in the home team's first innings, the best figures for the match.

The South African tour read very similarly to the 1948 UK tour. Australia won the Test series 4–0, and was unbeaten in every game, playing 26, winning 18 and drawing 8. Many games were won by huge margins. Hassett, a most likeable, capable character, was making his own mark. But his winning ways had a familiar ring. He would first bat his opponents out of the match, then use a strong bowling attack to dismiss the opposition twice. His predecessor's shadow was long.

Miller had made important contributions in four of the five Tests. Harvey dominated the batting averages with 660 runs at 132.00. Miller was a respectable sixth with 246 at 41.00. He was fifth in the bowling with 17 wickets at 22.94. These numbers disguised his impact with the ball in blasting through the opposition top order. He had worked hard after his dumping to maintain his established position as a match-winner for his country. He accepted, with a degree of disappointment, that it might now be difficult to perform with just the bat for his country.

***

Gus Glendinning received a telegram from Miller. It read: 'Meet me at the [Fremantle] wharf or else ... Dusty.' Glendinning drove down to the wharf at 9 a.m. to meet Miller's ship, the *Athenic*. He found the wharfies on strike. Another ship was already docked where the *Athenic* was meant to be. It was stuck at Gage Road, in Fremantle Harbour. Glendinning waited for a couple of hours and left.

Meanwhile, a photographer, Bill Watt, from the *WA News*,

managed to get aboard the *Athenic* to take shots of the cricketers. Miller took him aside. 'Do you know Gus Glendinning?' he asked. The photographer said he did. 'Could you give him this?' Miller said, handing the man an envelope. The photographer nodded.

The next day Glendinning dropped by the newspaper to collect the envelope for Miller. It contained four sizeable diamonds, which he had 'acquired' at the Kimberley mines, when the team was taken through them. This way Miller avoided any questions from customs, which was always diligent about searching luggage from South Africa.

The *Athenic* finally docked in the late afternoon. Miller met Glendinning that night at the Palace Hotel and the envelope was handed over. Diamonds, and good mates, it seemed, were forever.

14
AS YOU WERE

Miller found a different feeling in Australia when he returned. The Federal Government had changed from Labor to a conservative variety run by the Liberal–Country Party coalition led by Robert Menzies. The tenuous links to war that seemed a permanent part of Miller's life since 1942 – the rationing of tea, petrol and butter – were over. Child endowment came in with the new regime, and it would mean something in the Miller household as the family grew.

The new prime minister was even keener on his sport than his predecessor Ben Chifley, who liked his cricket, but did not romanticise it as Menzies did. The new leader, patrician in manner and voice, and superior in education and profession to average Australians, did come down from his lofty perch to connect with them in his appreciation of cricket and football. Sport was the great leveller and vote catcher. An enthusiastic supporter of Carlton (in the VFL) and cricket everywhere, Menzies gave a new perspective to Karl Marx's cynical observation that religion was the opiate of the masses. There was more than a grain of truth in this observation in his era of the mid-nineteenth century. But Menzies, a century later, recognised that sport was at least an opium derivative of the people. He was a believer in politics being off the front page, except when it suited him, and sport on the front and back pages. This kept the electorate distracted while he and his government got on with running the country.

Menzies loved his cricket and let everyone know it. He kept only two pictures in his Canberra office. One was a tiny Tom Roberts Australian landscape. The other was a photograph of Miller finishing a cover drive.

> The feet beautifully placed, the lithe body balanced yet leaning out of balance with the shot [Menzies wrote], the blade through over the left shoulder, the head triumphant, the eye looking at the boundary. It is not only the greatest action photograph of a cricketer I have seen; it is in two dimensions a beautiful piece of sculpture, and it would have provoked immense joy in ancient Athens.

Menzies was not after the gay Greek vote in Melbourne or Sydney. It was 1950, and anyone in that demographic was firmly locked in the closet. He meant it.

Miller would have liked to be remembered for that shot and many others. He still harboured desires to prove himself with the blade and looked forward to the next season, 1950–51, when England would tour Australia.

In the meantime, he spent the winter of 1950 in Sydney consolidating his journalistic and writing experiences. Miller had a family of four and had to work harder at his trade to provide for them. He was not playing football, cricket or baseball. He had time to broaden his skills. Apart from his usual writing on the magazine *Sporting Life* he was given general, non-sports assignments on its affiliate paper, the Sydney *Sun*, where his friend Whitington had a desk. The Miller byline appeared on a variety of topics. He and Whitington began collaborating on cricket books in a most fertile off-season period. The books were to be published by London's Latimer House. Miller had met its owner, Clifford Gibbs, in 1948. Whitington would do most of the research, writing and structuring. Miller would provide some ideas and his name. His lively and photogenic image was to be used liberally.

The first result was *Cricket Caravan*. It featured reminiscences and judgements on the game. They focused on Bradman. In this regard John Arlott judged it as neither idolatry nor enmity. '[The book is] written on a literary standard far higher than that of most books [thanks to Whitington] by outstanding players,' he noted in *Wisden* 1950. Arlott added encouragingly, 'it ought not be the last written by these two, who work smoothly and interestingly in double harness.' *The Times Literary Supplement* had the generosity to recommend *Caravan* to Test players, but apparently no one else.

During this busy time, *Sporting Life* lifted its circulation to 245,000. It was able to take on a junior assistant named Richie Benaud, who was seconded from AANL's accounts department. The 19-year-old was an all-rounder, who hit hard and bowled a fair leg-break. He had shown more than promise in the 1949–50 season for New South Wales. He looked up to Miller, 11 years his senior, as a sporting role model and mentor.

Miller began the season of 1950–51 in October with a determination to score big. Against Queensland in Brisbane, he was a solid, if unspectacular 65 not out on day one, with his team on 2 for 278. In front of a Saturday crowd of 6,647, he ploughed on to a 100, 150 then 201 not out. The innings was chanceless. Miller took very few risks. Just when the crowd was nodding off, he would hit a six. In the end they were jolted five times – every hour and a half on average. Miller batted his longest innings yet, taking 7 hours 18 minutes. The swashbuckler of Lord's in 1945 was nowhere to be seen. In his place was the cricket ghost of Bill Ponsford, without the crab shuffle to counter the spinners. Captain Morris declared at 9 for 529.

The skipper used his outstanding resource wisely. A tired Miller was back to his RAAF days being used as the fifth change. He bowled just 7 overs in the first innings and 10.5 in the second. This set a pattern. It depended on how much Miller took out of himself with the bat. If his back injury played up, it was another legitimate excuse to avoid rolling his arm over. Morris would act according to his needs and Miller's mood. Morris knew his man. The competitive Miller would never sit back and refuse a bowl if he were fit, especially if there was a champion bat in and about to cause trouble.

In the return match 10 days later, Morris tossed him the ball only when the other five bowlers couldn't remove opener Ken 'Slasher' Mackay, the left-hander with a jutting derrière and minimal backlift. Mackay, one of the gutsiest cricketers ever to wear the baggy green, chewed gum like a cow and could be as slow as one on a hot day. Miller got rid of him with an away-swinger that he nicked behind. Morris then put his mercurial paceman out to pasture after a four-over spell to preserve him for some more batting at number three.

He was in at 1 for 12. He and Morris (101) put on 133. Miller took a little over two hours in another responsible knock, to make 63. Morris held him back in Queensland's second innings, then let him loose opening in New South Wales's chase of 225. They were allowed 130 minutes and took 118. Miller hit 138 not out. He had taken less time to make more than twice the runs scored in the first innings.

Commentators might well have asked: would the real Keith Miller please stand up? The performances showed he had two gears when previously he struggled with one. One complemented the other. Even in the smashing second performance, he built his innings early with the precision of a diligent engineer. Then, having calculated the worth of the bowling, the attitude of the opposing captain and the pace of the pitch, Miller constructed a power innings with just 1 six and 16 fours. Most boundary shots were drives. He was in the best form of his first-class career in Australia, and was ready for the clash of the year so far: New South Wales versus the visiting England (MCC).

Burly, crimson-faced amateur Freddie Brown led the tourists. He was your average country squire type with a bit of British bulldog for extra bite. He put on a brave front for the press, but underneath he was concerned that his team was not up to winning back the Ashes. Compton had a bad knee, Hutton had a troublesome thumb and half the team had little Test experience. Old-stagers Bedser and Wright would carry the bowling department's burden, while Brown, with medium-pace cutters, and Bailey would add support. There was 37-year-old Eric Hollies, past his best; there was also paceman John Warr, a 23-year-old Cambridge undergraduate, who had not reached his.

Brown was mustering all his considerable dynamism for the fight with strong New South Wales. The state would be a measure of just where the tourists were after more than a month on tour. A hand injury prevented him from playing. He looked on as Morris and Miller put on a masterful batting display on the rain-delayed first day, 10 November, reaching 1 for 274 at stumps. Morris out-paced his steady partner to dominate with 150 not out. Miller, 99 not out at stumps, lost Morris the next morning in front of a 27,000-strong Sydney crowd for 168 in 261 minutes, but went on to a chanceless 214 (3 sixes and 15 fours) in approaching a day at the wicket. It was a superbly timed knock in more ways than one.

Alan Davidson, a young left-arm medium-fast bowler and handy bat, will always remember one shot: 'It was the second over from Bedser with a new ball. Keith hit it as if he were using a 2-iron. The ball went like a bullet.' This innings established Miller (with Morris) as the form batsman for the Australians, and put his selection beyond any doubt. Second, it put the tourists in a defensive state of mind a few weeks before the Tests began.

Morris was able to declare at 3 for 509. Compton's knee was able to stand up for 92 runs and Hutton's thumb registered 'up' for a century, which allowed England to record a modest reply of 339 in a game that was allowed to stagger to a draw. Morris didn't give Miller a bowl. He wasn't up to it after his day's batting, and that was reason enough to hold him back.

After this psychological triumph over the international competition, New South Wales travelled south to the MCG for the first Shield game of two against Victoria. This was now the hottest of the domestic matches. The press and the public felt the heat of competition between the two old rivals, and they created real interest. The Test players in particular hated their home side to lose. There was a special 'grudge' match within a match for Hassett and Johnson from South Melbourne versus Miller, formerly of South Melbourne. Niceties were forgotten, bumpers were frequent. Miller and Lindwall said no beg-pardons as they tried to dislodge Hassett. But according to the *Age*, Hassett's 'brilliant parade of rapid scoring shots in the "classic" style' in compiling 179 won the day. He faced the full fury of Miller, Lindwall and Walker sending missiles at and over his head. At one point he said to an umpire at the bowler's end: 'If this does not constitute intimidatory bowling under the rules, perhaps you can explain to me what does.'

Miller heard the remark and said: 'Get on with the game, Lindsay. Leave it to the umpire. It's nothing to do with you.'

Miller couldn't contain himself. He just had to bowl in this sort of competitive environment. In his effort to generate pace, he sent down four wides in the first innings. He delivered just four bursts for the match that amounted to 20 overs, a hail of bumpers and no wickets. His only joy came from three catches, including one from Johnson (76). Miller told Ian Johnson he would 'keep' for the next encounter.

When New South Wales batted, Miller was removed lbw by Loxton for a duck. It was a rare double 'failure' for Miller in the tough contests between these two ancient rivals.

Apart from the desire to win, he and all the New South Welshmen were intrigued to get a sight of Jack Iverson, who was creating a sensation with his very different, unorthodox style of spinning. He gripped the ball in his right hand between his thumb and bent middle finger. The bent digit was used to propel the ball. If the thumb pointed straight it was the top-spinner, which bounced straight through. If the thumb pointed to the leg-side, the ball would turn from the off. It came out as a kind of wrong 'un bowled with the wrist over the ball instead of under it. He had bamboozled first-class batsmen in the previous domestic season (1949–50), taking 46 wickets at 16.12, and again in New Zealand on tour with a virtual Australian Second XI under Bill Brown. Iverson secured no less than 75 Kiwi wickets at the amazing and miserly rate of 7 runs each. Only Lindwall was able to combat him with confidence in the state game.

Iverson had played the MCC without startling results, which made him less than a secret weapon. But had he held back something under instruction from Hassett? 'Big Jake' (who stood 195 cm tall and weighed 95 kg) excited the skipper and the selectors. His recent record and his form in 1949–50 meant he would be chosen for the Tests.

Hassett (36 years old) had known Iverson (who was 34) since their schooldays at Geelong College. Diminutive Hassett was always the talented bat destined for bigger things. Iverson had been a battler without prospects in the game, but during the war he played with the concept of his different spinning technique. Post-war he made his way through the ranks to the state team, under Hassett's watchful eye. He recognised the potential element of surprise, and knew that Iverson, a temperamental individual, had to be shown the way and protected. He was ungainly, guileless and without the on-field savvy necessary for top cricket. He had spent years working on his amazing bowling tricks. Yet once a batsman called his bluff he was found wanting. A tactic such as batting out of the crease to smother his spin would throw him. Instead of varying his pace or direction, Iverson would deliver from short of the bowling crease. In theory this might have worked, but it never did. When Iverson was delivering from further back, the batsman would play him off the back foot and score.

Once when playing Queensland, Iverson was having trouble bowling to left-hander Ken Mackay. The batsman had blocked him for two overs. Iverson became frustrated. Fellow spinner Doug Ring came over and whispered: 'Give him a single.' Iverson had not thought of that. He thanked Ring when he got Mackay away from the strike this way. Iverson was also a poor bat, runner between the wickets and fielder.

Hassett's instinct for nurturing was being tested and perhaps taken too far during practice for the First Test at Brisbane. Miller and Morris wanted to face Iverson in the nets. They would not only have their reactions examined; they would also hope to learn much about his bowling and demeanour at the wicket, which would be useful intelligence for their return bout against Victoria in Sydney in January. Hassett refused to let Iverson bowl to them. Miller and Morris complained in a joking way to Hassett that it was disgraceful that Shield competition should be taken to that extent. They were all playing for Australia, weren't they? Hassett was as phlegmatic as ever but non-committal. It was clear to Miller and Morris that he was putting the Shield competition above the Tests. His intent was even more manifest when the Test began.

After such a blistering start to the season, Miller was in a batting slump that lasted into the Tests. He failed to entertain the scorers against South Australia. Then he managed just 15 (caught off Wright) in the first innings of the First Test as Australia struggled to just 228 on a slow wicket on day one, 1 December. It poured on day two. Miller and Compton went to the Brisbane races. They kept in touch with the Gabba by phone to see when the game would resume. The rain allowed them to stay out all day and enjoy themselves.

On day three, England was caught on a sticky and managed just 68. Miller delighted in picking up his favourite bunny, John

Dewes, for 1, and the ebullient Brown for just 4, in taking 2 for 29. Hassett then found himself in a situation similar to that at Durban in January, except this time it was he who had to make up his mind on how long to bat. He called a halt to the destruction with Australia on 7 for 32 (Miller 8, caught off Bailey). Hassett gambled that England would not make 193 to win batting last on a dreadful strip. Lindwall and Johnston did the early damage. Miller contributed by, as usual, picking up Dewes (9) batting at three.

Iverson came on to tackle the middle order. Miller sauntered to his usual position in slip. But Hassett motioned for him to field at silly point. Miller was astonished, but he soon realised the cunning behind the move. The slipper, next to the keeper and looking straight down the wicket, always had the best view of what the bowler was doing. It was his job to pick the spinning technique and be ready for a catch by determining the likely batting miscalculation. At silly point, the main objective was to watch the batsman. There would be only a glance at the bowler to see when he was delivering, not see *how* he was delivering.

It hadn't been necessary to expose Iverson in the first innings when Johnston removed half the opposition. In England's second innings, Iverson sent down 13 overs. Nerves made him a trifle loose. But on more occasions than any other bowler in the Australian side, he was unplayable. His figures of 4 for 43 were a more than promising start. Only Hutton resisted. He batted at eight and scored a sensational 62 not out – more than half the team total of 122. Australia was away with an uncomfortable, fortunate 70-run win.

Even before the end of the Test, Miller and Morris were planning to go after Iverson in the upcoming New South Wales versus Victoria match. But he was only the proxy. The New South Welshmen had Hassett and Johnson in their sights.

Miller was drinking at the bar of Brisbane's Lennons Hotel with journalists after the match. John Woodcock of *The Times* was on his first trip to Australia covering the tour and had his initial meeting with Miller. Woodcock was surprised that Miller was nearly as disappointed as he was at England's bad luck with the weather that cost it the match. His sympathy was genuine. 'Keith's sense of fair play in the arena of sport was one of his most disarming characteristics,' Woodcock said. 'He knew that justice had not been done, and that England, as the weaker team, would find recovery harder.' The journalist was aware of Miller's affinity with England and several members of the team, but he was still taken aback.

The Miller charisma was evident at the bar. He knew how to work the press without it being obvious. He was a newspaperman himself, and this helped in creating his positive media image. Journalists stuck together and drank with other reporters. It was a brotherhood. Sisters were few and far between, especially in male-dominated sports. And the brotherhood had a code, unwritten and understood: *you do not report on your own.* (It stands today.) This protected characters like Miller, who, no matter what they did, would not receive unfavourable media attention.

At the end of the chat with Woodcock, Miller said goodbye and added: 'I've got a sheila to meet.' (In keeping with the code, the *Times* reporter mentioned this remark only in his obituary for Miller, 54 years later.)

Miller batted himself out of the slump mid-December with an encouraging display for an Australian XI on an easy Sydney wicket against the tourists. Morris captained the side, and kept the psychological hold on England with a century. Miller stayed 135 minutes for 63 and hit just 3 fours. There was hardly a moment when he opened his shoulders. Morris declared at 9 for 526. He used Miller sparingly, leaving the heavy work to Walker, Noblet and Ring, who were vying for a Test spot.

England was always behind, being dismissed for 321 and forced to follow on. Morris maintained Miller as a shock bowler, and brought him on for energetic bursts that would secure wickets and unsettle batsmen for the other bowlers to topple. It was sensible captaincy. Miller was a match-to-match proposition, especially with games so close and travelling around the country taking up time and energy.

A few days later the national team was in Melbourne for the Christmas Test. Compton, sporting a closed eye, pulled out of the game. Its acquisition was a mystery. Had he been in a punch-up in a Melbourne bar, or had he stepped on a long-handled shovel?

Miller was keyed up for a performance in front of his family (except Peg, who was expecting their third child in two months time) at the MCG. A crowd of nearly 36,000 turned up with Miller's parents under good conditions. Les Sr and Edie were pleased that he received a fair ovation when he entered the stadium before lunch on the first day, 22 December, at 2 for 67. The wicket gave some help to the bowlers early. He struggled against Bedser, with his tell-tale lunges out of synch, and was lbw to Brown for just 18. But as ever, a failure in one department served only to fire him up for the other. After England's fine all-round display of bowling and fielding reduced Australia to all out 194 on day one, Miller took part in removing three batsmen, which had the tourists reeling at 6 for 61. Miller ended with 2 for 39 off 13 overs. Iverson, that new nemesis for England and future target for New South Wales, snared another 4 for 37 in front of his home crowd.

The crowd of more than 48,000 got its money's worth with England sneaking ahead by three runs. Australia was 0 for 25 at stumps. Then the game was halted for two days over Christmas Eve and Day, and was resumed in front of 60,000 on Boxing Day. This meant that the third day was played on a fifth-day pitch. It showed. Cracks appeared after a baking by the sun over the break. The ball sometimes leapt and other times shot through low.

Miller came in at 2 for 99 and was bowled by Bailey with one that kept low for 14. Only Ken Archer (46), opening, reached 40.

Australia was humiliated again, this time for a miserable 181. England's target was 179. Hassett called on Iverson in the short period before stumps on day three. He took two wickets. England was 2 for 28 at stumps. The game was evenly poised going into day four in front of another big attendance of more than 46,000. The pacemen – Lindwall and Johnston – took seven wickets, despite Hutton (40) again standing up with his unmatched technique under tough conditions.

England fell 28 runs short. Two tight Tests had gone Australia's way, more through luck than superior play. Miller had failed with the bat four times but had been an integral part of the bowling line-up's assault on the opposition. His intention to dominate with the bat had been arrested by the intensity and conditions of Test match cricket and the need for him to contribute more in the bowling department. Morris had assisted his ride with the blade, but Hassett, like Bradman, had to think first about what combination of bowlers would do best to win a Test. Miller was always prominent in their thinking, as he would be in the mind of any national team leader. He was too good a bowler to ignore.

The confrontations continued. The tourists took on New South Wales in the New Year at Sydney. The run of events seemed predictable. Morris won the toss. Miller replaced Moroney at the wicket early. Rain intervened and restricted the first day to 150 minutes. The wicket wasn't run-laden, but Morris continued on his way as the country's top batsman, reaching 105 in just 135 minutes, and leaving Miller 53 not out to carry on to 98 before his five-year adversary Wright took his wicket again. It was another patient knock, taking just under three hours, with 3 sixes and 6 fours. It put Miller back in touch with his terrific early season form.

But there was a turn rather than a twist in this game. New South Wales could manage only 333. England started badly. It was hard not to when the openers had to face Lindwall, Miller and Walker. But this time the wicket gave them no help. Hutton

(150) got together with Simpson (259) for a 236-run stand. England reached 553. And Miller found himself the packhorse for the first time in the season. New South Wales stumbled to 6 for 130 (Miller bowled by Brown for 1) and were lucky there was not another day's play. It would have seen them easily beaten.

Was it a turning of the wheel? Had England found a way mid-season to counter the 'old firm' of Lindwall and Miller? They had seen enough of them. Perhaps they had worked out how to punch back. Maybe the old firm was more old than firm.

Fans didn't have long to wait to find out. The Third Test, in Sydney, began two days after the New South Wales match. Media attention turned to Compton's availability. Miller's paper, the *Sydney Sun,* asked him to contact his English mate. It wanted a photo. Miller arranged for a photographer to go to his hotel. The resultant picture was of a dishevelled man just out of bed. Compton was England's Miller. He was known to be a party boy, but never allowed anyone to photograph him looking as if he had had a heavy night. Compton had a commercial image to protect. This was not good. He looked like the before part of an advertisement for a hairbrush company or Brylcreem, for which he was the featured star. Miller apologised but told Compton he should not have let the photographer take a shot. A little feeling lingered on into the Test.

England began more or less where it had left off against New South Wales and was travelling well when Hassett brought on Ian Johnson. He tossed the ball just wide enough of the off stump to tempt Washbrook into a late cut. Miller, at slip, threw himself to his right and was parallel with the ground when the ball stuck in his prehensile right hand centimetres above the turf.

Simpson joined Hutton and these big scorers of the New South Wales match looked set for something similar. At 128 Hassett threw the old ball to Miller, who was asked to bowl from the Paddington end. He then produced one of his finest ever bowling bursts, in four overs taking out Hutton and Simpson and uprooting Compton's stumps for a duck. Perhaps it was Miller's protest against the tardiness of Hutton and Simpson. Maybe something had riled him. Hassett wondered what he had eaten for lunch. Whatever it was, he had swung the game. England was 4 for 137, and Miller had a hand in all of the dismissals.

The tourists reached 5 for 211 at stumps, an insultingly slow day for the Friday crowd of nearly 50,000. It didn't turn off the more than 50,000 fans who turned up the next day, no doubt hoping for some more sparkle. England reached 290. Miller had the figures with 4 for 37. Bedser poured cold water on the Morris spark plug by bowling him for a duck. The spectators had to be content with a tight struggle. The bowling, the pitch and the tension were not going to allow anyone to break free. Miller was subdued. The Test atmosphere had imprisoned him, as had his desire to make Ponsford-like scores. He was 96 not out at stumps on the Monday in front of a third 50,000 crowd. The game had packed fans into Sydney as they had in Bradman's best days, but without the pay-off. Yet the game was appreciated for the battle. Australia was 6 for 362 (Johnson 64 not out), with a 72-run lead.

On the Tuesday, Miller was late. Team-mates were reminded of Newlands and countless other occasions when he had made a last-minute arrival. But this was a Sydney 'home' Test. He was 4 runs off a hundred. No one could recall a player being late in this situation. But Miller was Miller. He could not push through the fans outside the Members' gate. He hurried to the Paddington Gate, squeezed into the ground, and rushed to change. Ian Johnson, feeling like a jilted bride, waited at the top of the steps to the stand for his tardy partner. Miller appeared from nowhere and joined him, saying he had been to the doctor for a conjunctivitis problem.

The rush might have unsettled anyone else. But not Miller, at least on this occasion. He went on to 145 not out. It had taken him just short of a day. He hit just 1 six and 6 fours. His capacity to curb his instincts to attack had given Australia a lead of 136. Johnnie Moyes thought this was the 'real Miller'. Yet this was

Moyes, steeped in the era of the steady build of a big innings, expressing his views on the way he thought Miller *should* play in Tests. Moyes had not been at Lord's in 1945. There, another Miller, perhaps the authentic one in terms of his character and desires, had batted more explosively.

Iverson on Tuesday afternoon in front of 30,000 worked his middle-finger flick magnificently, especially from the off, taking 6 for 27. England failed by 13 runs to make Australia bat again. Iverson had reached a marvellous peak in a story-book rise. His tale was one of the ordinary bloke with ordinary cricketing skills who had found a way to be a superstar. But he could not bring other important skills to the game to complement this steep climb. Iverson's mental application, among other things, was suspect. Miller at slip and Morris at point watched in awe as he had every England bat, including Hutton and Compton, playing and missing and shaking their heads.

It was even more incentive for the New South Welshmen to go after this cricketing freak in the next game against Victoria before he embarrassed them in the same way.

Iverson's amazing performance did not supersede the all-round luminescence of Miller. This was his finest Test effort ever, and the most satisfying. He had hit a big score to win an Ashes series for Australia. He had taken the catch of the match and delivered one of the most vivid bowling bursts in history. It's doubtful that even his wildest day-dream in a quiet lunch-hour beside the oval at Melbourne High could have imagined this. His sudden burst of growth between 16 and 17 years had thwarted his premier dream of becoming a great jockey. That apart, he had attained every major goal in his sporting life.

Miller always needed challenges. While his state skipper was a clever planner, he needed to topple a rival. He and Morris were in accord over what was required to beat Victoria at the SCG, 17 days after the Third Test. A prime objective would be to disturb the phenomenal Iverson. It didn't take rocket science to learn how, just observation and the application of aggression. The Englishmen had played him from the crease. He had to be attacked. Big Jake's art was a mechanical one. There was a feeling from playing him in the nets that if you attacked he lost composure. The ball had to land on the pitch to make work that deceptive, almost unpickable delivery that looked like a leg-break coming but which spun in to the right-hander. If the spin was killed by a defensive shot or drive, the menace subsided. The whisper was that Iverson's frustration would subside into fury and depression.

First, Victoria had to be subdued when it batted on a winter-like day of rain breaks, which reduced play to just 219 minutes. Hassett was the roadblock. He and Johnson were the key targets for Miller, Lindwall and Walker. When these two were batting late in the day Miller plied them with bumpers. It was overdone. Science gave way to intimidation. There was a clear sense that Miller would love to hurt both batsmen, and they in turn would love to humiliate him. The batsmen wore no helmets or protective clothing beyond a box, gloves and pads. They had to watch the ball at all costs. If the eye was taken off it, then the ball's stitching might leave an imprint on arm, chest or head.

After stumps a reporter asked Miller about his barrage. 'They [Hassett and Johnson] were batting too slow,' Miller was reported in the *Sydney Morning Herald* as saying. 'They annoyed me.' This was whimsical Miller at his best. He turned schoolmaster and was punishing the opposition bats for tardiness. It was true that he would rather see shots played, but not off his bowling. If that were done, he would be even more angered. The batsmen could not win.

Hassett (82) and Johnson (29) were picked up the next morning. Victoria's mediocre 280 seemed to justify the bombardment. Every New South Wales batsman was primed to attack Iverson. They jumped at him at every chance, and Big Jake stumbled and became frustrated, then down on himself. Hassett kept encouraging, and Iverson showed more ticker than expected.

But his rhythms were upset. He, and all the bowlers, were dealt with by Morris (182), but he did snare Miller (83), caught by Hassett trying to hit a second six. Yet it was too little too late. New South Wales was able to declare, always a slight humiliation for the opposition, at 7 for 459.

Iverson took 3 for 108 off 29 overs, and was much less expensive than Johnston and Johnson, who went for five an over in the riot of run-making. But Iverson had become used to controlling the opposition even at Test level. If he could not do that, he lost patience and interest. The game ended in a draw, but New South Wales held the high ground and had seen off the Iverson threat to New South Wales Shield supremacy.

Miller entered the last two Tests intent on capitalising on his good form with bat and ball. He felt fit and strong enough to excel at both. His wish was to bat first, giving him every chance to put his initial energies into his batting. Hassett pleased Miller by winning the toss at Adelaide in the Fourth Test and batting. Morris hit a double century. Miller, Hassett and Harvey all added their support with forties. But England persisted through Bedser and Wright, knocking over the last seven wickets for 90. Australia reached 371, not quite enough to ensure that it could not lose. Hutton (156 not out in 370 minutes) countered Morris's fine effort with a gutsy performance of his own in carrying his bat as England battled to 272.

Moyes' Miller turned up again in the second innings at 3 for 95, and played another accountable innings that was much the same as his Test century at Sydney. Except that it was the century that wasn't. On 99, Wright delivered him an unplayable fast leg-break that turned a long way and clipped his off bail. It was the sort of ball received once a match. But Miller's conscientious approach put the game beyond doubt in much the way Hassett liked.

A 7-year-old Ian Chappell, a future Test captain, was watching this game. His father told him: 'Look at Miller; watch what Miller is doing.' It was similar to the instruction Les Miller Sr gave a young Keith Miller observing Ponsford 20 years earlier.

Chappell, like the rest of the crowd, was disappointed when his hero was dismissed one short of a century. Yet thanks to the application of Miller, and Burke in scoring his first Test century, Australia was allowed the luxury of declaring at 8 for 403 – a lead of 502. Johnston on the afternoon of the second-last day, and Miller (3 for 27) in a burst at the middle order on the final day, finished England. The tourists went down by 274 runs. Miller's all-round effort would have given him the player-of-the-match award, if there had been one, for the second successive Test.

There wasn't much interest left in the final Test in Melbourne with Australia up 4–0. Attendances were mostly less than half those of the Second Test. Miller failed with the bat, going down to Brown twice caught and bowled for 7 and a duck. But he returned the best bowling analysis with 4 for 76 in England's only completed innings. The tourists won comfortably by eight wickets. No one begrudged Freddie Brown and his lads a win.

Some English scribes spoke bravely about the Test being a 'turning point'. But the Australian press remained smug about superiority in Ashes contests. Australia had lost the Ashes just once since 1930, or more than two decades ago, and time was putting that loss in the Bodyline series as an aberration, or at least something abnormal, which it was for more than one reason. Australia had now won two series comfortably since the Bradman era, and there were no overt signs that its dominance in world cricket had peaked.

Miller had been a part of four successive Test series wins. He was 31 years old and had to be at, or near, his own peak. This was his sixth year of international cricket if his Victory Tests were counted. Despite failing in six Test innings in the 1950–51 Ashes, he topped the batting averages with 350 runs at 43.75, just ahead of Hassett, Harvey and Morris. His 20 first-class innings presented even betting reading: 1332 runs at 78.35, the best average of all batsmen, including the tourists, for the season. It was his finest so far, ahead of his 72.50 in England in 1945, and 75.12 in Australia in 1946–47.

Miller's bowling figures were strong in the Tests: 17 wickets at 17.70. The great Hutton was the sole batsman who consistently countered Miller's bursts of vigour and speed. The bowler dismissed him just once. Only Iverson (21 at 15.23) headed Miller in the Tests. Sadly Miller's assault with Morris put paid to the Victorian, who became dispirited after it, in spite of his Test success. Iverson faded from view and never played another Test.

***

Soon after the Tests, Peg gave birth to their third son. He was named Denis Charles after Denis Compton. Miller's hope was that he would turn out to be as charming, carefree and gifted as his namesake.

In March, Miller had a tricky writing assignment. His editor wanted him to appraise the season. Miller wanted to say something about the spirit in which the first post-Bradman Ashes series was played in Australia. He reckoned there was a much better atmosphere without Bradman's on-field involvement. There were examples of a different mindset among the Australian players under Hassett. Johnson exemplified it after feathering a ball to the keeper off the unlucky paceman John Warr in the Fourth Test. The umpire said not out. The keeper gave a token appeal. Johnson noticed Warr's sadness and decided to give him the only Test wicket in his career. Johnson walked. He left the wicket with Australia 6 for 297, nearly 400 in front and heading for an unassailable mountain of runs. Miller's point (not mentioned in the proposed article) was that Johnson would not have walked had Bradman been sitting as skipper in the dressing room and not Hassett.

Miller's article asked whether Australia wanted another Bradman era. He acknowledged that period – 1928 to 1948 – produced record gates and outstanding batting from 'one or two individuals' (Miller had Bradman and Ponsford in mind). But it nearly killed the Ashes when England introduced Bodyline to combat Bradman's 'undoubted genius'. Then cricket lost its 'real value as a sport. It became war.' Miller was trying to be diplomatic while making his point. What was on his mind was Bradman's approach in crushing England after England's captain Jardine had targeted him in 1932–33. When Bradman became captain he was uncompromising in pursuit of victory. The hardness in this, Miller was saying between the lines, had spilled unnecessarily into the post-war era. Now that Bradman was off the scene, Miller maintained, cricket was becoming friendlier. It was a brave point to make, even if it were debatable. Bradman was sure to read it with interest.

Whitington worked hard on his second book with Miller: *Catch! An Account of Two Cricket Tours*. The formula was now established. A notable character – this time Denis Compton – would provide the foreword, then Whitington would write an account of the Tests; in this case two series: the Australian tour of South Africa in 1949–50, and the just completed 1950–51 Ashes. They were described with insider detail in, as Arlott observed, 'Runyonesque narrative' style with occasional bursts in the present tense. Arlott was unfamiliar with just one word in the text: *akimbo*. R. C. Robertson-Glasgow, writing in *Tatler*, was effusive also about the 'unfolding insider story' that distinguished *Catch!* from the conveyor belt of 'How to play' cricket books.

With such support and good sales figures in England and Australia, the 'partnership' of Miller's name and Whitington's words would carry on.

WWW.RAMADHIN.
VALENTINE

They were never a website, but should have been. Weekes, Walcott and Worrell, the three world-class West Indian batsmen who toured Australia in 1951–52, were billed as the biggest threat to Australian cricket supremacy since Bodyline. They had been in the West Indian side that thrashed England 3–1 in Tests in England in 1950. They, along with Allan Rae and Jeffrey Stollmeyer, had carved up England. Charming Everton Weekes was called the 'black Bradman'. The charismatic, suave Frank Worrell hit a Test 261 in 335 minutes. It was the highest Test score ever at Trent Bridge. And the forceful 95 kg Clyde Walcott, who also kept wickets, averaged in the mid fifties in Tests.

Hassett, Morris and Miller made diplomatic public statements saying how much they were looking forward to the challenge of these five and the great spin twins, 21-year-old Indian Sonny Ramadhin and 20-year-old Alf Valentine. They had taken 59 wickets in the four England Tests – at an amazing rate of 15 wickets a Test. It was all hype to bring the crowds in.

The West Indians had not toured Australia in 20 years, and then they had been a flop. Many cricket fans had long memories and had to be convinced. In private, Australia's big three and Lindwall were not convinced themselves. They read the press reports and looked at the statistics. They were both helpful and misleading. But they could not lie about the paucity of the

England bowling attack. Hollies, Bedser, Bailey and Yardley were the mainstays again with some new names. But only Bedser had taken more than 10 wickets: 11 at 34.27. In short, the West Indian heavy scorers had not beaten much.

The Australian bowling brains trust had a plan similar to the Miller–Morris strategy to defeat Iverson. Again, it didn't need Mensa Club members to work out their approach. Miller and Lindwall would pulverise the West Indies batting order and test them in a way that the English bowlers could not.

More problematic were the opposition spinners. Ramadhin, all 160 cm of him, terrorised the fine England batting line-up. Only Hutton, Washbrook and Bailey had answers, but not often. He could deliver leg and off-spin, and no one, not even the keeper, could pick him. 'All you see is the blur of a black hand, a white shirt with sleeves buttoned to the wrist, and a red ball,' Compton remarked. 'You have to guess the rest.' Bespectacled Valentine was a left-armer, and a perfect foil for his partner. Miller's approach to these two 'sheiks of tweak' would depend on the moment. It was one thing to measure a player's temperament and then attack but another matter if the spinner thrived on aggressive opponents, in which case a different tactic would have to be invoked.

While working out how to obliterate the visitors on the field, Hassett, Morris, Miller and Johnson, as the team's leaders, were conscious of making them feel welcome off the field. The White Australia policy to prevent non-white immigration to the country had been on the statute books since Federation in 1901. It provoked a negative attitude and ignorance. It was in part a reason for the neglect of Australia's own black population. The country had been going through a cultural shift with a post-war influx of different peoples, which was forcing the bulk of the Anglo-Celtic population to accept and accommodate 'new Australians', mainly Europeans. But there was not a black or Asian in sight, apart from the Chinese who had roots in nineteenth-century Australia before the 'whites only' policy was introduced. Exceptions were made for non-white sportsmen. If they could play cricket, then they had to be acceptable. If they could thrash England in England as convincingly as Bradman's Invincibles, there was even room for some respect.

The fact that these black men smiled, were polite and friendly, and were led by two whites – 32-year-old Barbadian John Goddard and 30-year-old Trinidadian Jeffrey Stollmeyer – made everyone breath more easily. Miller was aware from his playing against a Ceylonese team when at Melbourne High and his 1945 tour of India that racist myths were ridiculous. These experiences caused him and the other team leaders in 1951–52 to go out of their way to welcome the West Indians. Miller went over to them at the practice nets in the week before the First Test in Brisbane and introduced himself. He was surprised to learn that his reputation on and off the field had preceded him. He had an immediate rapport with Worrell and Weekes. He became good friends with them through the season.

The West Indies was at a disadvantage. They had only one warm-up match versus Queensland, in which the players seemed under-done. Yet the Brisbane Test would be played on a pitch more suitable to the spinners. The fear factor had also hit the Australian team. Batsmen were perplexed about the tourists' spin twins and in a quandary about how to play them. Morris and Barnes had done a little espionage by watching them play at Newcastle against a New South Wales Country XI. They sat near a sightscreen and viewed the bowlers through binoculars. But they came away none the wiser. In fact, seeing Valentine destroy the opposition bats, who seemed all at sea when trying, or not trying, to pick the spin, only increased their fears. The key Australian batsmen were looking for some clue to a technique with which to counter him and Ramadhin. They all knew the statistics for the West Indies in England, which had been emphasised in the newspapers, especially Ramadhin's 135 tour wickets at 14.88.

'I was reading too much about what happened in England,'

Morris said, 'and this didn't help. I could not pick Ramadhin at all. Later (in the West Indies in 1955) I managed to pick him in the air, but not in 1951–52.'

Miller was querulous, but tried not to let the problem get inside his head. He discussed it with Lindwall in their hotel the night before the game. Their plan when bowling was all-out attack against the three Ws, Rae and Stollmeyer. They would see how they played the short ball. After all the talk among the Australian batsmen and their worries about the spinners, Miller and Lindwall decided over a few quiet beers that they would forget all the theories and go after Ramadhin. He seemed to be the hardest to 'pick' of the two.

The West Indies batted first, and its key batsmen were uncomfortable under the speed barrage. Lindwall began the series by bowling Rae third ball for a duck. After that, none of the reputable opposition recovered to a point where Australia was threatened. The speed duo used the bumper freely, even against tail-enders. Only Goddard resisted until Miller bowled him for 45. The West Indies' 216 seemed to set Australia up for a win, if its top batsmen could overcome both the phobia about, and the actual spin of, Ramadhin and Valentine. They failed on both counts.

Miller came to the wicket at 3 for 80, now batting below Archer, Morris, Hassett and Harvey. He was not on form, having failed with the bat in his games for Manly and in his one Shield match. His overriding thought was: 'If Ramadhin pitches up I will hit him.' Aggression when out of form was the better part of valour. Miller could not pick Ramadhin's deliveries. 'I just hit,' he said. The spinner's first ball to him was swept for four. It had been Miller's policy in tight moments before. Sometimes it worked, sometimes it didn't. On this occasion it was somewhere in between. He missed a few and was dropped twice. First ball after lunch he walloped Valentine straight for six.

Lindwall joined Miller at 5 for 129, and was inspired by his tactic. They moved the score on 59 before Valentine caught and bowled Miller for 46. Lindwall went on to 61 when the medium-pace swinger Gerry Gomez bowled him. The unscientific hit-if-you-can policy lifted Australia just 10 runs ahead. Valentine had removed half the side for 99. Ramadhin had 1 for 75.

The tourists did a little better in their second effort with 245. Australia had 236 to make on a turning wicket. This time the spinners' figures were reversed. Valentine took 1 (Miller again, for 4) for 117 and Ramadhin 5 for 90. They sent down nearly 81 overs between them while Australia struggled to win by three wickets.

It was clear that Goddard was going to put complete faith in his spinners for the series. It seemed well placed. Miller had a problem with Valentine, who beat him twice in the match. No batsman looked comfortable against him, and to a lesser extent Ramadhin. Miller didn't get a chance to learn more about the spinners in the next game for New South Wales against the tourists. Prior Jones removed him for 30 before Valentine was on. But Miller kept the West Indies under pressure by turning in another match-winning performance. He took eight wickets and a catch and was involved in the dismissal of all but three West Indians. The tourists fought back but fell 24 short of the state side in a game in which Miller was supreme with the ball.

In the next Test in Sydney on a batsman's wicket, the West Indies batted first on 30 November and compiled 362. In response, Miller joined Hassett at 3 for 106. The captain used his skills off the back foot. The taller Miller used his reach to strive forward. 'I started to pick Ramadhin,' Miller said. He could now tell the difference between his leg-break and his off-spinner and top-spinner.

Miller also tried to put the Trinidadian orphan off his game by calling him 'Shorty'. This was 'Weedy' lashing back at his own early years, when he was himself under-sized. Miller had endured taunts about his height until he was well into his seventeenth year. He had hated it, but learned to live with it. He expected everyone to have his mental constitution and accept the barbs or lash back. But not everyone was as thick-skinned. 'You're a nice little chap,' he would say, 'but you haven't improved your bowling much since the last match, have you?' The patronising put-downs hit their mark. Ramadhin was angered and hurt. But instead of fighting back he went through the motions of delivering and then didn't bowl to Miller at all. It was a major victory for the Australian.

Hassett (132) and Miller hit centuries (129 in 246 minutes with 15 fours). Valentine took his wicket for the third successive time, but not before he and Hassett had demoralised Ramadhin. Before the Second Test was over Miller's psychological harassment had disengaged one half of the best spinning combination the world had seen since O'Reilly and Grimmett 16 years earlier. Ramadhin sent down 53.3 overs and took 1 wicket for 196. 'He also had a lean time against Len Hutton,' Miller boasted, 'although the Englishman mastered him more by his great defence. I attacked him.'

Ramadhin could not spin the ball as much on Australia's harder pitches. The spinner had to 'exaggerate' his finger action to extract bite. The effort was spotted first by Miller and later by others as the bowler lost confidence, tensed up and made ever more obvious finger movements. Miller began discerning his deliveries through the air as well, and backed his good form in going out to meet the ball before it hit the deck and spun.

He noticed a different mental make-up between Ramadhin, who dropped his bundle after the continual belting and sledging, and Valentine, who never gave up. The bespectacled spinner grinned and stared at Miller, who was never cocky against him. Miller rated him highly, even better than England's Tony Lock.

Once again Miller could claim to have dominated a match. After Australia reached 517, he took part in dismissals of half the West Indies team. Dependable batting and brilliant bowling and catching indicated that he was in the best all-round form of his Test career. Australia was unlikely to lose while he was in touch to this degree. It won the game by seven wickets and had a strong grip on the series.

Wisden complained that Lindwall and Miller were using 'relentless bumper tactics'. But the West Indians didn't complain. The description 'Bodyline' came up when Stollmeyer ducked into a lethal ball from Lindwall. But the Australians were delivering nothing like 'fast leg theory'. They used two men close in on the leg side and another player in the deep. But there was more emphasis on catches in the slips and gully on the off side, which was different from Bodyline in principle and execution.

The weather conspired to bring the West Indies back into the competition in Adelaide in the Third Test when 22 wickets fell on the first day. Worrell and Johnston, who both took 6 wickets, exploited a wet patch at one end. Miller was one of Worrell's victims. He retaliated by bowling Worrell for 6, but it was a lean match for Miller. He took that one wicket, and only his battling 35 in the second innings was something to salvage from Australia's six-wicket defeat. The tourists' victory lifted their spirits. Interest in the series was renewed.

***

Miller took time to visit the Bradman home in Adelaide's Kensington Park. His purpose, apart from savouring the Bradman hospitality over dinner, was to see Don's son John, who was suffering from poliomyelitis. John, 12, was incapacitated in a steel frame, where he would stay for a year. Don had given up all cricket administration duties, and was taking much time off from his broking business to assist his wife Jessie in nursing John. They had to bath and give him therapy every day.

John was proud of his father's achievements but had been just 7 years old when Bradman played his last Test series in Australia and 9 when he retired. Miller had become John's playing hero, and the visit was a tonic for him. They talked for some time. Miller read him stories. John would never forget this kindness. They became friends.

***

The Fourth Test began on 31 December 1951 and attracted nearly 60,000 Melbourne fans to the MCG on day one. Miller appreciated the atmosphere more than before. It helped his nerves that he could bowl first. He did not have to wait to bat, but instead was able to take full advantage of the tension generated in the colosseum. With the crowd behind him, he built great pace and was more than a foil for Lindwall. Miller sent back the openers K. R. Rickards and Stollmeyer, and Johnston removed Weekes, all with just 30 on the board, in the first hour. A century by Worrell restored some order for the West Indies, but it managed only 272. Miller took 5 for 60. He followed this up with 47 runs in the only meaningful partnership for Australia: 124 for with the dashing Harvey (83). Australia fumbled to be all out 216 on day two. But just before stumps Lindwall struck twice in his first over to leave the tourists on 2 for 20.

Miller's 2 for 49 helped dismiss the West Indies for 203, a lead of 259. Hassett's expertly composed 102 was not enough to challenge the target. Australia slumped to 9 for 222, bringing last-man-in Bill Johnston to the wicket with Doug Ring. More than 30,000 spectators were resigned to seeing the West Indies win and level the series. The sergeant in charge of Victoria's police contingent at the MCG had seen these two bat before. He was convinced the game was all but over. He sent his men around the boundary, ready to stop the charge towards the sacred pitch.

But these two unflappable Victorians, despite their limited batting skills, had other ideas. They began to scrape the runs together. Goddard seemed to panic. Ramadhin found the pressure too much. He left the ground. Miller, in the dressing room, began offering bets that the two Victorians would do it. He had no takers. No player dared move from his seat in case it disturbed the equilibrium and fortune on the field. The runs were acquired and Australia won by a wicket. It gave the home team the series.

Once more Miller had provided the best all-round performance, taking the largest number of wickets for the match (7) and
staying in a vital stand with Harvey. His consistently brilliant
form was maintained in the last Test in Sydney, where he took
another 7 wickets and hit 69 in Australia's second innings, the
second-highest score in a low-scoring match. Gomez' 10 wickets
was a fine performance.

A highlight of the game was a battle of wits between the
pacemen and Weekes. The West Indies began the final day on 2 for
112, needing 416 to win, a possibility given their strong batting
line-up. Miller and Lindwall began the first session with a rush of
bumpers. In his sixth over of the morning Lindwall bounced
Weekes, who hesitated and missed an attempted hook. Vice-
captain Stollmeyer was batting up the other end. He directed
Weekes not to play the shot. Lindwall heard the command. He
gave Weekes another short one. The batsman was tempted but
ducked. Stollmeyer repeated his command.

Miller took a few steps forward from slip. 'Who are you to tell
him how to bat?' he asked provocatively.

Lindwall sent down a third bouncer. Weekes refused to strike
back, although he was an accomplished hooker. The bowler sent
down another. Weekes shaped up, went half-way through with
the shot and was caught behind. Lindwall and Miller had
combined to win the battle, but brought criticism.

In the press box, Bill O'Reilly was angry over the tactics until
Lindwall reminded him that it was he who had first encouraged
the speedster to use the short ball as an intimidating weapon.

Miller's capacity with the bat might well have given him the
player-of-the-match award for the third time in the five Tests.
There could be little argument that he would have taken the man-
of-the-series award had there been one. He topped the bowling
statistics with 20 wickets at 19.90, and put in steady performances with the bat, scoring 362 at 40.22. Only Hassett (402 runs
at 57.43) had better returns.

***

Two weeks after the Tests Miller captained a 'Commonwealth XI' against a touring MCC side in Colombo, Ceylon. He had been reading about the success of Pakistan's Fazal Mahmood, a strong, medium-fast bowler, who delivered leg-cutters in the Bedser manner. Miller met him at the Colombo Hotel the day before the match. 'We've got to beat them [the MCC],' Miller told him.

'I will try,' the 24-year-old Fazal replied.

'It's not a matter of trying,' Miller said firmly. 'We must beat them.'

The MCC had been on a tough tour since early October through India, Pakistan and Ceylon. 'They went to Ceylon hoping to relax from serious cricket,' *Wisden* noted, 'but found themselves opposed to the strongest side they met on tour.'

Miller's attitude promised tough competition. The Commonwealth XI, including two other Australians, Harvey and Hole, batted first. Miller continued his form against the West Indians by compiling a forthright 106. Harvey (74), and C. I. Gunesekara (135) were in superb touch also as the team compiled 517. The pitch was fast. Miller made the ball fly and enjoyed the discomfort of the England batsmen, bowling both Robertson and Donald Kenyon for ducks. He also delighted in removing Donald Carr (17), whom he had first terrorised in a Victory 'Test'. The MCC was all out for 103 and forced to follow on.

Fazal was straggling off the ground after taking 4 for 46 when Miller came up to him. 'Fazal, you can't go off the ground,' Miller said, 'you'll lose your concentration.' The Pakistani was looking forward to putting his feet up. Miller faced him, placed his hands on his shoulders and repeated his directive.

'He was very determined to thrash the MCC,' Fazal said. 'We sat on the ground outside the pavilion and discussed the strategy to get out the MCC in the second innings.'

'Fazal,' Miller said, 'give them 100 and then finish the match.'

The Pakistani was buoyed by Miller's confidence in him.

Miller took the first wicket, again removing Robertson for a duck in the first over. He called for Fazal to bowl from the other end, and then surprised him by saying quietly about 24-year-old Tom Graveney, who had come to the wicket: 'Fazal, don't get him out. Give him 20 runs. This guy has to play against us next season [in the 1953 Ashes]. I want to find out his weak points.'

A stunned Fazal thought about the directive. 'Twenty-odd runs,' he said. 'Granted.'

He had removed Graveney for a duck in the first innings. Now he had to restrain himself. It made sense as he watched Miller in slip, arms crossed, a hand cupping his chin. This was cricket espionage at its most direct. Miller would absorb Graveney's style, and there was plenty to take in. He had a complete array of elegant strokes played mainly off the front foot. Miller tested him, first with a searing bumper, then some short balls, which took him off his beloved front foot. Graveney went on to 48, and Miller learnt all he wanted to know about the dashing England batsman, who was billed as a player with the ubiquitous 'great potential'. This was now a phrase used before a new player faced the Australian attack, which was still the best in the world.

When Mankad had dismissed Graveney, leaving MCC 4 for 97, Miller said to the team: 'Right, let's finish this off.' Somehow, Fazal felt, this supreme confidence was infectious. MCC was rolled for 155 and thrashed by an innings and plenty.

Another sense of the Miller style of leadership occurred in a pre-1952–53 season game for the state, when he was made captain in place of Morris, who was unavailable. 'Keith was so casual about the whole thing,' Bob Simpson recalled. He was just 16 years old and playing his first game for New South Wales. 'As we were walking on to the field an attendant drew him aside and said: "Mr Miller, something seems to have gone wrong. You're taking 12 men on the field." Keith had forgotten to nominate a twelfth man. I was pretty nervous. I was the youngest player there and felt I'd be the one sent back to the dressing room. How was he going to work out the strategy? Should he drop a batsman, a quick bowler or me? Keith solved it as only he could. He simply turned round to the team and said: "I say, would one of you chaps piss off?"'

'The entire team returned to the pavilion,' Alan Davidson recalled. 'Keith came to us, and said, "Righto, you funny fellows."'

Davidson and Simpson returned to the field, and another player, who expected to be twelfth man, stayed in the pavilion. The teenager, in awe of the legend Miller, was intrigued by the way the skipper would set his field when he took the new ball to open the bowling himself. Simpson was already a fine slipper. Would he be placed there? Would Davidson be in the gully near him? While the possible field permutations were running through his mind, Miller turned and said: 'Scatter!' Miller's explanation for this was that the players knew their positions. Only one or two of the younger members of the team wandered like lost sheep until given further instruction. Once everyone was in position more or less, he would calibrate the field with some fine-tuning.

While these incidents would become part of the Miller legend, this was only a practice match. He would never be a grand planner. Instinct, the moment, the way rhythms developed – or did not – in a game would be more likely to dictate his decisions than sitting down with a pencil and paper before a game.

***

Whatever his team-mates thought, they were about to receive much more of Miller's methods. Shortly after the pre-season game, he was in a Hong Kong bar in October 1952 when a Chinese journalist informed him that he had been made captain of New South Wales. He didn't call for champagne.

Arthur Morris was in the same city playing with him in a tournament celebrating the centenary of the Hong Kong Cricket League. New South Wales won the Shield for the second time under Morris's outstanding leadership in 1951–52. He had been Hassett's deputy in the national team for the past three Test series and was regarded as a calm, highly knowledgeable and competent leader who led by example at the top of the batting order. For reasons never fully explained, New South Wales's five-man selection panel decided to dump him. A Sydney press campaign had been pushing for Miller. It was suggested that he was a more dynamic cricketer and that he would bring more flair to games and attract more fans through SCG turnstiles. The New South Wales Cricket Association was worried. It had made a loss of £6,000 in the previous season. Its administration had to be seen to be doing something.

These reasons had some merit but were wafer thin. Yet Miller, who had earlier been on the end of a woeful national dumping decision, was entitled to a break from an administration. He would rather it had not been done at the expense of his friend Morris. Miller did not cabal against Morris. He did not lobby for the job, and Morris was aware of this, which helped to smooth the transition. Morris gave Miller his full support.

The state administration's arrogance was matched by its parochialism. Morris would be subordinate in state games. But Miller would be under Morris, the national team's vice-captain, whenever they played for Australia.

The confusion and lack of logic aside, Miller now had his chance to strut his stuff as a leader. He had his eyes on the main job as national leader once Hassett stepped down. Moving into the captaincy was just the challenge needed to inspire him. He was approaching 33 years of age during the initial burst of leading New South Wales five times before the Tests versus South Africa began early in December 1952. His style of leadership was of great interest from the first match against Queensland in Brisbane. Miller took his role seriously, sacrificing any adventurous tendencies from his first innings of 108, which was his slowest recorded so far. It took 4 hours and 20 minutes.

His most important game as skipper in this period was against South Africa at Sydney, beginning 14 November. The bold Miller style was evident. He won the toss, sent the opposition in, set a very attacking field without fine leg or third man, and opened with the right–left combination of Lindwall and Davidson. In 10 minutes, the tourists were 3 for 3 and never fully recovered. New South Wales went on to win by five wickets.

After those five games, he received high marks from most observers. Test leg-spinner Peter Philpott played under him at Manly from the age of 15 and later for New South Wales. 'Miller was totally unconventional and innovative,' he told me. 'He would never let a game slow down or die. He never went for containment [bowling with defensive fields to hold a batsman in check]. Miller was always on the attack.' Philpott said the New South Wales team felt they would never be beaten. 'We had Miller,' he said, 'and it was a huge advantage to feel he would always do something special if we were challenged.'

Batsman Ian Craig said Miller was the greatest bowler he had seen. 'That he could change the course of the game with a brilliant spell,' Craig said, 'was as much a reflection of his talent as his captaincy.'

Several of Miller's charges, including Burke, Philpott and Davidson, could mimic his nervous cough, voice, walk and mannerisms. This indicated the extraordinary influence of the man, his character and his style on the cricketers under him. Where others admired and mimicked Miller, Richie Benaud idolised him and copied his manner, even in the way he unbuttoned his shirt in the field. It could be that Benaud's oft-mimicked pronunciation of the scoreline '2 for 22' was a conscious or unconscious homage to his skipper.

After his playing days, in more mature reflection, Benaud compared Morris with Miller: 'Morris was always a quiet skipper but a very thoughtful one. He led the side just as well as Miller but in a much less flamboyant manner.' Benaud found that Miller's unorthodoxy made him a good captain. 'I learnt a lot from him in this department of the game,' he said, 'particularly by way of trying something a little unusual, if all orthodox methods failed.' There was always 'plenty of thought behind everything he did'. Benaud, like Lindwall, found Miller 'a nervous character. His suggestions would be proffered boldly but with a characteristic cough and much hand waving. But the players who took his advice or asked for it invariably benefited.'

Miller was prepared to buy a wicket by enticing a batsman to hit out. In leg-spinner Benaud's case this would mean putting men in the deep for the lofted catch or miscue, rather than placing fielders in purely defensive positions. Not all bowlers like being hit. Benaud was prepared to let it happen and cooperate with his captain. 'I took many wickets in first-class cricket that in some way could be traced back to a pointer produced by Miller. It may have been a change of pace or some little weakness in a batsman, undetected by myself. Or it may have been something to do with the pitch or the amount of zip being gained from the surface.'

Miller's advice suited Benaud. He, too, was always keen to try something different. Miller, like all strong captains, wished to lead by example. There were abundant opportunities with bat, ball and in slips. He was always in the game. Yet he did not ignore his troops. He studied them and cared about their morale and energies. If a batsman was having a run of low scores, he might change the batting order and send him in against opposition bowlers who were worn out after a long New South Wales partnership. If a batsman had been sitting for hours waiting to go in, Miller might tell him to take his pads off and relax. Another batsman might be told to pad up.

Miller did not regard the batting order as inviolate. He fiddled with it to suit the team's needs. Against South Australia in Adelaide on the day after his thirty-third birthday he demonstrated his all-round leadership skills even if not everything he tried worked. He reversed the batting order when Phil Ridings sent New South Wales in on a pitch ill-prepared because of rain.

Lindwall opened and made 70, but no one else could manage 30 in New South Wales's mediocre tally of 148. The move failed. It brought him criticism, as did his sending in the opposition, on some later occasions, when he won the toss. But, as Benaud observed, his moves were always thoughtful and based on what was best in his mind for the team. Flexibility was a key to Miller's style.

In this game, he led the New South Wales fight-back by mowing down the first five South Australian batsmen. His burst of sustained ferocity put the game in the balance by 5 p.m. when drinks were taken on blistering hot day. New South Wales twelfth man Sid Barnes in a double-breasted suit came on to the ground with a steward. They offered squash, cigars, combs and mirrors to players. Miller was amused. He ordered a second drink. The steward walked unhurried off the ground to fetch it. Photographers crept on to the ground. Barnes posed smiling for the cameras.

Phil Ridings, who had been batting in a rearguard action against the hostility of Miller and Lindwall, was angered, especially when the break was extended to more than 8 minutes. Ridings was a national selector. He believed Barnes, who had just been overlooked for Test selection, was causing the disruption to upset him. The Saturday crowd of 9,155 had been amused by Barnes' antics at first. But the long delay in the hot sun turned their laughs into boos as he left the ground.

Miller continued to lead from the front in this match. Evidently the captaincy had not impaired his performance. He took the largest number of wickets for New South Wales (8) and top-scored in its second innings with 71. South Australia scraped in by three wickets, thus inflicting the first defeat on New South Wales in the Miller-led era. Miller kept up a remarkably similar rate to his aggregate Test performances of more than 300 (335) at an average of just over 40 (41.87) with the bat. The bowling figures kept up his regular output with 21 wickets at 21.9. His catching was sharper than ever in slips.

The SACA (South Australian Cricket Association) wrote a letter of complaint to the NSWCA over the Barnes incident, and Miller was called before it for a 'please explain'. Miller assured the sombre board members that it was a harmless prank and that it would not happen again. Barnes was dropped from any calculations for the upcoming 1953 Ashes tour.

***

Jack Cheetham's South African team surprised all commentators by playing above themselves throughout the Test series of 1952–53. The basis of its success was fielding. Cheetham realised they would find it tough to match the Australians in batting and bowling. He thought laterally and developed his players' throwing, catching and chasing skills. Athleticism and fitness would be features of his young side. They were highlighted in the Second Test in Melbourne.

Miller was travelling well on 52 after 100 minutes at the wicket in pursuit of South Africa's 227. He wound up and hit a ball from off-spinner Hugh Tayfield with all his shoulder power straight and flat. People behind the sightscreen began to take evasive action. Russell Endean flew from nowhere to take a high catch in his right hand within a step of the boundary. It changed the course of the match. Miller applauded the catch. He had blasted out South Africa's early batsmen with the ball, and had been in charge with the bat. Now he was on his way. Australia moved only 16 ahead. It was nearly Endean's game. He scored 162 not out in 18 minutes less than 8 hours and earned the sobriquet 'Endless Endean'. South Africa won by 82 runs, reversing the result in Brisbane, where Australia got home by 96 runs. This was South Africa's first victory against Australia since 1910–11. Miller was Australia's best all-round performer in the game. He also reached the double – 100 wickets and 1,000 runs – when he dismissed John Waite a second time. It was his thirty-third Test.

He maintained his strong form in the Third Test at Sydney with 55 (once more Tayfield's victim, lbw) in Australia's only innings, and taking 5 for 81 in the two innings. Australia won easily by an innings, mainly because Harvey played 'one of the most dashing innings of his career', according to Sydney's *Sunday Herald*. His 190 took 6 hours.

Miller had a lean (drawn) Fourth Test, making just 9 and pulling a ligament in his back, which he believed was connected to the wrestling injury that had plagued him for nine years. Not coincidentally, Lindwall broke down too with a damaged leg tendon. The two of them had carried Australia's front-line bowling now for more than six years. The strain was beginning to show. They were not fit for the Fifth Test at Melbourne. It allowed South African batsmen greater freedom, and they won by six wickets, levelling the series two-all – despite a great double hundred by Harvey. The physical decline of Miller and Lindwall had coincided with Australia's being brought back sharply to the field.

Miller's bowling figures for three and a half Tests (13 wickets at 18.53) were on a par with his usual returns. But his batting – 153 runs at 25.50 and no century – was below his standard. Decline in form, injury and illness – he had a throat infection in the First Test when he scored 3 and 3 – combined to reduce his effectiveness with the bat.

***

Miller had only a few weeks to get fit before taking the boat to England for the 1953 Ashes. He said his goodbyes to Peg and the boys, aged 5, 3 and 2, who were off to Boston and the Wagner family during the northern summer for the duration of the Australian tour of England. Peg accepted her life with grace and without complaint, and was already used to the demanding role of being the nearest thing to a sole parent.

Australia was without Bradman on an Ashes tour of England for the first time since 1926. This, plus the injury clouds over its two great bowlers, was causing England pundits to search for other omens, pointers, portents, coincidences and some history that would suggest that England had a chance to win an Ashes series at home for the first time in 27 years. They mentioned that England had been weak after World War I, which ended in 1918. In early 1925 in Australia, seven years after the war, England had won the last Test of a lost Ashes series. It then went on to win in the 1926 Ashes in England. Similarly, a weakened England in 1951, six years after World War II, had won again the last Test of a lost Ashes series. The message was that England was strong once more and would win. Lighter imperial minds were pointing to the Queen's coronation. England just *had* to win in 1953.

Whitington again did most of the work on his third book with Miller, *Straight Hit*, published in 1952. Indian great Duleepsinhji wrote the foreword. The first third of the book was composed of general essays, including a Whitington article on Miller. The other two-thirds covered the tour by Goddard's West Indies. 'The quick staccato style of the match accounts is not always soothing,' *Wisden* noted, 'but these two can never be dull; they amuse and they argue with the reader, but they never quarrel.'

The formula would work as long as Australia kept winning.

16

CHANGE OF
FORTUNE: 1953

The *Orcades*, carrying the Australian Test squad, stopped at
Colombo and Bombay, and made its way through the Suez Canal
before pulling in at Naples in early April 1953. Miller saw the
ruins of Pompeii with Johnston and Lindwall. They lunched and
had half an hour to spare before their ship sailed.

Miller insisted they go to the San Carlos Opera House where
rehearsals for *La Bohème* were in progress. The doorkeeper tried
to stop them going in, explaining that it was a private rehearsal.
The three large men ignored him and went inside. They
wandered around the building before looking at their watches.
They had to return to the ship. They retraced their steps to the
door. They tried it. It was locked from the outside. They could see
the doorkeeper. He pretended not to understand their pleas. The
minutes ticked by. The doorkeeper kept looking in the direction
of the street. Miller realised that their vengeful jailer had phoned
the police – the *carabinieri*. That called for action. Lindwall
gripped the door handle. He pulled it with all his considerable
force and broke the lock. The three prisoners made a dash on foot
for the dock where the *Orcades* was preparing to leave for the next
stop, Marseilles. They just made the gangplank before it was eased
away. Instead of languishing in a Naples police cell, Australia's
front-line bowling line-up made it to Southampton after four
weeks at sea.

The annual book product of the Whitington–Miller collaboration was *Bumper*. Its publication was timed to coincide with the second day of the Australian tour. 'Again, they [the authors] are discursive,' wrote John Arlott, 'ranging from Larwood to the press box – for the last time? – the rights and wrongs of the method known as "Body-line", and closing with an analysis of Cheetham's 1952–53 South Africans in Australia.'

There was a controversial reference to Hutton's superiority in leadership over Hassett. The authors – it was assumed that Miller at least approved of his writing partner's words – thought the England skipper 'could develop an advantage for his country in the sphere of captaincy'. They thought Hassett had become too cautious. He tended, they said, to miss chances to be bold. He was apt to avoid taking chances because he was afraid that he might make the incorrect move. 'Daring captaincy demands willingness to accept the blame if the bold stroke goes astray,' the book said. It added that Hassett didn't like criticism, the implication being that he was afraid of it. 'He [Hassett] was also schooled for summers under the most cautious, albeit wide-awake of captains, Bradman.'

The co-writers suggested that Bradman made his plans half an hour ahead of the changing plot. 'Hassett deals, or fails to deal,' the book claimed, 'with things as they occur.' The collaborators thought that besides Bradman, Hutton had the shrewdest cricket brain since Gubby Allen. They believed he could reach the highest ranks of leadership in the 1953 Ashes.

The comments were honest opinion. Many agreed with them. But the timing, albeit perfect for book sales, was woeful for team morale and feeding ammunition to the enemy press – for that's what they were whenever tourists looked threatening – in the psychological warfare that was so much part of Test cricket. London's *Evening News* had a banner headline: 'Keith Miller Criticises his Captain.'

The night the story broke, all 890 pairs of eyes turned to

Hassett to see how he would react at the Journalists Association's welcoming dinner at the Savoy. He began introducing his team. Each member rose from his chair as his name was mentioned. First, his vice-captain, Morris. Then Miller. He got to his feet self-consciously, running his hand through his hair, which was always a sign of nerves. Hassett waited until Miller was standing tall. He paused for dramatic effect.

'There is Keith Miller, whom you all know well,' Hassett said, poker-faced. He paused again, forcing the audience of journalists, dignitaries and others to let go a ripple of nervous laughter, then added: 'I hear he has written a book. I know nothing about it.' Miller grinned. The audience laughed uproariously at Hassett's dry under-statement before moving on to Bill Johnston. The English press played the story for more than it was worth. But there was no dissension in the Australian ranks.

The squad had its problems. The older members – such as Hassett, Miller, Johnston, Lindwall and Morris – tended to group and imbibe together. The younger members, Ian Craig, Benaud, Davidson, Ron Archer, Colin McDonald, Graeme Hole and Jim de Courcy, avoided alcohol and formed their own group. The team used to travel mainly by bus to each match without a day's break. The bus ride became a pub crawl whereby the older members of the squad, led by Hassett, Miller and Lindwall, would stop for a drink, leaving the younger members disgruntled and waiting in the bus.

Perhaps there could have been more mixing. Maybe it didn't matter. Some of the players needed more nurturing than others. But there was no on-going dissent. Miller's collaborative criticism of his leader was left on the printed page. He did not repeat it in public or even in private. The press's attempt to create a cleavage in the Australian ranks failed. Hassett did not reprimand Miller in public or private. The matter was buried before it could undermine the tourists' chances in the Ashes. But Hassett, who had the capacity to conceal his true mind, would store away this episode for later consideration. Like Bradman before him, Hassett would turn 40 in the year of his final Ashes tour. He would retire at the end of it. As skipper, he could lobby for his successor, and have some influence. He was unlikely now to suggest that the person should be Keith Ross Miller.

***

Miller had other, deeper things on his mind in those first days in London than worrying about misguided book publicity. One of them was his Cockney mate in Putney, whose wife had been slain by his daughter. Miller visited him, and later again went to see Christine in a psychiatric hospital. He would also see her on other trips to London.

'That was Dusty,' Glendinning commented. 'His loyalty to mates and friends, and family in his way, knew no boundaries.'

***

The team's manager George Davies made a gaffe early when he told a reporter that the Australians would not bowl bouncers on the tour. Hassett stepped in and reclaimed the option of the bumper by saying it was still a legitimate delivery. It would not be ruled out. But there would no bumper war on Australia's part. Miller looked at Lindwall and smiled, bringing a grin to his speed partner's rugged countenance, which was noted by reporters. The press, and now TV, were keen to build up the images of this pair. They had roughed up Hutton, Edrich and Compton in 1948. Would they still be a menace to England's finest in 1953? It made good copy and pictures.

A net was set up at Alexandra Palace. The two speedsters were asked to bowl straight at the camera, which was protected by the net. Without a batsman to defend or strike the deliveries, they rocketed through. As the balls whizzed straight at the lens, they 'grew' fast on the camera, giving a graphic illustration of the batsman's plight in facing such pace.

It was not comforting for any of England's Test or county players, who would have to stand where the camera had been. But by misadventure, within two weeks of the team's arrival the tourists' speed department received a set-back. Bill Johnston injured a knee. It gave way in a warm-up, 13-a-side, one-dayer against East Molesey, a minor club situated on the Thames in Surrey. It was celebrating its centenary.

It was an unnecessary event from the tourists' point of view. Even the Duke of Edinburgh, who turned up on the afternoon of Sunday, 26 April as patron, must have wondered what the fuss was all about. He spent more time speaking to Miller than any other player. He was a hit among the royals, it seemed, and not just Princess Margaret, although the latter would see less of him on this tour. She was having a (so far) discreet affair with Group Captain Townsend.

The Duke noticed Miller had a roughed up nose. 'What have you done?'

'Oh,' Miller replied with a grin, 'you should have seen the other fellow.'

The Duke laughed. Miller was adamant that he had bumped into a lamp-post.

John Arlott was another personality of note who renewed acquaintance with Miller. The gravelly-voiced bon vivant had long admired him for his approach to the game.

In the speeches after the match, Hassett told the influential official who had managed to secure Prince Philip's patronage at the Australians' first tour game: 'My congratulations to you, sir, for scooping all the clubs in England, and for not only being the first man to get an Australian team to East Molesey – but also the last!'

Johnston's injury limited Australia's bowling resources. The left-armer, in his less obtrusive way, had been as effective as his partners since 1947. Not having him available for the pre-Test games was a blow to preparations. Worse than that, Johnston would not be the same bowler again when he came back. It would mean that more would be expected of Miller, Lindwall and 23-year-old medium-fast left-armer Alan Davidson.

The cricket season captured Britain's heart, and the Australians' arrival for the summer hastened the beat. Miller was not at full pace in the opening work-out against Worcestershire. He sent down 28 overs for 56 without taking a wicket.

It was a vastly different proposition with the bat, when he began at full clip. Miller came to the wicket when Australia was 3 for 28 and seemed intent on making a statement in much the same way as he had in 1948, when he stroked a double hundred in the second game of the tour against Leicester. This time he followed in the Bradman tradition of a big double hundred in the opening game against Worcester. Along the way he shepherded Hole (112), Benaud (44) and Archer (108) to some touch on their first games on English soil.

Benaud enjoyed his own knock and Miller's advice. Miller walked down the pitch at the end of each over. 'Get forward, son, this is a slow, low pitch,' he told Benaud, 'get forward.'

Miller's 220 not out took six and a quarter hours. It was a commanding performance. The trick for him was to keep up the momentum, which often depended on his interest in events on the cricket field as opposed to those at nearby race meetings. In an easy Australian innings win at Leicester in early May, Miller was run out for 42 after a scintillating partnership with Harvey (202 not out). Miller was stationed at square leg near the doyen of English umpires, Frank Chester. The two chatted between balls about the upcoming race events and what the best bets were. Miller thought him as agreeable as ever, and they got on well. Umpires are human, and Miller always thought it was useful to keep up at least a civil relationship with them. But during the game, he noticed a slightly hostile reaction from Chester to his appeals. 'Nart art!' he would snarl. Miller was surprised but said nothing.

At Bradford a few days later in another big innings win, Miller was dropped in slips on 20 and made Yorkshire pay with another patient knock. Benaud again benefited from a partnership with

Miller. 'Different pitch, son,' he said to Benaud. 'You still need to be forward because the ball's moving off the seam, but you'll need some back-foot play here as well.' Benaud was a good listener when it came to his role model. He made 97.

Miller reached 159 not out in 330 minutes. This was the new, more solid Miller. He was slow-handclapped for the first time in his career. Five years after Bradman had admonished him in his headmaster's report for six-hitting on the 1948 tour, Miller had curbed his natural instincts to a point where the crowd was complaining. Yet he remained unperturbed and not tempted to be the crowd-pleaser. His command of the situation was shown in a close run-out, in which the amateur keeper, Don Brennan, appealed. After umpire T. J. Bartley judged Miller not out, he made a mock hit on the keeper's backside. The Bradford crowd was amused. Miller was still Miller in the sense that he was in control of himself and the spectators. They did not slow-clap him again.

By 7 May he had scored 421 runs without being dismissed by a bowler. He was now a good bet to score a thousand in May, which would put him in the most select company. Only one touring batsman, Bradman, at that point had done it. Miller told journalists that if opposing captains now set a defensive field, he would not take them on. He would play the same defensive game and wait for the loose delivery or turn over the strike.

The press was now laying bets that Miller would reach the thousand. But he could not resist the siren call of the racetrack, in this case Newmarket, which was about 20 kilometres from Cambridge and the beautiful Fenner's ground, where the tourists were set to play the students on 13 May. A jockey friend, Billy Snaith, gave him a hot tip. Miller prevailed on Morris, the skipper for the game, to let him open the batting. Miller 'had a dash' and was caught off T. Hare for a bright 20. He rushed to change and take a taxi to Newmarket, confident that the Australians would bat all day. Snaith's tip failed, coming in fourth. Miller backed five

Meaning business: Lindwall and Miller, one of the great opening bowling combinations of all time, looking just as formidable in suits as they walk on the deck of the *Orcades* on arrival at Southampton in 1953.

You should have seen the other guy: Miller, Australian Test captain Lindsay Hassett and the Duke of Edinburgh chat during the Ashes season in England, 1953. The Duke had enquired about Miller's black eye.

Youth versus maturity: Miller (centre) introduces England captain and veteran Len Hutton (aged 37) to 17-year-old Australian Ian Craig at the Savoy Hotel before the lunch given to the 1953 tourists by the British Sportsman's Club. Miller's book, which criticised his captain, Lindsay Hassett, had just been launched.

Mentor and protégé: Miller with Richie Benaud in 1953. Benaud idolised Miller, copying his approach to the game, even down to an unbuttoned shirt on the field.

Follow-through flourish: Miller was a stylish batsman with all the strokes.

Family reunion: Miller and Peg and their three sons, (from left) Peter, Bill and Denis, reunite after the 1953 Ashes series in England. Families were not allowed on tour. Peg and the boys spent their time during the series in Boston with her family.

No miss-fire: Miller's *Cricket Crossfire* was an unusually candid book, which, although ghost-written, captured his mentality and approach. It was published soon after the end of his Test career.

Will you give me odds?: Miller shakes hands on a bet over a golf game with Australian champion golfer Peter Thomson. Witnesses include Australian Test cricketers Peter Burge (far left) and Neil Harvey (far right).

Compton, you must stop!: Close friends and ...iers, England's Denis Compton with Miller in ...4. During riots in Calcutta, a leader of Indian ...estors told Compton he had to leave the ground ... game against the Australian Servicemen. The ...tive became the greeting for Compton and Miller ...he rest of their lives.

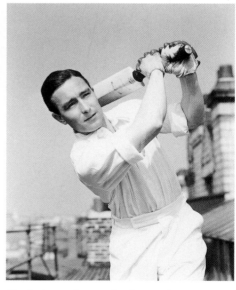

The Brylcream boy: England's great batsman Denis Compton, looking every inch the model for Brylcream hair gel. Miller also advertised the product.

Coming at you: Miller at the MCG Ashes Test on 31 December 1954. After Prime Minister Robert Menzies had suggested he bowl despite a knee injury, Miller dismissed Len Hutton, Bill Edrich and Denis Compton for just five runs off nine overs in the pre-lunch session in front of 64,000 spectators.

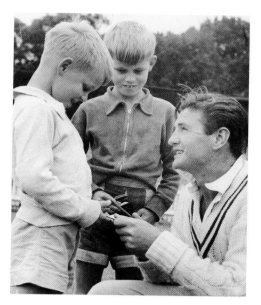

Shaping up: Prime Minister Robert Menzies arranged for Miller to receive a lucrative bat franchise in 1955, but Miller did not capitalise on the opportunity. Business was not his forte.

Hero to all: NSW captain Miller signs autographs for young fans at practice before a state game against Victoria in the 1954–1955 season. He was one of the most popular cricketers of all time.

On the attack: A typical Miller drive early in an innings. He used the lofted shot forward of the wicket to break shackles.

A great day at Ascot: Miller with former Miss Victoria, Beverley Prowse, outside the Australian team hotel in South Kensington, London, on Royal Ascot race day in 1956. That afternoon, he received a big job offer from the *London Express* newspaper.

On the run: Miller leaving a London cab in 1956. His active social life on tour matched his on-field performances.

A career flicked: Miller leaves Lord's in 1956 after taking ten wickets in his last Ashes Test at the hallowed ground. With typical nonchalance he flicks a bail into the crowd – a symbol of his own generosity and rapport with the Lord's crowd. They had supported him as if he were one of their own for over a decade, since his mighty performances in the Victory 'Tests'.

Empire decorations: Australian cricket captain Ian Johnson and Vice Captain Miller in July 1956 after receiving their MBEs from the Queen at Buckingham Palace.

Mixing with the Establishment: Miller enjoyed mixing with England's elite. Here he chats with British Prime Minister Sir Anthony Eden in 1956.

All smiles: Miller was the centre of media attention the day after attending a dinner party with Princess Margaret on 7 July 1956 at the home of Lord Mountbatten at Romsey. Miller remained discreet in public and did not respond to press questions.

Lest we forget: On the 1956 tour Miller photographs a memorial to six friends who were killed when a Wellington bomber crashed on moors near Horwich. Miller honoured those who had fallen during World War II and regularly visited graves to pay his respects.

Fine sweeping: Miller sweeps fine during the Leeds Test, 1956.

One in the eye: Miller was given a black eye by a short ball, which slid off his bat in his last appearance at Lord's, playing against the Gentlemen of England on 29 August 1956.

Portrait of an all-round champion: Miller, in pensive mood, during his last year of Test cricket, 1956.

Victory-year celebration: August 1970, Australia House, London, at a dinner to celebrate the 25th anniversary of the 1945 Victory 'Tests'. From left to right: former pre-war England Test captain Gubby Allen; former West Indian Test player Lord (Learie) Constantine; Miller; and former post-war England Test captain Sir Leonard Hutton.

Batsman's nightmare: In Perth in February 1970 there was a get-together of four great Test bowlers: (from left to right) Fred Trueman, Ray Lindwall, Miller and Richie Benaud.

Pooling his resources: Miller became a media relations consultant for Soccer Pools in 1973. Here he receives some promotional assistance in 1976 from models and the Sydney Opera House.

These are your siblings: Miller, aged 57 (at left examining fingernails), on *This is Your Life* in 1977 with siblings Ray, Snow and Les Jr. Compere Roger Climpson is at right.

RAAF mates: Miller (left) on *This is Your Life* with (left to right) his navigator, Jim Brown, navigator Bert Berriman and pilot Gus Glendinning.

That Miller charm: Miller, aged 62, in 1981. The good life he had been leading had etched itself in his face in his maturity.

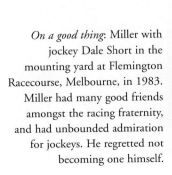

On a good thing: Miller with jockey Dale Short in the mounting yard at Flemington Racecourse, Melbourne, in 1983. Miller had many good friends amongst the racing fraternity, and had unbounded admiration for jockeys. He regretted not becoming one himself.

Invincibles forever:
Miller (left), aged 70,
with Neil Harvey in
1990. They remained
life-long mates.

Major supporter:
Miller (right) with
Prime Minister John
Major in London in
1992. At left (wearing
spectacles) is novelist
and controversial
British Conservative
Party stalwart Lord
Archer.

Cricket's philanthropist:
John Paul Getty Jr was a
close friend to Miller in
his last 15 years. Getty's
addiction to heroin
was supplanted by his
addiction to cricket, which
helped save him from a
dissolute life. Miller's
reputation as a free-
spirited player and his
fellowship was greatly
valued by the billionaire
American. In turn, Miller
enjoyed his company and
generosity.

In the 'Parade of Champions': Miller was honoured when this fine bronze statue, sculpted by Louis Laumen, joined the 'Parade of Champions' outside the MCG in February 2004. It joined others of Sir Donald Bradman, Ron Barassi, Dick Reynolds, Betty Cuthbert, Shirley Strickland and Haydn Bunton (which was added in April 2005).

other losers and ran out of cash. He was about to return to Fenner's when he received a tip to back a horse called Pinza, ridden by Sir Gordon Richards. Miller checked his wallet and tapped his pockets. He had nothing. He stayed to watch Pinza win.

'If I had backed it [Pinza] at Newmarket,' Miller wrote, 'I should have followed through and backed it in the Derby [where it won again]. I lost quite a bit of money by being broke that day.' More 'if onlys' for the perennial punter.

Miller also bemoaned his choice of sacrificing his run spree for the lure of the course. He had a few more matches in May. In the first against MCC he was bowled by Bailey for a duck at Lord's. As ever, he was rarely out of the match. He pushed himself while bowling in MCC's second innings and removed both the openers, Reg Simpson and David Sheppard, with just 15 on the board. Lindwall had done a similar thing in the first innings, and England was left with problems about the 'old firm', which still had some life in it.

Miller's second spell in the second innings brought him wickets from a full toss (Freddie Brown) and a round-arm (Godfrey Evans). At the end of the day over a beer, Alec Bedser, who had been a spectator, asked Miller about the two wayward deliveries. 'Well, they took wickets, didn't they?' Miller responded. 'You should try slinging up that sort of stuff from time to time. It can come off, as you saw.'

In Miller's next game versus Oxford, the students batted first. Several of his lbw and caught behind appeals were turned down by Frank Chester. The hostility noted at Leicester was still there. Miller sensed an 'anti-Australian complex'. It didn't matter too much. Oxford scraped together only 70 and 174. Miller took 5 wickets for 27 for the match.

He was set to make a big score in Australia's only innings when a nervous 21-year-old J. M. Allan, a left-arm spinner, was brought on to bowl. He had an unusual winding run up to the wicket.

When he stepped it out, Miller called to the umpire. 'Which pitch is he going to bowl on?'

Miller patted back Allan's first ball. The second got through his defences and bowled him for 19. A few balls later Allan had Ian Craig, in the horrors with the bat, stumped for a duck. The over was a maiden, and a memorable start in first-class cricket for the undergraduate. It also wiped out any chance Miller might have had of scoring a thousand by May's end. He had yet to score 500 and, with only the prospect of one or two more knocks, he had missed his opportunity. But Miller was true to character. He would have loved that status, yet could not resist being the risk-taker, somewhere, somehow. He was being circumspect with the bat. There was no way he could be restrained from making a 'sure' bet.

While the team played Minor Counties at Stoke-on-Trent, Miller received an invitation to spend the weekend of 23 and 24 May with Princess Margaret and Peter Townsend on the Isle of Man. Their relationship was blossoming but still private. 'Keith had the weekend off with them,' Alan Davidson recalled. 'He was very discreet about this kind of invitation, indeed all his other [non-cricket] activities.'

In the next tour game the Australians drew with Lancashire at Manchester, but all eyes were on a Test trial match going on at Edgbaston, Birmingham, between an England XI and the Rest. The rain curtailed this game, too, but not before some assessments could be made of the home team's strengths and weaknesses. Some Australian journalists spied on the game. Miller's collaborator Whitington indulged in some psychological warfare by singling out Yorkshire's speed hope Fred Trueman, 22 years of age, for some criticism. He had made a dramatic entry into Test cricket in the previous season, terrifying Indian batsmen and taking 24 wickets in three Tests. Trueman sent down 31 overs in two innings in the Test trial, taking 0 for 89.

After chatting with Miller, Whitington reported in the English press that 'to call Trueman "another Larwood" is unfair to both him and to Larwood'. The slap was made harsher by the article quoting Miller as saying, 'Trueman is just another bowler.' C. B. Fry admonished Trueman for not tying his bootlaces properly. 'Detail is important,' Fry maintained. More sensibly and poignantly, *Wisden* noted that Trueman was a 'disappointment . . . he lacked fire and control'. Assessments of this kind went some way to delaying the entry of this outstanding, if untamed tearaway into the Ashes Tests.

The Australians' game against Nottinghamshire was cut short to two days in order for them to see the coronation on Tuesday, 2 June. But when they reached London they were told they were too late to watch the show live. The day was saved for the tourists by Ronnie Cornwell, a British 'entrepreneur' (which in this case was a euphemism for 'fraudster'), who had earlier on the tour thrown a lunch party for the squad. He 'arranged' for the tourists to view the coronation from seats in a building under construction. The tourists were unaware of it at the time, but the connection to Ronnie Cornwell was a brush with literary history. The brilliant depiction of him by his son David, better known as John Le Carré, in the novel *A Perfect Spy* is one of the better characterisations in twentieth-century fiction. (Or, as Arthur Morris said, Cornwell had a brush with sporting history meeting the Australians.)

Miller pulled rib muscles on 4 June playing against Essex. It meant that he could play but not bowl at Nottingham in the First Test, which began a week later. The drawn game was Bedser's match. He exploited the wet conditions best, with prodigious swing and cut, taking 14 for 99, and reaching 189 wickets in Tests. This gave him the England Test wicket-taking record formerly held by the great S. F. Barnes. The 80-year-old was present at the ground and one of the first to congratulate Bedser.

Miller came in to bat on day one with the score at 3 for 128. He made 55 in a link with Hassett of 109 before hitting out at left-arm wrist spinner Johnny Wardle and being caught well by

Bailey at mid-wicket. Bailey and Miller were vying for the title of 'best all-rounder'. They worked that little bit harder against each other and often took each other's wicket.

Miller was caught for 5 off a deliberate full-toss from Bedser in the second innings. 'Thanks for the tip at Lord's,' Bedser said to Miller as he passed him on his way to the pavilion.

Miller captained the side against Yorkshire at Sheffield's Bramall Lane in one of two games before the Second Test at Lord's. Yorkshire won the toss and batted all day on the Saturday. Miller had one over in which he still felt some rib soreness. It was enough to stop him bowling, but not partying. With manager Davies, Hassett and Morris back in London, Miller was determined to lead the seven young members of the team astray. He had a party at the team's hotel at Grindleford, a resort in a valley some way from Sheffield. It went on until Sunday afternoon. Miller and Lindwall were the last to leave. They went to their rooms and slept 'soundly'.

They were awoken on Monday morning by the hotel's manageress and journalist Basil Easterbrook. There was panic as a taxi could not be found. The game was minutes away from recommencing. The two bleary-eyed cricketers were aware that there would be a furore in the press if the full house of 30,000 at Bramall Lane was kept waiting. And what would the team hierarchy back in London say? Miller had been left in charge of the team with a local minder while skippering an Australian XI for the first time. He would be in trouble if late. The quick-thinking Easterbrook got on the phone and hired a hearse from a local funeral parlour. It ferried the cadaverous Miller and Lindwall post haste to the ground.

'Pay the cab, Basil,' Miller said as he struggled to pull on his cricket clothes, 'and collect it from Davies.' (Easterbrook did attempt later to collect the two pounds from Davies, but the manager refused to pay because Miller and Lindwall had been late.)

Meanwhile, in the dressing room, the rest of the team sweated.

Where was Miller? Who would lead the team? The infirm old firm arrived still adjusting their cricket gear. With the clock showing the commencement time of 11.30 a.m. precisely, Miller led the team out on to the ground where the batsmen and umpires were waiting. Yorkshire meandered on to the highest score against the tourists so far: 377.

Miller opened the batting with Tallon and Craig, the two most out-of-touch batsmen in the squad. Both failed. It was left to Miller, still with alcohol in his veins and batting like it, to 'rescue' the tourists. He lived a charmed life at the crease – dropped five times and lucky to avoid a run-out. Miller's Luck was running on the day. He was last out for 86, having batted 195 minutes. Through the hangover haze, he had somehow managed to stay at the crease. This performance, with fifties by Hole and Harvey, avoided the ignominy of being forced to follow on and perhaps a loss. Australia stumbled to 323.

Hutton didn't attempt to go for a win. Instead he celebrated his thirty-seventh birthday – 23 June – with a technically perfect, methodical 84. It was a piece of fine-tuning for the Lord's Second Test and an ominous sign for Australia.

***

Miller came hurrying out of London's Park Lane Hotel looking tousled – a wrinkled suit, a dark red tie – and sporting a 'morning after the night before' appearance and a black eye. Four young English autograph hunters swarmed around. They had scored most of the autographs from the Aussie stars earlier. Only the big one – Miller's – was left. 'I have to get to Lord's,' Miller said, brushing past them and hurrying for a taxi. 'Want to come?' The boys couldn't believe their luck. They piled in and chatted with the superstar while he signed all their autograph books. They swept through the Grace Gates. Miller arranged for them to watch the Australians practise.

Towards the end of the session, the Duke of Edinburgh arrived at Lord's to open the Imperial Cricket Museum. He noticed the

Australians practising. He told manager Davies that he would like them to meet him in the Long Room after the ceremony. Miller overheard the request. Later he made his way to the Long Room. No other member of the team was there. Davies had ignored the request. He had taken the rest of the squad back to the Park Lane Hotel.

The Duke was not impressed by the apparent snub. He came over to Miller to ask what had happened and noticed that he had a black eye. 'How's her husband?' the Duke asked with a grin.

'I fell down some stairs,' an embarrassed Miller explained.

The Duke laughed and, turning to a nearby Australian journalist, asked: 'You don't believe that, do you?'

Miller and the journalist spent some time talking to the Duke to appease him.

Hutton kept his Bramall Lane form going and held England's first innings together with 145 in the Second Test. Miller was again dismissed by Wardle in the first knock for 25, but lifted when it was vital for his country in the second innings. Hassett promoted Miller to number three. He came in at 1 wicket for 3. His batting was a performance of restraint early when holding out until stumps one evening, and grace the next morning on a better paced wicket. He reached his first Test century in England. It was a joy that he had done it at his favourite run-hunting ground. Members in the pavilion rose to him. Many fans had seen his 1945 efforts and had a sense of nostalgia. He was dismissed on 109, with Australia safe from defeat at 4 for 235, a job professionally done.

His rib injury was manageable when he batted and bowled. He took only one wicket in 42 overs, but it was the satisfying one of Bailey, caught and bowled for 2 in England's first innings. Miller threw the ball twice in the air in glee. It was a demonstrative act for the era, which was not lost on Bailey.

England looked beaten going into the last day on 3 for 21, still 321 short of Australia. The lack of queues outside Lord's was a silent demonstration of what the fans thought of their team's chances of even a draw: next to nil. But battling innings by Compton, Bailey, Watson and Freddie Brown held off Lindwall and Miller, the nemesis of England for the past three successive Ashes. After honours were even in the First Test, Australia just had the upper hand at Lord's, with England at the close of the final day on 7 for 282 and 60 short. The fluctuating fortunes made it impossible to predict which team would come out on top. Yet England gained an enormous amount of self-confidence from being able to resist the might of Australia.

The equivalent to a fraction over two days' play was possible in the drawn Third Test at Old Trafford. The rain won again. Miller bowled his fast off-breaks and captured Tom Graveney's wicket for 5. Bedser bowled Miller for 17 in the first innings. Jim Laker revelled in the conditions of vicious spin in Australia's second innings and had him stumped for just 6. The tourists were reduced to a morale-destroying 8 for 35 in the second innings, after a respectable 318 in the first innings and England's only innings of 276. Australia led by just 77 when the game finished. The confidence built in the England team after the resistance at Lord's had been supplanted by a sense of superiority over Australia not seen since Hammond's team won the first two Tests of the 1936–37 Ashes.

Miller had a heavy bout of drinking with Bill Edrich after the first day of the tour match against Middlesex at Lord's on 18 July. Edrich was only good for a stodgy batting effort on day two, staying 3 hours for a painful 46 out of the county's laborious 150. The Queen and the Duke of Edinburgh arrived for the afternoon's play in time to see the Australians batting. Strong speedster Alan Moss bowled Hassett for 24, bringing Miller to the wicket.

'Pitch it up, Mossie,' Edrich called. 'He hasn't been to bed.'

Miller crashed a four. 'You still think I'm pissed, Mossie?' he asked the bowler.

Miller proceeded to attack, aware that the royals were

watching. 'It flashed through my mind that I ought to try to enliven their visit,' he said. 'Jack Young, the slow left-arm spinner, was bowling so I jumped out and clocked him into the Nursery for six.'

Miller crashed his way to 71 before Moss exacted some revenge by bowling him. De Courcy took up Miller's lead and hammered 5 sixes, making 74 in a little over an hour. 'It was right royal entertainment,' the *Express* reported.

Three days after this jolly respite in London it was back to the grim business of Test cricket, this time at Leeds, where Australia had never lost. Hassett won the toss and sent the hosts in on a wicket affected by overnight rain that had seeped under the covers. It was the first time the Australians had done this since 1909. Lindwall had completed his warm-up in the dressing room. He straightaway bowled at full tilt to Hutton and yorked him second ball in front of a home crowd of 30,000. The impact stayed with England when Miller trapped his good mate Edrich lbw for 10. The scoreboard said 2 for 33. England concentrated on defence, forcing long, gut-wrenching spells from the Australian speed pair.

Miller and Lindwall were doing plenty of appealing. Chester, umpiring his first Test of the summer, kept turning them down. After the umpteenth appeal and rejection, Miller said, 'Okay, but I don't like this snarling manner of yours.' It was not a comment to win umpires and influence decisions.

Soon afterwards a further query was turned down. Chester didn't bother to respond. Instead he turned his back on Miller. The speedster was riled. He steamed in and had the stubborn Graveney caught for 55. Miller took the new ball from Chester. He rocketed in at the hapless Simpson, who had come in to face the lethal pair at their most hostile with the score at 4 for 98. A delivery reared sharply off a good length and crashed into his leading left elbow. It left the batsman's arm numb and useless. A few overs later Simpson recovered enough to clip Lindwall wide of mid-on. Hassett gave chase. Miller ran from mid-off and hovered over the wicket at the bowler's end. Simpson decided on a third run. Hassett skimmed the ball in so that it bounced 10 metres in front of Miller and straight into his hands over the bails. He whipped them off. Miller turned to see that the batsman was still short of his ground by a metre. It was a clear run-out that would not have needed a signal for adjudication from a third umpire, had there been one.

'You've got him!' Lindwall yelled, 'You've got him!'

Miller turned to Chester. 'How's that, Frank?' he asked. It seemed just a formality.

Chester was out of position, even after the batsmen had run three, and off balance. 'Nart art!' he grunted.

Miller made four more appeals for the same incident. Chester kept shaking his head. 'I nearly went berserk,' Miller said. 'So did others in the team.' In the tightest of Test matches in the closest of series, this was a tense moment. Justice seemed to prevail within a few overs when Lindwall had Simpson caught behind for 15.

England grafted its way to 167. Lindwall took his third bag of 5 wickets for the series in an artful display of speed bowling, ably backed up by a hostile Miller, who bent that troublesome back more than ever for 2 for 39 off 28 overs. Only Harvey and Hole scored fifties in Australia's response of 266. Much to a tired Miller's chagrin, he was caught by friend Edrich off not so friendly Bailey for 5.

The lead of 99 was substantial given the conditions and bowling dominance. The battle continued. The game was interrupted by the weather and sustained by defiance from England's bats against fire from Miller, Lindwall and now Archer. The Australians peppered the batsmen with bumpers. Lindwall collected Compton a bruising blow on the hand. Miller, at his blistering best, had Willie Watson caught in the gully and Simpson in slips in successive balls. England went to stumps on 5 for 177 with one day to go.

Miller and Lindwall were booed as they left the ground. Having given all his energies for Australia, Miller was in no mood for such a reaction. He trudged up the Headingley pavilion steps. One member was particularly aggressive. Miller turned around and walked down to the aisle where the member was. Miller challenged him to a fight. The member went white, and declined him. 'I thought so,' Miller grunted with a look of contempt, then trudged up the steps.

Compton did not resume the next morning, but was replaced by Evans, who joined Bailey. Miller was still in an offensive mood. He quickly had Evans caught at square leg for 1. In the space of 11 runs, with interruptions for rain and the overnight break, he had taken three wickets to swing the game Australia's way. Bailey, who was earning the doubtful sobriquet 'Barnacle', and the unlikely Laker put up courageous resistance.

Bailey used gamesmanship. It irritated and exasperated Miller. The batsman pushed forward, ball after ball. It became a contest between the attacking, volatile cricketer, who wanted a true contest between bat and ball, and the negative cricketer, who was doing everything to avoid the contest. Bailey held up play; he had endless conferences with his partners; he made frivolous light appeals. At one point, he put his hand up when Miller was well into his run. Australian observers who knew Miller thought he might confront Bailey. Instead he wandered over to Lindwall, shaking his head. The two fast men sat down. Bailey was ready. Miller waved to him, got up and strolled back to his mark. He let go a beamer – a full toss aimed at Bailey's head. There was no signal from Miller that the ball had slipped. It hadn't. The crowd booed and catcalled. Miller was the 'bad boy' again; Bailey, the darling.

The Yorkshire crowd didn't care that there was a trickle of runs. They saw this as a terrific rear-guard action in a situation just right for a stonewaller. Bailey had become one of the best. He had limited scoring shots. About the only one employed in this innings, once every hundred balls, was the swing to leg. The late cut was even rarer. But he managed a four with it. The spectators cheered and clapped as if he were scoring at a run a minute.

Australia's misery ended when Davidson had him caught for 38. Compton resumed his innings with his injured hand bandaged. He had not been back in the centre more than a few minutes before he pushed at a ball from Lindwall. It flew low to Hole at second slip, who appeared to catch it at shin height. The Australians moved to congratulate him. Compton, who had not followed the ball after he edged it, stayed put. Umpire Frank Lee indicated his view had been blocked by Lindwall. He referred the decision to Chester at square leg.

'Nart art,' he said with a vigorous shake of the head. 'Nart art.'

Miller at first slip was angered. He was certain it was a catch.

Umpires sometimes have bad matches, or upset a fielding side by giving a string of poor decisions. If it had been Chester at the bowler's end who was unsighted by the bowler, the Australians would still have been irritated. They had lost confidence in him. His snarling at Miller and Miller's responses had turned the tourists' collective opinion against Chester. The Hole decision had no influence on the match. Lindwall soon afterward trapped Compton lbw for his overnight score of 61. But the impression of being hard-done-by stuck with the Australians.

England hung on to reach 275. Miller sauntered from the field at the end of the England innings. He was spent, having sent down 47 overs for the best return of the Australians with 4 for 63.

As he reached the pavilion a member yelled: 'You bloody great Australian prawn!' Miller turned, grabbed who he thought was the offender, an elderly well-dressed man, and wheeled him off to a policeman. The man protested that he was not the abuser. A tired Miller later good-humouredly told the press that he might have detained the wrong man. Later in private, he said he had the correct culprit.

Hassett spared him and Lindwall, who was also dripping sweat after delivering 54 overs (3 for 104), the need to bat by dropping them well down the order.

Australia needed 177 in 115 minutes. It was not a matter of the number of overs that had to be bowled but how little England could bowl to restrict the run gathering. Much to the disgust of Miller and Hassett, Bailey was brought on to waste as much time as he could by bowling leg theory – rubbish wide of the leg stump – off a long run. Memories of Merchant's unsporting approach in 1945 in India haunted the Australians. Bailey didn't employ a slip but stacked the leg side. Harvey was incensed that he had to face the bowler coming around the wicket and spearing the ball wide down the left-hander's leg-side. Keeper Evans was standing more than two metres wide of leg stump. Every delivery would have been a modern one-day wide, making Bailey impossible to score off. But umpires Chester and Lee were not about to signal 'wide', despite the fact that the balls were unreachable.

Harvey made 34 in 35 minutes before Bedser trapped him lbw. At that rate, had Bailey been bowling normally, Australia would have won the game with plenty of time to spare. But the tourists were 30 runs short at the end on 4 for 147. Bailey was hailed as a hero for his gritty batting and negative bowling. England was lucky to get away with a draw. It was the fourth successive result without a win. The Fifth Test at the Oval would decide the series. Would one team crack, or would it be a fifth draw in a rain-soaked series?

Hassett fired the first salvo by writing to the MCC requesting that Chester not be appointed for the final contest. The umpire was reported to be ill and unavailable to stand the game. The Australian skipper's second initiative was to give Miller and Lindwall four days off at the Royal Automobile Club (RAC) at Epsom about 30 kilometres south of London. They arrived there on the night of 11 August and were told not to reappear at the team's London hotel until 14 August, the night before the Fifth Test.

The Fifth Test was a big disappointment for Miller. He still disliked the Oval more than any other cricket arena, and his feelings were portentous. He managed just 1 in the first innings, falling lbw to Bailey, which made the experience all the more galling. Laker, whom he had tormented with six-hitting in the past, had revenge by having him caught by Trueman at short leg for a duck in the second. His dismissal was one of 4 Australian wickets to fall for just 2 in 19 deliveries.

Miller's walk back to the pavilion brought out the most depressing aspects of the Oval for him. The members were standing and cheering, which he expected, but not quite with enthusiasm that bordered on hysteria. He could see people on the top decks of buses waving newspapers and umbrellas. Those dreaded non-paying spectators in the flats were not sitting down with cups of tea but standing at their windows jumping up and down. Miller responded by putting everything into his bowling and was never easy to score off. The wicket was not to his liking. His off-spinners, perhaps in his desire to extract life, were erratic.

Trueman, with his marathon run to the wicket, was a hit in his first Ashes Test. His unsettling speed secured 4 wickets and complemented Bedser's swing and the spin of Laker and Lock, who took 9 Australian second innings wickets.

Lock's suspect 90 km/h faster ball – it was a throw to most neutral eyes – annoyed the Australians, but England's better use of the turning pitch in the last days was the difference. It was left just 132 to win. Miller, always striving and never capitulating, continued with his off-spin, employing a leg-side field and no slip. He managed to snare Peter May. Lindwall fought to the end but could not break through. This was the moment when Australia needed an extra spinner. But Benaud and Ring were glum spectators among the cheering, ecstatic throng.

England won the game, the series and the Ashes. There was jubilation beyond even that which had greeted the coronation a few months earlier. England's nearly three-decade inferiority complex with regard to Australia over the national game was over.

A disappointed Hassett was seething in private over Lock's 'bowling' but remained publicly gracious in defeat. He announced his retirement from cricket. The Australians let their feelings go in the dressing room. Three dozen bottles of champagne were consumed to fuel their emotions. Someone hurled a ball at the room's clock, shattering it. The older drinkers insisted on their younger team-mates getting drunk. It was easy for Archer, who had hardly ever touched champagne before. He suffered later.

Back in the hotel room, Miller, no less depressed than his captain but with no thought of retirement, rang Peg in Boston to convey the sad news of the loss and to make arrangements for his family to join him on the journey home on the *Strathaird*. 'So someone won at last?' she enquired, having been always bemused by the thought of a contest going on for five or six days without a result. The boys were interested in talking to their dad, although the result meant little to them either. Somehow their concern for him rather than any worries about winning and losing put the result in perspective. No matter what celebrations went on in England it was only a game. It was not war, no matter what the papers implied.

Miller had an ordinary Test series by his standards, scoring just 223 runs at 24.77, and taking 10 wickets at 30.30. His batting had suffered again from the energy expended while bowling and from the conditions. Only six centuries – two by Hassett – had been scored in the five Tests by batsmen of both sides. In turn Miller's bowling had not been allowed to flourish on spinner-friendly tracks during a soggy season.

***

Miller forgot any lingering woes about the Oval result by travelling to a race meeting at Bath. He was not 'ahead' on his betting for the tour and hoped that his Australian jockey mate Scobie Breasley could bring him some luck. Breasley had two mounts, one at 2 to 1 and the other at 12 to 1. The latter odds looked good to Miller, and his favourite jockey was in a positive mood. Miller put down £20 for a win. He stood to collect £240, a big win in 1953, given that it was about a quarter of the eight months' cricket tour allowance of £938.

But there was a hitch at Bath. The bookie with whom he dealt short-changed him a fiver in a cash pay-up of £160 and a cheque for £100. Breasley thought this was all suspect. Then Miller found that the cheque bounced. Another Australian jockey, Billy Evans, advised him to complain to the Bookmakers' Protection Association. Miller was told he would get the outstanding money. (The claim was settled soon after he sailed from England.)

***

There was still some more relaxed post-Ashes cricket to negotiate. Miller enjoyed Australia's win over the Gentlemen of England back at his favoured Lord's, where he scored a stylish 67 and did not slacken off with the ball. Australia's vulnerability to spin, and England's depth in this department, was emphasised by the Gentlemen's off-spinner Robin Marlar bowling all his five victims in Australia's first innings.

Miller, freer now that the Ashes loss was fading in his mind, was determined to make some sort of late statement against the Combined Services at Kingston. Miller belted a hundred before lunch and was severe on Trueman. He and the other not-out batsman, de Courcy, joined journalist Whitington for a champagne lunch in the marquee. Whitington had repeated his 'just another bowler' denigration of Trueman during the Fifth Test, despite the Yorkshireman's good performance. Irate fans had sent the journalist parcels of manure postmarked 'Yorkshire'.

Over several glasses of Moët during the break, Miller indicated he would keep going after Trueman. He continued to 262 not out (with 34 fours) in a 377 fourth-wicket stand with de Courcy (204). The partnership lasted just 205 minutes and was Miller's most liberated big knock since the Dominions game in 1945. Both batsmen kept on punishing Trueman, who took 0 for 95 from 14 overs, and was most reluctant to bowl when the new ball became available. When the servicemen batted, Miller bowled him for 6, just to complete the drubbing, while taking 3 for 17.

It was a fitting last game for Miller for the tour. He finished the season with 1,433 runs at 51.17, which was second only to Harvey (2,040 at 65.80), if Johnston's freakish average of 102.00 (created by only one dismissal in 17 innings) was excluded. Miller was the only Australian to hit two double hundreds on tour. He took 45 wickets at a good average of 22.51, to give him another impressive tour double.

Wisden honoured him as one of its 1953 Five Cricketers of the Year, along with Harvey, Lock, Willie Watson and Wardle.

Even the Golden Age of cricket would have been enriched by a character so colourful [*Wisden* said of Miller]. Had he consistently applied himself to all situations with the determination he has produced at moments of crisis, his batting and bowling averages would have been higher. In his 40 Tests, he would already have exceeded the 2,325 runs and 127 wickets of Wilfred Rhodes. Maybe so, but that would not have been Miller.

Post-mortems on Australia's loss and inability to win a Test were rife at the end of the 1953 season. Jack Fingleton, on tour as a correspondent, wrote that Miller, in the interests of his batting at the age of 33, 'must now be allowed to die a very honourable death as a bowler'.

AUSTRALIAN
VICE-CAPTAIN

Miller had no intention of hanging up his bowling boots, although he put more of his energies into batting in 1953–54. He matured as a captain, trusting his instincts even more than he had done in the previous domestic season. His astuteness as a leader was seen from the first session of the first match of the 1953–54 season at Brisbane. Miller threw the ball to Benaud to bowl leg-spin after just five overs of pace that had not troubled the Queensland openers. This was an innovative move for the Gabba, which excited the small Friday crowd. Benaud was a reluctant starter. He was used to delivering a ball with the shine off it – a sphere that he could grip and which would not do strange things through the air.

Miller reassured him, then let him set his own field. Miller bowled off-spin, and could produce a fast, well-disguised wrong 'un. But he never professed to be a master of the intricacies of the leg-spinner's art. Once Benaud was over the shock of coming on so early, he saw a terrific opportunity. Ringing in his ears was advice he had been given by Bill O'Reilly on 10 September in England during the tour match against T. N. Pearce's XI. Over dinner the great ex-leggie told Benaud to develop a stock ball; not to try to take a wicket every ball; and to give the batsman nothing. The young spinner had a poor previous domestic season with the ball. The 1953 Tests had been woeful for him, and his tour record had been spasmodic. Benaud, 23, was at the crossroads. Another domestic season like 1952–53 would have seen him banished to club cricket.

Friday, 13 November was his chance. He grabbed it and took 5 for 17 before lunch. The uplift from this saw him bat like a dynamo, hammering 158 in just over three hours. Miller had read the pitch and his protégé well.

Hassett had retired from all cricket, allowing Ian Johnson to step up to the Victorian captaincy. Johnson was 35 years of age. He had been dumped from the Test team after one Test against the South Africans, and did not tour England in 1953. This would have spelt the end for most cricketers in Australia. But Hassett took him aside late at a New Year's Eve party after two poor Shield matches and accused him of not trying. Johnson was shocked at the abruptness of his long-term team-mate and friend. Hassett suggested that if he applied himself, lifted his perform-ances and won the Shield, he could become the Australian Test captain in the next season, 1954–55.

Hassett never mentioned Miller. But encouraging someone else to be captain when Miller was the media and public favourite to take over from Hassett seemed very much as if there was the prospect of an anointment. A former captain could influence the choice of his successor, although he did not have a vote. Selec-tors would consult him. He would give his opinion. The selectors would present a squad. They would also proffer an opinion over the leadership to the 13-man 'Star Chamber' of Australian cricket: the Board of Control.

Had Hassett bottled his feelings about Miller's ill-timed criti-cism of his captaincy – or the mischievous Whitington's interpretation of them – at the start of the 1953 England tour? Did Hassett believe that Johnson was better equipped for the demands of the Australian leadership? Certainly, Johnson was a more accom-plished diplomat, who was effective at saying the right thing at the right time. Miller seemed more of a loose cannon to Hassett.

Australia had made a tradition of selecting a team and then

choosing the captain from it. England tended to choose the player whom they considered the appropriate leader, then build a team around him.

No one could dispute that Miller was a superior cricketer. He was also highly regarded as a leader, especially in New South Wales where he had led the state well. Critics suggested that he could not cope with the off-field demands of long tours: the endless receptions and speeches. It's true that Miller was not the conscientious or disciplined type. He had made a habit of being late for games and turning up hung-over. But the captaincy did strange things to rebels, especially if they were natural leaders. Swashbucklers stopped striking their own or their opponents' shields. Cavaliers maintained their gallantry and lost their disdainful and supercilious side. Selfish men became selfless. There is no doubt in the minds of close observers of Miller that he would have risen to the challenge.

His opponents listed Miller's schooling as a drawback. Hassett had been at Geelong College, Johnson at Wesley College. But some of the best leaders (before and after Miller) had come from non-private schools. Two greats who preceded him were Harry Trott and Bradman. Then there was Woodfull, a teacher at Melbourne High, which was regarded in Victoria as superior to most private schools. More the issue was Miller's personal capabilities, development and experiences. If the main concern was the tour of England, by far the most demanding of all, then Miller's natural affinity with that country's elite, from its royalty and aristocracy to its military and media, not to mention Marylebone Cricket Club, the controller of cricket, made him better qualified for leadership than anyone in the history of Australian cricket.

On New Year's Day 1954 there was no real issue, only the beginnings of speculation. Johnson's 1952–53 form and his returns so far in 1953–54 would see him overlooked for Test selection, which would leave two possible Test captains: Miller and

Morris, both from New South Wales. That would lead to a fascinating choice. Miller led the state side and Morris was his deputy. On tour in England Morris was Hassett's deputy and Miller was third in line. How would the Star Chamber sort that out?

Johnson had only a few hours rest before going to the MCG to lead Victoria against South Australia on New Year's Day. He won the toss, batted and did not have to bat himself until a few minutes before stumps. After a good night's sleep he was fit for the rest of the match, in which he took 4 wickets in each innings and a catch to be instrumental in winning the game. Hassett's direct advice had struck home. Johnson was a rejuvenated man with a mission. He transformed his fitness by extra running, gym work and boxing.

Morris was selected to captain one of the sides in the Hassett testimonial, which doubled as a trial game from which the Test side for the next season would be chosen. This indicated that the board still preferred Morris to Miller. But Miller continued on his winning ways as captain and batsman. For the first time he struck a century in each innings of a first-class match. In the first innings for Hassett's XI, he and the game's beneficiary put on 205 in 107 minutes. He also took a couple of wickets. Johnson, who seemed to have given up on his batting, took a thrashing with the ball in the first innings, going for 10 an over. But he persisted. He took 4 for 182 in the Morris XI's first innings and 4 for 86 in the second innings. His 8 dismissals was the best haul for the match.

The return Shield game versus Victoria at Sydney galvanised Miller for a big performance. He delivered in his second dig, scoring 143 in four and a half hours of chanceless, top-class batting. His performance held his state together while Johnson pegged away with the ball, returning the best figures in the second innings of 3 for 44. Perhaps more pertinently, Victoria won and inflicted New South Wales's only loss for the season.

New South Wales won the Shield just ahead of Victoria. Miller had the best first-class batting average: 71.10 for the season, but his poorest bowling figures: 16 wickets at 38.75. Johnson was the dominant bowler, taking 45 wickets at 22.75. If his dogged performance in the Trial game, which did him no harm, was removed, Johnson was the stand-out state bowler for the season, taking 37 wickets at just 16.37.

Selectors Bradman, Ryder and Dudley Seddon (New South Wales) would almost certainly choose Johnson in the 1954–55 Ashes team if he could retain that form at the beginning of the season. The board now had a third option for the captaincy.

Hassett's advice and Johnson's response had made the retired skipper a prophet of sorts. He had done the numbers. It was certain that all three Victorian selectors would vote against Miller and for Johnson. South Australia's delegates – Bradman, R. F. Middleton (the Australian board's chairman) and A. J. Baker – were rumoured in the press to be also voting against Miller and for Johnson, making it 6 for Johnson and 3 for Miller, assuming that the New South Wales delegates would vote as one.

Bradman's leanings fascinated the cricket world, but his influence was overrated. When I raised the issue of the Miller captaincy with him in 2000, Bradman (at the age of 92) reminded me heatedly that he had only one vote of 13 and that he was not chairman of the board. It was an issue that he had dealt with long ago, and he did not like me raising it yet again.

There are plenty of examples of his being in the minority at the selection table and at board level. The most recent and important instance was his support for Sid Barnes, who in different ways was a rebel like Miller. Bradman, along with Dwyer and Ryder, had chosen Barnes for the Third Test against West Indies in 1951–52. The board (for the first time in history) vetoed his selection. Three of its members, Bradman, chairman Aubrey Oxlade and Frank Cush, opposed the veto.

Bradman remained mute about the way he voted concerning the captaincy. On the surface, there were straws in the wind and some indicators to which way he *might* have voted. He was a friend of Ian Johnson's father, Keith, a former national selector. Bradman wrote to me after Johnson's death in 1998 saying that he regarded him as a 'loyal' supporter. In six years of discussions, Bradman only ever spoke positively about Miller. He chose him in his best ever Australian XI. But when I was interviewing people about Bradman for my biography, *The Don*, he did not list Miller as someone I should speak to. (I had my own list, which included Miller.) Bradman was always very conscious of the demands of touring as leader – England was his only experience – in 1938 and 1948. It was likely that he would choose Johnson over Miller as a 'safer' choice for having the capacity and desire to carry out the duties and demands of leadership on and off the field, after judging them on his personal standards and expectations.

Miller had a different attitude and approach to leadership, which might have been no less valid or effective on tour.

There was further illogical speculation that Queensland members were intending to vote for a compromise candidate: Morris. That left one vote each from the poor cousins of the Shield competition: Western Australia and Tasmania. Yet no one in the press knew which way the actual votes would go. The media and the public would have to wait until later in 1954 when the white smoke would come from the board HQ's chimney after a meeting of the Star Chamber when the team and its leader would be announced.

The building battle for the leadership would have been front-page news but for Prime Minister Menzies directing political events that would ensure his continued leadership. The question of KGB infiltration in Australia had precipitated into the Petrov Affair in which a Russian KGB agent and his wife had defected from the Soviet Embassy. Menzies built the fear factor about the communist menace and Labor's apparent intransigence over the issue. The cricket captaincy was restricted to the back pages. Menzies' shrewd political manoeuvring and timing caused him to be re-elected on 29 May 1954.

With that matter settled, the media wanted Menzies' views on the most vital issue of leadership of the Test team. The Prime Minister remained out of the debate that began to rage as football finals around the nation finished by early October. Menzies was torn. He was fond of Johnson, not the least reason being the fact he too had gone to Wesley. But he also admired Miller, whose image he gazed at adoringly every day at his office.

***

Off field, Miller had the future beyond cricket on his mind. *Sporting Life* magazine, which had employed him for seven years, closed its doors. Miller would get a little work in journalism, and there were some endorsement opportunities with Brylcreem and other products. But it was not regular or secure income. While he played cricket, there was again the old problem of earning a living. He expected to tour the West Indies in early 1955 and had his eyes on his third visit to England as a Test cricketer in 1956. After that he would reassess his future. Until then he would have to make do with augmenting his meagre salary for Test and state cricket.

One way to do so was by keeping the books coming. Number 5, *Gods or Flannelled Fools*, came out in 1954 with a preface by Miller's friend Sir John Barbirolli, the leader of Manchester's Hallé Orchestra. The essays about cricketers from C. B. Fry to Graeme Hole gave the book its title and comprised the first half of the book. The defeat in the 1953 Ashes reduced the Australians' enthusiasm, and that series took up just half the pages.

But *Wisden's* Arlott was still kind. 'Because these authors have a rare gusto for people,' he wrote, 'and for life off the field (especially when Australia lost) as well as on it, there is a constant bubble of variety about their interests, the unexpected reference, the odd quotation, of minds alive to human values as well as incident.' Arlott found some books 'effective soporifics' but the Whitington–Miller combination was bold and arousing rather than dull.

***

A clue to the selectors' thinking about the national captaincy came in an early game of 1954–55 when only Johnson was sent west to play for a Combined XI against the MCC touring side at Perth, beginning on 22 October. Yet Johnson was not made captain. He deferred to Keith Carmody, failed with the bat twice but returned the best bowling figures, removing three worthy batsmen – Simpson, Graveney and Bailey – for 44. It was more fuel for the pro-Johnson faction. His form from the previous season was still evident, and he had troubled the tourists. The selectors' cards were clear for everyone to see in the next choice of Johnson leading an 'Australian XI' eleven days later on the MCG. Again Miller and Morris were not selected. Johnson took another notch up by returning the best figures for the match – 6 for 66 – in the MCC's only innings.

The selectors had given Johnson every chance to show form and stake his claim for a Test spot and the national captaincy. The Melbourne *Sun* said of his performance against the MCC: 'Johnson's experience and cunning cricket brain played a much more important part than his spinning fingers in gathering a harvest of wickets.' This comment was the first salvo in the parochial war between the states to have their man as Australian captain. The *Sun*, the *Age,* the *Sporting Globe* and the *Argus* in Melbourne pushed for Johnson. In Sydney the *Daily Telegraph*, the *Sun* and the *Mirror* all supported Miller. Only the *Sydney Morning Herald* stayed neutral.

Miller was in touch with the bat when his belated turn came to face the MCC on 12 November. He scored 86, and led New South Wales to a dominant position against the tourists when the match ended in a draw. Two days after that game, the board met on 18 November to make its selections. Johnson was captain and Morris vice-captain. Miller, the more imaginative, daring and qualified choice, had missed out.

He was disappointed, not the least reason being his personal rivalry with Johnson. But Miller joined the ranks that closed behind the nation's new leader. The team had a tough set of opponents led again by Hutton, who, despite his own decline in form, would be ruthlessly determined to hold on to the little urn of burnt bails.

***

Hutton was thinking too much when he put Australia in on a good batting wicket in the First Test at the Gabba, commencing 26 November. He was suspicious that the pitch would be lively early, and he dreaded facing Miller and Lindwall with that prospect. The home side responded by batting well into the third day and amassing 8 for 601 (Morris 153, Harvey 162). Johnson, in the tradition of his predecessors, had batted England out of the game.

Miller, who had hit a bright 49 in 86 minutes, contributed with the ball by knocking over opener Simpson for just 2 in the first innings and his old rival Hutton for 13 in the second. England was tired after its marathon in the field, and its batting capitulated to a good all-round bowling display by the Australians.

It was a false dawn. A recurrence of an old football knee injury kept Miller out of the Second Test at Sydney, beginning on 17 December. He and Johnson, who had a knee injury also, were forced to sit and watch as their team led by Morris encountered the amazing speed of Northamptonshire's Frank Tyson. The mild-mannered 24-year-old schoolteacher loved his literature as much as his cricket. He had been poetry in motion in the first innings when he had taken four good wickets. But after Lindwall knocked him out with a bouncer in England's second innings, the Englishman came back to bowl with more menace than anyone had seen from him. Australia's small chase of 223 seemed gettable in two days until 'Typhoon' Tyson, as he was aptly dubbed, cut down his run and took six more wickets. England had a stunning win by 38 runs.

During the game, Miller was at a reputable Sydney club when a well-known racing identity and big gambler approached him.

The man took Miller aside and suggested he 'throw' one of the remaining Test matches. The deal was that Miller should get out for low scores in both innings and bowl 'like a dog'. 'It will be made worth your while,' the man said.

Miller had been targeted because he was a well-known punter and gambler. The briber had the right man, but not the right character. Miller was affronted. 'Get out of here!' Miller yelled.

The man was stunned by the reaction. He backed off and left the club.

Tyson's performance made Miller's return for the Melbourne Third Test over the New Year an imperative. But he would play, he said, on the understanding that he would not be called on to bowl. That knee was still 'dodgy'. On the morning of the match he did some deep knee bends and knee-to-chest jumps in his hotel room. The joint held up. It was good some days but not on others, just like his back, which seemed to fare worse in cold climates. The weather might well have had something to do with it.

The last day of 1954 was a scorcher. Miller decided to walk the short distance to the colosseum. Almost 64,000 fans braved the awful heat conditions to see this match instead of going to the beach at holiday time. There had been much hand-wringing by administrators and analysis by critics about the decline of cricket as a spectator sport. But if an attractive cricket show were put on, the fans would come. There were very few things in sport as riveting as a once-in-a-generation speed merchant like Tyson roaring in and delivering at 160 km/h to the finest bladesmen in Australia, including a drawcard like Miller.

Miller had the whiff of combat in his nostrils. He wanted his former home crowd to appreciate his skill and ability with the ball. He could not resist it. He felt the thrill of many visits, both as a spectator and performer in two sports at the amphitheatre. He was inspired. His step was quick as he joined the spectators on the short walk across the Fitzroy Gardens to the ground. His parents, brother Ray, sister-in-law Molly and adored nieces Jan,

Joy and Eleanor would be there to cheer him on. He was daring himself to consider bowling.

Inside the bowels of the concrete members' stand he bumped into Prime Minister Bob Menzies, who had just inspected the wicket. 'How's the knee?' the Prime Minister enquired.

'Not bad . . .'

'That's good. There is a slight ridge on that wicket out there, Keith. I've had a good look at it, and it's just where it could help you. Why don't you try a couple of overs? Your knee might stand up in this heat, and it's vital that we get a good start.'

Coming from a prime minister as imposing as 'Ming' – Menzies' self-explanatory nickname – and one who knew his cricket, it almost made Miller honour-bound to have a bowl.

Johnson lost the toss. England batted. Miller, inspired by Menzies, told his skipper he was ready to try out his knee. The heat had settled it down, he said. Mindful that his doctor had told him to bowl only in short spells, if at all, Miller had one over and declared himself right to keep going. He used his outswinger to have Hutton, Edrich and Compton – a magnificent trio at any time, anywhere – all caught and back in the pavilion by the lunch break. Each time a wicket went down, the mighty crowd roared. It was as sweet as any Beethoven concerto to his ears and added even more flourish to those nervous hand movements that brushed back his long hair. Miller felt vindicated. He bowled unchanged through the entire session, sending down 9 overs for 8 maidens while taking 3 wickets for 5 runs. He was spent at the break.

A century by Colin Cowdrey saved England from humiliation. Its tally of 191 was poor for a day's tight cricket.

Australia staggered to 8 for 188 in reply on the shockingly hot New Year's Day of 1955 in front of more than 65,000 fans. There was little doubt that the crowd had ignored the beaches again to see the confrontation between Tyson, billed as the fastest man since Larwood, and Australia's batsmen, particularly Miller, who was expected to stand and deliver. The show was a fizzer. Miller was removed for just 7, caught behind off the steady, accurate and fast Brian Statham, who dismissed half the Australians. Tyson was bothersome, taking out Morris lbw, and Hole bowled with sheer pace.

Day three was a rest day, and the pitch, which showed signs of cracking in the extreme heat, was expected to cause the match to finish before the close on Monday. Miller played golf with Lindwall and Australian champion Ossie Pickworth. Meanwhile a curator had flooded the wicket area. The impact was to firm up the pitch, making it a far better batting track than the disaster that was expected. Pitch watering was an illegal cricket act, but England was not going to complain. It now had a chance to build a lead. The Australians, too, let the matter subside. It was, after all, better to have the possibility of batting last on a firm pitch than one that would crack and make batting well-nigh impossible.

The better Monday wicket allowed Australia to slide 40 runs in front. But now the home team had the challenge of pegging England back. Johnston removed half the England team in a war of attrition over more than day's batting. Australia was set 240 to win, which was 17 more than at Sydney. Strong crowds totalling another 120,000 attended days three and four. The game was on a knife-edge going into the fifth day. Australia was 2 for 75. It needed just 165 runs with eight wickets in hand.

Fifty thousand more fans turned up at what was expected to be a thrilling Australian win. Yet there were overwhelming hurdles. The pitch, which had been held together on Sunday by watering, deteriorated on Wednesday in the way nature – that is, hot weather – intended it to on Monday.

Australia faced cracks and the bowlers, who made the ball fly high and shoot low. Tyson, the cyclone of Sydney, had whirled his way to the MCG. He struck with his seventh delivery. Harvey glanced one down leg side. Evans ran and threw out his right glove to send one of Australia's two great hopes on his way for 11. Miller came to the wicket at 3 for 77. Tyson's first ball beat him.

In the next over, Statham, whose outstanding strength was wonderful accuracy at speed, sent him four straight shooters. Miller jammed down on three. The fourth was met by an inelegant, unplanned French cut that slid away for four. Tyson got one to lift in the next over. Miller fended it off. Edrich caught him close to the wicket for 6.

A procession followed. The crowd remained mute. Tyson, the schoolmaster, dismissed six Australians, who trailed off the ground like a procession of schoolboys being sent to the headmaster for canings. He collected 6 victims for just 16 and ended with the school under-12 cricket figures of 7 for 27. On that final day only Archer – 15 – managed more than 6 runs. Australia collapsed for 111 right on lunch.

England won by 128. It had a 2–1 lead in the series. In a flash, Hutton's secret weapon had put the tourists on top. Had England lost the game, there would have been pressure for the result to be cancelled and the match replayed. The tourists' victory allowed the Melbourne Cricket Club to continue its cover-up over the watering fiasco.

Miller had some consolation between the Tests by wrapping up the Shield with a comprehensive win over Victoria – without an injured Johnson – in two days at Sydney. His five-wicket haul in Victoria's second dig closed the game off.

***

The selectors named a squad for the West Indies that would leave just two weeks after the Ashes series. Johnson, who had done nothing wrong in his first stint as skipper, was given the tough job of leadership in the troubled Caribbean. But Miller replaced Morris as vice-captain. This was taken as indicating that Miller would take over as Australian captain for the next Ashes tour of England in 1956. There seemed no other logical explanation. Johnson was expected to stand down after the West Indies tour. Miller, in private, was encouraged. Vice-captain was a step up and recognition.

It was over to Adelaide for the Fourth Test commencing on 28 January in a game Australia had to win to keep its Ashes hopes alive. Tyson had changed the dynamics of Australia's batting order. Morris and Favell, who had opened at Melbourne, were dumped. Morris slipped back in for the injured Lindwall, but his confidence was down. Yet he wasn't alone. No Australian batsman faced Tyson with any degree of security. Gutsy Colin McDonald came in to open. Only he and Miller showed any real capacity to defy the England attack. Yet it was hard going. Miller's 44 took 149 minutes. Every Australian except Davidson got a start, but only Len Maddocks (69) could manage a half century. Tyson had everyone bluffed or beaten. He was ably supported by Statham, Bailey, who revelled in the defensive atmosphere, Bob Appleyard (bowling fast off-spin) and Wardle. Even so, the Australians managed 323.

Miller had very little option but to respond to the team's dire needs since Lindwall had dropped out. He bowled steadily. No batsman dared take liberties with him. Yet he lacked penetration, taking Compton's wicket only. England edged ahead by just 18 runs. Australia fell apart and again could not get past the Nelson: 111. Tyson, Appleyard and deadeye Statham, who bowled Miller for 14, shared the wickets. England was left 94 for victory.

Could Miller repeat his sensational performance at Melbourne and shock England? More than 23,000 spectators stayed to find out on the fifth day of another well-attended match. Miller responded as if he were saying, 'Whatever Tyson can do I can do better.' He bowled Edrich with the first ball he faced in his first over. He had Hutton caught in his second. Then Cowdrey was removed, caught in his third. In 20 balls Miller had England 3 for 18. Suddenly 94 seemed a long way away.

Hutton was fretting in the dressing room and cursing the 35-year-old Miller, who had given him nightmares now for a decade. The dream of retaining the Ashes Down Under was fading. If Miller kept on this way, the series would be level with two all and one to play. Hutton could not cope. He turned his back on the play just as three RAAF jets swooped low over Adelaide Oval and dipped their wings. Was it an orchestrated recognition of Miller's service in the past and right then?

Moments later May sent him back a tough return catch. He couldn't hold it. Hutton looked around. Maybe England might win it yet. Australia lamented that the other shock merchant Lindwall had not been there to blast out the old enemy from the other end. But he was languishing in the dressing room, feeling as impotent as Hutton.

Miller had given it everything and had to be rested as Compton and May dug in for a long haul. At 49 May drove hard at Johnston. Miller took a brilliant catch in the covers. England was 4 for 49. He had performed a near miracle. But the tourists crawled to a five-wicket victory. The Ashes were blown away for a second successive series.

The victorious MCC played Miller's New South Wales in mid-February in an anti-climactic game that was still fiercely competitive.

'The Sydney groundsman, Bill Watt, was under the thumb of Lindwall and Miller,' leg-spinner Peter Philpott said. 'He produced green tops. The wicket on the first morning was a real green top. We all thought Miller would bowl. But I don't think he even looked at the wicket. We batted. They had Tyson, and Bedser, who was desperate to get back in the Test team.'

New South Wales was reduced to 5 for 26 (Miller making 11). It took Philpott (46) and Brian Booth (74 not out) to restore some respect. Bedser demolished half the state with a perform-ance to remind selectors that he was still around and more than serviceable. Alan Davidson did something similar in his gradual rise to top-drawer status, and both teams were locked on 172 after their first innings.

New South Wales climbed into a position of competitiveness on day three. Miller showed his style as a leader by ordering his batsmen to hit out late in the day. He wanted a win. It was his way, but it would also mark him out from both Hutton and Johnson in his approach. He led the way with a quickfire 71 in 57 minutes and declared at 8 for 314, leaving the MCC a tricky period before stumps. It negotiated it without loss and considered the 315 target gettable, if its early batsmen were allowed to settle on the final day. Miller juggled his bowlers with alacrity, skill, instinct and luck, trying eight in all, including Brian Booth and Jim Burke, who both took a wicket. This 'attempt anything' approach paid off. New South Wales won by 45 runs, and became the only team to defeat the tourists for the entire summer outside the Tests. Thanks to Miller's inventiveness and attacking leadership, New South Wales remained unbeaten by any England touring team.

Rain washed out three and a half days of the Fifth Test, and no one really cared when the game finished in an inevitable draw. England had won the series 3–1. It did not have one batsman with an average of 40 or more from more than three innings. Hutton, Compton and Edrich all failed. One key bowler, Tyson, with 28 wickets at 20.82, was the difference between the two sides. He was made more effective by outstanding support from Statham.

Miller was now part of a team that had not won any of the last three international series. This followed six straight series wins since the war. Apart from Miller, only Lindwall and Morris had played in all of the nine rubbers since the war. These three, along with Johnston and Johnson, were the ageing nucleus of a once-formidable combination. Harvey, at 25 years old, was the only 'veteran' who could look forward to as much as another decade at the top. Yet the players coming up behind had not yet threatened any of them.

Miller was not happy with his batting. He had failed to score a fifty in a series for the first time since he had broken into international cricket in 1945. His average of 23.86 was his lowest yet, and, of those who played more than four innings, he ranked below Johnson (a flattering 58.00), Harvey (Australia's stand-out bat), Morris, Len Maddocks and Lindwall. His bowling returns were fair for him – 10 wickets at 24.30 – but did not reflect the impact of his dynamic bursts. Yet his body had not let him deliver more than these explosive moments with the ball.

Still Miller believed, at 35, that he could deliver sustained, top-class bowling as well as anyone, if he were fit, and even while carrying injuries. He refused to believe that physical problems were catching up with him.

Miller packed his coffin for another overseas mission. The only consolation for Peg and the boys was that this time it would be for five months, not eight. Australia would travel to the West Indies by plane for the first time.

WONDERS IN THE
WEST INDIES

The Australian team arrived at Palisadoes Airport, Kingston, Jamaica, after perhaps the most circuitous route ever taken by an international team visiting another country. It took 54 hours via Fiji and Canada and avoided the US because of costs and the board's attitude that *all* expenses should be spared. The weary squad had to negotiate 11 stops, many time zones and a severe storm. More than 3,000 people, including Alf Valentine – just a face in the crowd – greeted them with steel bands, smiles and waves.

Johnson and Miller by-passed the British press and made for the local journalists. 'Hullo, I'm Miller,' he said, 'What's your name, and what do you want to know?' It was part of a conscious up-front act by the two of them to gain goodwill in the West Indies, where there had been agitation for self-government and against British colonial rule in the 1953–54 tour by Hutton's team. The England team had not engaged the West Indies crowds or media, and its players had kept to themselves. Disputed umpiring decisions had led to riots. Johnson and Miller were determined to go the other way, embrace the locals, enjoy themselves and have a happy, positive tour. Menzies had suggested the tour two years earlier, before the British visit, and political tensions had mounted since then. Johnson and Miller were the right leaders to handle the situation. Both turned on the diplomacy and charm, determined to be good ambassadors.

It was not that tough for either of them, or indeed any member of the Australian side. Captain and vice-captain together had enormous experience. They were both good mixers and adept at small talk when required. They both enjoyed a drink and a joke, and they were both proud of their Australian backgrounds and achievements as international sportsmen. The West Indians appreciated their approach and intent. They soon saw that the team members were there to mix, see the sights, go to the races and have a few rum punches with them.

First impressions were good and lasting from both sides, which set the scene for an exciting Test series. But it wasn't England. There was to be one warm-up game with Jamaica before the First Test. Johnson, the diplomat, was there also to win. His reputation was on the line as a leader after the Ashes loss. He wished to return home with a series win, which would be appreciated by the board, especially if it were accompanied by a successful tour off the field. Johnson put aside the rum by the pool and insisted on solid, regular training sessions, team meetings every day and not so much a curfew as a one-on-one reminder to each player that he should get to bed at a reasonable time.

Miller was at first bemused by these directives as Johnson set out to perform as a leader like disciplinarian Monty Noble in the early twentieth century. Miller played along and supported his captain, although it went against his instincts, which were to let the players be themselves and work out their own routines. Johnson was a planner like Bradman but with more strictures and guidelines. Miller remained spontaneous but was prepared to accede to the skipper's wishes. After all, the team had not won a Test series since they last played the West Indies three years ago. A new winning edge had to be found.

The crowd of 4,000 who turned up for the opening match against Jamaica at Melbourne Park were intrigued to get a look at Lindwall. He had a reputation as a 'killer' bowler, and many fans were surprised that he wasn't bigger. Yet when he bowled they understood a lot more about Lindwall's dimensions. He maintained their awe with his silent, sleek, shark-like fluency, rhythm and aggression. But it was Miller who grew on them faster. He clowned in the outfield, pulling on a local cap and conducting a steel band. When one spectator handed him a Coca-Cola bottle, Miller sipped from it and pretended to wobble as if drunk. The crowd roared. He didn't do much with the ball in his long first spell. Nor did he star with the bat. But what he did do by belting a couple of sixes into the mango trees surrounding the ground was to send a message about his own character and determination. Lindwall was the initial drawcard. Miller had joined him after that first drawn trial game.

Johnson, however, provided the photo opportunity that would define the tour. When he was leading his team off the field on the last day, youngsters surged towards the Australians. Johnson, with a huge grin, picked up a little boy, held him at eye level, engaged him in a quick chat and then set him down among his friends. It was a spontaneous act, which sent the right messages to West Indians. The Australians, including their determined, sometimes grim-faced leader, were fun, just like their hosts.

The Australians went to the fights at Kingston Stadium two nights before the Tests. Some sought inspiration; others relaxation. But the boxing was not high class, and the players left disappointed. On Test eve, the squad dined at the Blue Mountain Inn in the hills outside Kingston. Johnson and Miller were confident the players were fit, acclimatised and ready.

Johnson was relieved to bat first on the sunbaked clay Sabina Park pitch. The openers were not so thrilled at first. It took them some time to adjust to big Frank King thundering in. When he reached the wicket the batsmen could see his reflection in the glass-like pitch emerging from underground. That and the crowd noise, which they were not used to in Australia, were challenges to overcome.

Miller came to the wicket at 2 for 137, and indulged in a form-finding batting display with Harvey (133) in a 224-run stand. Miller went on to his highest Test score: 147 with 15 fours. It erased the stigma of his run of low Test scores in Australia and boosted his confidence. Miller enjoyed the good batting wicket and duelling with Valentine and Ramadhin. When 100 runs were registered in Valentine's bowling figures on the scoreboard, Miller took off a glove, marched up to the bowler and shook his hand. He did the same with Ramadhin. The two spinners sent down 100 overs between them in Australia's 9 declared for 515.

Johnson was hit on the foot by speedster Frank King and could not take the field when the West Indies batted. This left Miller in charge in a Test for the first time in his career. Australia's mammoth score was no guarantee of an easy win. He still had to find a way to overcome a fine batting order: Jackie Holt, Weekes, Walcott, Worrell, Collie Smith and the home team's captain, Denis Atkinson. The pitch was not going to aid the bowlers. Johnson's injury meant that Miller was short one bowler, who happened to be the team's most effective spinner.

He manipulated his speedsters – Lindwall and Archer opening, then Johnston and Benaud – with instinct and skill. The Australians were aided by an avoidable run-out when Weekes called for an easy single and ran through only to find that Holt had stayed put at his end.

'Why didn't you answer me, man?' Weekes said to Holt as he departed.

Miller's quirky humour came to the fore. He hummed singer Nat King Cole's song 'Answer Me' when he passed Holt. The incident unsettled the batsman. Lindwall had Holt caught soon afterwards. (Miller found a record store the next day before play, bought his friend Weekes 'Answer Me' and presented it to him.)

Walcott and Smith provided a 138-run partnership that examined the makeshift skipper's tactical ability. Miller would not die wondering about moves that could lead to a wicket. One of his tactics was pressure. His instinct was to put even the most vainglorious batsman under tension when he least expected it. And here Miller's standing as a batsman came into play. He knew what bladesmen at the top felt. He hated men close to the wicket within his vision. It was an insult. But how did an outstanding bat handle it? Did he ignore it, adjust his stance, calibrate his stroke-play to avoid a catch, or try to blast the fielder away from him?

The experienced Walcott found two silly points in position for the first time in his illustrious career. The move was a challenge to his cover-driving and cutting. The fielders retarded him, but he remained at the crease.

Miller delayed using the second new ball until he and Lindwall were fresh and there appeared to be something in the wicket on day three. The West Indies was on 5 for 239. He and Lindwall came on as if they were at the beginning of an innings. Miller had the centurion Walcott caught, and Lindwall dismissed Smith lbw. The home team collapsed to be all out 259. The blitzkrieg capacities of these two were still active.

Miller then enforced the follow-on. It was a gamble. All his bowlers were tired. Apart from Johnson, Archer was also injured and could not bowl. By tea on the fourth day the West Indies was 1 for 114. Miller's move was being questioned. But the pitch was beginning to turn. Benaud enticed an edge behind from Holt. Miller then applied a pressure tactic again. Weekes arrived at the wicket. Miller knew that his friend was impulsive, often impatient. Miller and Benaud took some time resetting the field. Weekes became agitated after scoring just one run. He drove at the spinner and sent back a catch.

Walcott and Smith, the latter being in an attacking mood, again held up the Australians. Miller detected some deviation off the pitch with the old ball. This caused him to reverse his tactic of the first innings and hasten the new ball's availability. Now the full force of the Miller personality as leader came into play. He set that double silly point up again, but this time added two silly mid-ons. If a batsman let this play on his mind, he would feel hemmed in. Walcott surveyed the field. He was being treated like a tail-ender who would pop up a catch or do something foolhardy.

These moves to silly extremes paid off. Lindwall quickly got rid of Walcott. Miller then swept up two wickets, making it three in as many overs. Once more the elderly firm had shown they had young legs, at least in bursts. Only young Collie Smith treated the field placings with disdain. He crashed 2 fours through them and continued on to a dashing century in his First Test before Miller had him caught by Harvey. It was enough to break the West Indies and give the tourists a nine-wicket first-up Test win.

Miller climbed into the team's bus a satisfied man. Johnson was technically the team's skipper. But his injury meant that Miller was in charge for the West Indies' two innings, which was more than half the game, and with all the major decision-making to do. He led from the front with a fine century and took 5 for 98 over the two innings, which nearly matched the figures of Lindwall, the game's other key bowler. The fact that he had captained the side well to a victory while performing so notably himself placed this Test as Miller's greatest ever.

The Trinidadian setting for the Second Test at Queen's Park, Port-of-Spain, was much to Miller's liking. The dark-green field was half-surrounded by white stands. Golden-blossomed poui trees studded the green mountains behind the stands. The mounds were 'reserved' for poorer blacks, East Indians and Chinese, who provided the excitement, *joie de vivre* and music. Despite this economic segregation, the atmosphere made it a joy to play cricket. More than 28,000 spectators – a record for any cricket match in the West Indies – had turned up for the clash.

Learie Constantine was at the game broadcasting with his rich baritone voice for Radio Trinidad. At a function before the game, he and Miller had reminisced about their mighty partnership at Lord's in the 1945 Dominions match. On air Constantine marvelled at the look of the newly laid turf pitch – the first ever for a Trinidad Test. West Indies won the toss and batted. He could be heard over radios on the mound saying that the batting conditions and pitch would help compensate for the loss of injured Worrell. Rain tempered Constantine's optimism and gave the new pitch some life. Miller and Lindwall steamed in. They were quick. Openers Holt and Stollmeyer (back as skipper) struggled. 'This is the fastest, most hostile bowling I have watched,' Constantine informed the momentarily hushed spectators, 'since I last watched Larwood in 1933.'

The strongest, most dangerous bowling combination in cricket for a blistering period shed the years and delivered like younger demons again. Memories of confrontations with Stollmeyer in Australia in 1951–52 were fresh. Lindwall removed both the openers in the fierce session that was cut to 85 minutes by the rain. It finished the day.

The next day Walcott and Weekes fought back with a terrific 242-run partnership as the sun took its toll on Australia's attack. Spinner Benaud was brought on to put a brake on the devastation. The batsmen were pleased. They had thoughts about lifting him into the ground's tamarind trees or over the stands. He began a burst that made his mentor proud by having Weekes (139) caught. Then he bowled Smith for a duck before the dasher could cause the tourists grief as he had on several occasions so far. Next to fall to the leg-spinner was Walcott, whom he lured from his crease for a good stumping by Langley. It was Benaud's most effective spell in a Test.

Miller applied himself as ever but contributed little in terms of runs and wickets in a game highlighted by a century in each innings by Walcott and lowlighted by the 'Archer incident'. The bowler had fumbled the ball when it was returned to him after having an lbw appeal against opener Jackie Holt turned down. It looked to observers as if he had thrown the ball down in anger, not dropped it. The Trinidadians halted their calypso music long enough to boo the bowler. A minute later, Archer slammed another delivery into Holt's pads. The bowler didn't appeal. The ball was a long way off the line of the stumps. But Gil Langley behind the stumps and the slips went up. Umpire Lee Kow raised his finger. The crowd became hostile. They saw the decision as a feeble square-off for not giving Holt out after the other appeal.

Spectators jeered Archer and Kow off the ground. It stopped there but demonstrated that the tourists could not afford to put a foot wrong in the sensitive region. Johnson took the initiative and said that he and the entire team had total confidence in the umpiring, which, he said, was up to Test standards.

Despite his ordinary game, Miller enjoyed the Creole restaurants, watched the calypso dancers at the dockside cafés and visited a nightclub. He also spent a night listening to music on a gramophone in Weekes' hotel room. Miller found some Beethoven. But the evening was dominated by the West Indian's collection of calypso and classical jazz records. The two spent many nights this way. It was their method of relaxing on what was a tough tour for both of them. The West Indians had to island-and country-hop just as much as the Australians in this 'national' cricket team drawn from several nations. It was a case of mates by night, competing gladiators by day.

Miller and Weekes continued to enjoy their duels on the pitch. When Australia played Trinidad, the West Indian took command. Miller and Lindwall were belted for several sixes. Weekes hit a century in the first innings and 87 not out in the second.

***

The Australians were prepared for trouble in the Third Test at Georgetown, British Guiana. Terrorists had blown up Queen Victoria's statue during riots in recent weeks and a communist government had just been thrown out of power, leaving unrest and uncertainty in its wake. The British had been keeping order with an installed governor backed up by two battlecruisers and a regiment.

The players were greeted by local press, but were uneasy about the poverty they encountered on the 40-kilometre drive into Georgetown's broad main street, which was dominated by a white cathedral. Journalist Whitington, on tour with the Australians, observed: 'A pink-robed effigy of Christ looked sadly and compassionately down [from the cathedral] on a strange blend of bicycles and black limousines, of night clubs and church, of saint and street singer.'

Miller had a second ordinary Test by his batting standards. Yet his 33 was a fair performance in a low-scoring game. He contributed with the ball by dismissing both openers early in the West Indies' first innings and by taking Holt's wicket a second time cheaply in the second innings.

One incident that would remain in observers' minds was Miller's nonchalance and uncanny ability to run up with rhythm no matter what the situation. In this game the ball slipped out of his hand as he was running in. Miller stopped, picked up the ball and continued on his way in to bowl. Any other bowler at this level of the game would have returned to the top of his mark. Not Miller. His delivery was accurate.

Australia won by eight wickets, with Ian Johnson turning in his best ever bowling performance of 7 for 44. The West Indies had contributed to its own defeat by not choosing Valentine and Ramadhin. The Australians remained mute about the musical chairs of the captaincy (Stollmeyer had replaced Atkinson) and the disastrous dropping of two key spinners on a turning wicket. In private, they could not believe their luck in moving to a 2–0 lead in the series with just two Tests to play.

***

The Australians had a week off in the sun in Barbados before the most challenging game outside the Tests for the tour. Barbados had a powerful side with batting strength the equal to any international team in the world. Its top six was Conrad Hunte, Clairmonte Depeiza, Smith, Weekes, Gary Sobers and Atkinson.

Miller rose to the challenge, returning the best single innings figures for the match with 4 for 51 in the opposition's first innings. Australia went on to win the game by three wickets. Weekes again won the personal battle with Miller, smashing 20 fours in his 132. Stollmeyer sustained a shoulder injury at Georgetown, which paved the way for Atkinson to return for the Fourth Test at Barbados. There had been a push just about everywhere else in the West Indies for Frank Worrell to become the first black to lead the West Indies, made up of nine blacks, one Indian and one white (Atkinson). But there was no support in Barbados itself.

Miller came to the wicket on day one with Australia's score at a comfortable 3 for 226. Within minutes the tourists lost three wickets. They looked in need of much comfort at 5 for 233 when Archer joined Miller. The latter decided on attack, and plundered 22 fours in a 206 stand. Miller's aggression in compiling a big hundred encouraged Archer (98) and a whirlwind century from Lindwall.

On 137, Miller cut at a fast delivery from Test debutant Tom Dewdney. Keeper Depeiza took the ball. Miller began walking. But no one appealed. Weekes in slips, like everyone behind the stumps and the bowler, was stunned. 'Lee [Kow] hasn't given you out, Keith,' he said.

Miller turned his head towards the umpire, who was lifting the bails for tea. Miller, in effect, had dismissed himself without the umpire's confirmation. Kow didn't think Miller had hit the ball, and would have given him not out if there had been an appeal. Miller, consistent in his sportsmanship, had 'walked'. He had done this through his cricketing life.

It was a six-day Test, and not even Australia's grand tally of 668 could ensure that Australia had batted the opposition out of the game on a perfect batting strip. The West Indies' intent was obvious from the early overs with Gary Sobers clipping Miller and Lindwall for several fours before Johnson brought his onslaught to a halt with the left-hander's score at 43. It was a blistering cameo in which a future champion showcased his fine skills and temperament. Miller was relieved from bowling duties after the onslaught, but came back for a devastating second spell, gaining revenge against Weekes, whom he had caught behind for 44, and snuffing out Smith in the same manner for 2.

Soon after this, with the West Indies teetering on the brink at 6 for 147, tensions that had lurked under the surface between Miller and Johnson broke out. Johnson took Miller off when he was running hot and put Lindwall on. This mistake allowed a remarkable partnership between Denis Atkinson and Depeiza to develop. Johnson juggled his bowlers, but the two West Indians had settled in. At one point an exhausted Lindwall was asked for another spell, and he refused. Miller, miffed at being taken off at the wrong time, came to the defence of Lindwall, saying that he should not have to bowl if he didn't wish to. It was the age-old problem of a desperate skipper attempting to squeeze an extra effort out of spent bowlers battling a long, dispiriting partnership.

Atkinson showed courage in compiling a double hundred in the wake of criticism of his selection. Had he not done so brilliantly with Depeiza (122) in a world-record seventh-wicket stand of 347, Australia would have won.

At the end of the fourth day's play, Miller complained in front of his team-mates about his removal from the crease after he had dismissed Weekes and Smith cheaply. The heat and the ball-chasing had frayed tempers. Miller attacked his skipper, saying: 'You couldn't captain a bunch of bloody schoolboys!'

Johnson listened as Miller threatened not to bowl again. The captain waited until he finished, then offered to settle the matter with fisticuffs 'out the back'.

Miller wisely did not take up this offer of a drastic means of dispute settlement, and the matter rested there. He knew that Johnson could box. He had seen him in the ring in the early days at South Melbourne and knew that he still trained with professionals. Miller himself had been in his share of stoushes and realised they rarely caused sensible resolution. A fight would see both or either of them damaged. Miller and Johnson returned to the hotel in the same car and cooled down further over a few beers. Yet some disputes cause permanent damage between friends. This was one of them.

Johnson himself removed Atkinson (219) after a day's batting, and the West Indies were all out 158 short of the Australian total. The pitch was turning. Johnson decided not to enforce the follow-on.

Miller was on 10 in the second innings when he was hit on the pads by a ball from Atkinson. The bowler stifled an appeal, realising that Miller had made contact. But the half-appeal was enough. Kow gave him out. Miller looked surprised but departed. 'Did you touch that?' Lindwall asked him in the dressing room.

'Yes,' Miller said, then with a grin added, 'Cow of a decision.'

At a function that night, the umpire asked Miller if he had made contact. 'I certainly did,' Miller said. Kow, aware of the Australian's reputation for scrupulous fairness, apologised.

The West Indies was left the impossible task of scoring 408 in 230 minutes. Its batsmen were content to play out a draw. As the home team approached 200 – the time for the new ball – the batsmen slowed the scoring rate. At 5 for 193, Miller hastened the new ball by what appeared to observers to be a careless over-throw for four. Lindwall joined him in an all-out onslaught for the last half hour, which otherwise would have fizzled to a draw. Instead it sizzled to the last delivery with the home team on 6 for 234. Many in the crowd reacted to the last fling of hostility. But they learnt much about the Australian attitude to winning.

The Fifth Test back at Kingston beginning on 11 June was the sort of dead rubber that drew out the worst in Miller. But this series had seen him find a new lease on his unmatched all-round skills. His leadership responsibilities and success as captain in the opening Test boosted him. His bowling had never been more effective over an entire Test innings. He struck early, removing Holt with pace, then in the middle stages took out Walcott (155) and the ever-dangerous Smith (29). Later he cleaned up the tail in one of those 'Miller-time' bursts, taking 3 for 15 and ending with 6 for 107. The West Indies reached 357, which was a serious challenge.

Miller's troublesome knee and back had stood up to a strenuous tour against a mighty array of batsmen on run-friendly pitches. He was exhausted after his 25.2 overs, and disappointed when Morris and Favell were both back in the pavilion with the score at just 7. But he was allowed plenty of rest as McDonald (127) and Harvey (204) put on a 295-run stand.

Miller arrived unhurried at the wicket with the score at 3 for 302 and Johnson's encouragement to go for his third century for the series. Australia was still 55 in arrears. Miller happily responded with 109. It ended up being one of five three-figure scores in the highest Australian score ever recorded: 8 declared for 758.

Johnson called for one more heave from his tireless bowling squad and got it. The five used shared the wickets. Miller led the way by yet again removing an opener. He, Lindwall and Johnson took two wickets apiece, while Benaud capped off a strong all-round series with 3 for 76 after his 121 with the bat. Only Walcott resisted. His second century in the Test made him the only person ever to do it *twice* in a series and to score five centuries in a series.

Australia won by an innings and 82 runs. The tourists took the series 3–0 and had the support and respect of the Caribbean. They had toured undefeated after 14 matches, with 8 wins and 6 draws. Miller's figures reflected his finest all-round Test series. He scored 439 runs at 73.17. It was his best performance with the blade since he first broke into Test cricket in the 1946–47 Ashes series. Only Harvey (650 at 108.33) and Walcott (827 at 82.70) did better. Miller took 20 wickets at 32.05, which was second, only and just, to Lindwall, who also accumulated 20 wickets.

The tourists climbed happily aboard SS *Rangitane* at Kingston for the trip home via the Panama Canal into the Pacific and on to New Zealand. They arrived home by plane from Wellington in mid-July 1955 a happy and united team with their prestige restored after a decisive series victory against a formidable foe on enemy territory. Miller's own reputation was maintained as the finest all-rounder in the world. His body had stood up to exceptional strain, and he was looking forward to a domestic summer, then the Ashes tour of England.

***

The sixth Whitington–Miller book appeared in 1955: *Cricket Typhoon*. The title was inspired by Tyson's dominance of the 1954–55 series, and included a chapter by C. B. Fry, 'Appointment with Speed'. Once more, half the book was made up of player profiles, and the second half covered the 1954–55 Ashes. A seventh book – an anthology of the six others – *The Keith Miller Companion* was also produced in the same year. But the formula and the partnership had become strained.

FINAL SEASON AT HOME: 1955–56

Miller began the 1955–56 domestic season the way he left off in the Caribbean, opening in late October 1955 with a day's batting for 164 against Queensland at the Gabba. This lifted New South Wales to 440. Queensland responded with 313. Miller, not bothering to bat himself in the second innings, declared at 6 for 147 in the early afternoon of 1 November, giving Queensland the tough challenge of scoring 275 in a session and a half. It was an un-Miller-like belated closure. But his mind was on other matters. It was Melbourne Cup day. He took 17 minutes in the changeover between innings (when it was supposed to take 10) to persuade umpires and administrators that the game should stop for the Cup's running and that it be broadcast over the loudspeakers.

Just after the first wicket fell with the score at 8, the game stopped for the race. Ken 'Slasher' Mackay waddled out to the wicket. He was on a pair, having been bowled by Davidson in the first innings for 0. It was not a moment to wait on the field for a hit. But he had no choice as the opposition players fell to earth for a welcome extra break from the heat.

The broadcast began. Miller was animated during the race. He had backed Rising Fast, which had won the previous Cup (1954) and was hot favourite to repeat the feat. It was beaten by Toparoa, ridden by a mate of his, Neville Sellwood.

Fully 13 minutes passed before play resumed. Slasher was a

nervous wreck when he faced Crawford and was bowled for a duck, giving him the dreaded pair. He straggled off the ground, complaining about the delay and with the Brisbane spectators also voicing their disapproval. But Miller was oblivious. He was still discussing the race as Mackay disappeared into the dressing room.

Miller's late declaration and delays of 20 minutes backfired. Queensland struggled to 7 for 87 at the close after being on the ropes. The game was drawn.

The next game, versus South Australia, began in Sydney on 18 November while Peg was in hospital expecting their fourth child. At close of play, the visitors were 0 for 2 at stumps following New South Wales's meagre 8 declared for 215. Peg gave birth overnight to a fourth son, Bob. Miller went out and celebrated through the night. He was up late the next morning. It was overcast and humid, and his rum-induced hangover matched the day. He sped across the Harbour Bridge, then remembered he had to pick up Peter Philpott at Balgowlah. Back he went, 22 kilometres. 'Keith's wartime air force experience came in good stead that day,' Philpott said. 'We flew very low, and landed inside the SCG gates just after 11 a.m., start time.'

The game had been delayed 17 minutes because of rain. Miller threw his gear on, not bothering to change his white shirt, white socks or underwear, or do up his laces. 'Keith was ready to lead the team out when I had just one boot on,' Philpott said.

The wicket seemed unaffected by the moisture. Miller had four balls to deliver from the interrupted over of the night before. 'There is nothing in it for me,' he said, breathing rum over Davidson. 'You have a go after Pat.' He tossed the ball to Pat Crawford, who bowled an over with a blustering south-easter behind him. Miller next tossed the ball to Davidson, who began striding out his 15 paces from the Noble Stand end.

Miller then changed his mind. He wanted to sweat the rum out of his system. 'No,' he said gesticulating to Davidson, 'I'll bowl. Give us the ball.' Miller walked back ten paces and steamed in.

According to Philpott at second slip, the first ball of his over 'nearly cut Les Favell in half. I can remember it clearly. The seam was perfectly upright, the rotation perfectly even. It was at about half-pace, which for Miller was still brisk. It hit just outside off stump and cut back from the off, whistling over Favell's middle stump.'

Everyone was alerted. There was something in the wicket, at least bowling from Miller's end. A few balls later he bowled Favell. It felt good. Miller's spirit was lifted. He told a couple of players about baby Bob's arrival, which was a fair excuse for his condition and rum aroma. He took the ball again and dismissed seven batsmen in as many overs. His figures were 7.3 overs, 3 maidens, 7 for 12. Five of his victims were clean-bowled. Crawford took the other three wickets. South Australia crumbled for just 27, the lowest-ever total to that point in the Sheffield Shield.

Miller's performance was one of the finest ever at the top level. He often had a nip of Scotch during a drinks break. 'I think I'll switch to rum from now on,' he joked.

The New South Wales team was in awe of his performance. 'There is no doubt in my mind,' Philpott observed, 'that he only bowled in the first place to clear his head and lift himself physically after a hard night.'

Miller asked South Australia to follow on. He showed little inclination to bowl himself and sent down just a lazy six overs in its second innings, leaving the load to Davidson and Benaud.

Philpott believed this game defined Miller. 'He had annihilated a state as few bowlers have annihilated any first-class innings,' he said. 'Yet on a wicket almost as responsive [as it had been in the first innings] he showed little interest in repeating the dose. This was typical Miller. He was never an accumulator of records, not particularly concerned with figures. Often he found it difficult to motivate himself consistently.'

Miller was in Melbourne for the Christmas 1955 match against Johnson's Victoria, and seeing family and friends. The

MCG was being prepared for the 1956 Olympic Games. The game was played at the St Kilda ground, where he had played many a match of football and cricket early in his sporting career. It was plagued by bad weather from the first morning. Outwardly the two state leaders were friendly. Underneath, tensions remained. Miller was keen to lead New South Wales to its third successive Shield win. Johnson's team had been runner-up in the last two seasons. Beyond that, there was also the residual feeling over the national leadership. Johnson's skilled performance on and off the field in the West Indies was sure to secure him the Test captaincy, yet there was still an undercurrent of support, especially from the Sydney press, for Miller.

One surprising switching of camps was made by Miller's co-writer, Whitington, who supported Johnson after the West Indies tour, following a falling out with Miller over several issues. One was Miller's refusal to discuss his reasons for selections on tour. Another problem arose over the contract for their book-writing partnership. Their link was broken, and no more books would be produced by the combination for the moment. But Miller was not concerned. He could always find another ghost-writer or collaborator if the need arose.

The journalist had moved to the Packer stable and was writing for the Sydney *Daily Telegraph* and *Sunday Telegraph*. A third factor in Whitington's switch of allegiance to Johnson was that Packer had on-sold his rights for coverage of the upcoming 1956 Ashes to Melbourne's *Argus*, making it useful that the journalist was now supporting a Victorian.

'I doubted among other things whether Miller really wanted to lead the 1956 Australian side to England,' Whitington wrote, 'whether he would be prepared to make the sacrifices such leadership would entail.' This now-loaded analysis was made when Miller had a fair idea that he would *not* be the team captain, which would influence his attitude to touring. If he had thought he might lead the side, Miller's attitude would have been different.

But he would have risen to the occasion as many others have done before and since when the responsibility was theirs. But as it was not, it would have been no surprise to anyone that Miller in 1956 would be like Miller in England in 1948 and 1953.

Whitington also referred to an incident when Miller was leading New South Wales in a warm-up game at Maitland at the beginning of the 1955–56 season. Miller was making a speech in front of the local mayor and other dignitaries at the town hall. He was responding to the mayor's welcome, saying it was great 'to be in this famous city of . . .' Miller then turned to a team member (Jim Burke) behind him, and asked: 'Where the bloody hell are we?' Whitington wondered whether he might deliver a speech 'in one of Britain's provincial cities to rival that unforgettable one' at Maitland.

Yet with good managers on tour, it's unlikely that Miller would have repeated such a gaffe. He was no orator, but when he had to speak it was poignant and from the heart, and he had a sense of humour. The goodwill that Miller had with the people who counted in the UK would have helped him carry the burden of off-field leadership. But this was speculation. Miller late in 1955 had next to no expectation of replacing Johnson.

'I never seriously thought I would be the captain,' he wrote later. 'I'm impulsive; what's more, I've never been Bradman's pin-up, and the Don rates high when it comes to policy matters in Australian cricket.' Bradman was still likely to give his vote to Johnson. But as before, he had only one vote of 13, and he would not be chairman again for a few years.

The knowledge that he would never lead his country did not lessen Miller's efforts to win for New South Wales, especially against Johnson and Victoria. The southern state could lay claim in the Christmas 1955 game to having a better batting side with Harvey, McDonald, Loxton and Len Maddocks. Johnson won the toss and batted. Miller soon had the prize wicket of McDonald, who had become the country's top opening bat with the retirement of Morris. Miller maintained a close-set, attacking field, and he and Crawford removed half the Victorians for 110.

More than 10,000 spectators were at the game. It began to drizzle in the afternoon. Miller had the option of taking his team off the field, but he opted to stay on at a disadvantage in the wet for both bowler and fielders. Philpott recalled chasing the ball as it caused a spray of water as it slid towards the boundary.

The press the next morning praised Miller. 'With almost quixotic gallantry,' the Melbourne *Sun* said, 'he kept the game going.' Miller's comment was that 'cricket has too much competition from tennis and other sports to afford putting on a poor show.' The game was washed out, and Miller didn't get a bat in New South Wales's only innings, which was a disappointment for the crowd. (It was more of a let-down than spectators – especially family and friends – would have realised. It was Miller's last game of cricket at any level in Victoria.) Not even he could stop the weather. Yet at least he tried to keep the game alive. His sentiment and thinking about cricket's plight was right.

In 1955 and 1956 there was much competition from tennis in which Australia was seen as producing 'winners', such as Frank Sedgman, Lew Hoad and Ken Rosewall. Australians were dominant at Wimbledon and in the Davis Cup. The latter, when played in Australia, was capturing the public mind during the summer, especially after the cricket team's decline in the Ashes. The fact that the Australians had performed at the highest level against a strong West Indian team had little or no influence with the public. There was no radio or TV coverage (TV itself began in Australia only in 1956) and, without the broadcast immediacy of the dazzling displays of Johnson and his mostly merry band in the Caribbean, the achievement went largely unnoticed. All they had seen weeks previously was the national team crumbling before Tyson and Statham. Australia was no exception. National sports teams from Russia to New Zealand and from Fiji to Sweden had to win or be ignored. Winners, not losers, sold newspapers. The nation had to be distracted from any sense of not being the best, or at least near it.

The coming Olympics (over two weeks from 22 November 1956) were more than a distraction. Any number of national teams could lose in the Olympic year as long as there was potential for wins during the games in athletics, swimming and an assortment of other sports from shooting to rowing. That would keep the media and the public content. It was the first Olympic Games ever in Australia and the biggest international event of any kind in the country's short history. It was a perfect time for failure in a non-Olympic sport.

***

Miller turned 36 happy in the knowledge that his form would be strong enough for him to tour England in 1956. The only problem was his fitness. Injuries were bound to catch up with him, especially after his tremendous effort in the West Indies. They did. His back 'went' in the second innings in the 1956 New Year game versus Queensland at Sydney. He was in pain leaving the ground on 59 not out. New South Wales masseur Charlie O'Brien gave him a rub-down. He felt a bit better but then had trouble walking to the wicket after lunch. Miller knew from experience that the problem came and went, sometimes with the weather, and sometimes for longer periods than others. He played three balls, then said to new Queensland captain Ray Lindwall, 'I'm useless. I'll have to go off.'

When he reached the dressing room his back went into spasm. This was the worst reaction in just over 12 years since he wrestled Englishman Ronnie James at Gloucestershire. He had to have novocaine to kill the pain and was immobilised for four days. He couldn't play cricket, but after a few weeks he decided to attempt golf. He collapsed again after seven rounds. Miller saw a specialist, who tried manipulative treatment. He began to improve. His confidence grew, and he felt he would be able to tour England. Miller had kept his problem quiet, although he had to keep withdrawing from games. There was speculation in the media about his future, especially since the national selectors were about to announce their touring squad on 1 February.

On 28 January Miller attended a cocktail party celebrating a hundred years of matches between New South Wales and Victoria. It was the night before a Sydney game between the states. Miller was chatting to Arthur Mailey. Bradman joined them. 'Ah, Nugget, how's your back?' Bradman asked.

'Good, Don. How's yours?' Miller replied.

Bradman, as a national selector, was keen to know whether Miller would be available. He probed about Miller's treatment and when he might practise again. Miller was evasive, saying he would not be playing any more cricket that season, which would end with the match against Victoria in a few days time. Bradman reminded him that the national team for the 1956 Ashes had to be chosen in a couple of days time.

'Okay, Don,' Miller said. 'You can pick it on this season's performances. If I remember rightly I was top of the batting and bowling averages [at the time he became injured].'

Miller was right. At that point in the season, he had scored 403 runs at 80.60. He had taken 19 wickets at 14.94. Miller was not about to tell a selector that he didn't think he would be able to bowl at all in England.

ASHES FOR THE LAST TIME: 1956

The family once more rallied behind Peg with her demanding brood of four vigorous boys, and Miller took off by boat for his third Ashes and fifth long-term tour in the decade since the war. He and Lindwall were leaning over the rails as the *Himalaya* slipped its moorings at Fremantle in March 1956. Miller dug his mate in the ribs. 'Take a good look at this scene, fella,' Miller said. 'It's the last time you'll see it as a player. Next time it will be armchair stuff for you.'

Lindwall didn't like the comment. 'I dunno about that,' he grunted.

Miller would have bet that neither of them would be on the next tour of England in 1961. Yet Miller's comment said much about the mindset of each man at that moment. Miller had come to accept that this would probably be his last tour. Lindwall was not yet ready to hang up his boots.

There was a bizarre episode at the beginning of the tour when Pat Crawford's wife Sheila was stopped from travelling with him by boat to England. The board had decreed that husbands and wives could not be together on tour. The stringent over-interference went further. No wife could stay in the same house, flat or hotel as her husband if she dared turn up in the UK while he was there. The ruling reflected the authoritarian, dubious mentality of the board, which in turn reflected Australian society in the 1950s.

The harsh ruling suited Miller, who preferred to be 'single' on all his trips. He could continue to pursue any woman he fancied and did so. Not that this was difficult. They pursued him. He was a sporting sex symbol in England for the fourth time since he first came to prominence in 1945. His appeal was universal; his charm, good looks and style enchanted even teenagers. In the first game of the tour in the beautiful grounds of Arundel Castle, the Duke of Norfolk and his family were hosts to the tourists. A picnic atmosphere prevailed on a fine spring day. The Duke of Norfolk's XI included the Rev. David Sheppard, Hutton (who had retired from the national team to make way for Peter May), Freddie Brown, Doug Wright and Robin Marlar.

Duck was very much on the menu. Lindwall reminded Hutton he had made a good career move by bowling him for 0. Miller disappointed the spectators outside the marquees under the oak trees when he too failed to trouble the scorers.

The Duke threw a party at the castle for the tourists. He showed Miller and a few others around, and introduced Miller to his four daughters, Jane, aged 11, Sarah, 14, Mary, 15, and Anne, 17. The girls had been allowed to 'wag' school – exclusive Woldingham Convent – to meet the cricketers. During dinner they appeared in the gallery above the dining hall where the Australians were feasting. Bold Anne called out: 'Mr Miller!' The team and their hosts looked up. Anne tossed down a sweet. Miller eased from his chair and caught the sweet as if in slips. The assembly cheered and clapped. The girls giggled and disappeared to bed. The next morning all four girls were down early for breakfast but were disappointed. Miller overslept. He was the last player to straggle in for breakfast. By that time the girls had returned to their convent. Despite this, it was unlikely that any of them would become drawn permanently to a nun's life after the fleeting meeting with the sporting heart-throb.

A tall, pretty young woman to receive more attention was 19-year-old Pat Williams, a receptionist, whom Miller often chatted with after he met her at the team's London hotel, the Park Lane, when it settled in there in April. Williams mentioned to him that she wished to come to Australia. Miller offered to sponsor her and be her legal guardian until she was 21 in two years time. 'You can live with us [the Miller family],' he said.

Williams thought she might take up the offer.

***

Miller had taken part in deck sports on the trip over and was optimistic about his back standing up. He warmed up in the traditional first net at Lord's, which doubled as a grand photo opportunity. But as soon as Miller bent his back for speed, he felt the tell-tale twinge. He went to a Harley Street associate of the Sydney doctor who looked after him.

'You've got a bit of fractured cartilage on the vertebrae,' the specialist told him. 'It slips out of position from time to time and presses against the nerve.'

Five minutes of manipulation corrected the problem. Miller was advised to rest it for another month and to concentrate on his batting. When he felt it was 'right' he could bowl. The specialist wrote him a note to this effect, adding that he should not bowl if he did not feel up to it.

Miller played his first game against Leicester. Captaining the side and coming in at 3 for 175, he batted for 390 minutes and compiled his highest ever score at any level of the game: 281 not out. He hit his customary six, a five and 35 fours. This brought him close to emulating Bradman's feat of three successive double hundreds in 1930, 1934 and 1938, to start the season followed by a century in 1948 when his fibrositis prevented from making it four. Miller started 1948 with 50 not out against Worcester, then a double hundred against Leicester. In 1953 he began with 220 against Worcester, and now he had gone close to a triple for the first time.

First Bradman then Miller symbolised the tourists' strength and intentions at the beginning of six successive tours from 1930 to 1956. Yet it was mere window dressing compared to the real examination by Surrey's 'twins', spinners Laker and Lock, in the game at the Oval, starting 16 May. Coming in at 3 for 124, Miller joined McDonald, who was living a charmed life but still handling the spin of Laker, who had removed the first three batsmen: Jim Burke, Mackay and Harvey.

Miller began carefully. He was determined to defy his phobia about the Oval, which was still his least preferred sporting arena. Miller played Laker from the crease. He was sluggish, collecting 18 in 120 minutes, which was his slowest session-equivalent in any form of the game on record. He was padding the ball away in an ungainly, yet effective fashion and using his front leg and long arms to smother spin. He loosened up against Lock, accelerating to take 36 runs out of 42 in half an hour as wickets kept tumbling at the other end. There were two successive overs of vintage Miller when Lock was carted for 11 and 14.

Laker ended with the rare distinction of taking 10 Australian wickets in an innings. Miller approached him, shook his hand, then whipped off the spinner's cap to ruffle his hair. It was a sweet acknowledgement for Laker, who had suffered at the hands of Miller in the past. But now he was on top. The Australians had no answers to his mature, hard off-spinning.

While he took 10 for 88 off 46 overs, Lock managed 0 for 100. Miller remained unconquered on 57, a singular triumph that would go almost unnoticed because of Laker's magical figures. Australia's ordinary tally of 259 was surpassed by the county by just 88. No alarms here. McDonald and Burke were soon facing spin again, and everything was going smoothly until Lock, making expert use of the poor, dusty wicket, ran amok, taking 7 for 49. Miller, like everyone else with the exception of McDonald, looked awkward against the left-armer and was one of his victims for 2.

Surrey won by ten wickets. It was the first time that a county had defeated Australia since 1912. The humiliation changed expectations and exposed the tourists' collective weakness against spin. The Australian spinners looped the ball higher at home to get more turn. In England, the best ball-turners obtained bite on the lower, slower wickets by delivering faster and flatter. Australian batsmen would have to make rapid gains to handle turn. Harvey, one of the finest players of spin ever, was out of sorts. The burden was on Miller to perform with the bat as never before. His start had been impressive, and his fifty in the first innings against Surrey had shown him capable. Johnson's plan was to use him primarily as a batsman, given that he had plenty of seamers at his disposal and himself and Benaud to deliver spin.

But Johnson's attitude had changed since the West Indian tour. He realised how vital a commodity Miller was in England. 'You can bowl when you want to,' he told his rival and friend of 20 years. This pleased Miller, and his respect for Johnson grew a bit.

The Oval match proved detrimental to the tourists in other ways. One was the concerted effort by several Australian journalists to have Johnson replaced by Miller as captain of the team. There was no chance of this happening at this stage of the tour after one cricketing disaster. But it was destabilising for the team, especially the younger members of the squad.

Miller still wished to bowl. His back strengthened day by day. He wanted to be a support to the front-line contingent, and was quite happy to be used as a 'shock' bowler in bursts if he could prove himself. He did at Lord's against MCC three weeks after his batting triumph against Leicester, coming through a 22-over work-out without restrictions. He looked very much the Miller of previous tours, which was just as well for Australia. Alan Davidson had broken his ankle – the same one he had damaged in the West Indies in 1955 – and this limited the tourists' speed bowling options.

Davidson remembered some depressing days stuck in the Kensington Palace Hotel in South Kensington, where the injured and those not rostered to tour and play remained in London. 'Keith gave me more support than anyone,' Davidson recalled.

'He came to see me every day he could. He took me to the races and to dinner. In conversations, he opened up just a fraction about his war days.'

Miller followed his performance against MCC with improved efforts against Oxford University and Sussex, which coincided with a dip in his batting form. Within weeks an unplanned role reversal was upon him. In the drawn First Test at Trent Bridge, which lost 12 hours owing to rain, Miller did most bowling for Australia, sending down 52 overs. Only Laker and Lock delivered more. Miller and Laker each took 6 wickets and were the most effective bowlers of pace and spin respectively for the match. But Miller's batting let him down. He struggled with defensive play against Laker, who dismissed him lbw for 0 and 4. Miller seemed to be in several minds about how to play his old rival. He used his pads, took block well outside leg stump and played back. Miller was not there long enough to become confident and use his reach to drive Laker off his length.

***

Miller dressed up in hired grey top hat and tails from Moss Brothers for the Royal Ascot races, and was photographed with one of his girlfriends, a former Miss Victoria, Beverley Prowse, whom he had been seeing much of on tour. The shot was taken outside the Kensington Palace Hotel where he and Prowse had spent the night. The picture was destined to make the Australian papers and the *Daily Express*, which was paying Miller close attention. 'I was the complete dude,' he wrote.

The first person who recognised him at Ascot was the Queen's jockey, Harry Carr. 'Good afternoon, your lordship,' he said loudly, with a poker face.

By contrast Scobie Breasley was amused. 'How do you do, Breasley?' Miller enquired in his best upper-class twit accent.

Another friend from his wartime flying days, Max Aitken, the son of newspaper proprietor Lord Beaverbrook, who owned the *Express*, met Miller for champagne. Aitken took him aside to make some tempting offers. The first and most important was a lucrative contract – worth £10,000 – to write a book, *Cricket Crossfire*, to be published as soon as possible in the UK and Australia. The *Express* would have world serial rights. Miller asked what the book should be about.

'Anything that comes into your head about your life, cricket, war, the races . . .' was Aitken's reply. 'Just pick a ghost [writer] and work with him.'

It was a good deal for Miller and an even better one for Beaverbrook. Miller's 'revelations' in a book, which was to be a collection of rambling thoughts, mainly about cricket under random chapter headings, such as 'Sir Donald Bradman', 'The War Years', 'Umpires are Human' and so on, would be sure to boost newspaper sales.

The experienced Aitken told him that it was imperative to publish the book in 1956. It was amazing how quickly a person's commercial appeal dropped off once they had retired or stopped being in the public eye. Those last thoughts struck Miller. This decision would see him retire, no longer to play the game he loved. Yet, he reasoned, he had had a good run. The injuries were catching up with him. Better, he always thought, to get out while still doing well. This was something else Aitken touched on. Commercial value depended very much on not staying too long in public view when you were past your best.

Yet the offer didn't finish with the book. Aitken also offered him £7,500 to cover the 1958–59 Ashes in Australia for the *Express* and the same amount again to cover the 1961 Ashes in England. The total offer was £25,000 coming in over the next five years. It was enough to live well on without doing any other work.

Miller knew by mid-afternoon that day at Ascot that he would accept the offer. It was momentous for him. Yet it was not a sudden wrench. If he played on, Miller was well aware that the next Ashes tour of Australia would be 1958–59. He would then be in his fortieth year. As he pointed out to Lindwall on the boat when leaving Fremantle, if they were to play on, they would not tour England again until 1961. Following Aitken's advice, Miller decided to engage Reuters cricket correspondent Reg Hayter as his ghost-writer for *Cricket Crossfire*.

At the end of the day's racing and socialising Miller was feeling in an outstanding mood aided by innumerable glasses of champagne. He had some serious security again, and his immediate work future was assured. With Prowse on his arm, Miller went to find his car, which had been made available to him for the summer by his friend Lord Tedder. He came up to a car-parking attendant. They both scrutinised each other. It was his commanding officer from Gloucestershire during the war, the one with whom he'd had an altercation that ended with Miller doing three weeks hard labour.

Miller had dreamt about such a moment ever since that incident on a dark country lane. He always fantasised about flattening this man. But the former CO was most fortunate. Miller had just had the best job offer of his life. It had been a marvellous day at Ascot. The champagne had made him even happier, and he had backed two winners on the day, not to forget having the attractive Prowse as a companion.

'How are you, *sir*?' Miller asked, when he was thinking *how far the mighty have fallen*. The embarrassed former CO responded, and there was a strained conversation for a minute. Miller kept calling him *sir*.

'You don't have to call me that,' the ex-CO said.

Miller was in a mood to forgive. He insisted that the ex-CO join him and Prowse for a drink at a bar.

Despite his convivial state, Miller did not forget to ring Peg later that night to tell her about the job offer, without too much information about how much time he would be away. Just the juicy detail about the money would suffice for the moment. He also explained a little sheepishly that the *Daily Express* for whom he would be writing had photographed him.

'I've already seen the photo, dear,' Peg said from Sydney.

'She was only some Australian model,' Miller added dismissively.

'Yes, dear. And if that's your story, you stick to it, dear.'

Later that day, Sydney reporters rang Peg to ask her opinion on the photo and the fact that Miller was reported in the *Express* as the most popular man in Britain with England's 'bobbysoxers' – young, trendy women. The report gushed that he was also on top of the polls for a wide range of women from 'elderly spinsters to the Nursery End'.

This white flannelled Casanova of the crease has replaced Denis Compton as the 'dream boy' walking back to the pavilion [the report went on]. Proof of this cascades into his sedate South Kensington Hotel room daily, worshipping fan letters by the sackful, 99 per cent from women. *They phone him. They camp-follow him from ground to ground. They send him presents. They adore him.*

The intrepid reporter visited Miller at his hotel and wanted to know more. Miller said he received love letters – 'all that sort of caper . . . most of them send me photographs, trinkets, cuff links, and things'.

When this story was put to Peg she laughed and said, 'I think the girls are just showing good taste. And I'm not worried a bit. Keith has always been a bit of a lady killer.'

The day before the Lord's Test, Charles Bray, owner of the *Daily Herald*, took Miller to lunch at the Savoy and made him an offer to write for his paper. 'I don't want this [the bidding for his services] to become a public auction,' he told Bray, saying he had already had an acceptable offer from another paper.

It was in the days before agents and managers, but even if they had been around, Miller would have gone for the paper and people with whom he felt most at ease. He wanted to earn good money, but it was not the first consideration for him. His flying colleague Aitken made him feel comfortable, as did the *Daily Express* with its banner headlines, more sensationalist, digestible, hard news stories and emphasis on heroes and villains.

***

Miller could not have felt better at Lord's. The business coups earlier in the week at Ascot and the build-up to the match put him in good humour for what he regarded as the high point of the summer. His back felt all right; his knee was standing up, although it was still a day-by-day proposition. It was just as well for Australia. Lindwall and Davidson, with a broken ankle, were out injured. Pat Crawford was in for his Test debut, as was Mackay.

McDonald and Burke did the right thing by the tourists by beginning with a fine opening stand of 137, the best by Australia since 1930. Miller arrived when the team had slumped soon after and managed to right the innings by stumps in failing light. He took most of the final assault by Trueman and Statham on bat and body and was a stubborn 19 not out at stumps on day one, with Burge not out 18. Australia was well placed at 3 for 180.

The next morning, Friday, was cold and cloudy. Miller never got going, and Trueman bowled him for 28 with a stunning in-swinger that kicked back his off stump. As Miller passed the bowler en route to the Long Room, Trueman, grinning broadly, stood mid-pitch, toes turned in and hands on hips. 'You must be just another batsman, Keith,' he said with a Miller-like flick of his own mop of hair. Miller laughed and doffed his cap to him. Trueman in many ways had modelled himself on Miller, just as Benaud had done. The result was more fight, electricity and excitement in the game.

Australia scrambled to 285, which was ordinary given the start. Then it was Miller's turn in the day's last session in front of a packed house. Crawford, after just 29 deliveries, pulled a muscle in the back of his thigh and could not bowl again for the match. This threw the onus on to a 36-year-old, who was likely to pull up lame at any time himself. Yet Miller, buoyed by the knowledge that this would be his second-last curtain call in a Lord's Test, was prepared to give it everything. Left-hander Peter Richardson obliged by waving like a demented monarch at everything outside the off stump, and Miller had him caught behind by the efficient Gil Langley. Then he knocked back Tom Graveney's stumps with an in-swinger.

England was 2 for 32 facing Miller in a murderous mood. May's first ball from him was a tortuous in-swinger. The batsman played it on to the top of the off stump. The bail jumped but was not dislodged.

In the press box, John Arlott's gravel voice had become even richer with Miller's performance. Back in Australia in the early hours of the morning, countless fans were glued to their radios. The commentators' words waxed and waned over the uncertain airwaves, but still left an indelible excitement in the arenas of listeners' minds.

May was just helping Cowdrey out of the crisis when the latter cut with tremendous power. All eyes looked to the boundary. Benaud in the gully caught the ball in front of his face in a reflex action. It was the catch of the season and a terrific way for Mackay to take his first wicket in Tests. England was 3 for 74 at stumps.

A third big crowd turned up on Saturday. The sun came with them for the first time in the match. Miller harassed May in the morning and beat him four times, but the lean, elegant England skipper remained. Miller had lifted another notch. The fifth ball of his third over of the morning hit Watson's bat and pad, and slid to Benaud in the gully.

Miller was later delighted to remove Bailey, who matched Mackay in stickability, for 32. Trueman proved to be less than just another batsman when he was caught behind off Miller, giving him 5 wickets for the innings. His effort was the prime reason for England's steady procession back and forwards to the pavilion. Its 171 managed to make Australia's modest first innings look more impressive. But before Australia could wallow in its 114 lead, it was in trouble at 3 for 69.

Miller emerged into the late afternoon sun, *once more into the breach*, with his country in trouble yet again. The standing ovation from the 30,000 spectators was heartfelt as he strode out, hair blowing in the breeze and shirt billowing. He gazed skyward as he had always done at Lord's, perhaps embarrassed by the attention, which he appreciated on one level and hated on another. Not only had he been at his best with the ball last evening and today; there was also a valedictory feeling in the applause. Miller was intent on smashing England, but the spectators had put aside patriotism. The welcome was sincere, yet not quite spontaneous. A current of thought ran through the spectators before he batted. This might well be his last appearance.

Miller responded by belting 30 majestic runs (7 fours) to revive his country's position. But Trueman had him caught behind and snuffed out dreams of his going on to a big score. Miller walked, perhaps pertinently giving himself out. As he turned to go he waved his bat to Trueman – an old bull to a younger one – in acknowledgement that a good delivery had finished him. Miller was, after all, an expert on such matters. It was his last chivalrous act with the bat in a Test at Lord's.

The crowd, who had gone up as one with Evans for the catch, rose once more to Miller, giving him a thunderous farewell. There was a feeling that this was it. Bradman, covering the Ashes as a journalist for the Melbourne *Herald*, sensed it. He asked, 'Did the people think it would be a last chance to show their appreciation?'

Australia was 6 for 115 at stumps and not yet on top. The papers and ex-players were fulsome in their praise of his bowling: 'Miller the moody,' the *Daily Sketch* reporter wrote, 'Miller the so very magnificent, always pops up like a fifth ace, unexpected and likely to disturb the balance of any game.'

Hutton (now Sir Len after his deeds in regaining and holding the Ashes) wrote: 'I cannot remember seeing Miller bowl better or with more vicious purpose. This was the Miller who nearly wrecked England's chance of winning the Fourth Test at Adelaide on my last tour [1954–55]. He was bowling firmly, with imagination and accuracy, and no two balls were alike. This [Saturday morning's] sustained spell of magnificent bowling clouded England's prospects.'

'In the main,' Hassett observed, 'his length was perfect and he varied his pace while he cut both towards and in from the slips. This control and variation, plus his ability to get the ball up sharply from the wicket, had all the batsmen worried.'

There was such a big crowd on Monday that Benaud, not out overnight with Mackay, was nearly late. 'In the course of the 50 metres [to the wicket],' Benaud said, 'I extolled [to] the dour Queenlander [Mackay] the virtue of making runs, quickly, slowly and any other way I could think of.'

At the pitch, the laconic Mackay, chewing relentlessly, glanced at Benaud and said, 'Just let's don't get run out.'

They didn't. Benaud thumped 97, in the best innings of his Test career, and hauled Australia's total up to an overall lead of 371.

It seemed enough, going on the game's pattern of low scores. Miller's first victim in the second innings always looked like being Graveney, who had yet to fulfil his outstanding promise. Miller drew him forward and into defensive mien, when he was a brilliant, natural stroke-maker. Miller then decided to bowl around the wicket. The change of angle confused the batsman. He edged a ball to Langley and was on his way for 18, leaving England floundering at 2 for 72 on Monday evening – needing an even 300 for victory.

***

Miller's constitution and will, were going to receive a severe examination on the final day of the Test. It did not stop him having a rollicking time with Prowse that night and in the morning. Ted Rippon, a former Essendon footballer and commentator, and a close mate of Miller's, arrived at his hotel room to pick up tickets for the final day. Rippon knocked on the door.

'Come in, Ted. The tickets are on the table,' Miller called.

Rippon walked in. He could see into the bathroom. Miller was in the shower with Prowse.

'He had tram tracks down his back,' Rippon said, and dined out on the observation thereafter.

***

Back on the field of play a few hours later, Yorkshireman Willie Watson saved Miller some labour when he defied a kindergarten dictum and hit across the line of a full toss. He was bowled middle stump for 18. Miller then toiled hard in spells during the morning and was unlucky not to have May with the new ball.

Yet whatever Miller had for lunch, or whatever went through his creative mind, caused him to raise his bowling to a ferocious level. His energy levels were high even after his grand effort in the morning and earlier with Prowse. His incentive was one last effort for Australia at Lord's. Miller delivered an even finer performance than in the first innings, bowling faster and more accurately. Evans, batting almost flippantly in chasing runs, flicked at one that was swallowed by his opposite number.

May was England's number one bat and captain, and Miller's main target. He succumbed with a nibble outside off stump, and Langley did the rest. Miller played cat and mouse with Wardle for a few balls before knocking back his off stump, making him his tenth victim for the match at a cost of 152 runs.

Only Cowdrey, Laker and Statham were not his victims at least once in the game, and that was by luck rather than good management. He moved the ball both ways in a marathon spell of 36 quality overs in the second innings and paid a price. His knee troubled him right through the second innings, but he kept going, pushing himself as he and Archer in strong support smelt victory, which was attained by 185 runs. It was Miller's one and only 10-wicket haul in a Test. If he had been given the choice of where and when to achieve it in his whole mighty career, he would have said this game.

A photographer with an eye for posterity captured a fine image. Miller, drained but contented, took a bail from umpire Emrys Davies and flicked it into the crowd. It was a gesture that said many things: flamboyance in an era when there was a certain amount of outrage for such things; rapport with the crowd, which was reserved for the game's characters; and farewell to a special throng of spectators who had always treated Miller well. The crowds at Bramall Lane and Nottingham had reacted over the years to his aggression. At Lord's, affection for him overrode other emotions.

It was over on the playing field he loved, but there were no tears. It was just a sporting arena after all. He had promises from Aitken in his back pocket, along with an offer from Aitken's friend, media mogul Frank Packer, who had been at the Test, for a prospective TV career in Australia. Miller would be moving on from the game. Besides, he knew he would be back at Lord's in lesser games this season and then other roles for decades to come.

***

Miller's knee was in bad shape. He had copious fluid taken from it before Johnson sent him off for 10 days holiday. The first part of the break was on Godfrey Evans' houseboat floating in the Thames Estuary. It was blissful until the second evening when he was stranded on a mudbank. On day three he drove down to Brighton with Prowse. They were sunbaking on the pebbles when a thief stole his jacket, which Miller had left in his unlocked car. The jacket pockets had his diary – his English little black book – and his wallet. The latter contained the official invitation for himself and two guests for his MBE investiture at Buckingham Palace in a few weeks time.

'The police were told to be on the look-out for a thief pretending to have an Aussie accent and boasting a date with the Queen to receive a medal,' Whitington noted, 'along with the telephone numbers of half the most attractive women in London.'

One of those women was Princess Margaret. In 1953 she was in a hush-hush love affair with Peter Townsend, but kept in contact with Miller with discreet invitations to visit her, once with Townsend present. The Queen and the Church of England had frowned on her desire to marry the divorcee Townsend, and the relationship was over by 1955. Margaret put royal duty in front of love and turned him down. It made her unhappy and occasionally wilful after being denied, and denying herself, the man she wanted.

Aware of her feelings, her close royal relative Lord Mountbatten had been understanding. He knew what cheered her up and the type of men she liked. He turned up at the Southampton ground where the Australians, led by Miller after his break, were playing Hampshire on 7 July. Mountbatten watched the end of the first day. After play, Mountbatten approached him. 'Miller,' he said, 'would you like to come to my place tonight and have dinner with us?'

This was a tempting invitation, but Miller was captaining the team. Hampshire was putting on a cocktail party for the Australians at the ground that evening. As ever, he was the star attraction among the tourists. But another thing worried him. He did not have any appropriate clothes, and he knew that guests would be in formal gear. He mumbled an uncertain response, stressing his responsibility. Mountbatten took the initiative, suggesting that he show up for the Hampshire cocktail party, then a car would pick him up from his hotel at 8 p.m.

'We're only 6 miles out [of Southampton] at Romsey,' he said. Before Miller could prevaricate further, Mountbatten added with a smile, 'I had better tell you who is coming. There will be Princess Margaret, a lady-in-waiting, my wife, my daughter Pamela, Lord Granville, Dominic Elliott, Billy Wallace . . .'

Miller didn't hear any names after the mention of Margaret. There was no doubt now that he would accept the invitation to

Mountbatten's spacious country home, Broadlands, in the beautiful Hampshire countryside, even if he turned up in his cricket gear. Fortunately he did have a suit with him. He attended the cocktail party, then dashed over to the team's hotel near the Hampshire ground and washed his only quick-drying shirt, which he had worn on the train down in the morning.

The First Sea Lord was known for his fastidious attention to detail, and had thought ahead to put his dinner guest at ease. When the chauffeur turned up at his hotel on the dot of 8 p.m. he had a note from Mountbatten for Miller. The postscript said: 'We are wearing dinner suits, but no doubt yours will be in London, so please come in your lounge suit.'

Miller arrived and was apologetic for not having a dinner suit with him, but was made to feel comfortable by his hosts. He was once more charmed by Margaret's conversation, humour, naturalness and lack of affectation. 'The Princess has the bluest eyes I have seen,' he remarked later, 'and is a most attractive person in every way.' Miller had felt out of his depth, but over dinner and with the wine flowing, he relaxed. After the meal, Mountbatten led them to a lounge room that doubled as a theatrette. The film threading through a projector was a thriller starring Edward G. Robinson. Mountbatten, directing seating arrangements, said: 'Oh, Mr Miller, would you please sit next to the Princess?'

Miller could hardly say, 'No, I'd rather sit in the back stalls', but he was more than pleased to oblige. He shared a settee with her in the dark, and occasionally spent moments whispering not sweet nothings but thoughts about 'whodunnit'. At one point Princess Margaret said, 'The butler did it,' and drew a laugh from Miller, who responded, 'He usually does.'

The next day, the press wanted to know all about the dinner. Miller remained discreet and would not even say whether he had sat next to the Princess or whether there had been music and dancing. 'It was an informal and entertaining evening,' was his diplomatic response. When asked by one journalist what time he left the party, which was a way of fishing for an angle on romance with the Princess, Miller replied: 'When the party terminated.'

His discretion was applauded. It was Miller's style in such matters, yet it was also wise. He had to think of his friend Prowse, who would have been wondering where she sat in the pecking order of women in Miller's life. More importantly there was Peg back in Sydney to consider. Her father Carl Wagner, the person responsible for Keith and his daughter meeting 13 years earlier, had just died.

***

Back on the field, Miller put his injured knee through 25 overs in Hampshire's two innings in the drawn game. It was not perfect. In the next two days before the Headingley Third Test, the knee deteriorated and fluid built up again. Miller told Johnson he could bat but not bowl. It was a blow and proved so in the game.

England's selectors, including chairman Gubby Allen, seemed certain that this wicket and the one at Old Trafford in the Fourth Test would be suitable for spinners. They chose only four bowlers: Trueman, Bailey, Laker and Lock. Statham was left out. Surrey's spin twins were expected to do what they had done so well for their county on turning wickets.

Peter May won the toss, and England was soon 3 for 17, thanks to Archer. Miller, looking on from the slips, would have been very frustrated. But he knew that if he put pressure on the knee it would collapse and put him out of the series. May (104) and a brave, 41-year-old Washbook (98), a selector who put himself back in a Test team for the first time since 1951, restored order for the home team, which went on to 325. Archer, Lindwall and Benaud each took three wickets and bowled well, but they needed the Miller spearhead to put more pressure on the opposition.

Australia was caught on a wet wicket, which never deteriorated to a sticky but which nevertheless was tough to bat on as it dried out in the sun. Miller came to the wicket at 4 for 59 late on day two and in failing light. Laker removed Mackay and Archer cheaply, bringing Benaud to the wicket at 6 for 69. By now it was black in the middle. The scoreboard lights were bright. Miller went over to umpires Davies and Buller. 'It's really getting bad,' he said. 'I've never known it so dark.'

Miller nearly had them agreeing, but the umpires conferred and decided to play on just for a few balls to see what transpired. Miller appealed twice more, and the men in white were even closer to drawing stumps. Then Benaud danced down to Laker and drove him superbly through mid-off for four. The batsmen had crossed. Miller came over to Benaud. 'What the bloody hell do you think you're up to?' Miller said. 'I'd just about talked them into giving us the light. But there's no chance now.' But despite the shot, bad light stopped play at 6.15 p.m.

The next morning Miller put up stubborn resistance. He played a superb innings of controlled aggression. But, just like his protégé Benaud (caught at deep square leg swinging at Laker), he lost his composure after 130 minutes at 41. Miller went down on one knee, swished across the line and was bowled neck and crop by Laker's slower ball. Only Burke (equal top score of 41), Miller and Benaud didn't look inept against spin, and even then they all got themselves out through lapses that were unnecessary. It was a woeful display against the wonderful right–left spin combination of Laker and Lock. Australia was dismissed for 143 and forced to follow on.

Ian Johnson, ever the optimist, gave a pep talk in the dressing room. 'We'll make 500,' he said, 'and we've still got a chance.'

Miller put down his racing paper and interrupted: 'Six to four we don't.' It was not the wisest remark, no matter how much the skipper was deluding himself and his team. It would be a reason for Johnson saying later that Miller, at times, could be 'selfish'.

As Miller's cynicism or realism predicted, it was much the same story of incompetence in the second innings. The Australian batting unravelled again. He was the only common denominator of determination and skill in the two innings. Harvey, perhaps taking up his vice-captain's odds, was at his valiant best.

Miller tried everything, it seemed, in his 135-minute stay to turn the tide. He hated the leg-trap set to the spinners and began, with Harvey, trying to remove them by force. The fielders ducked and covered their heads, but the ball was turning sharply and this belligerence didn't quite work. Miller tried using his pads, and seemed to get tired of it. He had a weapon and liked to use it. He went back to the turning ball and looked competent yet uncomfortable. Yet still, Miller was encouraged by his little mate Harvey. They were in a groove that could have blossomed the way their partnership did at Headingley against Laker in 1948. But that was on a good wicket, and Laker then was not the assured technician that he had become by 1956. Nor did he have in 1948 the irritating menace of Lock backing him up at the other end with overs delivered in less than two minutes, and which kept relentless pressure on the batsmen.

Miller broke the shackles late on the fourth day with two prodigious sixes: a sweep and a pull off Lock. But Laker's figures told a story. His last 10 overs of the day cost 5 runs. That was the equivalent of a dash up half the pitch by the batsmen every over. Australia went to stumps on 2 for 93 with Harvey 40 not out and Miller 24 not out. Overnight showers on the uncovered pitch had again dampened the wicket. Laker and Lock had more pace, lift and turn than before in the match.

Runs were at a premium as two fine players of spin faced the best combination since Grimmett and O'Reilly more than two decades earlier. The wicket, however, made it less than an even contest. Miller, on 26, played back to Laker's faster ball. He edged it into his pads. The ball flew low to the outstretched fingers of Trueman at very short square leg.

Harvey battled on to 69, but the rest of the Australians were without hope. Australia was rolled for just 143 and 140. Laker and Lock took 18 wickets between them. The tourists had no answers to their bite and turn on a poor wicket. England won by an innings and 42 runs, levelling the series at one-all. With the prospect of more spin at Old Trafford, momentum was with England.

***

The Fourth Test was just nine days after the Third, which meant that the Australian selection panel – Johnson, Miller and Langley – had to choose the team early. Johnson was badly out of form. He had no penetration with his looping spin, and he was out of touch with the bat. In short, the captain was a passenger. The Australian press was baying for the skipper's blood, hoping that this would cause him to fall on his sword. Journalists wanted Miller as captain.

When the selectors sat down at their London hotel on 18 July, Johnson was in an awkward position. If Miller and Langley were against him, he would go. Miller opened the discussion. 'I think Craig ought to come in,' he said.

Langley and a relieved Johnson nodded their agreement. Craig would replace Burge. That was the only suggestion. The team remained unchanged. Miller and Langley would have agreed to drop Johnson had he suggested it himself. But he did not, and the matter rested there. It was not even tempting for Miller to confront his long-term rival and friend. The team disharmony at this stage of a series, he judged, was simply not worth it. He would have loved to lead his country. But the moment was not right in Miller's mind, and now never would be. He would be forever known, among innumerable accolades, as the greatest captain never to captain his country. Had the team been down 2–1, it might have been a different story. But on paper, Australia was well in the series, with one win each and two to play.

Johnson and Miller were still thinking they could win the Ashes back after two miserable series losses when they went to Buckingham Palace on 21 July to receive their MBEs. The Queen made the awards. Photographers outside the palace gates surrounded both men. They stopped to pose with the medals, and it was not difficult to get them to smile. A crowd gathered. A

12-year-old boy produced an autograph book and asked for Miller's signature. Miller opened the book and was about to sign on a page with the scrawls of Sir Donald Bradman and Sir Len Hutton.

'Not there!' said the boy. He opened at a page headed 'Miscellaneous'.

Miller was amused at not being ranked with the great knights. The lad was placing him on his honour rating and not all-round cricket ability or performance. Or perhaps the young fan had never seen him make a century at Lord's. Maybe he ranked him lower because he had never seen Miller at his best. After all, 1945, when he dominated the summer with the bat, and 1948, when he and Lindwall were supreme with the ball, were eight to eleven years ago. Miller took the rebuff, jokingly, as a reminder that he had been in the game a long time. It really was time to move on. But not before the Ashes job was completed.

***

The home selectors dumped Trueman, who had been at home at Leeds, and brought in Statham, who would be in his element at Old Trafford. Doug Insole made way for a spiritual revival in the form of the Rev. David Sheppard. England was without their finest post-war pacemen next to Statham: Tyson (still under an injury cloud) and Trueman. This said something about what was in store for the tourists at Manchester.

Doctoring of wickets to suit the home team was the usual practice in all countries. In England, whether it be at Test, county or league level, it was as common as bad weather, and often paralleled it. Fast bowler Martin Ashenden, who partnered Tyson at Northamptonshire in the late 1950s and 1960s, recalled the pattern at county level:

The wicket would be 'shaved' from the batting crease to an area up the wicket, which would be bare of grass. It would take spin immediately. In our case, George Tribe and Jack

Manning – both Australians – would come on straight away, rubbing the new ball in the bare earth. Frank Tyson, the fastest bowler in the world at the time, was innocuous under these circumstances.

The curator at Old Trafford, Bert Flack, knew what he had to do. He made no secret of the fact that he had been instructed to prepare a spinner's wicket. The directive had come from England's chairman of selectors, Gubby Allen.

When interviewed more than 20 years later, Allen admitted inspecting the wicket on the morning of the match and thinking that it would 'go' – that is, deteriorate – by tea on the first day. Seconds after Allen's inspection, Flack's boss, the chairman of the Old Trafford Grounds Committee, asked Allen if he wanted any more grass cut off. Allen replied: 'It wouldn't break my heart.' He must have wanted the wicket to go by lunch. Coming from such an eminent MCC person and England selector, his remark was taken as an order. Flack was told to cut the grass further, which left the wicket bare.

Yet the directive to retard the Manchester wicket had come much earlier from Allen. The ideal wicket for England would be just like the one at Surrey earlier in the season when Laker had taken his 10 wickets in an innings. Flack put marl, which provided a surface, on the wicket about 10 days before the game. It was not watered enough and did not bind or mix with the wicket's soil. The pitch was too dry. The surface marl had flaked and cracked the day before play was due to begin. It would keep peeling off until the pitch was a dustbowl. This meant that it would be a spinner's paradise and a batsman's nightmare as early as the second session.

Miller looked at the pitch soon after Flack had done Allen's bidding and mowed the grass out of sight. Miller said to umpire Lee: 'I think three days will see this through [the match won and lost].' The umpire agreed with him.

Nothing was going right for Johnson, and he lost the toss. England (Richardson 104, Cowdrey 80) batted superbly, reaching 3 for 307 at stumps, after withstanding the turn that Benaud and Johnson were managing on the already tricky wicket late in the day. The game was effectively over. England batted on to 459 with the Rev. Sheppard (113) and Evans (47 in 29 minutes) playing the innings of their lives.

Australia began batting 20 minutes after lunch on day two. England's phantom opening bowlers – Statham and Bailey – went through the motions of delivering when in reality they were there for the formal reduction of the shine. The opening bats for Eton College's Third XI, which was having a good year, could have played this pair with ease, such was the docile nature of Flack's sad handiwork. McDonald and Burke, in fact, batted well. But when Laker came on, Eton's Thirds would not have done much worse than Australia. At 5.15 p.m. in the middle of the next session the tourists were all out for 84. Laker had removed 9 of them for just 37. A combination of the worst pitch in Ashes history and a master off-spinner humiliated Australia.

There was more to come in the second innings. Only McDonald (89) again and Craig (38) seemed to have any idea, or will, in playing Laker. This time he repeated the unrepeatable 10 wickets in an innings, making it 19 for 90 for the match. Perhaps this was justice. No one should be able to take all 20 wickets in a game or average 100 in Tests. Just like Bradman, Laker was left a fraction short of statistical perfection. Or maybe the door would be left open for near eternity for a bowler to take the maximum possible dismissals in a Test, or a batsman to average 100 after 20 years at the top.

Laker's return was amazing, but devalued because of the shocking nature of the pitch, which even Eton's Fourth XI, if there were one in 1956, would have refused to bat on. Yet Miller, among many observers and participants, would say later that even if the Australians had batted first, Laker and Lock would have been too good for them. The Test and the Ashes were England's under substandard conditions, but conditions equal to both sides under cricket's laws.

Miller left Old Trafford without a wicket, and scores of 6 and 0, falling both times to Laker, which were the worst returns in a Test for the finest all-rounder to that point in cricket history. This alone demonstrated that Old Trafford was a farce and that it should never have occurred.

And what of poor Bert Flack? He received his doctorate in pitches and went home fed up with all the publicity and the notoriety that would be his for cricketing eternity, thanks to the instruction from higher up.

The last person the tourists wished to face again soon after the humiliation and disgraceful conditions at Manchester was Jim Laker, now unofficially King of England for season 1956. But after trailing their coffins back to London on 1 August, the day after the Test, they now had to play Surrey on 2 August in what turned out to be a sadistic piece of match scheduling. The torture was worse when play was rained off on day one of the match, and the team had to bat against Laker on a rain-affected pitch on day two. The off-spinner, like all top-line bowlers, was a glutton for wickets. Laker, too, had a long memory of humiliation at the hands of the Australians. He was going to push their faces where he had rubbed the ball to get the shine off it.

The depression in the Australian dressing room was palpable as wickets tumbled with cautious strokeplay from a team that was shot of confidence. Laker was again on early. He took 4 wickets, including Miller's, for just 11. Only Davidson, back from injury and without the terrible scars of failure at Leeds and Old Trafford, had the right mental approach. He used his bullock-train driver's shoulders to belt Laker and Lock in an innings of 44 not out in 50 minutes. A Davidson six off Laker almost reached the gasometer. Australia still tumbled for 143 in a continuation of the run of poor scores that Eton's Thirds would have scorned.

Miller had the all-rounder's capacity to strike back. And he was in a mood to do it. Despite knee swelling, he fired up for a tremendous opening spell, ripping through Surrey's early order, including Ken Barrington (15) and May, whose stumps he shattered for 11. Miller was on when Laker was batting, but fortunately for the spinner, Davidson bowled him for a duck before he could face his long-term foe. Miller ended with 5 for 84, showing that just his batting but not his spirit had been thwarted.

Surrey captain Stuart Surridge, in the process of leading the county to its fifth successive championship, declared 38 ahead and put the tourists back in for a nasty final hour. As if England needed any more of a psychological advantage, Laker (1 wicket) and Lock (2 wickets) had Australia on the ropes for the tenth time in the season.

Miller missed a morale-lifting thrashing of Glamorgan at Swansea but returned as skipper at Birmingham against Warwickshire on 8 August. He and Ian Johnson had death threats through the mail suggesting that they would be murdered if Australia beat the county. No one was clear why. Had Miller and Johnson offended a disgruntled fan on this tour or a previous one? The unsigned one-page letter was half-typed, half-scrawled in an almost illegible hand. It said: 'You will be shot dead if you win.'

'I don't know if the writer is fair dinkum,' Miller told the press, 'but I haven't got a bodyguard.'

It didn't affect him, his performance (46 not out and 2 for 13 in the only innings he bowled) or the innings victory outcome for the Australians. Electric bursts against Lancashire back at the dreaded Manchester in the first innings by Lindwall (7 for 40), now fitter and running into form, and Miller in the second (5 for 29), gave the Australians their third successive win. The trend continued down at Southend against Essex, where Miller accumulated 50 in a most circumspect manner and took 5 wickets over two innings for 78.

Miller would have preferred Lord's to end his Test career, but he had to set aside negative sentiment about the Oval, a place he had grown to like even less in 1956 because it was the home of Laker and Lock, not to mention damp wickets. It also harboured memories of that 1953 lost Ashes game and series.

He went on television on the evening before the Test and announced that he would be retiring after this tour, which was to take in Pakistan and India on the way home. The board outlawed media appearances during a tour, and Miller risked a fine. The retirement announcement turned media attention to Miller and Compton, who had been selected to play after a knee operation. His troublesome patella had been removed. The media focused on the concept of the two great 'cavaliers' (read 'sportsmen, womanisers, drinkers and gamblers') and mates facing each other in a titanic last tussle.

Miller missed bowling him by a whisker first ball, which allowed Compton to turn back time for a masterful 94 in England's modest 247. This was a further coup for the selectors, who had also brought in Washbrook and Sheppard with success each time. Miller (4 for 91), Lindwall, and Archer (5 for 53) enjoyed a greener wicket to take the wickets. Miller arrived at the crease mid-afternoon on day two with Australia at 5 for 47 after Johnson had promoted himself on a rain-touched pitch. Tyson, back only to play third fiddle to the spinners, then Laker and Lock had done their usual early damage. Miller began scratchily then attacked, lifting Laker for a sweet six before sweeping hard at anything the spinner hurled down on leg stump.

Benaud joined Miller at 7 for 111 and used a controlled, intelligent approach to take the initiative and score a forceful 32. Miller, in his best innings of the Test series, was playing Laker and Statham with ease and grace. Australia had recovered to 8 for 198 at stumps with Miller on 57 not out and Lindwall on 22 not out.

Rain, predictably, intervened on Saturday morning before the third day, yet the wicket had dried just enough to allow play to begin on time. Miller decided to 'have a go' in the difficult conditions and was caught off Statham for 61. Australia crawled, exhausted, to 202, but Miller had his team in the game. England responded with 3 for 182 spread, because of awful weather, over Saturday, Sunday (a rest day and perfect weather), Monday and the final Tuesday.

May declared at 4.10 p.m., giving the tourists 2 hours to make 228. There were only thoughts of survival, and even that looked doubtful when Australia lost 3 for 5. Miller came in. He had decided to go forward to Laker in this game. It had worked in the first innings and did again now. His theory was to give fewer chances to the leg trap, which had been so successful for the spinners. Miller succeeded, but Australia was going nowhere at 4 for 10. He was back in his game for South Melbourne against Carlton as a 16-year-old defending with immaculate, fleet-footed forward defence, mixed in with a bit of pad play. At 5 for 27 with Miller on a dogged 7 not out, bad light and rain ended Australia's misery. A tame draw resulted.

With the sun peeping through the showers, Miller waved his bat to the crowd, and walked off to warm applause for the last time in a Test in England.

He might well have won the player-of-the-match award for making runs against exceptional opposition in tough conditions in the first innings; batting to save the game in the second; and his top bowling, especially in England's first innings. Opposed to this was Laker's outstanding bowling across two innings, when he took 7 for 88, and Compton's 94 and 35 not out. His newspaper-to-be did some pre-advertising with the headline: 'King Miller', dislodging King Jim for a day.

England had won the Ashes 2–1, but this did not reveal the one-sidedness of the series. Bradman ranked England's 1956 team at the Oval – Richardson, Cowdrey, Sheppard, May, Compton, Lock, Washbrook, Evans, Laker, Tyson and Statham – as its best ever side. He admired the team's balance and winning combinations with ball and bat. There was no disgrace in being defeated by such an elite XI. Yet that was not the way the media and the Australian public would see the decline. Knives would be out to cut away the dead wood and the aged. Miller, Lindwall and Johnson were mentioned, but only Lindwall was planning to play on anyway.

Miller was disappointed at bowing out in a team that capitulated to England in three successive Ashes series. But he happily put things in perspective, and had few regrets. He had played in dominant post-war teams for seven years, and now the wheel had turned full cycle placing the main victim of those golden years under Bradman and Hassett – England – on top.

***

Miller had to mop up some business in the last month, including his book, *Cricket Crossfire*. The method of its construction was tortuous. Miller would meet one of his 'ghosts' for this exercise, journalist Reg Hayter, in pubs up and down England and, towards the end, in Fleet Street. Hayter's problem was Miller's unpunctuality. He was always, without exception, late. Over a painless drink, Miller would talk and the journalist would take notes. These would be passed to Basil Easterbrook, who was composing the book itself.

It was a tough assignment. Easterbrook often found himself out of copy and would have to arrange for Hayter to speak more with Miller. Some sections were harder than others. The war years would be of interest in England and Australia, but Miller was reluctant to speak about them. He had burnt his log book long ago and had trouble recalling dates. Miller was equally unforthcoming in the chapter 'Miller and Royalty', but he did find his verbal flow when it came to discussing Bradman, Frank Chester and Len Hutton. The self-explanatory last two chapters, 'Random Thoughts' and 'More Random Thoughts', aptly demonstrated the Miller–Hayter–Easterbrook method and the two ghosts' frustration.

The *Daily Express* serialised the book, and this once more broke the Australian board's rule, which disallowed any player writing on cricket while still under contract. The serialisation added to his misdemeanour of appearing on TV, and went towards a £100 penalty. Bradman had been fined in much the same way in 1930 for writing in a newspaper. Yet he was not on the board sitting in judgement of Miller, who appealed against the ruling and lost. (Later a Melbourne confectionery-maker would pay the fine.)

Miller still had some enjoyable games to play in the United Kingdom. The first, against the Gentleman of England beginning on 29 August, was another rain-ruined drawn match. Johnson stepped aside to allow Miller to captain the side for his final appearance at Lord's. He had time for an ignoble end when he was given a black eye by a short ball that slid off the bat. Then he hit his wicket and was out for just 17. Next was an easy final game against a strong T. N. Pearce's XI – an English Test team but for Laker and Lock – at Scarborough, which Australia was pleased to win. Miller bobbed up to lead the Australians to a win once more against the Minor Counties, then had one final fling against Scotland. But Miller's heart was not in it any more. The rain and the mediocre opposition dampened his enthusiasm to do more than send down 27 economical overs and score 3 in his final innings representing his country on British soil.

***

Miller's relationship with Prowse continued, and he took her to Colin McDonald's wedding to his wife Louise at St Columbus Church in Knightsbridge, London. There were plenty of photographers at the event, with Ian Craig, Len Maddocks and Jim Burke and best man Ron Archer attending. Miller had to be smuggled in through the rear of the church to avoid the media at the front.

Miller's returns for his last Ashes series and tour were consistent with his career in bowling but not with his batting. He was fourth with just a 22.55-run average, yet he topped the bowling with 21 wickets at 22.23. His first-class batting statistics were down also, with just 843 at 36.65. Once again, his bowling stood up with the top return of 50 wickets at 19.60.

Even rising 37, Miller could have gone on for one or two more series. His batting had not fallen away, but it had suffered from an abnormal season. His technique was as effective as that of any of the Australians in the struggles against the spinners. But Miller had timed his retirement about right. He cited 'family reasons', which were doubtful; future work, which was authentic; and 'a desire to retire' before he was thrown out, which was debatable.

The Australians had a brief holiday in Europe before moving on to Karachi for their first ever Test against Pakistan. The setting was National Stadium. The pitch was covered by matting, which was a new experience for most of the tourists. The Australians were in first.

Miller was batting at five five. He put on his pads, called the team's liaison officer, Munir Hassain, and settled into a chair, arms folded. 'Wake me when I'm due to bat,' Miller said. At the fall of the third wicket at 24, Munir did as instructed, shaking the slumbering Miller by the shoulder. He uncoiled himself, rubbed his eyes and reached for his bat and gloves. 'Is McDonald batting?' Miller asked.

'No, back in the pavilion.'

'What about Harvey?'

'He's out, too.'

'Who got the wickets?'

'Fazal,' Munir replied, referring to Miller's friend from his match for the Commonwealth XI in Colombo five years earlier.

'Oh, he is running hot again,' Miller said, walking towards the gate. 'Don't disturb my bed. I'll be back soon.'

Miller top-scored with 21 – out caught off Fazal – in the team's pitiful 80. After the humiliation at Old Trafford this was the lowest point for Australian cricket post-war. Pakistan was 2 for 15 at stumps. Just 95 runs were scored in the day, the smallest tally in a full day's play in Test history.

Miller removed the gifted Hanif Mohammad for a duck and the attractive stroke-maker Waqar Hassan for 6, to help reduce the home side to 6 for 70. But Hanif Mohammad's elder brother Wazir (67) and Abdul Kardar (69) pushed Pakistan to 199. Miller contributed only 11 in Australia's second innings of 187 in which Benaud (56) and Davidson (37) looked comfortable. Fazal took a record 13 for 114 for the match, including three wickets in four balls in the second innings. Pakistan mopped up the 69 required to win, losing just one wicket.

During the game, Miller and Fazal were entertained to dinner by the Nawab Junagarh at his home. Fazal was Miller's best friend on the subcontinent, and their friendship was apparent on the night of the farewell dinner put on by the ruling Pakistan cricket body, the BCCP. Although Fazal was Pakistan's vice-captain, he had not been given a seat at the top table. Seeing this, Miller stood up and shouted, 'Where's Fazal's seat?' Officials hurried to find him a place. 'Right here,' Miller ordered, indicating a seat next to him. As Glendinning and other close friends in his life would attest, if you were 'in' with Miller, you were really 'in'. He was loyal under all circumstances.

Miller's knee was in such poor condition that he could not play in the three Tests in India. He was a spectator in the first game at Madras, where Australia won its first Test in India. It was dominated by Benaud and Lindwall with the ball. Miller was hardly seen at the drawn Second Test at Brabourne Stadium, Bombay, where Burke (161) and Harvey (140) found form.

He spent much time with a slim, beautiful Indian named Crystal, who looked remarkably like Princess Margaret. After their first evening together on 30 October she gave him a photo momento of herself inscribed: 'To Keith, with tons and tons of soul and a big kiss, from Crystal.' After a night together on 31 October, she inscribed a second photo: 'Keith . . . so you will not ever forget me! Love: Crystal xxx.'

Unlike Miller's girlfriend Prowse, the lovely Crystal would not

415

be invited to visit him in Australia. That would be too much of a complication, even for Miller, especially at a time when his family was moving from Dee Why on Sydney's northern beaches into a big rambling home at Nullaburra Road, Newport, still within walking distance of the surf. Peg had inherited £60,000 from her father and had bought the £6,500 property to better accommodate the growing boys. She could now look after the boys on her own account if her wandering husband decided to leave forever.

Miller had to forsake his new *amour* in Bombay and move on with the team as just a passenger once more to Eden Gardens, Calcutta, where Burge (58) in Australia's first innings, and Harvey (69), at his scintillating best against spin in the second, gave the tourists a chance. Benaud, emerging now as an all-rounder to replace Miller, took 11 for 105 to secure a win and the series.

It was the second time Australia had toured in tough conditions under Johnson and Miller to achieve wonderful series wins. But as with the West Indies tour that followed the drubbing in the 1954–55 Ashes, the Indian tour would be overshadowed by the disintegration of an Ashes series. Once more there was not the media coverage to capture public imagination about these more exotic and exacting visits to far-off lands.

***

Few all-rounders had comparable records to that of Miller. At the end of his 55-Test career he had taken 170 wickets at 22.97, with seven 5-wicket hauls and one 10. But as good as these figures were, they did not register the quality of batsmen he removed and when, which tell an even more impressive story with the ball. Similarly, the cold batting numbers of 2,958 runs (with 7 hundreds and 13 fifties) at 36.97 do not account for the number of times he came to the wicket in a crisis and restored order. There is no doubt that his fatigued condition after bowling stints impaired his batting on occasions. Then again, he was an all-rounder. Despite starting several seasons with determination only to bat, he became drawn into the exhausting bowling vortex by a cajoling captain or by his own irrepressible desire to take on the best opposition batsmen at state and Test level.

Miller was hoist with his own petard of competitiveness when it came to his batting and bowling. But by doing both when most players found the demands too much, his great skills and energy – not to mention a killer instinct when he felt like it with bat or ball – placed him in the top bracket of all-time great cricketers.

PART 5

LIFE AFTER CRICKET

21 ENDLESS SUMMER

In his last three weeks in England Miller went on a BBC TV training course in anticipation of beginning a career at Frank Packer's Channel Nine as a sporting commentator. But the medium was not to be his. Miller was too nervous and agitated. TV did not then, and never has, catered for characters who were *too* animated. Flamboyant types who wave their hands around, don't sit still and fluff their lines, whether remembered or read from autocues, are not acceptable. If they were commentators and newsreaders they were in people's living rooms almost every day. And, according to producers, no one wanted a chronic hand-waver in the corner of the room inside a little box disturbing the tranquillity of suburban Australia. At least that's what advertisers told producers and producers told advertisers. The strength of Miller's personality, wit, expertise on cricket and other sports, sonorous voice and outstanding looks were overridden by the need for sometimes less frenetic or even dull commentators and anchormen. The preference was for punctual performers, who could sit on their hands and not upset the great new audience for TV.

Miller didn't enjoy his experiences in front of the big-eye cameras in London and later in auditions at Channel Nine when he returned to Australia. He was not going to be chosen as a front or anchorman, but he was to work here and there for Nine's sports department as a commentator.

It didn't help Miller's adjustment to life after playing cricket. He was restless through the New Year into 1957 while trying to settle back at the new home in Newport with Peg and the boys. After being in so much of the action on and off the field in England, Miller craved more and could indulge his desires because he had the money to do it. Peg's financial independence increased Miller's own independence. He could spend all his income on his own pursuits if he wished.

This period of readjustment saw him drinking more than ever. One evening after a bad day at the Randwick races, he came home drunk and in a foul mood. Bill, 8, and Peter, 6, greeted him at the front gate. 'We were just happy to see him,' Peter recalled, 'but he was in an angry mood. He wanted to belt me. I ran. He chased me.' Bill watched as his father chased Peter down the side of the house. Peter, being small, managed to get under the fence. Miller tried to jump the fence, but fell flat on his face, much to Bill's amusement. Peter was so frightened that he spent three days at the home of a neighbour a few doors down the street.

Miller's relationship with Prowse had become serious and for the first time threatened to break the family unit. Miller installed his lover in a house at Bungan Beach, which was a few kilometres from his home. He had never before 'played' on his own doorstep, which was an unwritten, even unsaid, rule between him and Peg. Miller told Peg that he wanted 'time to himself to sort things out'. Peg, understanding as ever, allowed him his 'space'.

A week or so into this arrangement, Peg took the boys around to see their dad. Miller opened the door. He was annoyed. 'Never come around again without warning me,' he said and shut the door.

'We were a bit stunned,' Denis Miller recalled. It was a moment of cold rejection that stayed in the boys' minds.

After a few weeks Miller was spending time at both places. The instability that his lifestyle and travelling had caused the family was made worse by this development, and Miller was faced with choices. Yet after some indecision he was not prepared to abandon Peg, who took this new distraction stoically and without giving up her unconditional love for her husband. Besides, divorce in the 1950s was an unpalatable, lengthy business, which could take five years. Adultery and desertion had to be proved among other grounds for separation. Miller had looked on with discomfort and distaste at the dirty linen aired in the 1956 divorce of his former colleague Whitington.

'Peg, the boys and the Newport home were Keith's bolt-hole,' Jan Beames, who witnessed this family crisis, recalled. 'They represented stability and security, which he needed. He would have been lost without Peg, who was a sort of compass for his life.'

The situation was made more complicated by the arrival in Sydney on 29 July 1957 of Pat Williams, whom Miller had promised to sponsor to Australia. He and Peg turned up an hour after Williams' boat docked. She was doing modelling work on the ship's deck for a Melbourne fashion house. Journalists and photographers crowded the new arrival and fired questions at the Millers. With her usual aplomb, Peg fielded probes. 'I don't know how long Patricia will stay with us,' she said sweetly. 'We're a bit crowded already with four children, but I guess there's always room for one more.'

Williams stayed a short while until she was settled enough to find a place with other members of her family in Sydney. Prowse eventually returned to England, and Miller kept up a relationship with her, although it was never again in such proximity to Peg and the boys.

The next Ashes were always going to be a lure. The thought that he could have played on another couple of seasons, then taken on the England team in the Ashes of 1958–59 in Australia, would remain in the back of Miller's mind. He had to be content with writing for the *Express* (and Australian papers in separate deals) and a book on the series titled, perhaps plaintively, *Cricket from the Grandstand*, which reflected his feelings. It began with a chapter 'Why I Quit Cricket' and used Lindwall as an example of what happened if you were out of favour with the selectors. Lindwall was dumped from the 1957–58 tour of South Africa. Yet Miller omitted to qualify this with additional comment on the mighty effort put in by Lindwall to come back in the 1958–59 Ashes. The chapter seemed as if Miller was attempting to purge the nagging thought that he had bowed out too early. He also criticised Compton for going on England's 1956–57 tour of South Africa after his return against Australia in 1956.

Several chapters touched on issues then current. Miller supported the idea of one-day cricket to generate excitement and revenue. He believed it would be inevitable if the game were to survive. The book then launched into the Ashes series, which was little more than a regurgitation of his articles for the *Express*.

The book, pointedly, listed *Cricket Crossfire* as his only other cricket publication, which indicated that Miller and Whitington were not over their rift. Miller wished to draw a line under his (non-writing) collaborations and strike out a second time with his own distinctive voice with Oldbourne Press.

The 4–0 series victory by Richie Benaud's team would have caused Miller mixed feelings. He would have loved to be a part of beating England again after the three successive losing series. The whole experience of following the Ashes around Australia would have been a factor a few months after the series in his taking up the offer to play cricket with the MCC in the 1959 England season. In preparation for this he decided to play first-class cricket again, with Nottinghamshire. There would have been no thought as he approached 40 of a regular comeback. Yet he wanted to test himself to see if he still had 'it', like Lindwall, who did well on his Test return in the last two games of the 1958–59 Ashes.

Miller was not out of touch with bat or ball. He had played the odd festival match as well as performing in 1958 in England in aid of the Pakistan Flood Relief Fund. His constitution was strong, and he was fit from his regular swimming at secluded Long Reef beach and playing golf during the long Australian summers. He put doubts about his knee aside and joined his old friend from RAF and Test playing days, Reg Simpson, captain of Nottingham, to play against Cambridge University. Notts was on the bottom. It normally attracted less than a thousand spectators to a non-championship match. But the publicity about Miller's playing drew more than 5,000. There was some irony in returning for Notts. The local crowd had howled at him on several occasions for short-pitched bowling for Australia. But on Saturday, 15 June 1959 he soon had spectators applauding and cheering as he swept away the three years of retirement for a strong, very typical all-round display. He came to the wicket batting in familiar circumstances with his team floundering on 3 for 23.

Miller received a bouncer and moved out of the way of it. The crowd roared. When the bowler tried another, Miller waved his bat at the bowler, feigning anger. The spectators laughed. Miller had them on his side in a flash. He batted without fireworks, as he worked himself back into the rhythms of first-class cricket. In scoring 62, he partnered M. Hall in a 128-run stand that allowed Notts to recover to 284.

Simpson then threw Miller the ball. He delivered a strong opening spell, dismissing E. M. Rose (8) and N. S. K. Reddy (0) and just failing to remove the other opener, young Henry Blofeld. The students were reduced to 4 for 24 thanks to Miller's burst, but recovered on Monday to 160. Simpson called for quick runs. Miller answered with a fabulous final knock of 102 not out that brought all his skills to the fore. His innings included 2 sixes and 13 fours, and took just 125 minutes. It would have given him mixed emotions to feel how easily the runs flowed. It might have flashed through his mind that he could have played on after 1956 – as a batsman only.

The match was the true end to Miller's first-class career, which would rank with the best in history. In all first-class matches he had 326 innings for 14,183 runs at an average of 48.90. This included 41 centuries and a highest score of 281. He took 497 wickets at 22.30 and held 136 catches.

Miller played for the MCC against Oxford University and took a wicket in an economical performance. But soon after he began to bat he pulled a calf muscle, which put him out for the rest of the season. Miller's mind and skills were up to the game at the highest level, but his body was not.

***

This season Miller again took time to indulge in a pastime that had preoccupied him since 1948: searching for graves of war comrades. He took friend and commentator Tony Charlton to the grave of an RAF pilot with whom Miller had flown. It was in a country churchyard outside Cambridge en route to Newlands racecourse. He laid flowers there, as he had managed to do on most visits since the war.

During the 1959 summer Miller travelled to Europe by car and met Prowse in Spain, where they vacationed together. She had remained his main girlfriend, but there were many in England and Australia. Miller continued to juggle his family life with Peg and the boys at Newport, and his other life as a single man, which was a pattern that had remained the same since 1943.

***

The 1960–61 clash between Australia and the West Indies was a welcome departure from stodgy cricket, which had dominated much of Test match cricket since World War II. Miller's lust for attractive play was satisfied. The tourists from the Caribbean led by his good friend Frank Worrell played brilliant cricket, which had to be matched by Benaud's team. In this series, Gary Sobers confirmed himself as the finest all-rounder in the world, and Miller found his own record being neglected in comparison by a fickle media with short memories.

Sobers played 93 Tests – 38 more than Miller – and his batting record was superior. He scored 8,032 runs at an average of 57.78 with 26 centuries, compared to Miller's average of 36.97 and 7 centuries. Sobers had a greater capacity for the big hundred. He hit 10 scores between 150 and 365 (which stood for more than 30 years as the world Test record score).

Miller did not reach 150 in a Test, yet he had a better record with the ball by all measures, taking 170 wickets at 22.97, as opposed to Sobers' 235 wickets at 34.03. Miller's economy rate and strike rate of balls per wicket were far superior. In addition, he was under more pressure with the ball, being called upon to open the bowling more often. His strike rate among top five batsmen was superior – 59 per cent compared to Sobers' 54 per cent. Miller also took more wickets per Test: 3.1 against 2.5. They were about equal as top-class fielders.

Miller's impact as an all-rounder, when all aspects of the game are considered, including tactical and leadership skills, was hard to separate from the great West Indian. Yet from that magnificent 1960–61 series on, Sobers' name was mentioned as the 'greatest all-rounder of all time', and Miller's record became an after-thought. This was, in part, because cricket received far more attention through television in Sobers' career (from 1955 to 1974) as opposed to Miller's Test lifespan (1946–56) in which TV played no part in Australia. Sobers was in the public eye for twice as long as Miller, playing 38 more Tests.

Miller himself remained unconcerned over the prevailing assessment in private and in public. He generously spoke of Sobers as the best all-rounder, but his own sense of achievement was set and understood by those who played with or against him and the legion of fans who would not forget.

***

Miller found a flat for himself from May to September in London's Earls Court, which was becoming an enclave for Australian expatriates. It prompted Barry Humphries to pen a typical ditty, which amused Miller:

I've been over here about a year,
In a bedsitter in Earl's Courty,
The beer over here ain't fit to drink,
And the sheilas are proud and haughty,
I wouldn't say no to a nice cold beer,
I wouldn't say no to a naughty . . .

By 1961 Miller had been following the sun for five years, spending half the year based in England and half in Sydney. A complication arose as the boys were growing up. They needed a father present much more often. Miller, because of his work commitments, and by inclination, was not prepared to be there for them. He was seduced by a celebrity lifestyle in London with Lord's, Ascot, race meetings, endless parties and innumerable women, none of whom – after Prowse – he stayed with for any length of time or was committed to. He loved the playboy life for half the year and a family life of sorts at Newport Beach for the rest.

Miller had now formalised that arrangement with the *Express* and his other newspaper outlets in Australia. He made his name post-playing as a hard-hitting reporter looking for the headline grabber. He worked well with professionals at the *Express* and Australian papers who turned his ideas or reports into items that added an edge to cricket reporting, often with a punchy thought or theme. Miller's stories were based on his experience and temperament. They called on his formidable memory, not for dates or the mundane, but for telling or quirky incidents that often touched on the character and spirit of the game. The defensive player would receive the brickbats and the attackers would be praised. Ageing players would be told to leave the game before they became an embarrassment. Selectors were advised to dump a skipper and appoint another. Sensational or unusual incidents would attract Miller's eye, as would intimidatory bowlers or chuckers. He was always on the lookout for changes, in the law and otherwise, to improve the game. Miller would never be concerned with writing a feature with depth or nuance, but he used his refreshing, independent mind to create headlines and sell papers. The *Express* appreciated using the Miller by-line for this reason.

The next series to excite Miller was the long-awaited 1961 Ashes in England. Both England and Australia had luckily beaten the West Indies, and the UK media, including Miller in the *Express*, promoted it as the clash of the heavyweights. This was one of the hardest fought series in the history of Test cricket. Benaud, Harvey, McDonald and Mackay, the remnants of the humiliated Australian team of 1956, were determined to hold the Ashes and prove themselves on English soil. England's remnants of its 1956 team – May, Cowdrey, Lock, Laker and Statham – were no less committed.

***

Les Miller Sr died 21 June 1961, a day before the Second Test, and Miller was upset. While the family gathered in Melbourne for the funeral, he had to carry on stoically covering the big Lord's match. As ever, he kept his grief very much to himself. His mate Harvey lifted his spirits by leading Australia to a win at the home of cricket in place of the injured Benaud.

Miller owed his start in the game that had brought him so much to his father and brothers, who had taught him more than the game's rudiments. Les Sr provided the essential things, the bat, the gear, the extra quid for travel. He had also encouraged Miller's football, and had been a loyal supporter throughout his playing career. Les Sr had also given him an appreciation of poetry and helped in his leanings towards classical music.

Miller reflected on how his father had enriched his life and especially the early days, which brought only good memories. He regretted not having had a chance to thank his father, and the fact that the last time he had seen him had been under stressful circumstances. Les Sr had had a mild stroke. In a senior moment he had wandered across the road from his home and had kissed the woman (his age) who lived opposite. It had caused a mild sensation in the Glen Waverley neighbourhood where he and Edie then lived, and distressed Edie. Miller flew down from Sydney to admonish his father, telling him if he did anything like it again he would 'kick his arse to hell and back'. Family members were surprised at Miller's vehemence. Les Sr had always been a 'player' himself, and Miller had followed in his father's footsteps.

Now the old boy had gone, and there was no chance to make any final resolutions. Yet Miller had an overwhelming number of positive memories and was grateful for a father who had cared.

***

The Australians won the Fourth Test at Old Trafford thanks to a mighty fourth innings bowling spell by Benaud. This win would not erase the memory of Laker on the substandard wicket at the same ground in 1956. Yet it was sweet revenge and gave Australia the Ashes. Miller, watching from the press box, was thrilled for his former protégé and for the team. The cricket wheel of success had turned a full revolution in five years.

Miller's work for the *Express* was not restricted to cricket. Racing was fast returning to its original ranking in his mind as the number one sport. Even when he was covering cricket in England, he would often retire to a hotel room and watch it on TV so that he could switch to the racing channel and place bets. Miller appreciated the racing fraternity as much as if not more than the cricket brotherhood. In keeping with his love of racing and regret at not becoming a jockey, he counted the best of the profession as his good mates, including Lester Piggott, Breasley, Ron Hutchinson and the Queen's own Harry Carr. Miller's mixing with Britain's elite saw him also rubbing shoulders with the big racehorse owners, including Lord Rosebery, the Aga Khan and the Duke of Norfolk.

A third sporting love was soccer. His trips back for the start of the cricket season often allowed him to see the end of the football season, including the FA Cup finals at Wembley. His friendship with Compton, who had been a top soccer player, saw him connected to the era's big names of the sport, including Sir Stanley Matthews, Billy Wright and Sir Stanley Rouse. Miller even began ranking soccer above his beloved Aussie Rules as a spectator sport, believing that the great skills required by the feet-only game were superior.

Miller used all these contacts and more in golf and tennis to report or pass on snippets to his paper. Wimbledon and the British Open were musts on his social and work schedules, which were often one and the same. His extended summers in England saw him on an annual loop of Wembley, Trent Bridge, Lord's, Wimbledon, Edgbaston, Headingley, Old Trafford, St Andrews, Birkdale and the Oval. Paris and the race meetings there would receive a Miller visit too, and there might be time to drop down to Spain to see Lew Hoad. More often than not he would be accompanied by a woman, but not often the same one.

At night, Miller kept up his interest in classical music. He was a regular at concerts and occasionally would take in the opera. In the early 1960s he began to enjoy the theatre. It was in abundance in London's West End, and he was soon at opening nights at the invitation of leading impresarios, such as Jack Hylton. This led to Miller sailing on Hylton's ocean-going yacht in the Mediterranean.

Only time limited his hedonist lifestyle. Come the end of September, like Cinderella at the ball, Miller would return 'home' to Peg and the boys and some responsibility. He enjoyed the beach and sun. The boys' lasting memory of their playboy dad was of him sitting in shorts in the back garden with a can of beer and a race form. Emanating from the transistor radio would be the nasal twang of racing commentators. Miller would scribble their tips and put on a bet. Later would come the race calls, which demanded silence. He was a regular at Randwick, and never missed the Melbourne Cup. If a concert was on in Sydney he would go. But less and less in the 1960s would he venture to the cricket. If he were not on duty for the *Express* he did not go to the matches. Unless it was real action, his nervous disposition of perpetual motion would not allow him to sit through it. The 1960s, apart from the West Indies visits, produced wars of attrition, which were not to Miller's taste.

He covered another lacklustre series, England v. Pakistan, for the *Express* in England in 1962 and was disappointed not to see his old mate Fazal, now aged 34, in the touring team. Pakistan was thrashed in the first three Tests. It called for Fazal to join the squad in an attempt to salvage some pride in the last two Tests. The headline to a Miller piece on him was: 'England is on trial, Fazal arrives'. Fazal had some influence in the Nottingham Fourth Test with a first spell of 20 overs, 16 maidens, 1 for 4. He went on to a marathon bowling effort, taking 3 for 130 off 60 overs when England scored 5 declared for 428. Fazal was easily Pakistan's best bowler.

It was enough for Miller. After the game, he berated the Pakistani manager for not having Fazal in the original squad. 'He is perfect for English conditions!' he shouted. Fazal was pleased and honoured to have such bolstering from a man respected by all Pakistanis for his support since the country's inception.

The 1962–63 Ashes series in Australia was boring for Miller. It was a slow series, with enterprising batting and adventurous captaincy at a premium. The result – one win each and three draws – told the story. The battles of the previous eight Ashes series had created such tension and carried such national prestige that the two teams had become frightened to take risks. Australia held the symbolic little urn and was determined to hang on to it, despite the fact that it never left the showcase in the Lord's museum. England, desperate to grab it back, again symbolically, was still petrified about losing. Miller was fed up. Even on duty, he spent as little time at the games as possible.

Yet in England during this period, he would play the odd game for the *Express* against the *Daily Mail.* TV chat show host and journalist Michael Parkinson played in the same team. He recalled Miller having 'a tic-tac man standing by the sightscreen so he [Miller] was kept up to date with the day's racing at Epsom'. He once took an astonishing catch, diving across Parkinson at second slip, rolling over and handing him the ball. 'I wonder what won that bloody race,' Miller said, casting an eye towards his tic-tac man.

Parkinson had been a Miller fan when a youngster. Like Ian Chappell later, he would grow to admire him more as he got to know him. Parkinson once walked with Miller from the Old Tavern around Lord's, and it took several hours. He stopped to talk to stewards, surgeons, politicians, 'the odd field marshal or two', newspaper sellers and just about anyone else – Australians and English fans – who greeted him. 'We had visited several bars, charmed a flock of barmaids and given a few quid to the sundry bookmakers,' Parkinson said. 'He was like some munificent prince returning home to his subjects. Keith Miller loved England and the feeling was mutual. He was our favourite Aussie.'

Miller also had a remarkable memory for names and faces. He might have met a person just once. If there were another meeting a decade later, Miller, ever the gregarious charmer, would recall a name or where they met. Parkinson remembered another pub crawl – this time in Sydney – with Miller when he spoke first to a neurosurgeon, then a jockey, 'who explained how he won a race by holding on to the arse of the horse in front'. At another pub a woman 'of great beauty and title' was smitten by Miller. This capacity to engage and enjoy people from all walks of life, and to remember them, was an outstanding gift that endeared him to almost all he came in contact with.

Miller's desire to reach out extended to those who had long departed. He continued to hunt for graves of fallen comrades. One that had eluded him for 15 years was that of his command- ing officer, Neville Reeves, who was killed when testing a new bomber in 1949, aged 28. Neville's son, also Neville, was born a few months after the accident. He and his mother migrated to Australia in the early 1950s and settled at Indooroopilly, Brisbane. In 1962, Neville Jr, then 13, read an article on the Brisbane Test in the *Courier Mail*. His mother told him: 'That man used to fly with your father.' Young Neville wrote to Miller, and he replied, telling the boy he had been searching for his father's grave. Did the family know where it was? The boy wrote back telling him his father was buried in a village churchyard at Ripple, 9 kilometres from Worcester.

In 1964 Miller accompanied Bob Simpson's Australian team to Worcester for the traditional opening game of the tour under the cathedral. On the first morning of the game, Miller drove to Ripple, found Neville's grave and paid his respects, leaving flowers for the man he called 'one of the finest men I've known and a very good mate'. Miller felt compassion for such colleagues as Reeves, who had not been able to live a full life. It was a way of salving his feelings about being one of the fortunate ones. As he grew older, and life continued to be good for him, he was even more conscious of what his dead friends had missed.

***

The 1964 Ashes series in England (won by Simpson's Australians 1–0 with *four* draws) was no better for Miller than the 1962–63 clash, and it took a contest in the Caribbean to restore his faith in the game. He followed the 1964–65 Australia versus West Indies Tests (won 2–1 by the home team) and was convinced the spirited play supported his theory that Ashes cricket was killing the game. He was uplifted by the fire of the West Indies pacemen Charlie Griffith, accused of throwing, and Wes Hall, and the response by Australia's batsmen, especially left-hander Bob Cowper. Miller decried the call for helmets for the Australians during the series and urged batsmen to counter-attack by hooking the bumpers. 'The batsmen ... were at fault,' he wrote back to Australian papers, 'for this idiotic habit of ducking to anything short.'

Miller left Port-of-Spain, Trinidad, on 18 May after the Fifth

Test and was in Edgbaston a week later to cover the first of six Tests in England, versus New Zealand and South Africa. An *Express* headline, 'See Who's Here', and photo of a fit Miller wearing his trademark double-breasted suit reflected the investment in him that had continued for nearly a decade. The story told of his recent travel from the 'exciting' series in the Caribbean: 'How do England compare with the world champions [acknowledged as the West Indies after their series victory over Australia]? What does he think of Freddie Trueman's return? Read his expert comment in the *Express* tomorrow . . .'

The formula of making Miller the paper's star reporter had been a long-running success. He provided the bite. Regular journalists, such as the experienced Crawford White, provided the general coverage of play. This limited the work demands on the *Express*'s celebrity, who looked for the startling angle or controversial moment, which sometimes caused Miller concerns, especially if he were to bump into players, which was often the case, at the ground or hotel. He made a habit of saying to a player he was about to attack, usually at the bar after a day's play: 'Take no notice of what I say. It's just to sell papers. Don't take it personally.' This eased the burden for many a star, who might have been hurt by 'Millerisms', although it didn't change the perception of *Express* readers, who liked Miller's direct, crisp style.

When the West Indies' ferocious speedster Charlie Griffith was nearing the end of his career in the Caribbean against England in 1967–68, Miller filed a report for the *Express*, which would be picked up by the wire services in Trinidad where the First Test was being played. Miller had been harsh on Griffith. Miller then went to the bar at Queen's Park Oval where Griffith was having a drink. 'Charlie,' Miller said, putting an arm around Griffith, 'don't read me in the papers tomorrow.' Of course, Griffith did, but Miller's public relations effort had eased the pain for the once menacing paceman.

***

Miller once said all children should be born at age 7. He was not alone among his generation with this attitude, which led to the family being brought up mainly by the wife and mother. In the Millers' case, it was left almost entirely to Peg. Yet as the boys grew he showed interest in their sport in the summer (he was rarely at home in the Australian winter). They were all competent cricketers at the local high school, Pittwater. Denis was most like his father in looks, mannerisms, interests (including classical music), right down to a nervous cough and his attitude to life. He was a good all-round cricketer, who, unlike his father, had the height and strength in his mid-teens to open the bowling for the school's first XI. Denis also batted in the top order.

'Like many sons of champions,' Denis said, 'I got fed up with the comparisons.' He, like John Bradman who was also a talented schoolboy cricketer, became tired of the expectations whenever he was thrown the ball or took block. 'Maybe I just didn't have the ability or the drive,' Denis added, 'but after school, cricket didn't interest me.'

The boys lived so close to the beach that it attracted them more. They all enjoyed surfing. Denis was keen on boxing. He would go with his father to the fights at Sydney Stadium and experience the trappings, such as ringside seats, that came from being with the popular, well-connected Miller. Like their father, the boys enjoyed their golf at the Long Reef club.

The boys were proud of Miller's fame. He was known, it seemed, to everyone, and part of his enduring popularity was his warmth and friendly nature. Everyone wanted to know Miller or to be with him. The boys in this respect were like all his friends. He was also a man's man, with his sporting interests and attitudes, which appealed to his sons. They just wished he were around a lot more.

A house at Newport was rented by Americans on leave from the Vietnam War. Some were heroin addicts. They brought drugs with them. Local youths, many of them surfers, became involved with the Americans, and this led to Peter Miller taking drugs. The rest and recreation soldiers introduced drugs to a generation that otherwise would have had vices similar to those of Miller's generation, which centred on alcohol. The explosion in heroin accessibility created a market for criminal gangs, whose main source of income had been SP bookmaking, prostitution and gaming. The gangs moved fast to take over this more lucrative trade.

There had been some debate within the family over whether Miller's lack of parenting earlier in the boys' lives had affected them and had led to their falling into trouble. Three of the boys – Bob (who had no problems anyway), Denis and Peter – did not think it mattered. Bill, whose troubles lasted longer, did.

Psychologists acknowledge that not even diligent fathers and mothers on the spot all the time could always prevent their children from dabbling in drugs, which could lead to addiction. If parents spoiled their children or expected too much from them, it could lead to rebellion and substance abuse. There was much to be said for encouraging independence and letting them find their own way. Yet if there was no discipline or care, it could lead teenagers down a path similar to that taken by the over-indulged. Getting the balance right and giving the best guidance in face of the drug threat was the biggest challenge ever faced in Australian family and social life. The only certainty was that a boy or girl had a better chance of not being drawn into addictions of any kind if both parents were mindfully present throughout their development. From this perspective, Miller's absence hindered rather than helped the boys' individual problems.

There was also some inconsistency in the boys' minds concerning discipline. It went from one extreme to the other. Peg always indulged them and never punished. This created a permissiveness that left them open to enticements and rebellion. Miller, when at home, would enforce discipline with the usual methods for that generation, which was still more verbal than physical. 'There would be the usual slap on the behind or the occasional clip around the ear,' Bob recalled. 'But it was more a look than any action. Dad could intimidate with a stare, which was enough for all of us to fall into line.'

Given Peg's attitude, Miller's approach might have also caused rebellion. And there was another confusion. Miller's own omnipotent image and his connections to influential people – media, politicians, businessmen and police – would have led the boys consciously or unconsciously to believe that there were no boundaries to their behaviour. They thought they could get away with things. Dad would always be there to help them out of trouble.

Denis had another similar story to Peter when it came to being sucked into the insidious new drug culture. Through a friend he was introduced to hashish, then cocaine and heroin brought in by Americans. Denis found some irony in Peg's activity with the American-Australian Society. She invited back to their Newport home some 'clean-cut' American soldiers from the Midwest. At the same time Denis was dealing in drugs with another group of less savoury types. Some of his 'comrades' were robbing chemist shops to maintain their supply of such drugs as pethidine and morphine and just about anything they could inject themselves with. Denis, still at Pittwater High, went to watch a school rugby match in the country. He and a friend planned to rob a chemist in a town along the way. They broke in but could not open the safe containing the drugs. Denis did not join in break-ins again. But he was hooked on drugs and caught in the vicious circle of addiction and dealing to feed it.

***

Miller flew down to Melbourne to see his mother Edie in April 1967, and was shocked to see her emaciated condition after a losing fight with cancer. It was too much for him emotionally, and he returned to Sydney on a Saturday evening after seeing her twice, against protest from family members who wanted him to shoulder some of the responsibility. Edie died early the next morning, Sunday, 23 April. Miller decided to fly down for the funeral the following Tuesday, but his plane was diverted to Mangalore, in central Victoria. 'I spent some of the worst moments of my life sitting on the tarmac in that plane,' Miller told relatives.

He was known in the airline industry as the celebrity who held up the departure of more planes than anyone else. But this time he had no pull to do the opposite and get one flying again. He missed his mother's funeral and arrived at the wake afterwards. For once, he could not be blamed for his unpunctuality. Yet his brothers were unhappy that he had not planned it better by flying from Sydney the night before the funeral. From their perspective at these testing moments, their famous sibling had always been the spoilt one, who never pulled his weight.

***

After another tight, last-man-standing Ashes series in England in 1968 – which was drawn one-win-all with three more boring draws – Miller pushed for abandonment of the Ashes trophy. He thought that the battle for the urn had 'ruined the competition between the two countries' after watching Bill Lawry lead his team with the main aim of *retaining* the Ashes. Miller said in the *Express* that Lawry would have been content with the result or even five draws and no wins, as long as Australia retained the trophy. Miller believed that if the tradition was dumped, teams would go for wins rather than draws. This was an extension of his argument in the mid-1940s when he said that the Ashes competition was killing the spirit of the game. Coloured by his wonderful experience during the Victory Tests of 1945, Miller was still fighting the same losing battle over freeing up the competition between the two greatest rivals in Test cricket. He believed in tradition, but not for tradition's sake. If it was bad, Miller argued, 'it should be discontinued'.

He saw the Fourth Test at Headingley as the classic example of tradition gone wrong. England was set 326 on the last day, but instead of going for a win, Lawry 'shut up shop', set defensive fields and prevented England winning. At the end of the final day's play, Ian Chappell threw his cap on the dressing-room floor in protest. 'If that's Test cricket,' he said, 'you can stick it up your jumper.'

'We've done what we came here to do,' Lawry replied firmly. 'That was to win the Ashes.'

Miller joined the English media in attacking Lawry, who was dubbed 'the corpse with pads'. Lawry had been a champion opener on tour in 1961, and was the key batsman of that series. But the captaincy had seen his defensive side come to the fore, and Miller wanted him dumped as leader. But Lawry's record against India in 1967–68, and now in England, at least in not losing the Ashes, meant that the selectors would not follow Miller's advice.

***

Soon after a good win at the races, Miller was at Northampton's county ground when he noticed that a certain pensioner, who worked as gate-man, was not there. Miller had chatted to him for more than 20 years whenever he visited the ground as player and reporter. Miller asked another gate-man what had happened to his old friend, and was told that he had become too frail to stand up all day. Miller found out his address, and that evening after play he arrived on a surprise visit to the man's terrace cottage in Northampton. The pensioner, then in his seventies, and his wife were delighted to give Miller a cup of tea and chat for half an hour.

He noticed that the couple had an old 1930s wooden radio but no television. 'Don't care for TV?' Miller enquired casually.

'Oh, we love TV,' the man said. 'We see it every now and again at our friend's place, but we can't afford it. The pension doesn't leave us enough to save for such a luxury.'

Miller nodded understandingly but did not comment further. Late the next morning, a TV set arrived at the couple's house. It had been paid for.

Later in the season, the day after having another win at the races, Miller was a little further north at Nottingham when, on a whim, he decided to drive to Great Massingham to visit the parents of a wartime girlfriend who used to save their food coupons so they could cook him a much-appreciated roast lunch on a Sunday. He could see that they were living frugally and wanted to give them money as a thank you for their kindness more than two decades earlier. He said he would send a cheque to their bank account and was astonished to find that they did not have one. Miller took them into a bank in the town, helped them open an account and deposited the money.

These examples were typical of his generous spirit. Not only did Miller remain loyal to friends, he also never forgot the kindness or generosity of others.

Miller was now spending his summer months in Putney, near the Thames in the flat of a friend who was a purser on an ocean-going liner, which meant he was never home. Miller had the run of the place whenever he wanted it. His son Bill, 20, had been in England since he was 18. Tall, good-looking and charming like his father, Bill was found a job by Miller in a new business development, a supermarket chain. Bill enjoyed a closer time with his father than ever before.

Miller helped all the boys out with trips to France and England. 'He got us all jobs,' Denis recalled, 'and introduced us to people we would never have met otherwise. He had amazing contacts. No one seemed outside his reach. He just loved life and people.'

But Bill was ambivalent about another irrepressible side to Miller that became apparent in his London playground. He had developed into a middle-aged roué. Miller was now pushing 50, but his female companions were remaining young. More precisely, age did not matter in his desire for company of attractive women. One long-time girlfriend was a duchess. Miller fancied her 16-year-old daughter Cathy. He asked Bill to go to her private school and tell the headmistress that he was a cousin from

Australia and that he wished to spend the day with her. This ploy worked. Cathy became one of Miller's girlfriends over several years. Relatives and friends were surprised, even shocked, when he would turn up with a teenage girl on his arm. Miller told some family members and friends he had a 'mother and daughter combination' with the duchess and her daughter, meaning he had sex with both at the same time.

Miller's conquistadorial approach and lust for young flesh seemed boundless, and it backfired on him. He told Bill about an occasion when a mother knocked on the door of his flat demanding that her teenage daughter leave him. Another time, Miller was asleep when an attractive Anglo-Indian in her early thirties visited him. Seeing that Miller was dead to the world, she took Bill back to her flat and seduced him.

Bill, who had been in England between the ages of 18 and 20, was still at an impressionable age, especially with such a famous father. Most men of the era admired Miller for his fun character, looks, fame, sporting achievements, seductive powers and capacity for big drinking. Bill was just like anyone in this respect. It was 'exciting' to be with Miller as he continued with his legendary exploits, but his father's behaviour created a problem for Bill. Seducing young girls would have been confusing and even threatening to any son. Such actions would have reinforced Bill's uncertainty and insecurity about his father and about his father's relationship with Peg. As the eldest son, he had become the man of the house when Miller was not there. He was Peg's main confidant. He was aware of his father's philandering, although Miller was more discreet in his extramarital relationships in Sydney, with the exception of Prowse. Now in England it was in the open, and Miller had drawn Bill, superficially, into his philandering, no-rules world. Miller's all-powerful, do-anything image and attitude was in stark contrast to most fathers' links to their sons, which would have been based on trust, boundaries and protection.

Bill's sensitivities were exacerbated when Miller gave Cathy his red Rover car when he was out of England, and Bill had to take the bus or Underground to get around London. This seemed to indicate that a 16-year-old girl, who could never have been more than a sexual toy for Miller, was placed ahead of his son in his affections. This sort of behaviour at times created a sense of betrayal and an overall confusion in Bill's attitude to his father. These emotions or reactions jumbled a sense of right and wrong. They blurred a differentiation between fact and fiction. They also made Bill vulnerable to taking drugs. This would apply if, like his father, he had an addictive personality, especially in getting rid of painful feelings. Again, similarly to Miller, he might have been just thrill-seeking.

Bill might also have felt a compulsion to impress Miller with his own shows of physical 'courage'. Once when driving together in London, a cab cut them off, causing Miller to swerve. He vented his feelings at the beefy cab driver, who volleyed back in a piece of developing road rage. The two vehicles ended up stopped by the side of the road. Miller and Bill got out of the car, as did the cabbie. Then the male passenger in the back seat of the cab put in his opinion with some vehemence. Miller turned his attention to the passenger. The cabbie insulted Bill with reference to his parentage and nationality. Bill, a strong lad of about 190 cm (6 feet 3 inches), punched the cabbie hard on the nose. The man went down.

Miller thought it wise to depart the scene. The passenger scribbled down the car's registration number, and the cabbie contacted the police. Members of the British constabulary visited Miller. The cabbie wanted Bill to be charged with assault, and it was up to the police to ascertain whether a charge were warranted. It seemed from the heated discussion with them that it might be. Miller then contacted several friends, among them Commander Wally Virgo of the murder squad at Scotland Yard. No charges were laid.

Miller had police contacts in England and Australia, as he said, 'for insurance purposes'. In Sydney he carried letters from three different New South Wales police commissioners in the glove-box of his car. The quaintly worded letters asked that he be looked upon kindly if he were pulled over or in trouble. Some family members and close friends knew of these connections. They once more demonstrated Miller's sense of omnipotence. He was inviolate in his own mind and to those around him.

On another occasion in England, Miller and Bill were at the Greyhound Derby, White City, London – a formal function – in which they both dressed in white tie and tails. They were in a special box to watch the event when a drunken Irish waiter became obnoxious. Miller refused to tip him.

'Hey, listen everybody,' the waiter said to the assembled diners, 'Keith Miller has not given me a tip!' The waiter repeated the comment several times at the top of his voice.

'Bill,' Miller said, leaning across to his son, 'get up and snot him.'

Bill obliged. He grabbed the waiter by the neck and banged his head against a wall several times. The waiter's boss was called. The man was fired on the spot.

These two instances with the cabbie and the waiter reinforced Bill's sense that he could do and say what he wanted. His father was leading the way and encouraging him.

Bill was getting a first-hand look at another dimension to his father. As far as women were concerned, it began with Les Sr's example to Miller. On top of this, Miller's life had been affected by the upheavals of war and a freer lifestyle during it. This in turn reinforced a licentious attitude that he could follow through on any desires without fear of serious repercussions. The same applied to violence. It was always an option in resolving any dispute, as even his mother Edie had shown by belting Les's lover in the street. Aggression was encourged in Australia's youth in Miller's generation, particularly in sport. It was viewed by many as virtuous (as it still is). Overriding this again was Miller's experience in war, in which he was trained to kill the enemy. There could not have been a greater reinforcement of the option of violence and intimidation in achieving any aim.

All this, once more, was without any concern about being stopped, let alone punished. It had to influence Bill's own future behaviour.

***

After the slow dogfight of the 1968 Ashes Tests, Miller covered another Australia versus West Indies series in 1968–69 – again unencumbered by the grim history surrounding the Ashes – that once more restored enterprising cricket to Miller's liking. He was inspired to mend his differences with Whitington and collaborate on another book, *Fours Galore,* which celebrated the renewed enterprise in Test cricket. Australia's batsmen, especially Doug Walters and Ian Chappell, led the way against the ageing bowling line-up of Hall, Griffith, Sobers and off-spinner Lance Gibbs, who all received hammerings.

Miller was pleased to report on just one draw, and even that was a nail-biter in which Australia's last-wicket pair – Paul Sheahan and Alan Connolly – clung on. Australia won 3–1, and Miller headed for England in 1969 a much happier reporter.

When he felt like it Miller was still seeing the duchess's daughter. He was also keeping the occasional company of Beverley Prowse and other women, including another Victorian friend, Marie Challman, a singer from Melbourne's Chevron Hotel, whom he had met a few years earlier. Prowse and Challman were part of a Melbourne set that included TV personality Joy Fountain and socialite Jenny Ham, who used to meet Miller and others at the bar of the Southern Cross Hotel, where he stayed when in Melbourne.

Weeks before he was to cover England playing the West Indies and New Zealand in two series of Tests in the northern summer of 1969, news came from Australia that Peg, a smoker, was gravely ill with lung cancer. She would have to undergo an emergency operation. Specialists were telling Miller she would not survive surgery. One doctor gave her 10 days to live. Miller rushed back to Australia to be with Peg. She made a miraculous recovery after having three-quarters of a lung removed. 'She was very strong spiritually,' said Jan Beames, who was then also in England. 'She was determined to be there for her son's wedding.'

Bill, now 21, was due to be married in England in July 1969, and Peg had been looking forward to the event. He was the eldest and the first of the boys to marry. His bride, Regi, was from Newport. Peg had been both mother and father to Bill, as she had all the boys, for most of his life and they were close. She did not want to miss this moment. Her will prevailed and she made it to England for the wedding.

It was held in a little country church at Harefield in Middlesex, which was chosen by Miller. In a corner of the churchyard, there was an Anzac cemetery containing the graves of AIF personnel and one nursing sister from World War I. They had died from wounds or illness at the nearby No. 1 Australian Auxiliary Hospital, Harefield Park. Also in the area was a former RAF base for Miller that was now a pig farm. Before the wedding, he took Peter to see the old runway there. The wedding was a memorable event. It was covered by the *Express*, with a photo of Scobie Breasley on Bill's back acting like a jockey. This was the first time Peg had been in England with Miller in the summer. Many of his friends in high places wanted to know why they had not before seen his gracious and classy wife.

When they returned to Australia, Miller arranged for Peg's blue-chip share portfolio to be taken over by broker Jim Burke from his Test playing days. Peg knew something about investments because of her father's profession. She complained that Burke was making more on commissions from her than she was receiving as return on the investments. Burke upset her further by selling off some of her blue-chip stocks during the Poseidon boom on the stock market that began in 1969 and was over by March

1970. In this feverish time mining stocks rose on rumour when they might have nothing in the ground. Bullock drivers and charlatans were rich on paper in the short term. The boom was titled 'Poseidon' because this stock exemplified the madness on the floors of Australian exchanges where the actual volume of shares changing hands topped even that of Wall Street on some days. Poseidon, an innocuous Western Australian nickel miner, was languishing on 71 cents in September 1969 and peaked at $280 in February 1970.

Burke was not alone in pursuing rubbish stock at the expense of solid companies, such as BHP. Just about every broking house was into mindless speculation. There seemed to be money in it, but it was the great illusion in Australian stock exchange history. When the hot air boom crashed, very few of the millions of punters were ahead. Peg lost a big chunk of her inherited wealth. She dumped Burke and found another broker.

Miller, no businessman, was more interested in speculative shares. He found the boom – a worse gamble than any race meeting – more than enticing. Like almost everyone else, he lost. Miller also favoured dabbling in futures. Once when he 'bought' a tonne of cocoa, he said to Peg: 'Hope you like cocoa.'

***

Miller supported Ian Chappell's captaincy, although he warned him not to take his criticisms to heart. He preferred Chappell's approach to leadership and believed his team could take the 1972 Ashes in England.

At the First Test at Old Trafford (won by England), Miller bumped into Basil Easterbrook. They had a laugh over the incident 19 years earlier when Easterbrook had hired a hearse to ferry Miller and Lindwall to Bramall Lane. 'Did you ever get that two quid from Davies [the Australian manager]?' Miller asked.

'No. He claimed it was your fault for being late.'

Miller took five pounds from his wallet and thrust it in Easterbrook's pocket. 'That's for Grindleford, Basil.' Easterbrook

447

protested that Miller had given him too much. 'Well, Bas,' Miller replied, 'there's been inflation and it's a long time.'

Chappell's team kept coming back in the 1972 series, winning the Lord's Test, drawing at Trent Bridge, losing at Leeds and winning again at the Oval to square the series 2 wins all. 'Forget the Ashes,' Miller wrote in the *Express*. 'This levelled series means Australia is on the rise again under Chappell with the right attitude.'

***

Miller returned to Australia as usual in the summer unaware that Denis and Peter, who was a bricklayer, were both taking heroin. 'Heroin was rife in the building industry,' Peter said. 'The older blokes used to use alcohol for sore backs, pains and other problems. Heroin was the drug for the younger guys.' The brothers would inject heroin together. 'Dad had no idea this was going on,' Peter said.

Yet Miller himself had an addictive personality, as shown by his gambling and big drinking. Heroin, in essence, was just another on the list of potential addictions. It happened to be more often and more quickly destructive than other drugs. It was not surprising that some of the boys would display similar characteristics in a conducive environment.

Peter and Denis were hooked with no apparent escape from the vicious cycle. It was a major problem in Sydney where no homes, from those of a future prime minister to ordinary families, were immune. Governments began imposing heavier penalties for importation and possession of heroin. But as its production increased in the Golden Triangle, an area bounded by Burma, Laos and Thailand, Australia was flooded with the drug. Access, although dangerous, was easy. Heroin was becoming one of the biggest import–export businesses in Australia. Three decades later, it is the world's biggest import–export business, worth around $500 billion a year.

CHANGE OF PACE

Miller's long-running summer party looked like being over in 1973 when the *Express* began a retrenchment policy during more stringent times. Miller was 53. The life he had been leading for 30 years had etched itself into his tanned face and longish grey, Brylcreemed hair swept back. There was the tell-tale look of the steady drinker, yet despite this and his maturity, he was still outstandingly handsome. Miller's waistline was kept under control by swimming and golf.

He was looking for different work knowing that he could no longer rely on the English paper for an income. His days of fame on the field were now dimming memories, and a new generation of cricket followers had grown up in the meantime. The concept of his stun-gun comments was now jaded, and he had to move on. The *Express* would take his copy on the next England Ashes visit to Australia and accommodate him once more in the summer of 1974, but his days as a well-paid roving reporter were over.

***

Miller had been close to his niece, 37-year-old Eleanor McKenzie, Snow's daughter, and there was a mutual respect and affection on the basis of their similar brilliance as sports all-rounders. Eleanor, if anything, was more accomplished than her famous uncle, having represented Australia in cricket, softball and basketball.

449

Sadly, she was dying of cancer in 1974. Miller was told just before he was due to fly to England.

Snow rang Miller, who was upset by the news. 'Will you come down to see her?' Snow asked.

'I can't, Snow, I just can't.'

'She wants to see you. She asked me to ask you to come.'

Miller knew that he might just be able to cope with elderly relatives and friends dying. But someone close to him and young was just too much. It brought out all the old emotion and guilt over being a survivor. 'I can't do it, Snow,' Miller told his sister, 'but I'll give her a ring.' He spoke to Eleanor and took off for England in late April. A few weeks after he arrived, she died.

***

In 1975 Denis, aged 24 and now a heroin addict, went to Indonesia with a friend, whose mother had passed on $10,000 of a lottery win to him. They became caught up in further heroin dealing in Sumatra and Bali. If caught dealing in the region, they could have been jailed for 15 years or even executed. Denis ran out of money. He tried to contact his father but couldn't reach him. He then met a Qantas representative, who loaned him the money to return to Sydney. A disgruntled Miller was then persuaded to repay the representative.

But Denis was still in trouble. Miller, realising his son's problem, tried to help by putting him into a Sydney rehabilitation centre, Odyssey House. This worked for a while, but when Denis left the centre he went back to dealing.

***

In 1975, after covering the 1974–75 Ashes series, Miller found himself home for an Australian winter for the first time in 20 years. He was having a trim at the local barber when he read an item about Harry Beitzel, a former AFL umpire, who worked for the Robert Sangster-owned Soccer Pools in Australia. Miller knew Sangster, a racehorse owner, and Beitzel, whom he had helped with media contacts when Beitzel took an Australian Rules team to Ireland in the mid-1960s. He phoned the latter, who was visiting Sydney to work on PR operations for the pools. They met at West Ryde where a training program for pools agents was being run. Miller was introduced to the New South Wales marketing manager, who hired him that afternoon.

Miller's new job was to use his media contacts to gain publicity for the pools, especially winners, who drew abundant media attention – particularly stories about garbage workers or heart-of-gold ironing ladies with six kids, who were suddenly rich. 'I was the link man between the pools and the press,' Miller explained to journalist Phil Wilkins in *Cricketer* magazine. 'Instead of sending out reams and reams of publicity handouts for editors to say, "Fuck it, fuck it, fuck it!" each day and put them on their spikes, I provided the personal touch and went and saw them myself.' The job allowed him to call on his prodigious memory and ability never to forget a name. He was given an office in the pools premises in Alfred Street North, North Sydney. But Miller was never going to be desk- or office-bound, just as he was never press-box bound in his cricket reporting days.

He was back in England for the following summer in 1976, dropping in at Lord's, seeing his good mates Geoff Burns, an Australian expatriate dentist, and Scobie Breasley, from whom he was forever attempting to pry tips. Miller had been on a losing streak, which sometimes made friends uneasy about advice or encouraging him.

A rat pack of Australians that included Miller, Burns, Breasley, Trevor Perry, an ex-RAAF World War II squadron leader, who had served in New Guinea at the same time as Miller served in Europe, and a couple of others, met for lunch in London. Everyone except Perry, who was on vacation from Australia, nagged Breasley for a tip in the 1976 London Derby. Breasley didn't respond. Near the end of the lunch, he took Perry aside. 'Trev, you're the only one who hasn't been at me for a tip,' he said, then proceeded to tell him the horse he thought would win. 'Put all your holiday money on it.'

Perry, a gambler, was most appreciative. Later, Miller, who had noticed the discussion, rang Perry and met him on King's Road. Miller asked him about Breasley's tip. They both went to a local betting shop. Perry put £1,500 (equivalent to around half the average annual wage in Britain) on the horse in question. Miller, bitten by a series of recent losses, still outlaid £200. These were big outlays in a small Chelsea betting shop in 1976. The two of them spoke loudly about the source of the tip. As they left, all the mug punters in the shop were lining up to place a bet on the same horse, which gave Miller and Perry a chuckle.

The Derby was run two days later. Breasley's horse won by a head at 3 to 1. Miller and Perry went to collect at the betting shop. When they arrived, the shop had run out of money from the pay-outs to mug punters on the horse, and they had to go elsewhere to collect.

The win fuelled Miller's desire to continue. But he had a further string of losses at race meetings in the next few months. At a country meeting English jockey Edgar Britt chatted with Miller, who asked for a tip. Britt recommended a horse he was riding that day. 'He's unpredictable,' Britt cautioned, 'but I sense he can win today.'

'Unpredictable?' a wary Miller said.

'He can be feisty, Keith,' Britt said, 'plays up a bit. But that's usually a good sign. He goes all out on those days.'

'How will you run him, Edgar?'

'I'll tuck him [behind the leaders] and make a move two furlongs out.'

Miller was desperate for a win. He put a £300 bet on for a win at 6 to 4 and had his glasses on the race. Sure enough, Britt had the horse placed nicely behind the leaders. He made his move as predicted, and soon the horse was placed close behind the front-runner. Then the horse leaned forward. His mouth seemed almost over the behind of the mount in front. Britt was astonished to see his horse bite the backside of the horse in front. It wasn't just a nip. 'It was a mouthful,' Britt said, 'and the flesh of the horse [in front] stretched.' The leading horse bolted and won by several lengths. Britt's horse came in second. Miller was down £7,000 (equivalent today to $100,000). His mythical luck had deserted him more than at any time in his life.

The Australian jockey fraternity in the UK heard of his continued misfortune. The next time he was at a country race meeting, one of them, a laconic individual who passed on only tips that came off, told him to put a big bet on an English jockey in race 4. Miller acted on the advice, and noticed that the six other jockeys in the race were all Australians, including the tipster. Each one of them, Miller knew, was far more experienced at riding and winning than the nominated English jockey. But being a true gambler, he was prepared to take a risk and act on the tip. He put £1,000 on the English jockey at 10 to 1.

The race began with the English rider well back in the field, but somewhere near the middle of the race, the jockey found himself in a never-imagined dream run through this tough and brilliant field. He pushed his mount to the front without being blocked. He took the lead, which he never lost.

Miller collected enough to pay off his debt and was left a few thousand pounds in front. His popularity rather than his luck had been in play this time.

***

Miller remained in contact with friends from the war. One woman, Betty, who had worked with the staff at Great Massingham, had come into a sizeable inheritance. She had moved to Cornwall in recent years and was living in a big house on a large estate. Miller visited her. A large, unkempt man answered the door.

'Who are you?' the man asked.

'I'm an old friend of Betty's,' Miller replied. He was suspicious of the man's manner. Miller took Betty to lunch in the local village.

'Who was that bloke in the house?' Miller asked.

Betty was fearful about speaking at first. Miller reassured her that he would help her if she were in trouble. She told him she had hired the man as a gardener. He had moved into the house and was trying to take it over, making her a prisoner in her own home. The man had told everyone in the village that Betty was going mad and not to have anything to do with her.

Miller took Betty home and went to the local police station.

'Don't worry about her,' a policeman said. 'She's a nutter.'

'Who told you?'

'Everyone knows . . .'

'Yeah, but who told you?'

'Well, the gardener . . .'

'I've known her since the bloody war,' Miller said. 'She has not changed. There is nothing wrong with her.' He tried to get the police to investigate, but they refused. 'You'll be hearing from me,' Miller said and left the police station. He then contacted Wally Virgo at Scotland Yard. The gardener was investigated. It was discovered that there was a warrant out for the man's arrest. He had manipulated other women in a similar manner. The man was arrested and later jailed.

***

At the end of the 1976–77 season, Miller was in Melbourne for the Centenary Test between Australia and England. He took the moment to announce his best Australian team selected from all players who had played between 1877 and 1977. In batting order the team was: Charles Bannerman (who played in the first Test), Bill Ponsford, Don Bradman, Victor Trumper, Stan McCabe, Keith Miller, Monty Noble, Don Tallon (keeper), Ray Lindwall, Bill O'Reilly, Clarrie Grimmett and Richie Benaud as twelfth man.

The Centenary Test was played at the MCG, and Australia won by 45 runs (which happened to be the same result as in March 1877 when the first Test was played). At the end of the first day's play, Miller was to be captured on the show *This is Your Life*. There was a problem. A key to the show was the surprise for the chosen subject. Miller was in Melbourne with his friend Marie Challman, whom he had known a decade. He had been with her to cricket functions, the races, where they had been photographed, and other Melbourne events. He had to be separated from her and somehow deposited at Channel 7 studios because Peg would be coming from Sydney for the show.

Miller's mate Alan McGilvray was assigned the job and succeeded. Miller did receive a surprise. At first, he found it an emotional experience that he would never encourage. One by one the family was paraded, including Peg, Les Jr, Snow and Ray; then the boys, Bill, aged 29, Peter, 27, Denis, 26, and Bob, 21. England cricketers visiting for the Test – Denis Compton, Godfrey Evans, Bill Edrich, Fred Trueman and the Bedser twins, Alec and Eric – made appearances. So did his own team-mates Ian Johnson, Arthur Morris, Bill Johnston and Laurie Nash. Bradman, who was genuinely otherwise engaged at the Centenary celebrations, Benaud and Sobers paid tribute in recorded items.

When Ray Lindwall emerged on the set, Miller said with a grin, 'Arh, Jackson!'

Also there for 'Dusty' were wartime comrades pilot Gus Glendinning, navigators Jim Brown and Bert Berriman, along with Todd Hylton, about whom Miller commented, 'He is a DFC, I might add.'

Miller was nervous at first. He warmed to the occasion and seemed to enjoy it more as it proceeded. He was proud of the gathering of close friends and family, who had been the key people in his life thus far. The show highlighted Miller's personality. It also indicated why the Sydney *Daily Mirror*'s survey of its readers at the time had Miller (14.88 per cent) just pipping Bradman (13.09 per cent) as the most popular Test cricketer of all.

***

In 1977 Denis imported 50 grams of heroin, which newspapers claimed had a street value of between $50,000 and $100,000 when it was far less. Denis would have sold it to friends at discounted rates. Narcotics agents intercepted the heroin, concealed in the drilled-out handle of a tennis racquet. He was charged with drug importation. Miller didn't attend the trial because it would have increased media attention, but Peg was there every day. Denis was convicted, given a two-year sentence and sent to Long Bay jail.

Miller thought it a tough sentence. 'I'm going to find out where the judge swims, go there and drown him,' he fumed, showing his loyalty and anti-authoritarian streak in one.

Peg and Denis's brothers were regular visitors to the jail, bringing fresh fruit and other food. Miller also turned up with them weekly when he was in Sydney. 'Peg was stoic throughout,' Denis said. 'All the family was supportive.'

He was released on parole after serving nine months. He checked himself into Odyssey House in a second attempt to get clean. It didn't work. Miller took Denis to London in a further attempt to remove him from the Sydney drug *demi-monde*. They spent time together, and it was probably the closest Denis ever was to his father. They went to Beethoven concerts, the races and cricket together. But Denis had yet to come to terms with his problem. He slipped back into drugs.

'Drug addicts and dealers sniff out their own,' Denis said, but recalled a seminal moment in his life. 'I was ripped off by a Putney dealer, a real low-life. As we parted, we waved to each other. I suddenly realised what I was involved with. It was the best wave goodbye of my life.'

Denis decided there and then, at the age of 27, that it was the end of his life as a druggie and dealer. Miller secured him a job at the Knights of St John pub in St John's Wood. Denis did not look back, and was grateful for his father's intervention and help. (Back in Australia soon afterwards, Miller found him work with international courier DHL, and he has worked for them ever since.)

Snow (Gladys) Miller died aged 71, in October 1978, and Miller flew down to Melbourne for her funeral. Peg wanted to come. Snow had been her support during the birth of all the boys, but Miller insisted that she would be too upset. He said he would be tearful enough without Peg becoming that way, too. Peg stayed at home more for her husband's sake than her own.

Miller had looked up to Snow, 12 years his senior, as a second mother, and she had given balance to the masculine influence of his two elder brothers. After Eleanor died, Miller predicted that a devastated Snow would not last long. A wake at Snow's home followed the tearful funeral. After that, Marie Challman collected Miller. This was the real reason he had dissuaded Peg from coming to Melbourne. The family was upset. Through loyalty to Peg, no one in the family, and least of all Snow, approved of Miller's relationship with Challman, or any other woman.

***

Miller did not join Kerry Packer's World Series Cricket when it shook the cricket world between 1977 and 1979. He had plenty of mates in Packer's organisation, but he was too closely allied to Marylebone Cricket Club to switch allegiance to the new regime. When WSC disbanded and Packer's Channel Nine was given the rights to televise cricket, the commentary positions went to those loyal to WSC, such as Ian Chappell and Tony Greig.

In October 1979 Miller was flown to London to appear in the BBC version of *This is Your Life* for Freddie Trueman. Miller returned home to do his usual publicity stint in presenting the weekly Soccer Pools winner with a cheque. Then he prepared to go to Hong Kong for a cricket festival. Another cricketer and his wife were at the Millers' Newport home when the trip was mentioned. The wife of the former cricketer assumed that Peg had been asked to accompany Miller when she had not. He had to ask Peg to join him.

In February and March 1980 Miller covered the Australia v. Pakistan three Test series in Pakistan for Australian newspapers and local television. He renewed his friendship with Fazal and others, while at the same time being embroiled in a dispute during the Second Test at Iqbal Stadium, Faisalabad. The game was delayed because of light drizzle after Greg Chappell had won the toss and decided to bat. The Australians wanted to play. Pakistan's captain Javed Miandad was at his intransigent best and would not bring his team on to the field. His team was one up in the series after winning at Karachi. He had less to lose by forcing Australia into a position where it had to take risks to win.

Chappell was irritated. 'Do you want to draw this match?' he challenged the unwilling Javed.

Miller was also annoyed. He inspected the wicket during the light drizzle and pronounced it beautiful for batting. 'It will last eight days,' he told his television audience. He approached Fazal and told him to tell Javed, 'There is nothing wrong with the wicket. It is absolutely all right.'

But Javed refused to play. The Pakistani umpires – including former Test player Javed Akhtar standing in his first game – could not make Javed budge. A complete day was lost to this folly.

When Australia finally batted on day two, Chappell told Javed: 'You want a draw so badly, I'll give you one.' Chappell came to the wicket at 2 for 21. He batted first in a 179 stand with Kim Hughes (88), then 217 for the fourth wicket with Graham Yallop (172), and went on to the then highest score – 235 – in a Faisalabad Test. Australia punished Javed by batting for the better part of two days and compiling 617. Chappell was true to his word. The game petered to a forlorn draw, and Miller supported Chappell's stand against Javed's poor sportsmanship.

However, Miller turned his disdain on the Australian captain for instructing his younger brother Trevor to bowl underarm on the last ball of a one-day game during the 1980–81 World Series. The order stopped the remote chance of the opposing New Zealand batsman hitting a six to win. Chappell cited mental fatigue for his decision. But no one, not even his brother Ian, would let him get away with that excuse, which was an unfortunate lapse in an otherwise spotless and brilliant career.

Miller, who aspired to the highest standards of sportsmanship through his career, was unforgiving. 'One-day cricket died that day,' he said, 'and Greg should be buried with it.'

***

Miller drifted into the 1980s, still with his pools consultancy but without any commentary role in cricket, although he could always pick up newspaper work in covering Tests.

Peter attempted to get off heroin through a methadone replacement program, and it worked for five years. Then he succumbed to the addiction again. But, in the early 1980s, a few years after Denis walked away from drugs, Peter made a successful break, too. He continued to work as a bricklayer. Bill, too, had fallen victim to heroin addiction in the mid-1970s, and it stayed with him on and off in the early 1980s. By this time, Miller was in despair over a third son being a 'junkie' and did not know what to do. He could relate to the results of excessive drinking. Many of his mates were alcoholics, although they would never admit it. But heroin addiction was in a league he knew nothing about.

In 1985 Bill checked himself in to the Phoenix Detoxification Centre at Manly Hospital with problems over alcohol and heroin. Bill, like his brothers, had the strength and will to survive. He worked various jobs over the decades, including that of a milkman.

Fourth son Bob was never into substance abuse. 'Because I was the youngest by four or five years, I saw all the problems and pitfalls,' he said, 'and managed to avoid them.' (Bob runs his own lighting business in the television industry.)

Miller was still travelling to London when he could, but there was a little more time at the Newport home, which three generations of Millers – the boys and families – frequented. (Bob is married and has one daughter. The other three have each been married and divorced, and each marriage produced a boy and a girl.)

Newport was a very busy household. It sometimes became too much for Miller, who locked himself in his study, known in the family as 'the Bunker', to avoid the noise of the grandchildren. Despite these odd moments it was an open, friendly household.

Miller's degenerative injuries to back, knee and now hip, triggered by his wartime experiences, bowling and football, began to irritate him. He grumbled a bit, yet carried on, even if it meant discomfort on those long trips to England. In 1982 he was a guest of the MCC, and played golf with Gubby Allen and Douglas Bader, the RAF Battle of Britain air ace with tin legs. Both had been Miller's friends since the war. Miller kept the golf ball that he played with as a memento of Bader, who, like 'Laddie' Lucas, was one of his heroes. Two weeks after the golf game, Bader died.

Invitations were always coming in. In the English summer of 1984, Middlesex asked him and Lindwall to be special guests at a dinner to acknowledge 50 years of service from Compton and Edrich. Miller was more popular with the British cricket establishment than he was with Australia's. He bemoaned the fact that the Australian Cricket Board had not seen fit to honour him in any way. Nor had the SCG trustees. There wasn't anything to commemorate his great decade of entertainment at the cricket ground. 'Not even,' he told close friends with some angst, 'a bit of bloody graffiti!'

A few months later back in Sydney, Miller found it hard to do simple chores around the house. His hip at the age of 66 was playing up. In April 1985 he had an operation, which was a success. Seven weeks later he was on a plane to Melbourne to meet up with Glendinning at the Flemington races. They drank later at the pub of former VFL footballer Brian 'Whale' (because he was large) Roberts. Miller said that the next time Roberts was in London he would show him the Long Room at Lord's. Roberts took him up on the invitation later and arrived at the hallowed ground during a Test. He was wearing shorts and thongs, a dress code unknown to the egg-and-bacon tie and jacketed MCC members.

Miller knew the doorman, Frank, who worked at the entry to the MCC members' area. 'Frank, this is Whale,' Miller said.

'I want to show him the Long Room. If you don't let him in, I'll throw you over the balcony.'

'That's fine, Keith,' Frank said.

Roberts was shown the Long Room. No member dared object.

Miller's life in this period seemed to be a non-stop reunion with mates from the past. As John Arlott observed 40 years earlier, Miller was living life as if he were about to run out of it. But the invitations kept coming to make sure he had plenty to enjoy yet. He and Lindwall were guests of the Lord's Taverners in London. A short time later they attended the fortieth anniversary celebrations of the Australian 1945 services team in England. This meant more to Miller than even Invincibles dinners.

He was still in demand for comment about cricket. Australia began a horror stretch in the mid-1980s, and Miller called for some very different options to pull the national team out of its trough. He wanted New South Wales' Greg Matthews to replace Allan Border as captain. He felt Matthews, an all-rounder, could provide the dynamic, attacking drive needed for Australia to rise again, and likened him to Richie Benaud when Australia emerged in 1958–59 to win the Ashes after three successive losses. Later he called for batsman Dean Jones to lead the team. Miller didn't like Border's approach, but Border did prove to be the right man for the time, leading Australia from bottom of the cricket heap to the point where it was the biggest challenger to West Indian dominance.

In August 1986, in line with the VFL's push for an Australian Rules National Football League, Miller took on a new role as chief commissioner of the New South Wales Australian Football Commission. He did the job without payment. He agreed with the national vision for Aussie Rules and wanted to follow his conviction about the sport's potential. He faced a big media contingent and said he wanted to do for 'footy' what 'Captain Cook did for Australia': put it on the map. His role was that of a figurehead, but he was a good choice for initial publicity. Miller's credentials – as a Victorian and New South Wales state football representative, along with his short but brilliant career with St Kilda – were second to none.

The new body – the NSWAFC – took over the running of the game in New South Wales from the various regional bodies. In 1987 it oversaw 40,000 players and 1,700 clubs in the state. The eventual aim was to establish Rules in the biggest state and to compete with the rugby codes. Miller, the most popular former sportsman in Australia, was there at the beginning of the most important expansion in the game's history. He still appreciated soccer's skill, but his passion was with the game with which he began.

And he knew how to extract some attention by needling rugby code journalists and supporters. He liked, he said, all forms of football, 'particularly those where the ball is moved around'. But he added, 'I've always wondered why in rugby, scrums are formed to get the ball in play after an infringement. Up come the heavy-weights, down go their heads like turkeys at feeding time. They push and shove and other things, I'm told, to get the game flowing again. A sharp contrast to the simplicity of soccer and Aussie Rules.'

Miller was to the point, just as in his *Express* writing days, or indeed on any occasion. 'I make this observation after reading of the $2.2 million pay-out to a schoolboy who became a quadri-plegic when a scrum collapsed,' he said. 'Sadly there have been other cases in recent years.' He then surprised journalists, who were unaware of his poetic leanings, by quoting without notes a verse from English poet Rupert Brooke, who died in World War I:

When first I played I nearly died
The Bitter memory still rankles
They formed a scrum with me inside!
Some kicked the ball, some my ankles,
I did not like the game at all
Yet after all the harm they'd done me
Whenever I came near the ball

They knocked me down,
And stood upon me.

***

The American scion of the Getty Oil fortune, J. Paul Getty II, befriended Miller through mutual friends Gubby Allen and MCC stalwart John Stephenson, a former secretary of the club.

'I would like to be reincarnated as Keith Miller or Denis Compton,' Getty told Colin (later Lord) Cowdrey once he had absorbed enough about cricket to be an aficionado. They were equal in his cricketing pantheon. 'They were so uninhibited,' Getty said. 'They had so much joy from the game. Miller got out of the game a fraction early, I'm told.'

Miller was intrigued when told of Getty's love of cricket. Why would an American billionaire turn to a game that was not played to any extent in his native land? Miller soon learnt of his background. He empathised with Getty's long, difficult past with substance abuse because of the experience of Miller's sons at about the same time. In the 1960s Getty could afford endless expensive drugs, especially heroin, and he became addicted to heroin and alcohol. In this horrid period of his life he endured the death of a beautiful wife from an overdose. His son was kidnapped in Rome in 1973, and his severed ear was sent through the post to Getty.

Getty became a recluse, living on fashionable Cheyne Walk by the Thames in Chelsea, or at the London Clinic trying to kick his habits. Mick Jagger, a neighbour and cricket lover, whom he had known well from their philandering, druggie days of the 1960s, taught him the fundamentals of the gentle game. Jagger would draw the field placings on paper, then explain how they related to different kinds of bowler. Getty was a baseball fan, and he used it as the starting point for understanding cricket. As Getty's comprehension grew and he emerged from a long, drug-induced haze, he began to like the sport's complexities.

Jagger used to drop in almost every day in the summer. He saw that Getty had grasped the fundamentals and wanted to know more: about the history, the fine points, the great players. Getty began his own reading on cricket and talking to his other English friends about the game. A whole world opened up that took him away from the insanity of his drug addiction. 'Cricket is far more interesting than baseball,' Getty said, after absorbing his new passion for a couple of years, 'which is child's play by comparison. I always tell my American friends that baseball is to cricket what checkers is to chess.' It always amused Getty to see their reaction.

Over a decade from 1975, he began to comprehend the game's nuances and could differentiate between styles and approaches. In 1977 he bought his own *Wisden*, a big moment for a cricket fan and a sure sign of being hooked by the game. He became an MCC member, and that's where he met his retrospective heroes, Miller and Compton, of whom he had seen videos.

Over the years he began collecting *Wisdens*, a sign beyond addiction and more like obsession. Then he bought a complete leather-bound set, and joined Bradman as the only other private citizen with one at the time. Yet Getty could go beyond even the Don. He bought the company.

Love of cricket changed Getty from being a drug addict, weak of body, spirit and mind, to a philanthropist interested in all the causes he helped. The best known donation was £50 million to London's National Gallery in 1985. This generosity prompted the Queen to appoint him an Honorary Knight Commander of the British Empire. He was entitled to be called *Sir* Paul Getty. Thanks to Jagger, and Margaret Thatcher, who encouraged him further to do something with his life, and others such as Miller whom he met through cricket, Getty was transformed. He also grew to love cricketers. 'Cricketers are wonderful people,' he said often, 'a breed apart'. And to him, Miller was the epitome of what it was, and should be, to be a cricketer and a fine human being.

Getty put £3 million towards building the Mound Stand at Lord's, then took a box in it and entertained the greats of the game. Apart from Miller and Compton, Sobers, Benaud, Cowdrey, the

Bedsers and many others made their way there. Getty had video and film equipment put in the box literally for rainy days so that he could watch old Test matches and his other passion, 1930s movies.

Getty's dream became to own his own cricket ground. One day while entertaining Miller at his art-cluttered apartment overlooking Green Park, he pointed to two works of art. One was an oil painting by Jacques-Emile Blanche. It depicted an Eton v. Harrow match at Lord's in the 1930s. The painting included men in morning dress and women carrying parasols. The other painting was a small watercolour, again of a Lord's scene, by Pissarro. 'That's what I'd really like to create,' he told Miller.

'Why not? It's a wonderful idea. Always follow your dreams, Paul.'

Getty pointed to another piece of art: a line drawing by George Frederick Watts of a cover drive by a left-hander, believed to be the great all-rounder Frank Woolley, of Kent and England. 'That's the kind of cricket I want to see [at the proposed ground].' Getty already had the location. It would be carved out of a cornfield at his Buckinghamshire estate, Wormsley. 'It really just came from an idle thought,' he told Miller. 'They used to play cricket in the local village. I have an old scorebook from 1900. I'd like to revive all that.' Getty's aim was to reinstate 'country-house cricket – cricket just for the fun of it, not caring which side wins, just for the pleasure of it'. No one had built such a pitch in Britain since World War II. Getty wanted to be the first.

This simple, anachronistic love of the game was his broad point of connection with Miller, who always played that way. It developed a kindred spirit between them, which is exemplified in a letter Getty sent him:

Dear Keith,

Jim Swanton has told me, in confidence, that you will be coming to England this summer, news that excites me enormously.

Victoria and I are just back from the West Indies, where we saw England win a famous victory. We then went cruising around the Grenadines and watched the Antiguan run-fest on TV.

We had such a good time that we are determined to send the yacht to Australia this winter.

Anyway, we miss you and look forward to seeing you a little later on,

Yours Always,

[signed] Paul

J. Paul Getty

***

Life for Miller was still more one long party than a chore or bore. He was always someone's guest for something special, somewhere. His great facility for friendship across the board from paperboys and garbage men to Lord's administrators and prime ministers (in the 1950s, Bob Menzies and Anthony Eden; in the 1990s, John Howard and John Major) was now legendary. Although it was not a prerequisite, it helped for a friend to have a strong constitution for drink, as actors Peter O'Toole, Trevor Howard and Spencer Tracy would attest. He walked with royalty and the common man (and woman) alike, which was part of his huge appeal as a human being.

Once when he was hobbling from his favourite lunch spot, the East India Club, to a betting shop in Jermyn Street, London, his mind was on the third race at Newbury and a tip he had just picked up from a horse owner he had been lunching with. He put the bet on and just stepped back into Jermyn Street when he heard a voice he knew. 'Keif, Keif mate,' Jack the Cockney paper seller called from his post at the lane to Piccadilly. 'Want you to meet a mate of mine. He dwives Concordes, don't he.'

Jack, a friend of Miller for 20 years, introduced him to a lean fit man of 40, a British Airways Concorde captain. There was a quick exchange. Miller suggested a beer at a nearby hotel lounge. They got on well. The next morning at nine Miller was sitting in the jump seat of a Concorde. He arrived early morning New York time and had time to slip into Manhattan for a drink with the captain, who would stay overnight. Miller returned to the airport to catch the plane in the early afternoon and arrived back in London by 10 o'clock that night. He had difficulty explaining to customs why he had no luggage and two bottles of duty-free spirits.

Garbage collectors loomed large in Miller's life. Those who covered London's Covent Garden Hotel, where he often stayed, invited him to lunch, and he went. In the 1980s he often lunched in Sydney's Chinatown with a group of garbagemen he had known for years. Bob Radford, then the executive director of the New South Wales Cricket Association, went with him one day. 'We stayed a bit late [into early evening],' Radford told Melbourne journalist Jon Anderson, 'and on the way back he [Miller] stopped the car and went to the boot, where he had stowed a dinner suit. He got changed on the side of the road, and then, half an hour after leaving the garbos, headed off to a reception at Government House.'

***

Miller gave little thought to the ending of his cocktail party of a life. Yet every now and again in the late 1980s and early 1990s he had reminders that he might have to slow up a fraction. His brother Les died in 1989. Once again Miller regretted not being able to thank his brother formally for his guidance with Les Sr and Ray in helping him on the road to sporting glory and his unmatched life of fun, fame and celebrity.

There were never-ending reminders, too, of how fortunate he had been. In 1990 Miller found a reference in an air force newsletter to an RAAF pilot, 'W.E. Young', crashing his plane in the French Alps during the war. Local villagers had taken bodies from the plane in 1944 and had given them a respectful burial with the help of the victims' nametags.

Miller discovered that this 'William Ellis Young' was his good mate from Broken Hill, with whom he first met Peg in 1943. Miller found Young's grave on his next visit to Europe and paid his respects to a friend who had died before his 20th birthday.

The first major threat to Miller's life since his war years came when he visited Melbourne for Cup Week in November 1991. He had a stroke and was in hospital for 16 days. Miller returned to Sydney when well enough to travel but fell over and broke the hip that had been operated on in 1985. It required a further two operations and was never quite right afterwards. At 72, much to his chagrin, he needed a walking frame, not all the time, but when the pain was too much.

He also had a continuing problem with skin cancer. He blamed it on playing a lot of sport in the sun and his love of the beach. He had only rarely worn a cap on the cricket field or at the beach, preferring to leave his trademark mop of hair free. Nor did Miller care much for sunscreen on those countless surfing days. As a result he had to have an ear lobe removed. But the skin cancer was widespread, especially on his legs. This and his hip problem prevented him getting about as much.

Yet despite the stroke, he kept up his communication with admirers. One was British Prime Minister John Major, for whom he had earlier obtained a signed copy of the *Bradman Albums* when they were published.

On 22 January 1992 Major wrote from 10 Downing Street:

Dear Keith,

I was deeply sorry to learn that you had suffered a slight stroke in November. But the tone of your letter of 17 January was very heartening in proving your sense of humour is as alert as ever, and that, I hope, you are well on the way to complete recovery.

How marvellous to have a signed copy of the splendid photograph of you that Robert Menzies prized. I can certainly see why he thought so highly of it, but had not realised it was Alec Bedser's ball which you were disposing of so brilliantly. I daresay he got his own back! Thank you so much.

Norma joins me in sending you our warm good wishes for a very speedy recovery, and a happy 1992.

[Major then scribbled:] I do hope you'll be fit enough to return to England soon – or that I can come to Australia. Norma sends her love.

Yours Ever,

John

Until Major's letter, he had not thought seriously about another England trip just yet. Miller's compensation was to sit on the phone for hours every day. He was saddened when one of his three great telephonic mates in the early 1990s, Bill O'Reilly, died in 1992. The other two were Harold Larwood and Alan McGilvray. But there were many others. Even Bradman, whom he would never count among his close friends, was someone he would yarn with.

With great reluctance Miller resigned from the Long Reef Golf Club. His hip problems would now keep him from his favourite sporting pastime since his retirement from big cricket. Miller would not succumb easily to the walking frame, despite being hospitalised or housebound for many months. 'Christ!' he said one morning to Peg early in 1992, 'I look like something out of Belsen or Buchenwald!'

He decided to build himself up. Miller worked hard to improve his condition to a point where he could hobble around with the aid of an aluminium stick. His fight back to fitness was buoyed by countless friends sending him good wishes. Getty invited him and Peg to England travelling first class. It was a helpful incentive.

After months of struggle and gradual improvement in his health, he put on weight and was prepared to make the tough trip half way across the world. Getty was a courteous, thoughtful and caring host, who loved having Miller in his company. He invited Miller to ask anyone he wished to the Mound Box. This allowed Miller, in turn, to repay a kindness to his hero 'Laddie' Lucas, the war ace, whom he had first met in 1943 when Lucas gave him that precarious airlift from Ouston to Northolt.

Also in the Getty Box in 1992 at the Lord's Test were other Miller mates: John Major, Lord Carrington, Denis Compton, former England captain Bob Wyatt (then aged 92) and MCC stalwart Colin Ingleby-Mackenzie (who would later be MCC president). Mick Jagger popped in, as did Rolling Stones drummer Charlie Watts, whom Miller and Peg enjoyed meeting. The champagne flowed and the Miller stories came in a torrent. All that effort in overcoming the hip problem – at least to the point of being able to travel – had been worth every drop of sweat and the pain. It was, in short, an incentive to keep living and enjoying life. For if Miller were to be cut off from his beloved England and all his contacts there, life would not be worth living.

Getty insisted that he return in the summer of 1993 for more fun and yarns and for the opening of his dream cricket field at Wormsley. Miller happily agreed, and this trip dovetailed nicely with the MCC's request that his portrait be painted. Miller had 15 sittings with artist Michael Christopher Corkney, at the latter's small studio near the Oval. Miller and Corkney, himself a cricket buff, ranged over topics from music and John Barbirolli to Cardus and the royals.

The result was a remarkable painting of Miller as he was at 73, drawn and leaner from his recent illnesses, but still with the elegance of an ageing big cat – a leopard or a lion – with which observers had often drawn analogies. Corkney added a nice touch and homage to Miller's youth and cricket brilliance. In the left-hand corner was the famous photograph of Miller, which graced Menzies' office in the 1950s and 1960s. In the right-hand corner was a photograph of Miller bowling.

The painting was later hung above the door at the rear of the Long Room, which led to the bar. Miller thought this was more than appropriate. The only other portrait of an Australian in the room was of Bradman, placed meaningfully above those of Len Hutton and Douglas Jardine. Miller's love for Lord's, its traditions and its symbolism in remaining a playing arena when the Germans were bombing London during the war, meant that he regarded the hanging of the painting in the Long Room as the greatest honour of his life.

During the time of the sittings, Miller made it to Buckinghamshire to watch cricket with Getty at 2,500-acre Wormsley, reputedly the most beautiful estate in England, and just 45 minutes drive from London. Pheasants could be seen in the fields. Miller took in a game between the Lord's Taverners and the Australian Taverners, both charitable organisations. Bob Simpson and Greg Chappell opened the batting for the Australians. Miller was a guest at the elegant Georgian mansion, which had an orange façade. Around the lake in front of the house was a deer park. About 250 deer filed down to the water for a drink in the late afternoon. Getty proudly showed Miller his new library in a mock medieval turreted castle built to house his priceless collection of original manuscripts and documents, which were insured for $100 million. They included the first-ever page of printed matter, Samuel Pepys's diaries, hundreds of embroidered bindings and ancient bibles, and Getty's most prized non-cricket possession: a 14th-century copy of the Magna Carta.

During these trips, a deep friendship was cemented between the two men. Each year from then on Miller would receive a first-class ticket to visit England for the summer and to stay at the Getty mansion. There was always another ticket for Peg, who accompanied Miller several times. Getty and his wife Victoria Holdsworth recognised her quality and understood more about Miller through meeting her.

His fortieth stay through an English summer in 1993 marked

half a century since he first arrived in England during the war in 1943. Getty's mateship and largesse meant that this arrangement was open to Miller for the rest of his days, or Getty's. Yet he wasn't the only patron. There was always somebody or some organisation that wanted Miller in attendance in England. In March 1994 the National Sporting Club of the UK and London's *Evening Standard* newspaper invited him for a tribute dinner for Compton at the Café Royal. On such occasions it rankled with Miller more than ever that nothing was being done to honour him in his own country. He was 74. He knew time for any accolades was running out.

Despite his stroke and some slowing down, Miller would not stop enjoying himself in the manner to which he had become accustomed over 50 years. There were now more celebrations for the Invincibles, who were being given increased recognition as the decades since their amazing 1948 Ashes season enlarged them to legendary status. There was a special bond between the team members, which had been a big factor in their success in the first place.

When he returned to Australia after enjoying the Gettys' hospitality, he heard that Invincibles team-mate Ernie Toshack was ill in a Sydney hospital. Miller visited him, smuggling in a bottle of whisky. When nurses weren't watching, they drank the bottle and enjoyed themselves. Miller was about to leave when he fell over and was knocked unconscious. He woke up in a concussed state but managed to climb into a second bed in Toshack's room. A nurse discovered Miller fast asleep the next morning.

Despite their differences in the playing era 1946–48, Miller, like all Invincibles, kept in touch with their captain. He would see Bradman when in Adelaide. Miller was there for the Australia Day Test of the 1994–95 Ashes series, using a friend's caravan at the tennis courts next to the ground to entertain anyone who cared to drop in. There was a steady stream of well-wishers. He made a point of popping up to see Bradman, then 86 years old, who sat in his usual spot in the Members' Stand. He and Miller chatted amiably.

Soon after the meeting, Miller bumped into friend Michael Parkinson, who had tried everything over the years to be granted an audience with the Don. But Bradman had never trusted Parkinson because he consorted over the years with such Bradman enemies as Bill O'Reilly and Jack Fingleton, who had appeared on his TV show. Bradman enjoyed eluding and rejecting Parkinson in his many attempts to see him.

'I have offered him money, attempted to lure him with limousines and expensive hotel suites, persuaded mutual friends to use their influence, even tried incense and prayer,' Parkinson wrote in the Melbourne *Herald Sun* at the time of the Adelaide Test. 'I still haven't interviewed Sir Donald.'

Bradman sent me this article a few weeks after it appeared. In a covering letter dated 15 February 1995 he wrote: 'I enclose an article about me by Michael Parkinson. He hates my guts because I refused to do a TV interview with him and [he] puts in a sly barb here and there.'

Parkinson once wrote in a December 1969 article in *Punch*: 'Like all nostalgics, I varnish real incidents with the gloss of my own imagination so that after a year or two the story I tell bears little relation to what really happened. This, of course, is not lying, merely the poetic licence which is the prerogative of all nostalgics.' Parkinson, the entertainer on screen and in newspapers, was too poetic for the Don's liking. Bradman had humour, but preferred his stories without varnish and his facts dry. He didn't appreciate Parkinson's repeating stories from detractors that bore little relation to *what really happened* decades ago.

Miller was a different character altogether, who also enjoyed a good reminiscence, apocryphal or not. Parkinson loved having him on his TV chat show more than any other guest. Parkinson periodically waxed lyrical about him in newspapers.

The Bradman–Miller cordiality continued. 'They [Miller and Bradman] had a mutual respect for each other,' said Richard Mulvaney, the Bradman Museum's director. 'They may have had their differences, but Keith went out of his way to help us on more than one occasion. That's something that Bill O'Reilly, for one, would never do!'

Miller and Peg made the now-annual trek across the world in May 1996 courtesy of Getty. The Millers were the only guests to be given three lunch invitations for the prestigious Box 3 at the Mound Stand during the England v. India Test. No one else appeared more than once on the guest list over the three days that Getty turned on a show. Miller was the most popular name on the list. On day one, Thursday 20 June, everyone, even the sometimes loquacious, other times insouciant Mick Jagger, had to cope with not being the centre of attention in the presence of the Millers and the Comptons. Jagger and his son James still enjoyed themselves, as did ex-Indian cricket star Dilip Doshi and his wife Kalinda. On the Friday, the Millers and the Gettys shared plenty of anecdotes in the company of Michael Parkinson and his wife Mary. Lord and Lady Carrington (Peter and Iona to the Millers) were also there reminiscing along with esteemed cricket writer Jim Swanton and his wife Ann.

On the big day of the Test, the Saturday, the Millers were entertained with Peter O'Toole (who loved drinking with Miller) and his son Lorcan. Ingleby-Mackenzie and his wife Susan were there too, as was the 'Big Cat', West Indian star Clive Lloyd, and his wife Waveney. Comedian Spike Milligan kept everyone and his wife Shelagh amused with zany impersonations of Prince Charles and Margaret Thatcher.

In the rare moments that cricket was the topic, Miller took pride in Australia's revival after Border had dragged the team to near the top. Mark Taylor, the skipper to follow Border, had in 1995 led Australia to a win against the West Indies in the Caribbean, which was at that point the toughest assignment in world cricket.

Miller loved those days and the company. He wished they would never end.

FADING AWAY

The recognition that Miller felt was due to him began to come late in his life. Apart from the Invincibles accolades, in 1996, in his seventy-seventh year, he was one of the original inductees to Australian sports' international hall of fame along with Fred Spofforth, John Blackham, Victor Trumper, Clarrie Grimmett, Bill Ponsford, Don Bradman, Bill O'Reilly, Ray Lindwall and Dennis Lillee. Yet the following year he was not thrilled to see the image of a cricketer, Bradman, honoured on Australian stamps. He felt that someone like his mate of old, Bill Newton, should be recognised before any sportsman. Miller told the media he thought Australia Post had 'its priorities all wrong'. It countered by saying that it had started the stamp series with the idea of using the images of people who had done something 'extraordinary for their country'. Australia Post intended to use people outside the sporting arena 'when it could'.

Miller had earlier fought to have Newton's name remain on the William Newton Steeplechase – the first race of every Anzac Day meeting – rather than that of a sponsor, Manchester Unity of Victoria. Miller's well-placed sentiment and sense of history won over money – the $27,000 sponsorship. Newton's name remained on the race. It was all part of his perspective, in which veterans were ranked above those who had not served or were simply sportsmen and not, in Miller's eyes, true heroes.

'If there was a cricketer and an air force veteran in the room with him,' son Bill observed, 'the air force veteran would get all the attention.'

He would make perhaps one exception: his close mate Denis Compton, with whom he spoke over the phone once a week and saw every summer. They chatted on Monday, 28 April 1997. 'Denis told me he was not feeling too good,' Miller said. 'It broke my heart. He said we would meet at Lord's for a beer in the summer and that would make him feel better.' Compton died the next day. 'I can't believe he's gone,' Miller told the London *Express*. 'He was like a brother to me. I shed a tear or two when I heard the news. To lose him after 50 years is very hard. There will be a big hole at Lord's now. It won't be the same watching Australia play England without him.'

Ian Johnson died in 1998. Miller in tribute called him a 'great diplomat, a great public relations man. He had the charm. The West Indies tour of 1955 was successful and he restored good relations. This was one of his finest achievements.' Miller rated Johnson a good captain and tactician. 'He knew his cricket. He was very thorough, perhaps a little conservative.' This was Miller himself at his diplomatic best. His rivalry with Johnson had gone beyond the cricket field.

There was further recognition from an institution he respected and was fond of: Melbourne High. In March 1999 the school's sports field was renamed the Woodfull–Miller Oval. Paul Sheahan, then head of Melbourne Grammar School, gave an eloquent keynote address with Miller in attendance.

Miller was also able to see a little more of his brother Ray. They spoke on the phone often, which prompted Miller to write a letter that he felt was long overdue:

Ray, thanks to you, Les and Dad, cricket has given me a most interesting life.

The places I've been to, the people I've met, is [*sic*] unbelievable, all because of my cricket exploits.

And it's all because of the endless hours, you, Les and Dad taught me in the backyard.

So this letter is to say thank you.

It's a sort of letter I should've writing [*sic*] when Les and Dad was [*sic*] around, but like many things "I'll do it tomorrow" style which never gets done.

So Ray, I finally made it.

All my cricket was due to the three of you – nobody else.

My most genuine thanks Ray.

Pop – Weedy [family nicknames].

Ray appreciated the gesture greatly. He died in December 1999. It was poignant moment, especially when Miller was told that Mozart's *Jupiter* symphony (No. 41) – to which Ray had introduced him – was the last music Ray ever heard. He was the closer elder brother, and had been Miller's main support and confidant. Ray's opinions were valued, and they often swayed his own.

Miller attended his funeral. Someone asked him if there were any members of his family left. Miller said nothing but pointed to his chest. He was now the last of his family alive.

Godfrey Evans also passed on in 1999, which meant Miller's three closest English friends from cricket – the others being Edrich and Compton – had now gone.

By September 1999 Miller needed a wheelchair more and more. He decided that his long-time Melbourne friend, Marie Challman, in her late fifties and a receptionist at Melbourne's Freemason's Hospital, could better look after him in his final years than Peg, who had done so for 56 years. Miller decided to leave Newport. Without so much as a 'goodbye', he said he was going to the 1999 AFL Grand Final, and flew out of Sydney never to return (except for one occasion, but not in Peg's presence). Peg, aged 82, was hurt and upset, as were the boys. There had been no major dispute between him and Peg.

'Keith always spoke to and of Peg in the warmest possible

loving manner,' said Jan Beames, who was close to both, 'and not once did I ever pick up any undercurrents [of disagreement] when I stayed there [at Newport].' Their four sons verified this. 'His great respect [for Peg] and his attitude are the main reasons Peg turned a blind eye to it [Miller's philandering],' Beames added.

All the family and the boys felt his behaviour in the last few years was uncharacteristic of the man before the major stroke in 1991 and a series of smaller strokes (transient ischaemic attacks or TIAs) that occurred in his last years. They felt that arrangements could have been made for their parents to have support together in their final years. But it wasn't what Miller wanted. He moved to Challman's home on the Mornington Peninsula, a 75-minute drive from Melbourne. He found better and easier care at the Peninsula Hospital a few kilometres from his new home. 'If I rang a doctor [from Newport] he took hours to get there,' Miller told artist Brian Clinton, who visited him at Mornington. 'The facility and treatment are far better here.'

More importantly, he needed a specialist to look after his problems with varicose veins, ulcers and skin cancer. The pain was worsening. No specialist in Sydney would operate on his legs. Miller had been treated by a Melbourne specialist for 20 years, and this was a main factor in his move. In his final years leg bandages needed changing at hospital three times a week. Challman became his full-time carer.

Despite his condition, Miller was determined to keep living the England dream, and Challman was able to nurse him and look after his every need. They travelled together to London again courtesy of Getty, who was also ailing. Even flying first-class was an ordeal, but Miller was prepared to do it, such was his love for England in the summer.

In 2000, Miller was named in Australia's 'Test Team of the Century', which was pleasing to him, as was his selection by Bradman in his personal 'best Australian team ever'. When told that Bradman had had a fall down the stairs at his Adelaide home,

Miller rang him to see how he was, and they had a long talk. The two men had not spoken since their meeting during the Australia Day Test in Adelaide in early 1995. Several other phone conversations followed thereafer. Bradman died in February 2001, and Miller was pleased that they had been on chatting terms late in his life. Miller told such acquaintances as Brian Clinton that 'we were not the arch enemies we'd been portrayed'.

Miller was touched by the death of Princess Margaret in February 2002. He kept an item in a British newspaper that mentioned his relationship with her, and treasured the memory of their times together.

***

Through this final period of living in Melbourne, Miller was struggling financially. He still liked to place a bet, but had long ago stopped being a mug punter. He had lost more than he ever won, and used to counsel people against gambling. Towards the end he was short of money. Now there was not the energy to pursue tips from racing industry mates at the track or anywhere else. Years earlier Miller's sheer force of will, knowledge of the horses, jockeys and trainers, and his hunger for tips would occasionally see him ahead on any given day. But these became fewer as he slowed down.

Miller had long refused to involve himself in memorabilia, but now he agreed for a fee to sign 500 prints of a painting by Brian Clinton. He also signed – for a $15,000 fee – 50 prints for the Bradman Museum of Bradman making his hundredth first-class century. Miller had been batting with him at the time against India.

Peg and the boys decided to sell off some items to retrieve some money for her. 'We thought we'd get enough to go out for a good dinner,' Bob said lightly. 'Peg always hated one item hanging on the wall – a painting of famous Sydney Hill barracker "Yabba" – and it would have given her some delight to sell it.' Denis took to Melbourne the Yabba painting, which was signed by Bradman and Miller, along with an old bat tipped at the bottom with polymer and one of his sleeveless Australian cricket jumpers. Denis saw a well-known memorabilia dealing identity, Michael Ludgrove.

Ludgrove then approached Miller with the thought of creating a bigger selection of his possessions, including his RAAF belongings. An angry Miller rang Denis to ask what he was doing with his memorabilia. It began a rift between Miller and Denis and the other brothers. Miller demanded back items that could be sold off, including some that the sons felt he had given to them as personal mementos. They were asked to part with an Omega watch that belonged to Hugh Edwards, a highly decorated World War II flyer, who had bequeathed it to Miller. 'It should have gone to a museum,' Bob said, 'and it was just not like Dad to start flogging things off like that. It was not cricket memorabilia.' Denis even had to part with a set of serviette rings that his father had given him as a gift some time ago.

By nature Miller was a generous person. His sons again put this turnaround down to his deteriorating condition. They, the rest of the family and some friends believed Miller was doing things contrary to all he stood for, such as his loyalty, convictions and generosity. Miller's Australian 1953 baggy green cap was advertised for sale at between $30,000 and $50,000. Ludgrove auctioned a wide variety of items, which were sold, he claimed, for around $250,000.

Four items were likely to remain on Miller's mantelpiece at Mornington and not go to the auctioneer. First, there was a crystal bowl that marked his induction into sports' international Hall of Fame. Then there was the silver eggcup presented to him by Woodfull in 1936 after he made 61 for South Melbourne against Carlton. It was the gift he cherished most. It represented the start of his great life as a cricketer. A third item that would be hard to part with was his favourite cricket photo, which showed the Australian Services team taking the field at Bramall Lane in

1945. Even after 55 Tests and nearly 60 years, he still had most nostalgia for and best memories of the unofficial Victory Tests of that year. His favourite photo of all would stay with him to the end, if he could help it. That was of Guy Gibson, VC, of Dambusters fame, sitting reading in a field of poppies. 'I just love that picture,' he would tell visitors.

Miller needed finance to remodel the bathroom and kitchen at Challman's Mornington home so that he could better access them with a new wheelchair that he also needed to buy.

Challman herself wanted further recognition – as the second Mrs Miller. This prompted Miller to serve divorce papers on Peg in July 2002. Notification of their marriage's dissolution arrived on 21 September, their fifty-sixth wedding anniversary. Peg was heart-broken. Many of their friends and the boys, aware of what she had put into the marriage, rallied to her. Ian Chappell's wife Barbara was chief among the many who supported Peg. In the meantime, Miller married Challman without telling any of his family. In one phone conversation to Peg, Miller said he had no regrets for anything he had ever done. 'That's all right for you, honey,' Peg responded, 'at the expense of your family.'

***

Getty died in April 2003, aged 70. Miller was deeply saddened for his friend. It also spelt the end of Miller's access to England, which was a kind of death for him, too. Yet he helped others enjoy in part what he had experienced by arranging for a Bradman Museum XI to play at Getty's Wormsley estate in the summer.

Again, Richard Mulvaney, director of the Bradman Museum, was grateful to Miller.

***

Peg died in November 2003. Miller by this time was not up to travel by plane. He missed her funeral. He was devastated by her death.

'She was ahead of her time,' said Jan Beames in her eulogy at Peg's funeral service, held at St Michael's and All Angels Anglican

Church, Newport, which Peg had regularly attended over nearly half a century. Pippa Burke, the daughter of Jim Burke, played the organ at the funeral. In earlier days, Peg too had played the organ there.

'Peg had her own sense of identity and life outside of being Mrs Keith Miller,' Beames added. 'People were drawn to this quietly independent, warm woman. She carved out a fulfilling, busy life for herself. Peg had her challenges with her health and in her personal life but irrespective of what was happening to her, or around her, she maintained a calmness, cheerful spirit and her dignity at all times.'

No matter what was happening or how ill she was, Beames noted, she would always respond to an inquiry about her well-being 'in that gorgeous husky voice': 'I'm just fine, thanks, honey.' Beames' moving tribute left many in tears.

***

The accolades for Miller kept coming. He was pleased to learn that a plaque recognising him appeared at the SCG's Walk of Honour, which was a lot more impressive than the graffiti he would have settled for. Denis accepted the honour on his father's behalf. In his speech, he referred pointedly to 'Mr Miller'. Some resentment remained among Miller's sons for what they saw as his desertion of their mother and for the memorabilia episode.

In 2003 Miller was added to the St Kilda Football Club Hall of Fame and was persuaded by Neil Roberts, a former Saints star, to appear at a dinner. He turned up in a tuxedo, in his wheelchair and Marie by his side. Miller was the centre of attention, with many people lining up for him to sign something.

Just as he had been thrilled with the recognition from the MCC in the form of his portrait at Lord's, so he was also gratified in February 2004 by an excellent large bronze statue by Louis Laumen of him in bowling action. It was one of several statues in a 'Parade of Champions' outside the MCG. Others nearby were of Bradman, Australian Rules champion coach and player Ron

Barassi, Essendon Football Club triple Brownlow Medallist Dick Reynolds and athletes Betty Cuthbert and Shirley Strickland. Miller, ever modest, was honoured to have his sculpted effigy join them.

Miller and Marie were at the unveiling, which was attended by friends but none of his family. He was still estranged from his sons. Miller was frail, and could hardly express through tears his gratitude, not just for the statue but also for the warmth of the assembled throng. He might have felt this would be his last public hurrah, which it was.

In August, Denis flew to Melbourne to reconcile the estrangement between him and his father since their disagreement over memorabilia a few years earlier. The meeting ended with Miller hugging Denis and giving him a kiss on the cheek. 'I'm eternally grateful I went to see him,' Denis told *Herald Sun* journalist Ron Reed.

A constant flow of calls came through to the Mornington home. He could entertain fewer and fewer visitors. Mates and loyal confidants, such as journalist Ken Piesse, saw him, each time knowing it might be the last meeting. Miller, the old soldier, who had done his duty – except to his family – and lived his life to the full without regrets, was fading away.

***

Keith Miller died in a Mornington nursing home on 11 October 2004, aged 84, the same day as American actor Christopher Reeve, who was famous for playing Superman in the movies. As one observer noted, two Supermen departed that day.

A minute's silence was observed for Miller during the Test match going on in Chennai between Australia and India, and in Lahore, where Pakistan was playing Sri Lanka. The Australian team members wore black armbands throughout the Chennai game. At Lord's, Miller's spiritual home, the MCC flag on the grandstand was flown at half-mast.

The media coverage in the cricket world following his death

was huge, especially in Britain and Australia. Only the deaths of Don Bradman and Wilfred Burchett, the radical communist journalist, of all Australians, commanded more attention in the UK since World War II. But the affection for Miller there was greater than for any other Australian public figure.

A State funeral was granted by the Victorian Government, and the service was organised by Marie with the help of Tony Charlton. It was held at a packed St Paul's Cathedral in Melbourne on a warm day, 20 October, and broadcast to the nation on ABC radio. Three mementos – his RAAF wings, the silver eggcup from Woodfull and Miller's baggy green cap – sat at the front of the church. The service began with the national anthem, but most of the music was by Beethoven, Miller's favourite, and by Bach, whom he liked almost as much. Trinity Grammar student Hamish Beeston recited Wordsworth's 'Upon Westminster Bridge'. Soloist Suzanne Shakespeare sang 'Sheep May Safely Graze' from a Bach cantata.

A theme developed through the event. It was evident – in the make-up of the audience and what was said – as people from the humble to the high and mighty of sport, politics and business stood shoulder to shoulder in the grand cathedral. Miller was the ultimate egalitarian Australian, who believed that all men were equal as characters no matter what their background or station in life. This attitude was prevalent among diggers after World War I, and continued as a tradition with returned servicemen after World War II. Fighting for your country was a great leveller. It united men in a common cause, in which courage, sacrifice and mateship superseded all else. That is why he was equally at home with anyone with whom he made day-to-day contact and with the elite of the societies in which he moved. It was the reason Melbourne Cricket Club barman of 39 years, Tom Portelli, turned up at the funeral, along with the State Governor, John Landy. It's why MCG cleaner Les Fehr, a stalwart of the South Melbourne Cricket Club, put a flower in the hand of the Miller statue outside the MCG after his death. It helped explain why four Australian captains – Richie Benaud, Ian Chappell, Steve Waugh and Ricky Ponting – came from interstate to pay their respects; why the country's Prime Minister John Howard, who was abroad, sent a message. In the audience, too, were Scobie Breasley and Ron Hutchinson, representing the many jockeys who related so well to the big-hearted horse-lover and punter. The Miller family was there in force, and included his seven grand-children and four great-grandchildren.

Tony Charlton delivered the eulogy and emphasised the clear theme of Miller's common, and not so common, touch. John Bradman spoke and painted a positive picture of his father's rela-tionship with Miller. It raised eyebrows. Many in the audience had heard different views. Yet it was true that the differences between Miller and Bradman were accentuated by gossip and media beat-ups over time. When they were together as players, and on the rare occasions afterwards, there was no real animosity. Their final phone calls not long before Bradman's death were a kind of rapprochement between two great but different Australians.

John mentioned that Miller and Bradman twice swapped caps, each gaining a better fit at the time, but delivering a nightmare to auction houses decades later when trying to establish their prov-enance. John Bradman, too, was speaking more for his own friendship with Miller, who had been his hero as a schoolboy. He made a telling point, saying that Miller was a man's man, who nonetheless expressed friendship more openly than any other man he had known. Neil Harvey, who was in the audience with two other Invincibles, Sam Loxton and Bill Brown, augmented Bradman's remarks when he said that Keith was a 'man's man and a ladies' man' as well.

Only Ian Chappell, another speaker, mentioned Peg. This pleased the family, who had not been invited to speak at the service. The lack of reference to Peg by others was a poor over-sight. She had been Miller's rock, main companion and focus of attention for the great bulk of 60 years from 1943, when they first met and he asked her to marry him, until her death in 2003. 'The greatest thing I can say about Keith Miller,' Chappell added, 'is that I had a boyhood hero who lived up to my lofty expectations.'

In his speech, Benaud put the obverse of the old axiom *don't believe everything you read* or heard about Miller. For once, he said, you could believe it, and to a point this was true.

Marie, in black and looking trim and elegant, also spoke of a man who had remained true to his motto: 'Be yourself.' 'I was blessed to meet him, privileged to take care of him, and honoured to be his wife,' she said, 'He was, is and always will be the love of my life.'

The service ran nearly an hour over time, and for once Miller could not be blamed. Or perhaps he could. There was just too much to say about him, too many memories to be fitted into a tight event.

Miller's sons, Bill, 56, Peter, 54, Denis, 53, and Bob, 48, and two grandsons – Peter's son Christian, 21, and Bill's son Ben, 31 – were the pall-bearers. As they carried the heavy coffin out of the cathedral and into the warmth of Swanston Street, several hundred people outside applauded. The spontaneity touched the boys. The funeral cortège, with a police escort, then made its way to the MCG, where Marie laid a wreath at the foot of Miller's statue. The mourners adjourned to the (recently named) Miller Room for the wake. No lover of funerals, it was the part Miller would have been looking forward to.

Miller lies buried in a Mornington cemetery, in a grave site for two. Marie intends to be buried beside him. The black headstone mentions Marie and Miller's four sons. There is no reference to Peg.

***

Miller wrote in 1956: 'I have numerous failings – but then, I have never set myself up as a shining example of propriety. Yet whatever my faults, I've no time for the half-truth. I like to call a spade a spade.'

Over the next half century, these failings remained evident, particuarly where his family was concerned. Yet his human virtues, of fellowship, of care and consideration for people less fortunate than himself, of courage, of loyalty, of conviction and of sacrifice in war, outweighed his weaknesses. Australia has never produced a better all-round sportsman. He was a once-in-a-generation cricketer. More than that, Keith Ross Miller was a once-in-a-lifetime character.

APPENDIX

KEITH MILLER: THE STATISTICAL RECORD

Born 28 November 1919; died 11 October 2004
Teams: New South Wales, Nottinghamshire and Australia
First-class debut: 1937–38

FIRST-CLASS RECORD

TEST MATCHES

Batting:

Against	Tests	Inns	Not Out	Runs	Highest Score	100s	Average
England	29	49	4	1511	145 n.o.	3	33.57
West Indies	10	16	1	801	147	4	53.40
South Africa	9	14	2	399	84	–	33.25
India	5	5	–	185	67	–	37.00
Pakistan	1	2	–	32	–	–	16.00
New Zealand	1	1	–	30	30	–	30.00
Total	55	87	7	2958	147	7	36.97

Bowling:

Against	Tests	Overs	Maidens	Runs	Wickets	Average
England	29	757.1	224	1960	87	22.56
West Indies	10	316.5	53	1047	40	26.17
South Africa	9	226	35	632	30	21.06
India	5	72	4	223	9	24.77
Pakistan	1	29	9	58	2	29.00
New Zealand	1	6	62	6	2	3.00
Total	55	1407	337	3905	170	22.97

UNOFFICIAL TEST MATCHES

Batting:

Against	Matches	Inns	Not Out	Runs	Highest Score	100s	Average
England 1945	5	10	3	443	118	2	63.28

Bowling:

Against	Matches	Overs	Maidens	Runs	Wickets	Average
England 1945	5	121	19	277	10	27.70

SHEFFIELD SHIELD

Batting:

For	Matches	Inns	Not Out	Runs	Highest Score	100s	Average
Victoria	10	17	2	965	206 n.o.	4	64.33
New South Wales	42	57	6	2838	201 n.o.	9	55.64
Total	52	74	8	3803	206 n.o.	13	57.62

Bowling:

For	Matches	Overs	Maidens	Runs	Wickets	Average
Victoria	10	65	4	231	11	21.00
New South Wales	42	767.7	104	2618	98	26.71
Total	52	832.7	108	2849	109	26.13

OTHER MATCHES IN AUSTRALIA

Season	Matches	Inns	Not Out	Runs	Highest Score	100s	Average
1945–46	3	6	1	273	105 n.o.	1	54.60
1946–47 v MCC	4	6	–	151	70	–	25.16
1947–48 v India	2	3	–	171	86	–	57.00
1950–51 v MCC	3	4	–	373	214	1	93.25
1951–52 v West Indies	1	1	–	30	30	–	30.00
1952–53 v South Africa	2	3	–	117	58	–	39.00
1954–55 v MCC	2	3	–	168	86	–	56.00
Testimonial matches	3	6	–	238	101	2	39.66
Total	20	32	1	1521	214	4	49.06

Bowling:

Season	Matches	Overs	Maidens	Runs	Wickets	Average
1945–46	3	29	2	162	6	27.00
1946–47 v MCC	4	58	9	160	6	26.66
1947–48 v India	2	39.3	3	112	6	18.66
1950–51 v MCC	3	43	7	102	2	51.00
1951–52 v West Indies	1	29.1	5	63	8	7.87
1952–53 v South Africa	2	48	10	127	5	25.40
1954–55 v MCC	2	29	1	85	3	28.33
Testimonial matches	3	41	1	198	4	49.50
Total	20	316.4	38	1009	40	25.22

OVERSEAS TOURS (matches other than Tests)

Batting:

Season	Country	Matches	Inns	Not Out	Runs	Highest Score	100s	Average
1946	New Zealand	3	3	–	227	139	1	75.66
1948	England	17	19	3	913	202 n.o.	2	57.00
1949–50	South Africa	8	8	1	331	131	1	47.28
1953	England	17	20	2	909	220 n.o.	2	50.50
1955	West Indies	4	6	–	168	39	–	28.00
1956	England	15	18	5	637	281 n.o.	1	49.00
Total		64	74	11	3185	281 n.o.	7	50.04

Bowling:

Season	Country	Matches	Overs	Maidens	Runs	Wickets	Average
1946	New Zealand	3	17	6	21	4	5.25
1948	England	17	293.3	75	686	43	15.95
1949–50	South Africa	8	121	22	338	27	12.51
1953	England	17	269.4	78	625	25	25.00
1955	West Indies	4	70	17	190	9	21.33
1956	England	15	224.5	58	513	29	17.68
Total		64	996	256	2373	137	17.32

TOTAL FIRST-CLASS

Batting:

	Matches	Inns	Not Out	Runs	Highest Score	100s	Average
Tests	55	87	7	2958	147	7	36.97
Unofficial Tests	5	10	3	443	118	2	63.28
Sheffield Shield	52	74	8	3803	206 n.o.	13	57.62
Other first-class games	84	106	12	4706	281 n.o.	11	50.06
Total	196	277	30	11910	281 n.o.	33	48.61

Bowling:

	Matches	Overs	Maidens	Runs	Wickets	Average
Tests	55	1407	337	3905	170	22.97
Unofficial Tests	5	121	19	277	10	27.70
Sheffield Shield	52	832.7	108	2849	109	26.13
Other first-class games	84	1312.4	294	3382	177	19.10
Total	196	3673.3	758	10413	466	22.34

THE TESTS

Season	Batting					Bowling		
	I.	N.O.	Runs	H.S.	Avge	Runs	Wkts	Avge
1937–38 (Australia)	1	0	181	181	181.00	–	–	–
1938–39 (Australia)	7	2	125	55	25.00	–	–	–
1939–40 (Australia)	11	1	298	108	29.80	–	–	–
1940–41 (Australia)	5	0	140	63	28.00	27	1	27.00
1945 (England)	13	3	725	185	72.50	336	10	33.60
1945–46 (India)	14	1	470	132	36.15	343	13	26.38
1945–46 (Australia)	9	1	463	105*	57.87	191	6	31.83
1945–46 (New Zealand)	4	0	257	139	64.25	27	5	5.40
1946–47 (Australia)	19	3	1202	206*	75.12	725	32	22.65
1947–48 (Australia)	17	0	791	170	46.52	940	33	28.48
1948 (England)	26	3	1088	202*	47.30	985	56	17.58
1948–49 (Australia)	13	1	400	109	33.33	265	11	24.09
1949–50 (Australia)	4	0	107	80	26.75	121	8	15.12
1949–50 (South Africa)	18	3	577	131	38.46	728	44	16.54
1950–51 (Australia)	20	3	1332	214	78.35	762	27	28.22
1951–52 (Australia)	17	1	584	129	36.50	680	32	21.25
1951–52 (Ceylon)	1	0	106	106	106.00	24	5	4.80
1952–53 (Australia)	17	0	558	108	32.82	684	34	20.11
1953 (England)	31	3	1433	262*	51.17	1013	45	22.51
1953–54 (Australia)	12	2	711	143	71.10	540	16	33.75
1954–55 (Australia)	12	0	381	86	31.75	489	19	25.73
1955 (West Indies)	11	0	577	147	52.45	791	26	30.42
1955–56 (Australia)	10	1	638	164	70.88	272	19	14.31
1956 (England)	29	6	843	281*	36.65	980	50	19.60
1956 (Pakistan)	2	0	32	21	16.00	58	2	29.00
1959 (England)	3	2	164	102*	164.00	87	3	29.00
TOTAL	326	36	14,183	281*	48.90	11,068	497	22.26

Fielding: Miller took 129 catches in his career.

FIRST-CLASS CENTURIES

1937–38	181	Victoria v. Tasmania at Melbourne
1939–40	108	Victoria v. South Australia at Melbourne
1945	185	The Dominions v. England at Lord's
1945	105	Australia v. England at Lord's (Victory Test)
1945	118	Australia v. England at Lord's (Victory Test)
1945–46	106	Australian Services v. West Zone at Bombay
1945–46	132	Australian Services v. Ceylon at Colombo
1945–46	105*	Australian Services v. New South Wales at Sydney
1945–46	139	Australia v. Auckland at Auckland
1946–47	188	Victoria v. South Australia at Adelaide
1946–47	153	Victoria v. New South Wales at Melbourne
1946–47	206*	Victoria v. New South Wales at Sydney
1946–47	141*	Australia v. England at Adelaide
1947–48	170	New South Wales v. West Australia at Sydney
1948	202*	Australia v. Leicestershire at Leicester
1948	163	Australia v. MCC at Lord's
1948–49	109	New South Wales v. Queensland at Brisbane
1949–50	131	Australia v. Eastern Province at Port Elizabeth
1950–51	202*	New South Wales v. Queensland at Brisbane
1950–51	138*	New South Wales v. Queensland at Sydney
1950–51	122	New South Wales v. South Australia at Sydney
1950–51	214	New South Wales v. MCC at Sydney
1950–51	145*	Australia v. England at Sydney
1951–52	129	Australia v. West Indies at Sydney
1951–52	106	Commonwealth XI v. MCC at Colombo
1952–53	108	New South Wales v. Queensland at Brisbane
1953	262*	Australia v. Combined Services at Kingston
1953	220*	Australia v. Worcestershire at Worcester
1953	159*	Australia v. Yorkshire at Bradford
1953	109	Australia v. England at Lord's
1953–54 }	100 101 }	Hassett's XI v. Morris's XI at Melbourne
1953–54	143	New South Wales v. Victoria at Sydney
1955	147	Australia v. West Indies at Kingston
1955	137	Australia v. West Indies at Bridgetown
1955	109	Australia v. West Indies at Kingston
1955–56	164	New South Wales v. Queensland at Brisbane
1955–56	128	New South Wales v. Western Australia at Perth
1955–56	106	Australian XI v. Tasmania at Hobart
1955–56	132	Governor–General's XI v. Prime Minister's XI at Karachi
1956	281*	Australia v. Leicestershire at Leicester
1959	102*	Nottinghamshire v. Cambridge University at Nottingham

ACKNOWLEDGEMENTS

Everyone contacted, it seemed, had a Keith Miller anecdote. Some were wrong; some apocryphal; most were true. They fell into many categories: his generosity, his womanising, his aggression on and off the sporting field, his gift for friendship, his loyalty to mates both living and dead, his good luck, his bad luck, his unpunctuality and his feats as a cricketer and footballer. I must thank scores of people in Australia and the UK for their stories and other information (including permission to include published and unpublished material). They include Martin Ashenden, Ron Barassi, Sir Alec Bedser, Eric Bedser, Richie Benaud, Loretta Breasley, Scobie Breasley, Pippa Burke, Les Carlyon, Tony Charlton, Chris Clark, Brian Clinton, Ian Craig, Alan Davidson, Alec Dodds, Mary Fitzgerald, Basil Grapsas, Dave Greener, Jack Grossman, Neil Harvey, Christopher Hodgkinson, Thos Hodgson, Ron Hutchinson, Richard Joslin, Philip Law, Philip Linstead, Michael Ludgrove, Lady Pippa O'Brien, Larry Maddison, Tony Maylam, Colin McDonald, John McWhirter, Rod Mater, Norman May, John Miles, Arthur Morris, Don Moyes, Peter Philpott, Ron Reed, Bruce Woodley and Ian Woodward. Those interviewed earlier, who have since died – including Sir Donald Bradman, Dr Geoff Burns, Denis Compton, Lord (Colin) Cowdrey, Godfrey Evans, Jenny Ham, Ian Johnson, Ray Lindwall and Trevor Perry – also told illuminating stories about the subject.

I'm most grateful to the Miller family, including Keith's four sons, Bill, Peter, Denis and Bob, who were open and candid about their relationship with their father and their own lives. Miller's niece Jan, her husband Colin Beames and Miller's sister-in-law Molly (wife of his brother Ray) were also most helpful. Jan Beames had a unique view, being close to both Miller and his wife Peg. She is also a psychotherapist, which allowed her to give insightful layers to her observations. Jennifer Greenway, a psychotherapist, also added her assessments, thus giving professional perspectives from inside and outside the Miller inner sanctum. Medical practitioners who knew and treated Miller were also consulted.

The family allowed me access to Miller's personal files, which were invaluable in creating a portrait of an intriguing individual, who was multifaceted in his interests, capacities and connections.

Miller's war has always been a mystery to most, including his family. Access to his war record was helpful, but his own file, plus the inside views, diaries and files of his closest mate in the air force, Angus ('Gus') Glendinning, added dimensions far beyond the official record. Thanks to them and a handful of other interviewees and respondents who knew Miller in those vital years 1943–45, we have comprehension of the loyal, wild-living, sentimental, big-drinking, cultured, hell-raising, poetry-reciting, courageous, Beethoven-loving, wartime bomber and fighter support pilot known as 'Dusty'.

I am grateful for assistance from Melbourne High's archivist Glen Turnbull and historian Alan Gregory, who aided my delving into Miller's school years.

My thanks also for interviews and information to Diana Barnato-Walker, who flew Mosquitoes during World War II, statistical archivist Andrew Bayles and St Kilda Football Club historian Russell Holmesby.

Thanks once more to Jane Palfreyman, publisher, Cathryn Game, editor, and Jessica Dettmann, project editor, for their expertise and professionalism.

Roland Perry
June 2005

REFERENCES

Allen, Peter, *The Invincibles*, Bradman Museum and Allen & Kemsley Publishing, Australia, 1999.

Arlott, John, *Gone to the Test Match*, Longmans, Green & Co., London, 1949.

Bailey, Trevor, *Sir Gary*, Collins, London, 1976.

Bedser, Alec, with Bannister, Alec, *Twin Ambitions*, Stanley Paul, London, 1986.

Benaud, Richie, *The Appeal of Cricket*, Coronet Books, 1995.

Bose, Mihir, *Keith Miller: A Cricketing Biography*, George Allen & Unwin, London, 1980.

Bradman, Sir Donald, *Farewell to Cricket*, Hodder & Stoughton, London, 1950.

—— *The Bradman Albums*, Vol 2, Rigby Publishers, Melbourne, 1987.

Carlyon, Les, *True Grit: Tales From a Decade on the Turf*, Mandarin, Melbourne, 1996.

Cutler, Norman, *Behind the Australian Tests 1956*, Putnam, London, 1956.

Docker, Edward, *History of Indian Cricket*, Macmillan, Delhi, 1976.

Dunstan, Keith, *The Paddock That Grew*, Hutchinson, Melbourne, 1985.

Fingleton, Jack, *Brightly Fades the Don*, Arcadia, Melbourne, 2002.

Flanagan, Andy, *On Tour with Bradman*, Halstead Press, Sydney, 1950.

George, Anthony, *A Statistical Supplement*, Harris Printers, Melbourne, 1986.

Grogan, Robert, *Our Proud Heritage: A History of the South Melbourne Cricket Club from 1862*, published by South Melbourne Cricket Club, 2003.

Harvey, Neil, *My World of Cricket*, Hodder & Stoughton, London, 1963.

Heald, Tim, *Denis Compton*, Pavilion Books, London, 1994.

Hill, Alan, *Peter May*, Andre Deutsch, London, 1996.

Hutchinson, Garrie, and Ross, John, *200 Seasons of Australian Cricket*, Ironbark, Sydney, 1997.

Lindwall, Ray, *Flying Stumps*, Stanley Paul, London, 1954.

Mason, Ronald, *Walter Hammond*, Hollis & Carter, London, 1962.

May, Peter, *A Game Enjoyed*, Stanley Paul, London, 1985.

McHarg, Jack, *Arthur Morris: An Elegant Genius*, ABC Books, Sydney, 1995.

McIntosh, Dave, *Terror in the Starboard Seat*, Beaufort Books, New York, 1980.

Millar, Alexander Crosbie, *The Tale of Two Millers, 1849–1999: One Hundred and Fifty Years of Millar/Miller History in Australia*, self-published.

Miller, Keith, *Cricket Crossfire*, Oldbourne Press, London, 1956.

—— *Cricket from the Grandstand*, Oldbourne Press, London, 1959.

Moyes, A. G., *A Century of Cricketers*, Angus & Robertson, Sydney, 1950.

—— *Benaud*, Angus & Robertson, Melbourne, 1962.

O'Reilly, W. J. *Cricket Conquest: The Story of the 1948 Test Tour*, Werner Laurie, London, 1949.

Perry, Roland, *Bradman's Best Ashes Teams*, Random House Australia, Sydney, 2002; chapter 6, 'The Golden Nugget'.

—— *The Don*, Pan Macmillan, Sydney, 1995.

—— *The Exile: Burchett: Reporter of Conflict*, William Heinemann Australia, Melbourne, 1988.

Philpott, Peter, *A Spinner's Yarn*, ABC Books, Sydney, 1990.

Pollard, Jack, *The Complete Illustrated History of Australian Cricket*, Viking, Melbourne, 1992.

Ringwood, John, *Ray Lindwall*, Kangaroo Press, Sydney, 1995.

Rosenwater, Irving, *Sir Donald Bradman*, B. T. Batsford, London, 1978.

Ross, Alan, *The Penguin Cricketer's Companion*, Penguin, 1981.

Smith, Terry, *Cricket Centuries*, Angus & Robertson, Sydney, 1991.

Wallish, E. A., *The Great Laurie Nash*, Ryan Publishing, Melbourne, 1998.

Webster, Ray, compiler, Miller, Allan, editor, *First-Class Cricket in Australia*, Vols 1 & 2, Melbourne, R. Webster, 1991.

Whitington, R. S., *Keith Miller: The Golden Nugget*, Rigby, Sydney, 1981.

—— *The Quiet Australian: The Lindsay Hassett Story*, Heinemann, Melbourne, 1969.

—— *Fours Galore*, Cassell Australia, Melbourne, 1969.

Whitington R. S. & Miller, Keith, *Cricket Typhoon*, McDonald, London, 1955.

—— *Bumper*, Latimer House, London, 1953.

—— *Catch!*, Latimer House, London, 1951.

Wilde, Simon, *Number One*, Victor Gollancz, London, 1998.

Wisden Cricketers' Almanack, 1938–60.

Woodward, Ian, *Cricket, Not War*, SMK Enterprises, 1994.

Wright, Graeme, *Wisden on Bradman*, Hardie Grant Books, Melbourne, 1998.

Documentaries

BBC, *Test Match Special*, 16 May 2001.

BBC Radio, *A Portrait of Keith Miller*, October 1956.

Channel 7, *This is Your Life*, March 1977.

ESPN, *Keith Miller*, 1996.

Articles, Periodicals, Annuals

AAP, 'Not "Bad Boy"—Cool with Don', *Herald* (Melbourne), 19 October 1949.

Alderson, Andrew, 'The Passionate Princess Who Loved and Lost', *Daily Telegraph* (London), 10 February 2002.

Anderson, Jon, 'Cricket Louts Rile Cricket Commentator', *Sun* (Melbourne), 10 February 1997.

Banks, Rex, 'Miller Bumps Them Down', *Sun* (Melbourne), 4 July 1959.

Benaud, Richie, 'Mighty Miller', *Herald* (Melbourne), 3 May 1971.

Baum, Greg, 'When They Were Kings', *Age* (Melbourne), 14 August 1998.

—— 'Just a Few Tears as Miller's Tale Celebrated', *Age* (Melbourne), 21 December 2004.

Bose, Mihir, 'Bradman was Feared But Miller was Cherished', *Times of India*, 12 October 2004

Brown, Terry, 'Packed House Says Goodbye to Keith Miller', *Herald Sun* (Melbourne), 21 December 2004.

Clark, Chris, *Air Force News,* October 2004.

Coward, Mike, 'Time Takes its Toll on an Immortal', *Australian*, 27–28 November 1999.

Derriman, Philip, 'Daredevil Who Burned Like a Star', *Sydney Morning Herald*, 14 October 2004.

—— 'A Great Aussie All-rounder', *Sydney Morning Herald*, 28 November 1996.

Doherty, Frank, 'The Thrust of Keith's Argument Floored Him', *Signature*, Diner's Club Magazine, November–December 1981.

Fitzsimons, Peter, 'A Gentleman and a Skoller to the Very End', *Sydney Morning Herald*, 16 October 2004.

—— 'Officer and Gentleman', *Sydney Morning Herald*, 6 May 1996.

Frith, David, 'Keith Miller Interview', *Wisden*, November 1993.

Hadfield, Tom, 'Craig Back on the Test Map', *Daily News* (Perth), 10 December 1955.

Hall, Ross, 'Miller Vice-Captain—and Ross Hall Writes an Open Letter', *Sun* (Melbourne), 9 February 1955.

Holmesby, Russell, 'Keith Miller, 1940–1946', *Inside Football*, 29 October 2004.

—— 'Nugget—All-Round Champion', *Southern Peninsula Gazette*, 3 July 1990.

Horan, Michael, 'Best of the Century', *Herald Sun* (Melbourne), 19 January 2000.

Hughes, Simon, 'Finding Utopia Through Cricket', *Long Room Magazine*, November 1998.

Humphries, Rod, 'Edie's Dash, Dashing Keith Top Moomba', *Sun Herald* (Sydney), 13 March 1977.

Hunt, Adrian, 'Veteran Breasley Still has the Master Touch', *Daily Telegraph* (London), 15 July 1990.

Lewis, Tony, 'Nugget Makes Lord's Homecoming', *Sunday Telegraph* (London), 17 July 1994.

Longmore, Andrew, 'Free Spirit of Golden Summer of Victory', *Times* (London), 4 May 1995.

Lynch, Steven, 'The Australian in Excelsis', *Cricinfo*, 11 October 2004.

MacDonald, John, 'For Parky, There's Only One Keith Miller', *Australian*, 20 February 1996.

MacDonald, Mick, 'Remembering My Mate Keith', *Manning River Times*, 15 October 2004.

Marks, Vic, 'Miller More Than a Hero of Yesteryear', *Observer* (London), October 2004.

McFarline, Peter, 'Aussie Heroes Pack Them In', *Herald* (Melbourne), 2 July 1985.

Millard, P. J. 'Schoolboy's Test Promise', *Herald* (Melbourne), 9 March 1936.

Miller, Keith, 'It's All Baloney About Bumpers', *Daily Mirror* (Sydney), 10 March 1965.

—— 'May is No Longer the Shy Stripling', *Sun* (Melbourne), 4 October 1958.

—— 'Umpires Must Move Now', *Sun* (Melbourne), 26 November 1958.

—— 'Keith Miller on the Tests', *Herald* (Melbourne), 13 January 1970.

—— 'Butter Fingers Says Miller', *Herald* (Melbourne), 13 January 1970.

—— 'Miller's Romantic Gamble', *Herald* (Melbourne), 5 March 1977.

Mitchell, Ray, 'Keith Miller', *Adam Magazine*, November 1968.

Mossop, Brian, 'Keith Miller to Pad Up Again', *Sydney Morning Herald*, 14 October 1976.

Nicholson, Rod, 'Nugget's Golden Day', *Herald* (Melbourne), 26 December 1980.

Palmer, Scott, 'Nugget's Aussie Rules, OK', *Sun* (Melbourne), 26 April 1987.

Parkinson, Michael, 'They Don't Bowl, Score, Shoot or Save 'Em Like They Used To', *Punch,* 3 December 1969.

—— 'My Life-long Pursuit of the Greatest Ever Cricketer', *Herald Sun* (Melbourne), 29 January 1995.

Parsons, Joanna, 'Trevor Howard Came in to Bat for an Aussie Film', *Woman's Day*, 26 April 1976.

Piesse, Ken, '1945—A Star is Born', *Age* (Melbourne), 29 December 1976.

—— 'Private Thoughts of the Don', *Sunday Herald Sun* (Melbourne), 6 October 2002.

Reed, Ron, 'Miller Still a Mighty Magnet', *Herald Sun* (Melbourne), 7 December 1996.

—— 'Re-running Past Times from a Golden Era', *Herald Sun* (Melbourne), 28 July 1987.

—— 'Millers Made Peace in Time', *Herald Sun* (Melbourne), 13 October 2004.

—— 'Australia's All-round Good Guy Hits 83', *Herald Sun* (Melbourne), 21 November 2002.

—— 'Re-running Past Times from a Golden Era', *Herald* (Melbourne), 28 July 1987.

Rostron, Frank, 'The Playboy of Cricket has Paid for His Rows on the Way Up', *Sun* (Melbourne), 12 February 1955.

Sheahan, Mike, 'Nugget is Still a Gem of a Bloke', *Herald* (Melbourne), 12 June 1985.

Smith, Trevor, 'London is Australia's', *Herald* (Melbourne), 6 July 1956.

Stephens, Tony, 'A $20 Million Salute to Our Extraordinary Ordinary Heroes', *Sydney Morning Herald*, 14 November 1997.

Steven, Alistair, 'Keith Miller, MBE, Cricketer', *Scotsman*, 13 October 2004.

Trengove, Alan, 'Miller Finds His Wartime Mate . . .', *Herald* (Melbourne), 22 April 1964.

Tucker, Dick, 'Test Cricket a Bloody Picnic', *Sunday Mirror* (Sydney), 12 October 1975.

Whitington, R. S., 'New Faces for England?', *Sporting Life*, October 1952.

—— 'Threat to Shoot Keith, Ian', *Argus* (Melbourne), 10 August 1956.

Wilkins, Phil, 'Miller: The Man from the Pools', *Cricketer*, November 1975.

—— 'Australia's First X', *Sydney Morning Herald*, 7 December 1996.

Woodcock, John, 'Mosquito Pilot by Night, Cricketer by Day', *Times* (London), 12 October 2004.

Wooldridge, Ian, 'Raise a Glass to the Magic of Miller, an Aussie in Excelsis', *Daily Mail* (London), 28 November 1989.

Zec, Donald, 'Dreamboy Keith is all the Rage', *Argus* (Melbourne), 5 July 1956.

Other
'A Spitfire of the Pitch', *Age* (Melbourne), 20 October 1984.

'A Star Revered for More Than the Numbers', *International Herald Tribune*, 14 October 2004.

'Australians in India, 1956', souvenir booklet.

'Ex-cricketer Bowled with Decree Nisi', *Truth* (Melbourne), Sunday 13 May 1956.

'Germans Sourly Look on as Their Teeth are Drawn', *Times* (London), 14 June 1945.

'Hammond Slated: Bradman Praised', *Sun* (Melbourne), 2 June 1950.

Hong Kong Cricket League, Souvenir Programme, Visit by Jack Chegwyn's Australian X1, 8–18 October 1952.

'John Arlott, A Poet', Test Match Special, BBC Sport, 16 May 2001.

'Keith Miller Brings Out a Briton', *Sun* (Melbourne), 29 July 1957.

'Keith Miller at Baseball', *Sun* (Melbourne), 19 May 1949.

'Legend Goes into Bat for Old Mate', *Herald Sun* (Melbourne), 2 April 1997.

'Mighty Miller—The Cricketing Cavalier', *Truth* (Melbourne), 13 December 1975.

'Miller Brings a Young Shield Team to Perth', *West Australian*, 8 December 1955.

'Miller Denies Ill-Feeling', *Herald Sun* (Melbourne), 14 November 1949.

'Miller to Join the Don at Lord's', *Herald Sun* (Melbourne), 28 November 1992.

'Nugget', *Sunday Telegraph* (Sydney), 31 December 1989.

'On the Air', *Punch*, 4 July 1956.

'Test Cricketers Train Battle to Regain Ashes', *Pix*, 2 October 1954.

'The Footy Story', *Argus Football Magazine* (Melbourne), November 1955.

'The Heroic Bluey Truscott', *Daily Mirror* (Sydney), 22 February 1989.

'The Invincibles', *Age* (Melbourne), 14 August 1998.

'The Mighty Keith Miller', *Truth* (Melbourne), 25 January 1975.

'The Passionate Princess', *Time* Europe, 18 February 2002.

'Trivial Facts, Figures with Bat and Ball', *Nunawading Gazette*, 14 December 1988.

'Truscott Commemoration', *Old Unicornian*, Spring 1993.

PHOTO CREDITS

The author and publishers gratefully acknowledge Newspix for permission to use the pictures captioned *Copybook drive*; *The Saint*; *Battered but unbowed*; *Beautiful body language*; *Cricket's philanthropist*; *Empire decorations*; *In the Parade of Champions.*

Thanks to Getty Images for permission to use the pictures captioned *The corkscrew*; *Relaxed and upright*; *The eyes have it.*

Thanks to West Australian Newspapers Limited for permission to use the picture captioned *Batsman's nightmare.*

Thanks to Australian Picture Library for permission to use the picture captioned *Victory-year celebration.*

Thanks to Empics for permission to use the picture captioned *Farewell to Lord's.*

Thanks to the Herald and Weekly Times Limited for permission to use the pictures captioned *You should have seen the other guy*; *Hero to all*; *Youth versus maturity*; *Mr Compton, you must stop!*; *Coming at you*; *That Miller charm*; *On a good thing.*

Thanks to the Miller family for providing all other photographs.

Every effort has been made to identify copyright holders and photographers of pictures in this book. The publishers would be pleased to hear from any copyright holders who have not been acknowledged.

INDEX

This card does not necessarily include the fall of the last wic

2d. Lord's Ground

ENGLAND v. DOMINIONS

(King George's Fund for Sailors, Australian Service Charities and New Zeala
Sports Fund)

SAT., MON. & TUES., AUGUST 25, 27, 28, 1945. (Three-day Ma

DOMINIONS	First Innings		Second Inning
1 H. Craig	c Davies, b Phillipson	56	c Hammond, b Davi
2 D. R. Fell	c Griffith, b Wright	12	b Davies
3 J. Pettiford	b Davies	1	b Wright
4 K. R. Miller	l b w, b Hollies	26	c Langridge, b Wrig
5 M. P. Donnelly	c and b Hollies	133	b Wright
†6 L. N. Constantine	c Hollies, b Wright	5	c Fishlock, b Hollies
7 C. G. Pepper	c Hammond, b Wright	51	c Robertson, c Hollie
8 D. R. Cristofani	l b w, b Edrich	6	b Wright
9 R. G. Williams	l b w, b Wright	11	c Hammond, b Wrig
10 R. S. Ellis	b Wright	0	st Griffith, b Hollies
*11 C. D. Bremner	not out	1	not out
	B , l-b 3, w 2, n-b	5	B 1, l-b 8, w , n-l
	Total	307	Total

FALL OF THE WICKETS
1—37 2—38 3—90 4—104 5—109 6—229 7—240 8—271 9—279 10—3
1—49 2—56 3—96 4—200 5—209 6—326 7—336 8—336 9—336 10—3.

ANALYSIS OF BOWLING

Name	1st Innings						2nd Innings				
	O.	M.	R.	W.	Wd.	N-b.	O.	M.	R.	W.	Wd.
Phillipson	16	2	40	1	2	...	2	1	1	0	...
Edrich	9	1	19	1	...	...	3	0	13	0	...
Wright	30	2	90	5	...	...	30.1	6	105	5	...
Davies	22	9	43	1	...	...	13	3	35	2	...
Hollies	20.2	3	86	2	...	...	29	8	115	3	...
Langridge	6	1	24	0	...	...	8	0	57	0	...

ENGLAND	First Innings		Second Inning
1 L. B. Fishlock	c Pettiford, b Ellis	12	run out
2 J. D. Robertson	l b w, b Constantine	4	c Fell, b Pettiford
3 James Langridge	l b w, b Cristofani	28	b Pepper
4 W. E. Phillipson	b Pepper	0	run out
*5 S. C. Griffith	b Williams	15	c Pepper, b Pettiford
†6 W. R. Hammond	st Bremner, b Pepper	121	st Bremner, b Cristof
7 H. Gimblett	c Pettiford, b Cristofani	11	b Pepper
8 W. J. Edrich	c Pepper, b Cristofani	78	c Pepper, b Ellis
9 J. G. W. Davies	b Pepper	1	b Pepper
10 D. V. P. Wright	l b w, b Pepper	0	b Cristofani
11 E. Hollies	not out	0	not out
	B 7, l-b 6, w 2, n-b 2,	17	B 6, l-b 5, w , n-l
	Total	287	Total

FALL OF THE WICKETS
1—8 2—23 3—26 4—52 5—78 6—96 7—273 8—287 9—287 10—28
1—25 2—42 3—128 4—160 5—200 6—200 7—283 8—309 9—311 10—31

ANALYSIS OF BOWLING
Name	1st Innings		2nd Innings
	O.	M.	R. W. Wd. N-b.	O. M. R. W. Wd. N